STAGING HARMONY

STAGING HARMONY

MUSIC AND RELIGIOUS CHANGE
IN LATE MEDIEVAL AND EARLY
MODERN ENGLISH DRAMA

KATHERINE STEELE BROKAW

CORNELL UNIVERSITY PRESS
Ithaca and London

First published 2016 by Cornell University Press

Printed in the United States of America

Library of Congress Cataloging-in-Publication Data

Names: Brokaw, Katherine Steele, 1980– author.
Title: Staging harmony : music and religious change in
    late medieval and early modern English drama /
    Katherine Steele Brokaw.
Description: Ithaca ; London : Cornell University Press,
    2016. | Includes bibliographical references and index.
Identifiers: LCCN 2016012108 | ISBN 9781501703140
    (cloth : alk. paper)
Subjects: LCSH: Religion and drama—History—16th
    century. | Dramatic music—England—16th
    century—History and criticism.
Classification: LCC PR658.R43 B76 2016 |
    DDC 882/.3093578—dc23
LC record available at https://lccn.loc.gov/2016012108

Cloth printing   10 9 8 7 6 5 4 3 2 1

For my parents, Tom Brokaw and Nancy Steele Brokaw

For as good Musike consisteth not of one, but of divers sowndes proportionablie answering together: so doeth the Commonweale of sundrie kinds of men keping themselves within the limits of their owne callings.

   —Thomas Rogers, *A Golden Chaine* (1587)

Musicians wrestle everywhere -
All day - among the crowded air
I hear the silver strife -
And - waking - long before the morn
Such transport breaks upon the town
I think it that "New Life"!

It is not Bird - it has no nest -
Nor "Band" - in brass and scarlet - drest
Nor Tamborin - nor Man -
It is not Hymn from pulpit read -
The "Morning Stars" the Treble led
On Time's first Afternoon!

Some - say - it is "the Spheres" - at play!
Some say - that bright Majority
Of vanished Dames - and Men!
Some - think it service in the place
Where we - with late - celestial face
Please God - shall Ascertain!

   —Emily Dickinson, 1861

Music is first and foremost a human practice. By that I mean that it is 'sounded' by voices and/or instruments by means of a disciplined set of embodied skills. Theology, too, is a practice, or more accurately, a complex set of practices. . . . Thinking, writing, and speaking theologically about God, the world, and being human moves in both contemplative and practical modes. . . . Could it be that such a beholding of the truth of things, as well as the source of goodness and beauty, may be embodied in the various arts, and most pointedly in music? Might this require attention to the dissonant, the tension-filled, and the difficult truths as well as the harmonious, the beautiful, and the praiseworthy?

   —Don Saliers, *Music and Theology*

Contents

ACKNOWLEDGMENTS

I have had the great good fortune to learn from and work with several mentors and colleagues over the years. Chief among them is the brilliant and dedicated Theresa Tinkle; she has been my and this book's best critic and supporter and my greatest intellectual debt is to her. I also owe much to my "book buddy" Jay Zysk, without whose incisive feedback and encouraging text messages I could not have completed this project.

This book has benefited immensely from the detailed reports of two anonymous readers for Cornell. I am also most grateful to Kent Cartwright, Steven Spiess, and Angela Heetderks for feedback on chapter drafts, and to Daniel Francis and Paul Prescott for editing assistance in the eleventh hour. I am thankful every day for my graduate education at the University of Michigan, and this project benefited from the early and in many cases continued guidance of W. B. Worthen, Steven Mullaney, Michael Schoenfeldt, and Peggy McCracken. Michigan's Linda Gregerson, Barbara Hodgdon, Cathy Sanok, Karla Taylor, Valerie Traub, Douglas Trevor, John Whittier-Ferguson, and Ralph Williams have also inspired and supported me. For the continued exchange of ideas and friendship, I thank fellow Michigan grads Kathryn Will, Rebecca Wiseman, Andrew Bozio, Leila Watkins (who all read very early drafts of some of these chapters) as well as Ari Friedlander, Amy Rodgers, Marjorie Rubright, Chad Thomas, and Gavin Hollis. I have also been sustained by the love and friendship of, among many others, Asynith Palmer, Linda Bates, Sarah Moss, Sarah Ehlers, Shanna Shipman, and Caroline Miller.

For conversation and encouragement, I am grateful to several scholars including Linda Austern, Sarah Beckwith, Gina Bloom, Seeta Chaganti, Margreta deGrazia, Michael Dobson, Frances Dolan, Noah Guynn, Bruce Holsinger, Jeffrey Knight, Erika Lin, Christopher Marsh, Carla Mazzio, Joseph Ortiz, John Parker, Bruce Smith, Emma Maggie Solberg, Scott Trudell, Claire Waters, and William West. For bringing this book to fruition with swiftness, competence, and assurance, I thank Peter Potter, Bethany Wasik, Susan Barnett, and Mahinder Kingra at Cornell as well as Michelle Witkowski and Elliot Bratton.

I have presented much of the work here at several conferences, and benefited from the intellectual communities fostered by meetings of the Shakespeare Association of America, the American Association for Theater Research, the International Medieval Congress at Leeds, the International Congress on Medieval Studies at Kalamazoo, the Renaissance Society of America, and the Modern Language Association. I am also grateful for the research fellowships given to me by the University of Michigan Institute for the Humanities and the University of California-Merced Center for the Humanities, and to UC-Merced's Center for the Humanities for a generous subvention grant to support this book's publication. Parts of Chapter 2 originally appeared in *Comparative Drama 44.3* (2010). Portions of chapter 3 appear in *Beyond Boundaries: Rethinking the Circulation of Music in Early Modern England* published by Indiana University Press, 2016.

I am lucky to have landed among such supportive colleagues at UC-Merced, and am particularly indebted to Susan Amussen, Jayson Beaster-Jones, Irenee Beattie, Gregg Camfield, Jan Goggans, Taryn Hakala, Nigel Hatton, Matthew Kaiser, David Kaminsky, Ruth Mostern, and Jenni Samuelson, for their encouragement as I have completed this book. Thanks are owed, too, to my undergraduate research assistants Alexandra Curtis and Kuljit Gill. I have too many longstanding debts to list, but must give public thanks to Charles Moseley at Cambridge for helping me fall in love with the English literary past. Several early teachers led me to literary, theatrical, and musical study, including Kathleen Clesson and Rodger Baldwin in my high school days, and Kathleen O'Gorman, Wes Chapman, Robert Bray, Daniel Terkla, Christopher Callahan, Bob Mangialardi, and Roger Bechtel at Illinois Wesleyan University. I am forever grateful to three brilliant spirits who have passed on from this world, three mentors I encountered as an undergraduate at Illinois Wesleyan and without whom I would not be an academic; this book, and all my work, honors the memories of the late John O'Leary, James McGowan, and Minor Myers jr. My greatest debts are to my family: my intrepid brother Stephen Brokaw and grandmother Ruth Steele, and my loving and ceaselessly supportive parents, Tom and Nancy Brokaw, to whom I dedicate this book.

NOTE ON THE TEXT

Wherever possible, I present texts with their original spellings; I do this even with the plays of Marlowe and Shakespeare, so as to not reinforce the notion that their plays are significantly more "modern" than the other materials discussed in this book. The fifteenth-century texts discussed in the first chapter occasionally make use of two characters no longer used in modern English. The thorn (þ) is the equivalent of our "th," and the yogh (ȝ) is the same as our silent "gh," as in "might." I do modernize the lettering of early modern print inasmuch as I update to our present-day usage of "s," "u," "v," "i," and "j" letterforms.

ABBREVIATIONS

EBBA English Broadside Ballad Archive
EEBO Early English Books Online
EETS Early English Text Society
OED Oxford English Dictionary

STAGING HARMONY

Introduction
Theater, Music, and Religion
in the Long Sixteenth Century

> Prest: Now, clerkys, with voicys cler, *Te deum laudamus* lett us sing.
>
> —The Digby *Mary Magdalene* (c. 1480)
>
> King Henry: Doe we all holy Rights:/Let there be sung *Non nobis*, and *Te Deum,*/The dead with charitie enclos'd in Clay.
>
> —*Henry V* (1599)

First performed over a century apart, the fifteenth-century Digby *Mary Magdalene* and Shakespeare's *Henry V* (1599) both call for the singing of the "Te Deum," a hymn of praise to God. In the intervening years, the context, performance, reception, and significance of such religious music underwent profound transformations. The audience of *Mary Magdalene* would likely have been treated to the glory of contemporary sacred polyphony familiar from church rites of the time: in Latin, often distinguished by intricate vocal lines and long melismatic passages in which singers extended single syllables over many notes. Such music exhibited the beauty of the composer's harmonies as well as the singers' voices. By contrast, by the time *Henry V* was first performed on the eve of the seventeenth century, the Church of England's services were conducted according to the Elizabethan 1559 *Book of Common Prayer*. This prayer book retains the singing of the "Te Deum" in morning prayers, but rejects florid Latin polyphony, indicating instead that the tune should, "to the ende people maye the better heare . . . be songe in a plaine tune . . . in Englyshe dayly throughe the whole yere."[1] That church music should be sung in English and to a "plain

---

1. Brian Cummings, ed., *The Book of Common Prayer: The Texts of 1549, 1559, and 1662* (Oxford: Oxford World Classics, 2013), 106. This text comes from the 1559 version, which would have been used in 1599.

tune" was the result of innumerable disputes throughout the sixteenth century that resulted in several changes to England's official musical liturgy.

As the action of *Henry V* is set in 1415, it would have been historically accurate for Shakespeare's actors to sing in a way that reflected early fifteenth-century practice, incorporating the Latin polyphony that had, by then, been excised from Elizabeth's *Book of Common Prayer*. If they did so, older audience members may have recalled such music being sung in their younger years, as Catholicism had been England's official religion as recently as the 1550s during the reign of Mary I. For performers and audience members alike, the older, Catholic tunes were charged with various theological, aesthetic, and political meanings. No singer, actor, playwright, or theatergoer could fail to feel, personally and profoundly, the tensions implicated by the sounds of this nostalgic, sacred music. As the performers sang and the audience attended, the experience mingled aesthetic sensibility with political and religious conscience; the hymn itself is in richly textured dialogue with the social order and the complex, inconsistent history of England's long sixteenth century.

As this book will show, the making and hearing of religious music on stage was crucial to the progress and reception of England's reformations. Staged music enacts and alludes to many theological and political debates regarding music's role in the salvation or damnation of Christian subjects, as well as the proper function of music in the church.[2] Because staged music gains affective and social force through its ability to evoke deeply ingrained memories, its effects are best understood by considering a long and consecutive history of music in churches and on stages.[3] The theatrical representations of religious music in *Mary Magdalene* and *Henry V* provide fine examples of the rich contrasts and (so to speak) dramatic changes that mark the period covered by this book, which aims to explain the how performances of music on early English stages reflected and influenced religious differences and transformations.

Staging Harmony demonstrates how theatrical music from the late fifteenth to the early seventeenth centuries contributed to contemporary discourses

---

2. Many scholars have taken to referring to England's religious changes as plural reformations, inspired, for example, by Christopher Haigh, *English Reformations: Religion, Politics, and Society under the Tudors* (Oxford: Clarendon Press, 1993).

3. Several historians have documented how the sensory, including acoustic, properties of the church's sacraments were crucial in forming religious memories and social ties. See, for example, Matthew Milner, *The Senses and the English Reformation* (Surrey, UK: Ashgate, 2011); Andy Wood, *The Memory of the People: Custom and Popular Sense of the Past in Early Modern England* (Cambridge: Cambridge University Press, 2013); and Bruce Holsinger, "Liturgy," in *Oxford Twenty-First Century Approaches to Literature: Middle English*, ed. Paul Strohm (Oxford: Oxford University Press, 2007), 295–314.

on the power and morality of music and its proper role in religious life, shaping the changes made to church music as well as people's reception to those changes. While debates raged about music's abilities to bring listeners and singers into harmony with their God—and its power to distract, corrupt, and manipulate—staged music could represent and enact the logical consequences of cases made by music's defenders *and* its detractors. As we shall see, staged songs and dances reveal that music's defenders and detractors were often both right: music's powers to charm and deceive are of a piece with its abilities to bring people together in the sensation of harmony. At the heart of this book, then, is my argument that plays performed throughout the long sixteenth century literally and figuratively "staged harmony." Through the performance and reception of music, participants in the contentious theological debates of this period found themselves—though perhaps reluctantly and often imperfectly—in dialogue with one another. Staged music provided a creative space in which it was at times possible for understanding and even tolerance to take tentative, fragile form. And as actors, playwrights, and theatergoers sought concord among diverse participants, they subtly refined the psychological and social tools that were vital to the construction of bridges across the theological and political chasms that divided England. In the process of staging harmony, they learned, honed, and sometimes exploited the art of concord itself.

For late medieval and early modern musical theorists, the idea of "harmony" suggests concord and resolution: the most beautiful harmonies follow discordant sounds. In the words of Charles Butler, "a Discord . . . in Musik" can "mak[e] the Concord following the sweeter."[4] The notion that musical harmony unifies and resolves dissonance translates to the social and political sphere, as Thomas Rogers's analogy (quoted in this book's epigraph) suggests, likening "divers sowndes proportionablie" to "sundrie kinds of men."[5] Playwrights understood the affective power of music as well as its metaphorical resonances, using performed songs and references to musical theories in their plays to unite audiences in the powerful sensory experience that is sound, and to suggest emotional and social commonalities among audience members that transcend confessional labels.[6]

---

4. Charles Butler, *The Principles of Music, in Singing and Setting* (London, 1636), 51. See also Jonathan Willis, *Church Music and Protestantism in Post-Reformation England: Discourses, Sites, and Identities* (Aldershot, UK: Ashgate, 2010), 235.

5. Thomas Rogers, *A Golden Chaine* (London, 1587), A3r.

6. Early theater audiences spoke of going to "hear" a play, rather than going to "see" it. I favor the term "audience" over "spectator" not only because I prefer the aural etymology to the visual, but also because I prefer to think of audiences as a mixed plural rather than a unified singular.

Between the mid-fifteenth and early seventeenth centuries, English musical, theatrical, and religious cultures were constantly adapting to the pressures of politics, protest, and popular opinion. At the same time, music, theater, and religion were mutually constitutive forces, constantly representing and shaping one another. Ballads voiced diverse religious viewpoints and retold theatrical narratives; psalms sung in church incorporated ballad tunes while reformers compared the Catholic liturgy to the theater; and actors staged religious rituals and re-performed music sacred and profane. Thus, the formation of the Anglican liturgy, the rises of polyphony, psalmody, and balladry, and the growth of the professional theater are related developments.

Debates about the source of music's power and its moral status mattered deeply in the long sixteenth century because music was so central to religious change. The rites sanctioned for churches went through drastic revisions in each of the periods discussed here. A mid-sixteenth-century reformist homily imagines the complaints of a woman parishioner regarding the recent acoustic changes to church services: "Alas gossip, what shal we now do at Church . . . since we cannot heare the like pyping, singing, chaunting, & playing uppon the organs that we could do before[?]"[7] The homily immediately chides the woman's sentiment: "we ought greatly to rejoyce and geve God thankes, that our Churches are delivered of all those thinges which displeased God so sore, & filthily defiled his holy house and his place of prayer." The tensions between the "pyping, singing, chaunting, & playing" many found spiritually powerful and the purity of the Protestant ideal of Word alone stretches across and beyond the scope of this book. Music historians have recently called attention to the centrality of musical issues to English reforms. They have noted in particular how the presence of Lollardy—a heresy associated with anti-music stances—at the dawn of England's reformations as well as Tudor monarchs' personal attachments to music meant that religious liturgy went through different transformations in England than on the continent.[8]

Wycliffite complaints against the vanities of orthodox musical ritual—a minority voice in the years around 1500—gave way to an official attack on the sounds of traditional religion when Henry VIII repudiated the Pope and

---

7. Printed in *The second tome of homilees of such matters as were promised, and intituled in the former part of homilees* (London, 1571), 271–72.

8. For recent analyses of these musical changes, see Robert Wegman, *The Crisis of Music in Early Modern Europe, 1470–1530* (New York: Routledge, 2008), 106–61; Willis, *Church Music and Protestantism*; John Milsom, "Music, Politics and Society," in *A Companion to Tudor Britain*, eds. Robert Tittler and Norman Jones (Oxford: Wiley-Blackwell, 2009), 492–508; and Roger Bray, "England i, 1485–1600," in *European Music 1520–1640*, ed. James Haar (Woodbridge, UK: Boydell & Brewer, 2006), 487–508.

declared himself head of the Church of England in 1534. When he closed and dissolved the monasteries in the 1530s, he also divested their choir schools, and under the influence of Archbishop Cranmer and Henry's minister Thomas Cromwell a slow but sure assault on "popish" musical practice spread. Henry himself wavered on musical rites, but reforms made under his son, Edward VI, stripped church ritual to the unaccompanied singing of psalms, and many organs and bells were destroyed during the realm of the boy king. Mary I's brief reign saw an attempt to rebuild traditional musical rites, but most parishes were soon back to unaccompanied metrical psalm singing when Elizabeth I came to the throne, despite the far more traditional polyphonic music she commissioned for her own Chapel Royal. By the time James I was crowned, there were several kinds of music being intoned in churches and cathedrals, including polyphonic anthems and traditional Mass elements sung in English.

Beyond the church, music was a key part of late medieval and early modern English life, and Christopher Marsh, Bruce Holsinger, and Bruce Smith, among others, have helped us to hear its pervasive and diverse sounds.[9] The printing press enabled the sale and circulation of broadside ballads, instrumental sheet music, and treatises on music and dance. Writing when Shakespeare was composing *The Tempest* and *The Winter's Tale*, the plays that conclude this book, John Taverner sums up long held views on music's universal appeal: "And sure itt seemes that naturall there is in man not onely a love but allso a kind of proneness to Musicke, w[hich] makes even children & infants delight & practise itt: And not onely for, but allso all men of what trade or fashion of life soever, very carters & plowman are not without their musicke."[10] Ever-popular and ever-changing musical forms were represented on English stages from pageant wagons to churchyards, from courts to professional amphitheaters. Drama is uniquely able to juxtapose sacred and profane music, and playwrights appropriated the affective and associative effects of tavern songs, liturgical music, ballads, dances, and magical chants. Song and dance marks the vices of *Wisdom* (c. 1475), the devils of Marlowe's *Doctor Faustus* (c. 1588), and *The Tempest*'s Trinculo and Stephano (1611) as immoral, even as music is sounded by angels in the Digby *Mary Magdalene* (c. 1480), by devout believers in John Bale's *God's Promises* (c. 1538), by a doomed

9. Christopher Marsh, *Music and Society in Early Modern England* (Cambridge: Cambridge University Press, 2011); Bruce Holsinger, *Music, Body, and Desire in Medieval Culture: Hildegard of Bingen to Chaucer* (Palo Alto, CA: Stanford University Press, 2001); Bruce Smith, *The Acoustic World of Early Modern England: Attending to the O-Factor* (Chicago: University of Chicago Press, 1999).

10. John Taverner, "Praelections musical in aedibus Greshamensibus," (1610–1611), MS 2329, Sloane Collection, British Library, 11v.

Queen in Thomas Preston's *Cambises* (c. 1558), and by seemingly magical forces during Hermione's reanimation in *The Winter's Tale* (1611). Stage music could be both sacred and profane at once, as in several examples of parodic religious rites intoned in the Digby *Mary Magdalene*, Bale's *King Johan* (1538), Nicholas Udall's *Ralph Roister Doister* (1553), and *Doctor Faustus*.[11] While Joseph Ortiz, David Lindley, and several other scholars have productively explored the way melody, voicing, and instrumentation are connotative forces in Shakespeare's plays, much less attention has been paid to the aural dimensions of earlier dramas.[12] But because an audience's reception of theatrical music is "ghosted," in Marvin Carlson's term, by the sounds of the present world outside the theater as well as the songs and dances of any play's recent theatrical past, it is important to view drama across the *longue durée* of theatrical history if we are to begin to understand music's affective and social power on the stage.[13]

Songs performed in a late sixteenth-century play like *Doctor Faustus* or *Henry V* could remind older audience members of melodies they had heard sung outside the theater that morning, of Catholic chants sung by their mothers years ago, or of tunes used with different words in older plays. As Smith points out, recollection of sound is somatic, not just cognitive, and theatrical music is socially and emotionally powerful in large part because it is a phenomenological experience. When audience members hear the melodies, voices, and instruments of the theater, both early modern musical theories and modern cognitive science point to the way that minds re-embody "traces of sound that were already lodged in the brain, lungs, larynx, and mouth."[14]

To hear and feel with these audience members, we must pay attention to what kinds of music were performed throughout and beyond the sixteenth

11. Throughout the book, I will be using the word "parody" in its literary rather than musicological sense, as in the way Ben Jonson uses it in his 1598 *Every Man in his Humour* when Edward Knowell says that the gift of a "parodie" is "to make it absurder than it was." *Every Man in His Humour*, in *Ben Jonson: Five Plays*, ed. G.A. Wilkes (Oxford: Oxford University Press, 1988), 5.5.24–25.

12. Joseph Ortiz, *Broken Harmony: Shakespeare and the Politics of Music* (Ithaca, NY: Cornell University Press, 2011); David Lindley, *Shakespeare and Music: Arden Critical Companion* (London: Arden, 2006). See also Erin Minear, *Reverberating Song in Shakespeare and Milton* (Aldershot, UK: Ashgate, 2011); Wes Folkerth, *The Sound of Shakespeare* (London: Routledge, 2002); and Gina Bloom, *Voice in Motion: Staging Gender, Shaping Sound in Early Modern England* (Philadelphia: University of Pennsylvania Press, 2007). Attention to music in earlier dramas includes Richard Rastall, *The Heaven Singing: Music in Early English Religious Drama*, vol. 1 (Cambridge: D.S. Brewer, 1996), and *Minstrels Playing: Music in Early English Religious Drama*, vol. 2 (Cambridge: D.S. Brewer, 2001); and Peter Happé, *Song in Morality Plays and Interludes* (Lancaster, UK: Medieval Theatre Monographs, 1991).

13. Marvin Carlson, *The Haunted Stage: The Theatre as Memory Machine* (Ann Arbor: University of Michigan Press, 2001), 1–15.

14. Smith, *The Acoustic World*, 112.

century and, for this reason, this book never jumps forward more than thirty years between chapters: it traces a steady progression from late fifteenth century religious drama to Shakespeare's last single-authored plays, from the time of late medieval Wycliffite "heresies" to the early Jacobean church. *Staging Harmony* demonstrates that scholarship on early English drama, so often focused on Elizabethan commercial theater and/or late "medieval" biblical drama, needs to be rearticulated to include the substantial impacts of early Tudor interludes, including reformist morality plays, schoolboy dramas, and court and household entertainments.[15] Each chapter details a specific historical moment that featured a different official religion as well as new innovations to music and drama. In each of these periods, religious, musical, and theatrical contexts must be understood in terms of each other, and in terms of the developments and debates surrounding them. The historical range of this book thus lets us hear how musical, dramatic, and religious changes unfolded over the course of England's complicated periods of religious reformation. The intensity and pace of religious changes in England were such that the representation of sacred music on the stage echoed with the sounds of recent state religions. Someone born when *Mary Magdalene* was first performed could live to see Henry VII's son and three grandchildren all become monarchs, dying as the country's parishes were filled with books of metrical psalms and dramatists were reworking Catholic morality plays into reformist polemics. And someone watching *The Tempest* could recall those polemical plays of the early Elizabethan years as well as Mary's Catholic reforms and humanist comedies like *Ralph Roister Doister*.

Theater is a form of "embodied social thought" in Steven Mullaney's phrase, and like Mullaney, I attend to the "affective core of individual and collective identities" to understand better the crucial role staged music played in shaping how people felt about and socially reacted to England's schizophrenic religious changes.[16] In the long sixteenth century, England went from Catholicism to two forms of reformed religion under Henry VIII, to evangelical Protestantism under Edward VI, to Mary I's restored Catholicism, to

---

15. Recent books that attend to a longue durée of drama, examining not only so-called "medieval drama" but also Tudor interludes, include Heather Hirschfeld, *The End of Satisfaction: Drama and Repentance in the Age of Shakespeare* (Ithaca, NY: Cornell University Press, 2014), and Alice Hunt, *The Drama of Coronation: Medieval Ceremony in Early Modern England* (Cambridge: Cambridge University Press, 2008). On literary periodization, see also, for example, Jennifer Summit and David Wallace, "Rethinking Periodization," *Journal of Medieval and Early Modern Studies* 37.3 (2007): 447–51, and Brian Cummings and James Simpson, eds., *Cultural Reformations: Medieval and Renaissance Literary History* (Oxford: Oxford University Press, 2011).

16. Steven Mullaney, *The Reformation of Emotions in the Age of Shakespeare* (Chicago: University of Chicago Press, 2015), 7, 6.

the "Elizabethan compromise," to King James I's Anglicanism in the aftermath of the Gunpowder Plot. The periods discussed in this book were marked by vociferous debates over religious controversies, heresy trials and burnings, uprisings and failed plots against monarchs, and zealotry of all kinds, but also by compromises, peaceful coexistence, and a lack of widespread violence (like the massacres that occurred in France, for instance). That there is evidence of compromise and tolerance during the course of England's contentious reformations is indicative of the great number of men and women who found their religious identity—or their performance of it—to be flexible enough to navigate rapid changes in state religion. In the words of Trinh T. Minh-ha, "despite our desperate, eternal attempt to separate, contain, and mend, categories always leak."[17] And indeed, historians have recently begun to see religious identity as far more fluid and unstable than can be explained by confessional labels that suggest "Catholics" or "Wycliffites" or "Protestants" or "Puritans" uniformly and consistently believed in any particular doctrines or theologies.[18] Reality, and the texture of religious conscience, are invariably more complex than such simplistic labels suggest.

This book builds on the premise that religious identity is performative, and that performances of religious identities are emotional and social. Music on the stage and in the church relies on the affective and socio-political complexity of religious identity: meaning many things at once to audience members, songs are capable of uniting or dividing their hearers, sometimes doing both at the same time. The stage exposes music's multifariousness, demonstrating that reformers borrow melodies no less than theatrical plots wholesale from the "Papist" traditions they disparage (as playwrights of early Elizabethan morality plays do), that there is inherent hypocrisy in reformist playwrights railing against music in prose while filling their plays with it (as John Bale does), or that melodies move rapidly across confessional markers, between social classes, and from church to tavern and back again.

---

17. Trinh T. Minh-ha, *Women, Native, Other: Writing Postcoloniality and Feminism* (Bloomington: Indiana University Press, 1989), 94.

18. I use confessional markers at times throughout the book because the late medieval and early modern English used these labels; at the same time, I acknowledge that everyone is a mix of religious identities and pure adherence to any one doctrine is impossible. For more on the fluidity of fifteenth and sixteenth century religious identity in England, see, for example, Stephen Kelly and Ryan Perry, "Devotional Cosmopolitanism in Fifteenth-Century England," in *After Arundel: Religious Writing in Fifteenth-Century England*, eds. Vincent Gillespie and Kantik Ghosh (Turnhout, Belgium: Brepols Publishers, 2011), 365 and passim; David Kastan, *A Will to Believe: Shakespeare and Religion* (Oxford: Oxford University Press, 2014), 75; and Peter Marshall, "The Reformation, Lollardy, and Catholicism," in *A Companion to Tudor Literature*, ed. Kent Cartwright (Oxford: Wiley-Blackwell, 2010), 15–30.

The complex webs of association to which staged music refers make it an inherently ambiguous performance tool. Sir Thomas Browne's articulation of how profane music stirs devotional feeling in him is an apt demonstration of music's interpretive promiscuity: "for even that vulgar Taverne Musicke, which makes one man merry, another mad, strikes in mee a deepe fit of devotion, and a profound contemplation of the first Composer, there is something in it of Divinity more than the eare discovers."[19] The sensory experience of sound, as Browne's statement implies, often transcends and synthesizes binaries like sacred and profane, Catholic and Protestant, past and present, high and low class, imagined and real, demonstrating that these categories are much less distinct than contemporary polemicists (no less than some modern scholars) claim. Theatricalized music can have an effect opposite to formal decrees of doctrine, moralized treatises, heresy trials, or religious executions that seek to define and solidify such categories. In representing social, affective, and religious life in all its intricacy, and in unifying auditors in shared acoustic experiences, staged musical moments suggest complexity, hypocrisy, resolution, and compromise rather than oversimplified, absolutist binaries worth killing or dying for.

It is by now almost a commonplace to understand religion and theater as mutually constitutive in the years covered by this book: Mullaney, Stephen Greenblatt, and Sarah Beckwith, among others, have demonstrated the ways in which theater's impact on and reflection of changing state religions mattered in the social, sensual, and emotional lives of audiences and congregations (groups that were, in large part, one and the same).[20] The effects of music upon the community, the body, and the heart (not to mention the soul) were contested raucously throughout England's reformations.

In the poem quoted as an epigraph, Emily Dickinson writes of music's ineffability—does its power come from the "spheres" or "the place" celestial; do the "Hymns from the pulpit" move people because they are natural,

---

19. Sir Thomas Browne, "Religio Medici," in *The Major Works*, ed. C.A. Patrides (New York: Penguin Books, 1977), 149. Ortiz speaks of music as "promiscuous" in its meaning-making in *Broken Harmony*, 2.

20. Mullaney, *The Reformation of Emotions*; Stephen Greenblatt, *Hamlet in Purgatory* (Princeton, NJ: Princeton University Press, 2001); Sarah Beckwith, *Signifying God: Social Relation and Symbolic Act in York Corpus Christi Plays* (Chicago: University of Chicago Press, 2001), and *Shakespeare and the Grammar of Forgiveness* (Ithaca, NY: Cornell University Press, 2011). See also, for example, Jennifer Waldron, *Reformations of the Body: Idolatry, Sacrifice, and Early Modern Theater* (New York: Palgrave Macmillan, 2013); Gillian Woods, *Shakespeare's Unreformed Fictions* (Oxford: Oxford University Press, 2013); and Huston Diehl, *Staging Reform, Reforming the Stage: Protestantism and Popular Theater in Early Modern England* (Ithaca, NY: Cornell University Press, 1997).

human, divine, or magical?[21] She echoes millennia of debate over music's power to connect to the divine, lure people to the devil, aid in worship and heal the sick, seduce people to lechery, create feelings of social harmony, or increase one's vanity in their exceptional skills; the longer history of this discourse is outlined in chapter 1. Marsh summarizes the centrality of these conversations in the era that concerns this book: "one of the early modern period's great cultural debates centered on the power of music for good and ill," and "the theatre . . . provides the best evidence we have that sophisticated ideas about the power of music circulated among a substantial cross-section of the population."[22] Throughout England's reformations, preachers, monarchs, playwrights, and ballad mongers attempted variously to enlist and to censure music's powers, keenly aware of its ability to suggest and promote either consensus or subversion. In listening closely to conversations about music, this book reveals that plays often embodied and enacted accusations against and testaments to music's powers. In the plays studied here, music becomes a shorthand for vice or virtue (in *Wisdom* and several later morality plays), singing choirboy actors embody musical educational ideals (in Udall's plays), and sacred music's proximity to profane song and dance is performed (in everything from the Digby *Mary Magdalene* to *The Tempest*). Staging anti-music polemicists' worst fears and musical defenders' greatest hopes, theatrical performance complicates both views. The nuances of this paradox are not lost, I argue, on Udall, Marlowe, and Shakespeare, but the performance of this dialectic matters to the reception of all of these plays. Theatrical performance reveals that the very qualities that make music alluring and socially beneficial are the same qualities that allow it to be deceiving and manipulative. This is why music is criticized and lauded; this is why it produces such complex effects on its listeners. Music is "compromised," or compromising, in several senses: it often reflects compromises in religio-political practice, it may bring about social compromise, and it may compromise the asserted principles of the people who experience it. Sometimes, as we will see, it is in compromising people's reformist principles or bringing out their hypocrisy that music is best able to bring about the social harmonies so productive in times of religious change.

From the "Te Deums" of *Mary Magdalene* and *Henry V* to the parodies of *Ralph Roister Doister* and *Doctor Faustus*, the theater represented—in various ways—the music of the church's present and past. Staging the feeling of social

---

21. Emily Dickinson, "Musicians wrestle everywhere - ," *The Poems of Emily Dickinson*, ed. R.W. Franklin (Cambridge: Belknap Press, 1999), 103.

22. Marsh, *Music and Society*, 32, 33.

harmony, exposing the hypocrisy of various doctrinal stances, and demonstrating the theatricality of church music, the cumulative effect of the plays performed during England's long period of reformations contributed to the affective fusion of musical devotional practice characteristic of Anglicanism.

In order to hear the music of humans long gone, this book attends to a limited number of extant melodies for stage music, other contemporary manuscript and print music, dialogue about music in the plays themselves, and musical discourses in religious tracts, sermons, theater records, proclamations, ballads, and songbooks. Writing in the early seventeenth century about ancient music, Taverner articulates the problem that the modern scholar faces, too: "Wee must call to mind thinges long since foregotten & allmost cleane worne out of memory, wee must search for things hidden in darknes. . . . For there is not any art which hath soe generally fellt the Tiranny of Time, as this of musicke."[23] While we can never fully reconstruct the sounds of the past, many modern musical groups—informed by musicological research—have recorded their best guess estimates of the kinds of music discussed in this book. These are widely available on CD or streaming audio services, and I suggest relevant recordings in the first footnote of each chapter.

---

23. Taverner, "Praelections musical," 61v.

CHAPTER 1

Sacred, Sensual, and Social Music
Wisdom and the Digby *Mary Magdalene*

> Yet when I find the singing itself more moving than
> the truth which it conveys, I confess that this is a
> grievous thing, and at those times I would prefer not
> to hear the singer.
>
> —St. Augustine
>
> It is after all a great bond of unity for the full number
> of people to join in one chorus.
>
> —St. Ambrose

In the early fifteenth-century treatise *Dives and Pauper*, a rich man (Dives) and a poor one (Pauper) debate liturgical issues. Pauper synthesizes Wycliffite sentiments about the need for sincerity of heart and the function of music in the church, rebutting Dives's objections to church music as vain "hackyn."[1] His response is "neither apology for the shortcomings of the clergy nor a plea for a Wyclifian reform of doctrine but rather something between the two."[2] Pauper gives the caveat that a singer must be intent on praising God: "And þerfor what we syngyn in our preyere we don non displesance to God but mychil plesance, inasmychil as we preysyn hym & worchepyn hym with our power, for every note syngynge to God in chirche or in oþir place with good entencion is a preysyng to God. . . .

---

1. Priscilla Heath Barnum, ed., *Dives and Pauper* (Oxford: Early English Text Society, 1976), 206. To hear the contrast between Gregorian chant and fifteenth-century polyphony, listen, for example, to Benedictine Monks of Santo Domingo de Silos, *Gregorian Chant: The Definitive Collection* (Milan Records, 2008), compact disc; The Tallis Scholars, *Music from the Eton Choirbook* (Gimell, 2005), compact disc; and Russell Oberlin, *Music of the Middle Ages, vol. 6: English Polyphony of the Fourteenth and Early Fifteenth Centuries* (Lyrichord Discs Inc., 1994), compact disc. Late medieval dance music may be heard on Dufay Collective, *A L'Estampida* (Avie Records, 2006). Recordings of *Wisdom* and the Digby *Mary Magdalene* may be heard as "Mind, Will, and Understanding" and "Mary Magdalene," on John Barton, *The First Stage*, Box M (Dover Publications, 1970).

2. Priscilla Heath Barnum, "Introduction," in Barnum, *Dives and Pauper*, x.

And but men preysyn God with song, . . . ellys þey synnyn grevously."[3] That is, Pauper suggests that music may be retained in church only if it is sung with "good entencion." The treatise thus offers a compromise between the view of music as a vain and sinful distraction (a stance taken in many Wycliffite tracts) and a defense of music as an essential devotional aid. The fifteenth century witnessed a growth in the composition of elaborate church music in England, but also continued conversations about music's potential dangers. While a written treatise like *Dives and Pauper* suggests compromise on these issues, it is through performance on the stage that these matters and the debates surrounding them can be more fully realized, and that compromise itself can be enacted.

This chapter will focus on fifteenth-century East Anglia and the music of two plays, *Wisdom* and the Digby *Mary Magdalene*. It will also use the particular dramatic content of these two plays and their social and religious context to set up issues regarding the interpretive flexibility of staged music and the confessional complexity of audiences, issues that resonate throughout the plays and periods discussed in this book and that demonstrate the importance of taking a long view of English theatrical and religious history. In the fifteenth century, more plays were produced in East Anglia than in any other region in England.[4] Examining the popular drama produced in this area reveals the crucial theological role staged music had in the years leading up to the Henrician reformations. It also highlights the social functions of musical drama, for while East Anglia was the center of late fifteenth-century theatrical life, it was also a region with relatively few persecutions of heretics and a complex and hybridized mixture of religious confessions.

Wisdom and *Mary Magdalene* stage and embody anxieties about the sensual nature of music that can be traced back to classical philosophy and early Christian theologians. These plays also engage with liturgical debates that stem from these anxieties, debates regarding the role of music in the church and in the life of a pious Christian. In order to explicate the depth and breadth of these issues, this chapter outlines the complexities of religious diversity among audience members and explains the problems we encounter when speaking about historical religious confessions in times of religious dynamism,

---

3. Barnum, *Dives and Pauper*, 206–7.

4. On East Anglian economic prosperity and its prolific dramatic output, see Victor Scherb, *Staging Faith: East Anglian Drama in the Later Middle Ages* (Madison, NJ: Fairleigh Dickinson University Press, 2001), 24–39; Gail McMurray Gibson, *The Theater of Devotion: East Anglian Drama and Society in the Late Middle Ages* (Chicago: University of Chicago Press, 1989), 19–24, 108; and John Coldewey, "The non-cycle plays and the East Anglian tradition," in *The Cambridge Companion to Medieval English Theatre*, eds. Richard Beadle and Alan Fletcher (Cambridge: Cambridge University Press, 2008), 215–16.

and more specifically in fifteenth-century East Anglia. It also traces a brief history of classical and early Christian musical theories, theories that continued to inform how audiences and playwrights of all the plays discussed in this book understood music.

After these religious and musical backgrounds are established, the rest of the chapter argues five major points about how staged music can contribute to religious discourse, using *Wisdom* and *Mary Magdalene* as examples that have particular implications for fifteenth-century East Anglia, but which at the same time establish recurring functions for dramatic music. Firstly, I use *Wisdom* to show that music can be employed to depict the moral status of characters, and that liturgical music is often theatricalized in order to portray the innocence or salvation of these characters. Secondly, I explain how *Wisdom* and *Mary Magdalene* stage the bodily sensuality that music provokes by using song and dance to index sin and temptation. Thirdly, I look at the parodic rite staged in *Mary Magdalene*, which I contest is open to multiple doctrinal interpretations even as it unifies audience members in the feeling of Christian solidarity against a perverted Saracen-pagan faith. Fourthly, I argue that staged religious music often capitalizes on the affective power of liturgy and sacrament, and I use *Wisdom* to show how music's emotional force empowers it to suggest and urge compromise or at least toleration of theological diversity. The chapter's final section looks at the way staged music—in this case the "Te Deums" that conclude *Mary Magdalene*—can be a socializing force that unifies people in the shared experience of literal harmony, building the sensation of concord even in the absence of real consensus. All of these readings of staged music assume a diversity of religious confessions among participants and audience members: it is to this diversity I now turn.

Confessional Identities: East Anglia and Beyond

When we think about the religious identities of late medieval East Anglian audiences—or any audiences—it is quite difficult to use simple confessional markers like "Catholic," "Lollard," or "Protestant." These terms mean different things in different times: it is anachronistic to refer to "Protestants" before the word exists; it is equally inaccurate to conflate the label "Wycliffite" with the often disparaging term "Lollard" or the overly vague "heterodox." While rituals of inclusion (like baptism) and of exclusion (like heresy trials and public executions) sought to stabilize the definitions of true believers and heretics in order to maximize the power of the official

Church (which is always also a state matter in these periods), the truth as lived and experienced by real people was far more nuanced. For example, the term "Lollard," as Andrew Cole explains, was in the fourteenth and fifteenth centuries a curse word used by those who wanted to employ the "greatest resources of secular and ecclesiastical institutions against individuals at Oxford and elsewhere," and at the same time a term used by self-professed Wycliffites themselves to describe ideas that were not entirely orthodox.[5] Because "Lollardy" is such a contradictory and historically weighty term, I will use the word "Wycliffite" to refer to ideas and tracts that are often labeled "Lollard" in contemporary documents.

Even the marker "Wycliffite," though, is an overgeneralization when used to describe a person or group, because of the interdependent and mutually constitutive natures of so-called orthodox and heterodox identities and ideas. Historians of religion have shown how discourses of heresy—which have *always* been present—influence the thinking of even the resolutely "orthodox."[6] In David Aers's words, the prolific doctrinal conversations of late medieval England "called into question what should count as orthodoxy and heresy," and the result of these sustained conversations was that "all who participate[d] [were] changed in the process."[7] J. Patrick Hornbeck II localizes this phenomenon in East Anglia: "It is important to note that the interface between mainstream and dissenting religious culture operated in both directions. Not only can dissenting groups be affected by developments within the wider community, but the presence of dissenting viewpoints can provide the impetus for mainstream institutions to stress certain ideas over others. . . . In East Anglia, the interplay of dissenting and 'orthodox' religious culture shaped the theological emphases of both communities."[8] Dramas like *Wisdom* and *Mary Magdalene* were a part of this "interplay," and they drew audience members into such a process of engagement. Scholars of late medieval England view the complex theological leanings of these potential audience members in terms of a "devotional cosmopolitism" that proposes a "radical openness to the suggestions of antithetical theologies" in which "difference

5. Andrew Cole, *Literature and Heresy in the Age of Chaucer* (Cambridge: Cambridge University Press, 2008), 72.

6. For a long history of Christian heresies, see Walter Bauer, *Orthodoxy and Heresy in Earliest Christianity*, trans. Georg Strecker, eds. Robert A. Kraft and Gerhard Krodel (Philadelphia: Fortress Press, 1971).

7. David Aers, *Sanctifying Signs: Making Christian Tradition in Late Medieval England* (Notre Dame, IN: University of Notre Dame Press, 2004), viii.

8. J. Patrick Hornbeck II, *What is a Lollard?: Dissent and Belief in Late Medieval England* (Oxford: Oxford University Press, 2010), 200.

is tolerated, re-thought, adapted, and appropriated in the interests of re-imagining Christian community in England"; as we will see, this descriptor could equally be applied to a number of people in the next century, too.[9] While East Anglian "Lollards"—as historical documents name them—had previously been persecuted, and three burnt at the stake, prosecutions of Wycliffite dissenters had become rare by the early fifteenth century.[10] Indeed, not only were many of the firmly orthodox tolerant of Wycliffites, it also seems that many people were neither die-hard Wycliffites willing to be martyred nor orthodox Catholics ready to expose their neighbor for heresy.

Finally, it is not enough to understand religious identity as a spectrum between stable categories of reformers or radicals occupying one pole and conservative traditionalists occupying the other, with a "great muddled middle" in between.[11] Not only was this muddled middle truly great, and not only did those ideological poles reorient frequently throughout the sixteenth century, but moreover individuals undoubtedly experienced significant changes in their own sense of religious identity. Surely this reflects a perennial truth: to varying degrees, everyone considers multiple perspectives on different doctrinal issues to create their own hybridized faith system. Anyone's views on various theological matters is likely in flux from year to year, possibly even from day to day. No matter the insistence of conviction expressed by a religious person, everyone goes through conversions and is shaped by their culture's dominant ideological discourses.[12] It is my contention that even among those who firmly identify themselves with—indeed, are willing to be martyred for—one particular confessional identity, uniformity of belief is impossible by virtue of the fact that credos are expressed in

---

9. Stephen Kelly and Ryan Perry, "Devotional Cosmopolitanism in Fifteenth-Century England" in *After Arundel: Religious Writing in Fifteenth-Century England*, eds. Vincent Gillespie and Kantik Ghosh (Turnhout, Belgium: Brepols Publishers, 2011), 365.

10. Theresa Coletti describes the population as hybridized: religious "hybridity was exceptionally active in East Anglia, where the religious culture sustained a wide range of options and behaviors, showing itself relatively tolerant of the nonconformity it harbored and bred while clinging at the same time to habits and beliefs of what [Eamon] Duffy has called 'traditional religion.'" *Mary Magdalene and the Drama of Saints: Theater, Gender, and Religion in Late Medieval England* (Philadelphia: University of Pennsylvania Press, 2004), 148. See also Margaret Aston and Colin Richmond, *Lollardy and the Gentry in the Later Middle Ages* (New York: St. Martin's Press, 1997), 4, 20–22, and passim; and Gibson, *The Theater of Devotion*, 30–34.

11. The phrase "great muddled middle" comes from Arthur Marotti, "Shakespeare and Catholicism," in *Theatre and Religion: Lancastrian Shakespeare,* eds. Richard Dutton, Alison Findlay, and Richard Wilson (Manchester, UK: Manchester University Press, 2003), 219.

12. Judith Butler writes of the way one can deny their former subjectivity in order to maintain contemporary subjectivity: "The traumatic repetition of what has been foreclosed from contemporary life threatens the 'I'. . . . The subject pursues its own dissolution through this repetition." *The Psychic Life of Power: Theories in Subjection* (Palo Alto, CA: Stanford University Press, 1997), 9.

language and thus interpreted variously by each person who encounters them. And, as we will see in the next chapter, those on the far ends of any religio-political spectrum are subject—as much as those in the "great muddle middle"—to contradictory and changing convictions, positions that are at odds with the implications of "official" dogma (which is itself in flux). So, while I will refer to "Wycliffite" and "traditional" positions in this chapter—and to other confessional labels throughout the book—I refer to these labels inasmuch as they demarcate the terms of debate, and to the extent that they represent the identity markers that were proclaimed by and inflicted on late medieval and early modern English people.

These labels were proclaimed and applied in polemical tracts, in sermons, and in textual and verbal acts of religio-political power like legal proclamations, trials, and executions; they functioned to rally people into groups of seeming similarity and against religious others, to make people *feel*, at any rate, that they were part of a unified, righteous whole against which they could understand another group—be they Wycliffite or Popish or Puritan or Saracen—as similarly unified in their corresponding wrongness.[13] In the plays explored throughout this book, drama moves discourses of polarizing divisions and confessional labels—the rhetoric of law, polemic, and persecution—to a more polysemous poetics and thus to a more moderate position, one that speaks to the diversity among audience members as well as the internal complications and tensions within their own consciousnesses. One of theater's greatest resources for creating theatrical polyvalence is music's interpretive openness.

The Music of the Spheres and Sonorous Bodies

In *Wisdom* and the Digby *Mary Magdalene* as well as several plays discussed in the following chapters, music expresses temptation, sin, and the entrapments of fleshly pleasures as well as religious transcendence, personal devotion, and spiritual ecstasy. The fact that religious music shares properties—and power—with sensual, sinful pleasures makes it a particularly contentious and interpretively indeterminate theatrical resource. Music's sensuality is a source of anxiety for everyone from Augustine to late medieval Wycliffites, from early reformers to Puritans and Anabaptists.[14] In order to understand the ways that

---

13. I am grateful to one of my anonymous readers for helping me think through how to articulate the complexities of these issues of inconsistent confessional subject positions.

14. Overviews of the long history of this debate and its implications in medieval and early modern England can be found in Bruce Wood Holsinger, *Music, Body, and Desire in Medieval Culture:*

Wisdom and the Digby *Mary Magdalene* dramatize debates about music's divine power and its potential for dangerous bodily corruption, it is important to understand the bearing that classical philosophy and patristic Christian theology have on late medieval—and early modern—conceptions of music. Throughout the historical periods covered in this book, there remains the persistent concern that music's sensuality undermines its ability to facilitate or present spiritual transcendence: that what makes music so alluring and promising as a vehicle for sacred experience is also *exactly* what makes it seductive, manipulative, deceptive, and dangerous.

The classical conceptual model of the music of the spheres remained persuasive in England until the seventeenth century. Pythagoras's notion that harmony was a consequence of perfect mathematical proportions that corresponded to the motions of the planetary spheres was expounded on by Plato and developed in Macrobius's *Dream of Scipio*. This Platonist-Pythagorean model posited an essentially harmonious universe in which the planetary spheres created a divine, celestial music that was inaudible to humans but that ordered the world and created the model of harmony to which all terrestrial music could aspire.[15] When patristic theologians created theories of Christian music, they incorporated these classical ideas and attributed the power of the music of the spheres to God.

Written in the early sixth century, Boethius's *De institutione musica* divides all music into three categories: *musica mundana* (the music of the spheres), *musica humana* (the music of the human soul), and *musica instrumentalis* (music performed on earth). For Boethius, *musica humana* and *musica mundana* were the proper domain of philosophers and theologians; *musica instrumentalis* was reserved for those who were merely slaves to material and bodily resources.[16] Boethius's categories of *musica humana* and *musica mundana* became the *musica speculativa* (speculative music), a philosophical study of the way music orders the universe and creates resonant human microcosms. This field continued to be developed—and to some extent privileged—throughout the fifteenth, sixteenth, and seventeenth centuries (speculative music is also crucial to

---

Hildegard of Bingem to Chaucer (Palo Alto, CA: Stanford University Press, 2001): 1–86; Robert Wegman, *The Crisis of Music in Early Modern Europe 1470–1530* (New York: Routledge, 2008), 62–88; Jonathan Willis, *Church Music and Protestantism in Post-Reformation England: Discourses, Sites, and Identities* (Aldershot, UK: Ashgate, 2010), 39–47; and Christopher Marsh, *Music and Society in Early Modern England* (Cambridge: Cambridge University Press, 2010), 32–106.

15. See, for example, Jamie James, *The Music of the Spheres: Music, Science, and the Natural Order of the Universe* (New York: Grove Press, 1993).

16. Boethius, *Fundamentals of Music*, trans. Calvin M. Bower and Claude V. Palisca (New Haven, CT: Yale University Press, 1989). For a succinct overview, see Joseph Ortiz, *Broken Harmony: Shakespeare and the Politics of Music* (Ithaca, NY: Cornell University Press, 2011), 78–80.

early modern "natural magic," as will be discussed in the context of what music means to Doctor Faustus and Prospero).

Boethius's biases toward speculative music echo classical writings about music that register an anxiety about the materiality and corporeality of music: *The Dream of Scipio*, for example, sees the body as a site of corruption, a collection of vulnerable, fleshly organs that cannot hear celestial harmonies. Augustine most influentially inscribes this nervousness about the bodily experience of music into foundational Christian texts. The corpus of Augustinian writings is often contradictory in its positioning on music, and it offers to medieval and early modern Christendom both a model of continued concern regarding music, and potential ways of synthesizing what Bruce Wood Holsinger calls the "sonorous body" with celestial musical models. Augustine transforms speculation regarding the music of the spheres into the divine incantations of Christianity; for him, music is both a system of eternal and perfect numbers and a dangerously sensual and vain stimulation. Augustine's writings, in Holsinger's words, "provide some of the most compelling examples of the wider philosophical and religious inconsistencies of music," and are central to the history of Christian theories of music and its pleasures.[17]

Late medieval and early modern English writers echo these classical and patristic theories of music and anxieties over music's corporeality. For Christian defenders of music, the platonic-Pythagorean music of the spheres becomes the songs of angels, the Boethian correspondences of celestial music (*musica mundana*) with the human soul (*musica humana*) become a sign of God's grace, and terrestrial music (*musica instrumentalis*) sung and played for the glory of God is authorized by the many examples of devotional music documented in the Bible.[18] For music's detractors, any music produced by and audible to humans is necessarily tainted by virtue of being made and consumed with the flesh, and earthly music is defended to varying degrees, if at all, inasmuch as it may be seen as glorifying God. Notorious antitheatricalists Philip Stubbes and Stephen Gosson, for example, rail against music's "massieness" in the late sixteenth century.[19] When it came to the music of the

---

17. Holsinger, *Music, Body, and Desire*, 61. The first two chapters of this book explore in detail the classical and patristic roots of musical-theoretical biases against the body, 27–86.

18. See, for example, Susan Rankin, "Naturalis concordia vocum cum planetis: Conceptualizing the Harmony of the Spheres in the Early Middle Ages," in *Citation and Authority in Medieval and Renaissance Musical Culture: Learning from the Learned*, eds. Suzannah Clark and Elizabeth Eva Leach (Woodbridge, UK: Boydell, 2005), 3–22.

19. Philip Stubbes, *Anatomie of Abuses* (London, 1585), 3O3r; Stephen Gosson, *The School of Abuse* (1579), ed. Arthur Freeman (New York: Garland, 1973), B2r–B2v. See discussion in Ortiz, *Broken Harmony*, 21–23.

church, the primary concern of many Christians, from Augustine to Gosson, was to what extent both singer and listener could be distracted by sensual melodies and harmonies so that they stopped paying attention to God's Word: was music devotional or deviant?

Concerns about this issue were voiced throughout England's many stages of religious reformation, and also by John Wyclif and his followers starting in the fourteenth century. Apprehension over music's potential for bodily harm is registered in a late medieval complaint about church music as "grete cnakkyng [singing with melismas] of curious song in menes eeris."[20] Another work refers to trills and melismas as an indulgent novelty, "a veyn knackyng of new song."[21] Criticisms of Catholic priests in a fifteenth-century Wycliffite tract are typical of concerns about distraction: "Also þei magnyfien more new songe founden of sinful men þan þe gospel of ihu crist . . . for þei bisien [solicit] hem fastere to kunne [know] & do & teche þis newe song þan to kunne & kepe & teche cristis gospel; & þis is merveile [terrible], for þis song distractiþ þe syngere fro devocion & lettith men fro consceivynge of þe sentence."[22] Such detractions, which are rearticulated by early sixteenth-century evangelical reformers and seventeenth century Anabaptists, found their ideas on the premise that earthly music is produced by and experienced in the body, and the body is by its nature fallen, susceptible to sin.

In late medieval drama, the tension between music's potential for divine communion and worship and its material foundation in the voices, instruments, and ears of the flesh is played out in the very site that was the object of contention, for music is voiced through actors' bodies. In the musical moments of the Digby *Mary Magdalene* and *Wisdom*, the sensuality of music is performed through singing, playing, and dancing bodies, which put music's spiritual and sinful valences in productive dramatic tension. *Wisdom* enacts a dialectical relationship between an allegorized inward soul and outward senses, a relationship that is demonstrated musically and has implications for musical theology. *Mary Magdalene* expands on the Gospel story of the fallen woman and uses the sensuality of song and dance to demonstrate her temptation and decline into a life of sin. Both plays exemplify the complexities

---

20. BL MS Additional 24202, ff. 25–28v. Anne Hudson calls this excerpt "Images and Pilgrimages" in *Selections from English Wycliffite Writings*, ed. Anne Hudson (Toronto: University of Toronto Press, 1997), 86, ll. 124–25.

21. Corpus MS X. F. D. Matthew calls this tract "Of Prelates," in *The English Works of Wyclif: Hitherto Unprinted*, ed. F. D. Matthew (Oxford: Early English Text Society, 1902), 76.

22. Corpus MS X. Matthew calls this excerpt "The Order of the Priesthood" in *English Works of Wyclif*, 169.

of religious attitudes toward music's dangers as well as its potential for devotion, godly praise, and the creation of harmonious feeling among people of mixed and contradictory religious confessions. In *Wisdom*, traditional liturgical words and melodies are represented on stage early in the play, but the drama's diverse representations of music make a singular interpretation of this liturgical music impossible.

Morality, Liturgy, and Music in *Wisdom*

Wisdom is typical of late medieval moralities in its thematic structure built on innocence, temptation, sin, and salvation, and in its use of allegory and music to signify each part of this structure.[23] Musical morality plays—because they often depict both sin and salvation through song—juxtapose sacred and profane musical moments on the stage; they thus perform music as both devotional aid and sensual entrapment.[24] The variety of music's significations in the play thus mirrors the theological crux of music's sensual appeal.

Wisdom reveals a faith in music's ability to aid one's salvation, while also acknowledging music's power over one's corruptible flesh. The play calls attention to matters of soul and body when it dramatizes the inward soul ("Mights") and the outward senses ("Wits"), and when it performs liturgical plainchant, sacred and secular polyphony (multipart singing), and dance

---

23. Scholars have posited several locations and contexts for *Wisdom*'s earliest productions, with its extravagant cast of forty actors, singers, dancers, and musicians. Donald Baker argues for a professional company in "Is *Wisdom* a 'Professional' Play?" in *The* Wisdom *Symposium: Papers from the Trinity College Medieval Festival*, ed. Milla Cozart Riggio (New York: AMS Press, 1986), 67–86. Alexandra Johnston suggests that the play had a secular commissioner and context in "*Wisdom* and the Records: Is there a Moral?" in *The* Wisdom *Symposium*, 87–102. Lawrence Clopper argues for a country house performance in *Drama, Play, and Game: English Festive Culture in the Medieval and Early Modern Period* (Chicago: University of Chicago Press, 2001), 259. Gail McMurray Gibson's conjecture is that the play was performed at Bury St. Edmund's for a mixed audience of monastic and lay clergy in *Theater of Devotion*, 125. John Marshall favors a performance by a religious guild in a place like King's College, Cambridge in "'Her Virgynes, as many as man wylle': Dance and Provenance in Three Late Medieval Plays, *Wisdom/The Killing of the Children/The Conversion of St Paul*," *Leeds Studies in English* 25 (1994): 123.

24. When I contrast the sacred with the "profane," I use this word according to its second *OED* definition, that is, "Not relating or devoted to what is sacred or biblical; unconsecrated, secular, lay; civil, as distinguished from ecclesiastical," a usage that is documented in the fifteenth century. As this book will often argue, however, distinctions between sacred and profane are often far blurrier than they at first appear. There are many instances in this book where I talk about the *OED*'s first definition of the word (also in use in the fifteenth century), that is, those things that are "unholy, or desecrating what is holy or sacred; unhallowed; ritually unclean or polluted; (esp. of religious rites) heathen, pagan"; I will usually refer to this as "desecration" or "parody."

music to reveal the shared sensuality of spiritual and profane music. Embody-
ing the inner soul and outward senses through theatrical allegory, the musical
journey from innocence to sin to redemption in *Wisdom* complicates distinctions between musical transcendence and musical temptation, between
bodily and spiritual experience, and between active and contemplative piety; it ultimately advocates for a synthesis between opposing ways of understanding one's spiritual life and music's role in it.

At the start, the play allegorizes the premise that the soul, played by the
female character Anima, consists of two parts: "sensualyté/wych ys clepyde
the flechly feylnge" and is served by the five outward Wits, or senses, and
"resone," which is the "ymage of Gode propyrly," and is served by three
inward Mights (ll. 135–36, 141–42).[25] This is explained to Anima by Wisdom,
a Christ figure who also describes the soul as both "blake and wyght, foull
and fayer" (l. 151). These descriptions are visually represented in the black
costuming of the women who portray the five virgin Wits and the white
clothing of the three male Mights, named Mind, Will, and Understanding
(l. 167, l. 324 s.d.) In addition to making these verbal and visual distinctions,
the play represents these aspects of the soul with music. In *Wisdom*'s first
scene, the Wits and Mights enter and exit the stage in musical procession
and demonstrate that the inner soul is musical, thus dramatizing Boethius's
musica humana. And while there seems to be a distinction between the sensual
Wits and the reasonable, spiritual Mights, there is reciprocity from the start
between these aspects of the soul: things are not, in fact, black and white.
The play's music reinforces the dialectic between inward and outward, sinful
flesh and soulful reasoning. Both parts of the soul sing liturgical music at the
start of the play, showing that the music of the church is an experience of
both body and soul, and is heard by earthly people as well as Christ (represented as the character Wisdom).

Late medieval English liturgy was sacramental and musical. The church's
many services followed prescribed orders for music, sermon, scripture, prayer,
and sacrament; all parts of the services were led and sung by clerics or monastics who had been trained to sing and had the authority to administer
sacraments.[26] Participation in the liturgy was social and cultural, "the arena of

---

25. Citations and line numbers come from *Two Moral Interludes*, ed. David N. Klausner (Kalamazoo, MI: Medieval Institute Publications), 29–100.

26. Says Gabriela Ilnitchi, "Almost no section of the various liturgical services was performed
without some musical enhancement." "Music and the Liturgy," in *The Liturgy of the Medieval Church*,
2nd ed., eds. Thomas J. Heffernan and E. Ann Matter (Kalamazoo, MI: Medieval Institute Publications, 2005), 589. See also Matthew Milner, *The Senses and the English Reformation* (Surrey, UK:

intense communication of cultural values and negotiation of power within social formations."[27] The use of liturgical music in *Wisdom* as well as *Mary Magdalene* negotiates the social and cultural implications of mixed confessional identities.

Anima introduces the female Wits, clad in black, as "five prudent vyrgyns of my reme" who are the "fyve wyttys of my soull wythinne"; she stresses the initial purity as well as the interiority of one's corruptible and outward physical senses (ll. 161, 162). Played by either boys or actual women, they enter singing of their blackness and their beauty; they are, as the stage direction indicates, "syng[ing] 'Nigra sum sed Formosa, filia Jerusalem, sicut tabernacula cedar et sicut pelles Salamonis'" (l. 164 s.d.).[28] Anima immediately translates their song into English:

The doughters of Jerusalem me not lak, [find no lack in me]
For this dyrke schadow I bere of humanyté
That, as the tabernacull of Cedar wythout, yt ys blake,
Ande wythine as the skyn of Salamone, full of bewty. (ll. 165–68)

That their outward darkness conceals inner beauty suggests that the Wits are fundamental not only to the soul's susceptibility but also to the soul's chances at redemption, which may indeed be achieved through such worldly means as the sacraments.[29] Crucially, the "Nigra Sum" the actors sing is a processional antiphon from Canticles (Song of Songs) 1:4, which would have been sung in either single melodic lines or in a polyphonic song showing off the actors' skills at harmonizing.[30] Regardless of the musical setting, the actors who represent outward senses "made in the ymage of synne" (in

---

Ashgate, 2011), 114; G.W. Bernard, *The Late Medieval English Church: Vitality and Vulnerability Before the Break With Rome* (New Haven, CT: Yale University Press, 2012), 91–93; and Jonathan Black, "The Divine Office and Private Devotion in the Latin West," in Heffernan and Matter, *The Liturgy of the Medieval Church*, 41–64.

27. Clifford C. Flanigan, Kathleen Ashley, and Pamela Sheingorn, "Liturgy as Social Performance: Expanding the Definitions," in Heffernan and Matter, *The Liturgy of the Medieval Church*, 652.

28. For more on the possibility of female performers in late fifteenth-century English drama, see Pamela A. Brown and Peter Parolin, eds., *Women Players in England, 1500–1660: Beyond the All-Male Stage* (Aldershot, UK: Ashgate, 2008), and for this particular context, Richard Rastall, *Minstrels Playing: Music in Early English Religious Drama*, vol. 2 (Cambridge: D.S. Brewer, 2001), 463.

29. Wisdom explains that out of the crucifixion "sprenge the sacramentys sevyn,/Wyche sacramentys all synne wasche awey" (ll. 124–25).

30. The possibility of polyphonic harmony is proposed by Rastall, *The Heaven Singing: Music in Early English Religious Drama*, vol. 1 (Cambridge: D.S. Brewer, 1996), 87, and by David Klausner, who supplies contemporary and plausible polyphonic scores for this song in his edition of the play, *Two Moral Interludes*, 94–95.

Wisdom's words) put biblical, Latin words to tunes that sound like a church procession.

In the play's opening scene, then, the Five Wits are the play's musical leaders, which demonstrates that music is both sensual and spiritual. After the white-and-gold clad Three Mights of the rational, inward soul are introduced, the Wits lead them offstage, singing "Tota Pulchra es," a processional antiphon from the Canticles, based on Song of Songs 4:7 and used on Trinity Sunday: "You are completely beautiful, my love, and there is no spot in thee." It is likely that all aspects of a Trinity Sunday processional are here quoted: the words, the music, and the solemn march (l. 324 s.d.). We do not know to what tune the actors sang "Tota Pulchra es"; it could have been a monophonic plainchant from the Sarum (Salisbury) Rite, which was the primary source for liturgical music from the time of its composition in the eleventh century until the English reformations, or one of the newer polyphonic settings of the fifteenth century. The key point is that the dramatic moment reproduces the sounds of the late medieval church, for music permeated almost all aspects of late medieval liturgical practice. If either of these initial musical moments used polyphony, they would be participating in the fifteenth-century trend—buoyed by increased funding to monastic choirs and collegiate musical foundations—of exploiting those mathematical potentials for harmony Pythagoras had described in order to create complex harmonies. The ornate music of the so-called Eton Style is at once derived from classical notions of universal harmonies that authorized its spiritual power and at the same time a highly sensual experience.[31] The late medieval church's musical sensuality was, in fact, part of its strategy for combating heresies. Archbishop Thomas Arundel's 1409 Constitutions explain how "Lollardy" might be addressed through the music, incense, and visual spectacle of the church, thus, "renew[ing] religious life through the traditional sacraments, ceremonies, doctrines of Catholicism."[32] But Arundel's need to defend the Church's sensuality reveals that many found the late medieval liturgical experience—that which *Wisdom* excerpts—to be indulgent, vain, expensive, and distracting.

As we have seen, Wycliffite objections to music are part of a longstanding tradition of musical detractors who associated music with the corruptible body. Late medieval heretical tracts from East Anglia often take cues from

---

31. Robert Wegman describes the so-called Eton style from this period as music that "could be elaborated into prolix settings that lasted up to fourteen or fifteen minutes in performance," *The Crisis of Music*, 149. See also Milner, *The Senses and the English Reformation*, 114–15.

32. Jeremy Catto, "After Arundel: The Closing or the Opening of the English Mind?," in *After Arundel*, 43.

Wyclif himself, who wrote that the devil uses church music as a sinful substitute for reading and learning about God's law: "Also bi song þe fend lettiþ men to studie and preche þe Gospel; for siþ mannys wittis ben of certeyn mesure and my3t, þe more þat þei ben occupied aboute sich bi mannus song, þe lesse moten [compelled] þei be sett about Goddis lawe. Þis stirriþ men to pride, and iolité, and oþere synnys, and so unableþ hem many gatis [paths] to understonde and kepe Holy Writte."[33] Wyclif's concern that music can "stirriþ" the body enough to lead men to "synnys" is replicated by later Wyclif sympathizers as well as post-Luther reformers. A commonly listed heresy for later "Lollards" was "that the divine services are not to be sung with music, and that God takes no delight in song of this kind."[34] It was thus a matter of debate, when *Wisdom* was written and performed, whether the meditative plainchant and prolix polyphony heard in official church services were approximations of God's celestial harmonies or vain indulgences that obscured the biblical word into meaninglessness. It is an oversimplification of the situation to suggest that there were orthodox and heterodox camps battling this out: it was rather more likely the case that people considered these issues and changed their minds, and that many had mixed feelings, enjoying church music while perhaps worrying at what point they were enjoying it *too* much.

In allegorical drama—as opposed to the verbal allegory of a tract or sermon—bodies on stage enact the entrapments of the Flesh associated with music. In *Wisdom*, the actors' bodies dramatize concerns about music by performing musical temptation sequences that depict the Mights falling into a life of vain singing and sensual dancing. But at the same time, the bodies of actors stand for the immaterial things that are supposed to animate and authorize divine music: the soul, Christ. In staging Anima and Wisdom with actors' bodies, then, the play always reveals the sense to which bodies both contaminate and enable any musical experience, be it profane *or* sacred.

The allegory and music used in *Wisdom*'s opening scene set up the play's soul-body dialectic and reveal the ways in which music is central to doctrinal and liturgical issues. While *Wisdom* begins by dramatizing innocence through the use of musical liturgy, *Mary Magdalene*'s first use of music establishes the fallen nature of its protagonist. In both plays, the juxtaposition of profane songs and dances reveals the dangers of music, while the staging of

---

33. John Wyclif, "Of Feigned Contemplative Life," in *Fourteenth Century Verse and Prose*, ed. Kenneth Sisam (Oxford: Clarendon Press, 1950), 123.

34. Wegman translates and quotes this phrase from fourteenth-century chronicler Henry Knighton's list of "doctrinal errors," *The Crisis of Music*, 122.

musical devotion exposes the unsettling lack of distinction between sacred and profane song.

The Dancing Magdalene and the Tempted Mights

The 2100-line Digby *Mary Magdalene*, performed most likely in the third quarter of the sixteenth century, has been the subject of much critical analysis, due to its theatrical and religious complexity.[35] Theresa Coletti, Gail McMurray Gibson, and others have done much to illuminate the play's relationship to fifteenth-century devotional practice, including its complex treatment of gender.[36] Coletti argues that the play's "word and spectacle" reinforce each other to create meaning; building on this suggestion I argue that sound is an equally important and mutually reinforcing resource of the play's "religious and dramatic epistemology."[37] The play's first musical moment, Mary's dance with the gallant Curiosity, is one of many musical theatrical scenes that demonstrate how dance indexes the physical dangers of sensual—and often sexual—music. But in staging, rather than merely describing, the carnal pleasures of dance, the play harnesses the power of embodied performance and enacts the very dangers the play's narrative purports to denounce.

The histories of music and sex are inextricably bound up in each other, and anxieties about music's sensuality are often sexual in nature.[38] In dance, the musical and the sensual are nearly coterminous in their bodily location. The Digby *Mary Magdalene* uses dance to suggest that when Mary interacts with Curiosity in a tavern, dance is not the only way she is moving her body:

---

35. Auspice theories are discussed by Coletti, *Mary Magdalene and the Drama of Saints*, 38. The play's dialect suggests a Norfolk origin, and the fact that it was owned in the sixteenth century by physician and collector Myles Blomefylde introduces a strong possibility that it was performed in Essex into the third quarter of the sixteenth century. John Coldewey suggests that the plays were also performed at Chelmsford in 1562: "The Digby Plays and the Chelmsford Records," *Research Opportunities in Renaissance Drama* 18 (1975): 103–21.

36. Coletti, *Mary Magdalene and the Drama of Saints*, and Gibson, *Theater of Devotion*, 137–78, are foundational studies; more recent works are cited below.

37. In Coletti's words, "The play . . . identifies words and theatrical images as parallel sources of sacred truth or illusion. . . . As resources of religious and dramatic epistemology, word and spectacle in the Digby play dynamically interact and mutually reinforce each other." *Mary Magdalene and the Drama of Saints*, 124. Other critics focusing on the play's visual spectacle include Clifford Davidson, "Middle English Saint Play," in *The Saint Play in Medieval Europe*, ed. Clifford Davidson (Kalamazoo, MI: Medieval Institute Publications, 1986), 31–122, and Victor Scherb, *Staging Faith*, 52–54.

38. For late medieval manifestations of the confluence of music and sex, see Holsinger, *Music, Body, and Desire*, 87–190 and passim.

Curiosity: . . . But wol yow dawns, my own dere?

Mary: Syr, I assent in good maner.

Go ye before, I sue [follow] you nere . . . (ll. 530–32)[39]

Here, Curiosity invites Mary to dance before following her offstage to partake in other activities. Portraying the Gospels' infamous whore as a dancer is part of a long exegetical tradition, and engages early patristic debates about dance.

Several Church fathers discuss the merits and perils of dance: Ambrose, for example, advocates for it as a potential companion of grace; Augustine warns against its frivolity.[40] They reflect the Bible's own ambivalence on this issue, where it is both devotional (Ecclesiastes 3:4, Psalms 150:4, Matthew 11:17) and immoral (Exodus 32:19–25, Matthew 14:6). A fifth-century Italian bishop, St. Peter Chrysologus, gives an example of the exegetical tradition the Digby play enacts, that of figuring Mary Magdalene's interactions with Christ at the house of the Pharisee (Luke 7:36–38) musically: "She beat a melody from her heart and body. She produced the organ tones of her lamentation, played upon the cithar by her long and rhythmical sighs, and fitted groans to the pipe. While she kept beating her breast in reproach to her conscience she made the symbols resound which would please God."[41] Discussing Chrysologus's description of Mary and the legends that figure her as a dancer, Holsinger writes of the ways this demonstrates how "musical predispositions of the body . . . are actualized in dance."[42] The characterization of Mary's whoredom through dance can be found in contemporary sources, too. Clifford Davidson has pointed out that the dance of Mary Magdalene is illustrated in a 1519 engraving by Lucas van Leyden, sometimes called "the Worldly Pleasure of Mary Magdalene."[43] Additionally, continental dramas like the Frankfurt Passion Play feature Mary as a dancer prior to her conversion; she requests to dance to the pipe.

The use of the dance highlights Mary's delight in sensual pleasure—the aural and tactile sensations of music and partner dance. While sermons and engravings verbally and visually represent Mary's sexuality and the dangers of dance, the musical and embodied dancing of the actors playing Mary and

39. All quotations from "The Digby *Mary Magdalene*," in *Early English Drama: An Anthology*, ed. John Coldewey (New York: Garland Publishing, 1993), 186–252.

40. See, for example, Judith Lynne Hanna, *The Performer-Audience Connection: Emotion to Metaphor in Dance and Society* (Austin: University of Texas Press, 1983), 30.

41. Peter Chrysologus, *Sermones*, ed. Alexander Olivar. *Corpus Christianorum, series latina* 24A (Turn-hout, Belgium: Brepols, 1975–1982), 575.

42. Holsinger, *Music, Body, and Desire*, 20.

43. Davidson, "Middle English Saint Play," in Davidson, *The Saint Play*, 83.

Curiosity perform live the very pleasures that music and dance detractors feared, that is, they are actually dancing to real music. Richard Rastall suggests that in its early performances at least, "they would perhaps have danced a *basse dance* to the music of shawms and trumpet," and he also suggests that a flautist and drummer or a single player with pipe-and-tabor would have been adequate.[44] The fact that this dance is likely the only use of instrumentation in the first half of the play guarantees that this is a moment that stands out acoustically and visually. The moment has a narrative function— it moves the story of Mary along; and it has an exemplary function—it reproduces the legend of Mary as a dancer. At the same time, it also transcends the referential features of drama in that the staged dancing reproduces the exact aural, visual, and tactile pleasures of extra-theatrical dancing, the sinful temptations of real taverns.[45] That is, the enjoyment that audience members get from Mary and Curiosity's dancing is similar to the kind of pleasure they would receive when they heard and watched people dance at any den of iniquity. The dance at once *exposes* the sensual dangers of music and dance, and *poses* a danger to the audience by the fact that these sights and sounds enter the auditor's ears and eyes. The lack of distinction between staged and extra-theatrical dancing is repeatedly denounced by anti-theatrical polemicists, as we shall see in subsequent chapters, but the staging of dance is an old theatrical trick by the time Marlowe and Shakespeare do it.

That partner dancing is tactile is also crucial, as part of Mary's identity is her desire to touch the risen Christ, to know him by touching him (which he refuses with his famous *noli me tangere*). Her desire for the transgressive touch, as many scholars have noted, is an important aspect of Mary's femininity and of her widespread appeal. Patricia Badir claims that Mary's conversion also represents an epistemological shift from this tactile knowledge to an understanding that comes through a withdrawal of the senses.[46] This dance sequence thus foregrounds Mary's later conversion from tactile pleasure and knowledge to ascetic spirituality. At the same time, though, there is a sense

---

44. Rastall, *The Heaven Singing*, 173.

45. In this way, it enacts what Jean Alter calls the "performant" function of theater, referring to the non-representational entertainments like processions, sports, and the circus. Jean Alter, *A Sociosemiotic Theory of Theatre* (Philadelphia: University of Pennsylvania Press, 1990), 39–46. As Erika Lin points out, when performant spectacles are represented on the stage, they are pleasing to playgoers and thus bring this performant function together with the referential function of mimetic, representational theater. *Shakespeare and the Materiality of Performance* (New York: Palgrave Macmillan, 2012), 109.

46. Patricia Badir, "Medieval Poetics and Protestant Magdalenes," in *Reading the Medieval in Early Modern England*, eds. Gordon McMullan and David Matthews (Cambridge: Cambridge University Press, 2007): 210.

to which her promiscuity, her penchant for bodily pleasure, is part of her redemption, rather than the antithesis of it. Emma Maggie Solberg has shown how the Blessed Virgin Mary's simultaneous status as whore and saint is crucial to her dramatic and theological power in the N-Town play and in late medieval devotion, and this Mary functions similarly.[47] In the scene that immediately follows, Mary waits in an arbor for her next "Valentine," resting among the precious balms "tyll som lovyr wol apere/that me is wont to halse [embrace] and kysse" (ll. 570–71). That lover turns out to be not another client, but the Good Angel, who heralds the entrance of Jesus. Erotic desire is thus transformed into sacred love, but not before this most sensual of women washes Jesus's feet and anoints him with good-smelling "precyus noyttment," as is described in Luke (l. 640 s.d.).

Mary, who experiences musical pleasure through her ears and arms and shows her love of Christ with her hands, is sent by Jesus to Marseilles, where the first miracle she performs is likely a sexual one.[48] So while the narrative logic of Mary's conversion suggests that she abandons musical pleasure for spiritual asceticism, her bodily abilities remain vital to her power as an evangelist. In Mary's dance, then, the play dramatizes music's sensuality. But instead of condemning music and dance as dangerous entrapments, it sets up a dialectic between sin and redemption, body and soul. In the allegorical *Wisdom*, the songs and dances of temptation expose the flesh's susceptibility to musical dangers in a somewhat similar fashion.

While music was crucial in establishing the solemn, ceremonial tone of *Wisdom*'s opening, it is also used throughout the play's temptation sequence to portray sin. The liturgical procession in which the Mights and Wits sing "Tota Pulchra es" is immediately followed by the entrance of Lucifer, who tells the audience that he is the originator of sin (l. 332). While the play's opening sequence might lead one to suspect that this agent of "syn" would interact with the Five Wits, Lucifer explains that corruption of the "flesche of man" is not sin until the Three Mights of the inward soul consent (l. 360). The play's temptation sequence stages the corruption of Mind, Will, and Understanding—the inward Mights—and it does so musically. That which is interior is susceptible to what is let in through sensory perception. This dual dramatic function for music—signifying inward purity (and later religious transcendence) as well as the entrapments of the outward flesh—mirrors

---

47. Emma Maggie Solberg, "Madonna, Whore: Mary's Sexuality in the N-Town Plays," *Comparative Drama* 38.3 (2014): 191–219.

48. I am grateful to one of my anonymous readers for pointing out that Mary's miracle for the King and Queen of Marseilles is to cure their infertility: the fact that Mary goes "to the kynggys bed" to do so implies that her bodily skills are as important as her spiritual ones (l. 1609 s.d.).

the anxieties of the church fathers regarding music. The combination of music and word activates the mind and body, but that which makes music spiritually and intellectually powerful can just as easily invite temptation.[49]

Lucifer reveals right away that it is through bodily pleasure that he will pull the Mights away from their lives of virtue, explaining why it is that he goes straight to the *inner* soul to do so:

And the flesche of man that ys so changeable,
That wyll I tempte, as I gees;
Thou that I pervert, synne noon is
But yff the Soule consent to mys,
For in the Wyll of the Soule the deyd ben damnable. (ll. 360–64)

Though the play does not stage the Wits' response to Lucifer, it is explained that the Mights receive their cues from these outward senses:

LUCIFER: What seyth sensualité to this conclusyon?
WYLL: As the fyve wyttys gyff informacyon,
Yt semyth your resons be goode. (ll. 478–80)

The play thus argues that the inner soul and outer senses are interdependent, mutually corruptible and mutually redeemable, before it has the actors embody and create the kind of sensual experience that tempts them into their sinful state.

Wisdom's rowdy temptation sequence includes songs and dances for each Might, which are indicative of the sins to which they are tempted. Whatever dance music was played, the tunes would have been upbeat, and the stage directions indicate that they were accompanied by a variety of instruments. The sudden use of instruments and actors' feet pounding on the floor means that these dances are the acoustic opposite of the (likely) unaccompanied liturgical songs sung by the Mights. As with Mary's dancing, the songs and dances are both referential—they function within the play's allegorized plot—and an experiential replica of the sinful song and dance of the "real world" that potentially entraps audience members into music's bodily pleasures. Mind welcomes six dancers and an unknown number of trumpet-playing minstrels to the stage for a devil's dance, which was associated with

---

49. In Milner's words, "When combined with music in singing, the voice offered a potent mixture of the intellective power of speech and affective consonant power of music restoring consonance between body and soul, or creating lustful discord." *The Senses and the English Reformation*, 30.

the Lord of Misrule when pipers and drummers would dance through the church.[50] Understanding does the "Madam Regent," a now lost popular dance, accompanied by a minstrel on bagpipe. The final dance most explicitly ties dancing and music to dangerous bodily pleasure: Will's "sprynge of Lechery" is done with dancing whores. Will introduces six masked women (real women, it seems): three are dressed as gallants and three as matrons. They perform a dancing brothel accompanied by minstrels playing hornpipes, representing lechery.[51] Six dancing women, half of them cross-dressed, whirling about in a couple dance—surely this would have been one of the defining moments of any production of *Wisdom*. This song and dance sequence forces everyone in the audience to experience sin, and then resist it; it exposes the danger of the dancing and music through performance.

The Mights don't just dance, though, they also sing together at least once, and possibly twice:

> MYNDE: I rejoys of thes, now let us synge!
> UNDYRSTONDYNGE: Ande yff I spar, evell joy me wrynge!
> WYLL: Have at, quod I! Lo, howe I sprynge!
>   Lust makyth me wondyr wylde!
>   A tenour to you bothe I brynge.
> UNDYRSTONDYNGE: And I a mene for ony kynge!
> WYLL: And but a trebull I outwrynge,
>   The Devell hym spede that myrth exyled!
>   *Et cantent.* [and they sing] (ll. 612–19)[52]

Taking the parts of "tenour," "mene" (middle part) and "trebull," the Mights engage in three-part polyphony for this unspecified song. There is a long medieval history that viewed polyphony sung by same-sex singers as a metaphor for sexual perversion: it gets vilified as effeminate and even as musical sodomy.[53] And many contemporary texts associate polyphonic music with promiscuous women.[54] Such polyphonic singing in *Wisdom* thus suggests sexual promiscuity almost as clearly as Will's dancing whores.

---

50. Pointed out by Mark Eccles in *The Macro Plays: The Castle of Perseverance, Wisdom, Mankind*, ed. Mark Eccles, EETS, o.s. 262 (Oxford: Oxford University Press, 1969), 211.

51. John Marshall suggests that the "Matrons" to which the text refers were probably wives, and some of them were then dressed as gallants. The women indicated in the *text* are the dancers, not the characters, who are described as matrons and gallants. Marshall, "'Her Virgynes,'" 115, 119.

52. Klausner suggests that Understanding's line "We woll be fresche and it hap *La plu joly*" (l. 512) cues another song. *Two Moral Interludes*, 65.

53. Holsinger, *Music, Body, and Desire*, 159, and chap. 4 passim.

54. See, for example, Ortiz, *Broken Harmony*, 28, 58–64.

While the Mights' three-man song(s), which may well have changed from performance to performance in order to accommodate whichever tunes were fashionable, certainly combined profane words with profane melodies (likely a bawdy love song or drinking song), profane polyphony implicates and reveals its kinship with religious polyphony in a theatrical context. David Klausner's edition of the play suggests a known fifteenth-century tune for this moment, one that "parodies the fauxbourdon style which was often used in a contemporary liturgical context."[55] If a contrafactum setting (putting profane words to melodies from religious music or vice versa) like this was used, then it would expose the similarities between the trendy ornate polyphony of the fifteenth-century church and the harmonies used in profane songs. At any rate, three-part harmony is a skilled type of singing. It would make sense that liturgical singers, for example, clerics at Bury St. Edmunds (one possible performance context for the play), could be cast in these roles. Or, if the performers were laymen, perhaps professional singer/actors, they would be demonstrating their ability to sing the most musically complicated types of liturgy. Singing the mass and singing a street ballad require the same skills, and the interchangeability of musical talent highlights the fine line between secular and spiritual entertainment. If the processional songs of the opening scene were sung in plainsong, "we should probably understand part-music to belong to the forces of evil," as Rastall suggests.[56] If these vice songs instead juxtapose profane polyphony with sacred polyphony, the play implies that sacred and profane multipart singing share the ability to pervert the senses. In either case, the play opens music up to the sorts of critiques of polyphony found in Wycliffite writings. The juxtaposition of sacred and profane music in *Wisdom* stages the paradoxes of musical experience, the ways in which it can aid in both piety and in sin. But even as the play's middle action stages the dangers of music, its conclusion, as we shall see, stages music's ability to express contrition and redemption.

The multivalence of performed music allows for many simultaneous interpretations. While *Wisdom* juxtaposes sacred and profane song, *Mary Magdalene* takes musical heterogeneity one step further to stage a parodic rite that sounds simultaneously of liturgical music and comedy. The rite satirizes the communities against which the play defines itself: the non-Christian people of the lands to which the evangelical Mary has been sent.

---

55. Klausner, *Two Moral Interludes*, 93. The tune he suggests is in the Henry VIII manuscript British Library Add. 31922, fols. 106v–107r. Fauxbourdon is a style of parallel harmonies popularized by Guillaume Dufay in the fifteenth century.

56. Rastall, *Minstrels Playing*, 456.

Profaned Rite in *Mary Magdalene*

In the second half of *Mary Magdalene* (beginning at l. 925), a fantasy of non-Christian practice is theatricalized in the form of a perverted mass for the King of Marseilles, at once a Saracen and a pagan, and one whom Jesus Christ has charged Mary to convert.[57] The multipart religious ceremony in Marseilles includes a dramatized pagan sacrifice, music, nonsense Latin incantation, and a "priestly" absolution of sin that echoes the sacrament of penance: dangerous religious difference is an inversion of Christian religious practice. To its audience members, with their mixed and fluctuating religious confessions, the perverted sacrament could seem truly threatening or aptly humorous, or perhaps an awkward combination of both. Speaking of fifteenth-century French dramatic farce, Noah Guynn writes: "farceurs used the contingencies of performance, the infelicities of performative ritual, and the sheer provocation of bawdy, earthy humor to put pressure on ecclesiastical traditions and authority and to bring blasphemy and heterodoxy into play as the irrepressible others of sacrament and dogma."[58] In this English play, too, a combination of bawdy humor and parodic ritual pressures late medieval ecclesiastic authority.

The preacher Mary serves as a foil to the Saracen/pagan priest and his followers in Marseilles, who are sexual as well as religious perverts. The priest ("Presbyter" in the text) performs his ceremony for the King and Queen, accompanied by his boy assistant. Before they begin, the boy explains that his lust is often fulfilled since his master's fatness causes women to avoid the priest and lay eyes on the boy instead, so he "can houkkyn" with them; the priest responds to this insult by threatening physical abuse, a threat he makes good on after the boy tells him to "fartt" and "kysse my grenne" (l. 1160, 1171). This scatological and violent humor sets up the profane puns of their ritual travesty.[59]

---

57. Marseilles became the naval base for the Franco-Ottoman Alliance in 1536, giving the overt references to Islam the veneer of historical validity. The conflation of pagans and Saracens (Muslims) is common throughout medieval literature, with "others" often praying simultaneously to Mahound, Termergant, and Apollo. See, for example, Jonathan Burton, *Traffic and Turning: Islam and English Drama, 1579–1624* (Newark: University of Delaware Press, 2005); and Daniel Vitkus, *Turning Turk: English Theater and the Multicultural Mediterranean 1570–1630* (New York: Palgrave Macmillan, 2003).

58. Noah Guynn, "The Wisdom of Farts: Ethics and Politics, Carnival and Festive Drama in Late Medieval and Early Modern France" (paper circulated for Merced Seminar in the Humanities, Merced, CA, December, 2013).

59. The priest threatens to whip the boy in graphic terms: "I shall whyp thee tyll thi ars shall belle [peal]" (l. 1169).

While this scene occurs after Mary's conversion from bodily temptations, the parodied rite entertains the audience here in a way similar to
Mary's temptation sequence.[60] The Presbyter's instructions to the boy evoke
the kind of props—altar, book, and vestments—that were necessary for late
medieval worship: "Boy, a boke anon thou bring me!/Now, boy, to my aw-
ter I wyll me dresse—/On shall my vestment and myn array" (ll. 1181–83).
The boy's "servyse of this day," chanted in mock plainsong, bears reproduc-
ing in full:

> *Leccyo mahowndys, viri fortissimi sarasenorum:*
> *Glabiosum ad glumandum glumardinorum,*
> *Gormondorum alocorum, stampatinantum cursorum,*
> *Cownthtys fulcatum, congruryandum tersorum,*
> *Mursum malgorum, mararayorum,*
> *Skartum sialporum, fartum cardiculorum,*
> *Slaundri stroumppum, corbolcorum,*
> *Snyguer snagoer werwolfforum*
> *Standgardum lamba beffettorum,*
> *Strowtum stardy strangolcorum,*
> *Rygour dagour flapporum*
> *Castratum raty rybaldorum*
> Howndys and hoggys, in heggys and hellys,
> Snakys and toddys mott be yower bellys!
> Ragnell and Roffyn, and other in the wavys,
> Grauntt yow grace to dye on the galows! (ll. 1186–1201)

The first line is the only real Latin, in a sense turning Turk the Christian
office: "the Book of Mahound, most mighty men of Saracens." But the mass
is all Latin doggerel and it is possible that this "suggests a deep level of theological criticism against the church with its high Latin" in contrast to Mary's
use of the vernacular when she later converts the King and Queen.[61]
    After the boy utters the service, the Presbyter invites the lords and ladies
of ranks "lesse and more" (l. 1202) to give their offering to Saint Mahound:

> And ye shall have grett pardon
> That longytth to this holy place

---

60. This point is also made by Susan Carter, "The Digby Mary Magdalen: Constructing the
Apostola Apostolorum," *Studies in Philology* 106.4 (2009): 412.
    61. Ibid.

And receyve ye shall my benesown [blessing]
And stond in Mahowndys grace. (ll. 1206–9)

While the scene does not feature the sinner's confession, it represents and perverts the priest's absolution. The joke, of course, is that unconverted pagans are irredeemable sinners who could never be granted grace by Saint Mahound. But the mockery could further suggest that sacerdotal authority to absolve sins is itself laughable.

The sequence of ritual in Marseilles suggests many meanings simultaneously. As any East Anglian regardless of their views on Latin ritual would have got the "in-joke," this moment might seem to unify its audience community. But some in the audience might laugh extra hard at the joke and think that it exposes the obscurity of the Church's Latinity and solemnity, which is set in contrast to Mary's clear, vernacular, non-musical preaching. The scene's effectiveness as comedy relies on the notion that sacrament—words, music, movement, and material objects that effect spiritual change when performed and handled by a priest—is in some measure absurd. The proximity of the scatological and parodic rite to a version of sacramental absolution could, for some, evoke Wycliffite critiques of the Church's insistence on sacramental authority. Audience members more sympathetic to Wycliffite critiques of church ritual could note how easy it is to mock the alienating effects of Latin gibberish, relics, sacraments, bell ringing, and religious music, to dialogize supposedly sacred ceremonies in pagan voices.

But another response would be that only truly wicked people could mock so sacred a ritual as penance; the scene merely shows the dangers of Saracen-pagan practice. John Parker writes about a similarly inverted parodic sacrament—an Antichrist's Eucharist—in the Chester cycle. For Parker, the Chester Antichrist play "redeems through laughter" the real Eucharist and reaffirms its questionable efficacy (if the Antichrist's mass is fake and dramatized, Christ's Mass of the church, by virtue of it being the opposite, is real).[62] This complex line of interpretation would be available to *Mary Magdalene*'s audience, but, as would also be the case for the Chester parody, the play does not univocally force this response. Thus, this entertainingly theatrical moment that mocks real ritual efficacy does something more profound than merely entertain. The audience's divergent and overlapping responses to the scene would have in common a shared disgust for the Saracens. The scene simultaneously points out the audience's different doctrinal

---

62. John Parker, *The Aesthetics of Antichrist: From Christian Drama to Christopher Marlowe* (Ithaca, NY: Cornell University Press, 2007), 82.

positions regarding sacraments while unifying them under a broader category of Christian identification.

Many have noted the potentially unifying effects of religious satire. In late medieval England, "satire could powerfully work to reform and to cleanse the church. Satire implies shared values, or perhaps values that ought to be shared, or, at the very least, lip-service to shared values."[63] In this case, musical religious satire, performed as it is in a play full of profane music, parodies ritual for its sensuality, for the way it delights the ears and base human faculties, like Mary's street dance. That Christian ritual was too sensual—including too musically sensual—was, as will be discussed in later chapters, a vulnerability of Catholic practice that became a basis for reform. It is largely for this reason that parodic rite became a common theatrical resource, one deployed time and again in Tudor comedies like Bale's *King Johan*, Udall's *Ralph Roister Doister*, and the anonymous *Misogonus*, as well as in *Doctor Faustus*. In several of these plays, musical parody's multivalence allows these moments to suggest doctrinal complexity, or even hybridity. It is to musical drama's ability to reconcile—or seemingly reconcile—doctrinal diversity and confusion that I now turn.

Affective Power and Doctrinal Hybridity in *Wisdom*

As we have seen, the beginning and middle sequences of *Wisdom* display music as a devotional aid and symbol of purity, and as a sinful bodily indulgence. In the play's final moments—the confession, forgiveness, and salvation of Anima—music is used to express contrition and redemption, and the affective impacts of these experiences. The play at this point has presented various musical perspectives, and its final musical moments synthesize the bodily and spiritual resonances of music by demonstrating the devotional benefits of music's emotional power. Sensuality is crucial to the power of sacrament, which is experienced through aural, visual, tactile, and sometimes olfactory sensation, and these bodily experiences in turn produce emotional effects. But while the play's closing moments assert the power of sacraments as devotional aids—despite or rather *because* of their sensuality—in the end the play also asserts the effectiveness of more intellectual expressions of religious piety that Wycliffite writers favored, like sermons, prayer, and ver-

---

63. Bernard, *The Late Medieval English Church*, 163. See also Evelyn Birge Vitz, "The Liturgy and Vernacular Literature," in Heffernan and Matter, *The Liturgy of the Medieval Church*, 525, 561.

nacular scripture. The play thus performs a hybridized understanding of religion, one that is consistent with the complex confessional identities of its audiences.

When Anima reappears after the sin dances, she is "in the most horrybull wyse, foulere than a fende" (l. 901 s.d.). Wisdom informs her that only "very contrycyon" will purify her soul—"all the preyer" that can be said will do nothing "wythowt sorowe of hert" (ll. 960, 965, 966). She is sent offstage, weeping and singing her sorrow. The stage directions for Anima's song instruct the actor to heighten the moment's emotional impact: "the Soule syngyth in the most lamentabull wyse, wyth drawte notys as yt ys songyn in the passyon wyke" (l. 995 s.d.). She sings two verses from Lamentations: the song of contrition, "Magna velud mare contricio," from the Good Friday Matins, and the song of nocturnal bitterness, "Plorans ploravit in nocte," from the Maundy Thursday service. Her emotive singing draws its impact from both its "lamentabull" delivery and its associations with Passion Week liturgy.

In contrast to these forlorn solos of contrition, the play's final representation of liturgical music has Anima reenter with the Wits and Mights after she has been presumably absolved off-stage. The nine of them enter "all havyng crowyns, syngynge in here commynge in 'Quid retribuam Domino pro omnibus que retribuit mihi?'" (l. 1065 s.d.). The actors thus sing an antiphon based on a psalm of forgiveness; the words are from Psalm 115, part of which is in the Sarum rite. Their singing may have been done in a polyphonic style—perhaps with the nine actors divided into three-part fauxbourdon—or it could have been nine voices singing the plainchant notes of the Sarum rite in unison.[64] Either way, the voices project a musical grandeur that is in stark contrast to the forlorn singing of the Anima actor in a "most lamentabull wyse." Music is thus used to express the depths of despair and the joy of finding God's grace; when Anima sings, she embodies Pauper's idea of singing "with good entencion."

These staged moments call on the audience to mourn and celebrate in sympathy with Anima. They gain some of their affective power because of their similarity to several moments of traditional late medieval liturgies— the doleful sounds of Kyries and Diriges, the jubilation of Te Deums and Alleluias. On stage and in church services, inner feelings of devotion are expressed with the resources of the body and then perceived by audiences and

---

64. Klausner gives musical settings for both Sarum use plainchant and three-part fauxbourdon, *Two Moral Interludes*, 99–100.

congregants with the outer senses. While *Wisdom*'s temptation sequences establish that the outer senses—"the Five Wits"—endanger the inward soul's "Mights," the play's contrition sequence demonstrates that the symbiotic relationship between body and soul in fact aids in redemption. When Anima expresses her contrition and redemption, she tells Wisdom that her "soule ys waschede by the passyon/Fro the synnys cummynge by sensualyté" (ll. 1070–71). But while sensuality brought her to sin, it also brought her to grace. She goes on to explain that she offended Christ with the "tweyn myghtes" of her soul, the inward and outward parts, and that she uses both of those parts to make sound: "wyth the wyche tweyn myghtys mercy I crye" (ll. 1074, 1078). Wisdom responds by explaining the acoustic impact of her cries: "It perrysschyt my hert to here you crye" (l. 1090). The sounds' physical resonance in bodies is thus essential to Anima's ability to confess and be absolved of her sins though, as we will see, the absolution does not seem to require priestly authority.

The fact that the senses are central to Anima's forgiveness is consistent with Beth Williamson's research on how there is, in medieval piety, a porous relationship between the conceptualization of inner and outer senses (which led to concepts like "the mind's eye"), and that this relationship is not merely a source of anxiety but also an explanation for why sensory perceptions could move the inner soul to greater spiritual feeling and devotion.[65] The spiritual productivity of bodily experience was praised by Augustine in his later writings, as he came to realize that the power of music is not that it transcends the body, but rather that it is grounded in the body. In the *Confessions*, he registers his lifelong ambivalence on the issue, and comes to an understanding that music's bodily grounding grants it spiritually advantageous affective power:

> So I waver between the danger that lies in gratifying the senses and the benefits which, as I know from experience, can accrue from singing. Without committing myself to an irrevocable opinion, I am inclined to approve of the custom of singing in church, in order that by indulging the ears weaker spirits may be inspired with feelings of devotion. Yet when I find the singing itself more moving than the truth which it conveys, I confess that this is a grievous thing, and at those times I would prefer not to hear the singer.[66]

---

65. Beth Williamson, "Sensory Experience in Medieval Devotion: Sound and Vision, Invisibility and Silence," *Speculum* 88.1 (2013): 1–43.

66. Augustine, *Confessions*, trans. R.S. Pine-Coffin (New York: Penguin, 1987), 10.33.5.

Wisdom embodies this Augustinian idea: it puts sonorous bodies on stage and redeems them through singing, suggesting the transformative power of emotion. This theatrical synthesis is consistent with late medieval defenses of church music, and with the proclivity of polyphonic compositions for the church in the fifteenth century. But the play does not make musical liturgy and ecclesiastic power the sole agents of Anima's redemption.

The musical display of Anima's emotional state when she enters in a "most lamentabull wyse" leads the audience to believe that she is truly contrite and thus ready for confession and absolution. It is the sincerity of contrition— not the authority of priestly absolution—that Wycliffite writers often asserted was the necessary condition for God's forgiveness and grace. The transformation of Anima from lamenter to rejoicer happens because she is—one way or another—forgiven while offstage. Julie Paulson reads the play as assertively orthodox and assumes that a priestly confession occurs offstage in order to avoid the "dangerous suggestion that sacerdotal confession and absolution are mere theater."[67] But whether or not this suggestion was avoided was open to interpretation depending on an audience member's doctrinal sympathies. An offstage moment does not positively affirm the necessity of Church-sponsored confession and absolution; despite Wisdom's assertion that Anima will be "reformyde by the sakyrment of penance," the play does not direct one to assume that a priest was present (l. 1112). The moment rather allows for multiple interpretations, which could affirm multiple doctrinal viewpoints on where the efficacy of contrition lies, whether in the heart of the sinner and in God's grace, as Wycliffite tracts often affirmed, or in the priestly absolution granted after auricular confession, as was required by the doctrine of the late medieval church.[68]

Recognizing that there were not discrete camps of "orthodox" and "heterodox" identities allows us to see that, even in rejoinders to Wycliffite heresies, there is evidence of the productive interplay of ideas. Andrew Cole has shown how heresies were vital to and constitutive of both Christianity itself and literary output since the religion's early days. He describes an "orthodox" tract that endorses Wycliffite recommendations for moderating meat and drink, for example.[69] One can also see evidence of Wycliffite influence on "orthodox" writing that addresses the sacrament of confession and church

---

67. Julie Paulson, "A Theater of the Soul's Interior: Contemplative Literature and Penitential Education in the Morality Play *Wisdom*," *Journal of Medieval and Early Modern Studies* 38.2 (2008), 276.

68. Wisdom does confirm the importance of sacraments early in the play when he tells Anima that "the sacraments sevyn" came out of Christ's sacrifice, "wyche sacramentys alle synne wasche awey" (ll. 124–25).

69. Cole, *Literature and Heresy*, 51–52.

music. In the early fifteenth-century tract of "Sixteen points on which the Bishops accuse the Lollards," the bishops respond to Wycliffite ideas on confession by saying, "Also we graunteyn þat schrifte of mouþe is needful to al suche þat ben counselid of God for to make it mekeliche [humble]. But ȝut [yet] very contricioun is more nedeful, forwhi [for indeed] wiþouȝten schrift of mouþe may a syneful man be saved in many a caas, but wiþouȝten veri contricioun of herte mai no syneful man of discrecioun be saved."[70] That is, while affirming the Church's official position that oral confession to a priest, "shrift of mouþe," is "needful," the "orthodox" bishops assert that being "contricious of herte" is the more important criteria for salvation. The same tract reveals a concession, too, to Wycliffite concerns about music: "But wane prestis or religious singen þe latanye for pride, for ipocrisie or for covatise, þan þei plesen not God, but þe fende and þe worlde, wich ben þe maistris þat þei serven."[71] That priests can be prideful, hypocritical, and covetous with their singing remained a criticism of liturgical music for centuries, but it is crucial that even representatives of the Catholic church expressed that concern in the fifteenth century.

Wisdom dramatizes the interplay of Wycliffite and traditional notions of confession and music that we see in these tracts. While the play asserts the spiritual power of religious music—and uses it to express the play's most spiritually transformative dramatic actions—it does not perform any of the seven Penitential Psalms, which were a salient feature of traditional late medieval rituals of penance, both ecclesiastical and private.[72] Rather than using the Penitential Psalms or a priestly absolution as part of Anima's contrition, the play includes rather a reasoned vernacular sermon delivered by Christ/Wisdom himself. The denouement of the play thus supplements sensual and sacramental experiences with devotional aids that are more consistent with Wycliffite preferences.

Immediately following Anima's sung laments and exit, Wisdom delivers a homily on the Nine Virtues, derived from work by the fourteenth-century contemplative Richard Rolle. The sermon goes on for sixty-six lines; Wisdom instructs the audience on a bare stage, as a preacher might (ll. 998–1065). A represented sermon is not a theatrical showstopper, but this moment performs the kind of ecclesiastic experience praised in Wycliffite writing. The

---

70. From MS Trinity College Cambridge B 14.50, reprinted in Hudson, *Selections from English Wycliffite Writings*, 20–1, ll. 69–73.

71. Ibid., 23, ll. 161–63.

72. Clare Costly King'oo, *Miserere Mei: The Penitential Psalms in Late Medieval and Early Modern England* (Notre Dame, IN: University of Notre Dame Press, 2012), 13.

tract called "Of Prelates" stresses: "prelatis ben more bounden to preche trewely þe gospel þan þes sugetis ben holden to paie here dymes [tithe]. . . . Also prelatis ben more bounden to þis prechynge, for þat is comaundement of crist before his deþ and eke aftir, þan to seie matynes, masse, even song, or placebo, for þat is mannus ordynaunce."[73] In his study of many such tracts, Hornbeck concludes that "almost every dissenting text we have considered emphasized preaching in preference to the administration of the sacraments and the other traditional duties of the late medieval clergy."[74] This formal sermon is wholly consistent with gospel teaching and emphasizes deeds and contemplation over ritual and ceremony. While Rolle himself was an orthodox mystic who directed his work to anchorites, his use of the vernacular to explain devotional fervor as well as his scriptural translations appealed to later Wycliffites, and his writings appear in several Wycliffite manuscripts.[75] The content of the sermon, then, would appeal to Wycliffites but would not disenfranchise orthodox Catholics, suggesting the common ground between religious mindsets. And while Wisdom says that Anima will be "reformyde by the sakryment of penance," the penultimate speech of the play features Anima explaining that she is "reformyde thorow feyth in Jhesum," a point she reiterates in Latin, quoting Romans 5:1 (ll. 1151, 1153).[76] Giving the final word to faith, rather than the church's sacraments, also encourages theological interpretations of the play that are more Wycliffite in nature (while using biblical language that will be central to sixteenth-century reformations).

Paulson argues that Wisdom appropriates the contemplative language of self-knowledge and "shows that such language is itself inadequate, and indeed incomprehensible, without the forms of self-recognition only available through Christian ritual practice."[77] Surely the reverse is also true, that ritual is inadequate and, perhaps especially, incomprehensible, without the thoughtfulness, deliberation, and directness of contemplation and spare, non-musicalized language. To clear the stage at the play's dramatic climax for

73. "Of Prelates," in Matthew, *English Works of Wyclif*, 57.

74. Hornbeck, *What is a Lollard?*, 172.

75. Fiona Somerset explains that the Lollard uses of Rolle attest to the wide appeal of spiritual alternatives to an audience much broader than the sort that would be inclined to the extremes of either martyrdom or abjuration. "Wycliffite Spirituality," in *Text and Controversy from Wyclif to Bale: Essays in Honour of Anne Hudson*, eds. Helen Barr and Ann M. Hutchison (Turnhout, Belgium: Brepols Publishers, 2005), 386.

76. Anima quotes Romans 5:1 in saying "*Justificati ex fide pacem habemus ad Deum*," or "Being justified by faith, we have peace with God."

77. Paulson, "A Theater of the Soul's Interior," 278.

nothing but a homiletic speech of some length (I calculate it would take approximately four minutes for an actor to give) does *not* show that language is "inadequate."

Anima is restored by *both* the sacrament of penance and by the intellectual sermon, and her redemption is celebrated through musical liturgy and spoken vernacular words. The fact that drama was so popular in fifteenth-century East Anglia affirms its necessity: the audience and performers needed drama to supplement available ritual practices.[78] Further, by performing religious and profane experience as part of the play's whole narrative, *Wisdom* reveals the independent deficiencies of both church ritual and secular daily life. Melody itself in the fifteenth century demonstrates the interdependence of the sacred and profane, because secular tunes were often used in the liturgical music of the Mass and other rituals; I will explore kind of contra-factum in more detail in later chapters.[79] The play's explicit arguments for a mixed life of active, worldly engagement and contemplation come from Lucifer's bastardized version of Walter Hilton's *Epistle on the Mixed Life*. The play may on the surface seem to advocate against a mixed life since it makes Lucifer the advocate of it. However, *Wisdom*'s overall logic discloses the necessity of profane engagements with the world, and the centrality of bodily experience to spiritual life.

The polysemous nature of music and drama allow them to enact the interdependence of body and soul, heterodox and orthodox, sacred and profane. *Wisdom* urges audiences to embrace this internal pluralism; it mirrors and perhaps shapes ongoing conversations about music's role in religion. We will see this kind of musical urging of doctrinal hybridity in plays as diverse as Bale's *God's Promises*, Wager's *The Longer Thou Livest, the More Fool Thou Art*, and Shakespeare's *Tempest*. While theatrical music can engage in religious debates and urge compromise and congruence, it can also stage mo-

---

78. I was inspired to think of drama as a supplement to religious experience by Derrida's use of the term. For him, a supplement is an extra added to something that is already seen as complete. Derrida thus argues that a supplement can only exist when there is an originary lack. Jacques Derrida, *Of Grammatology*, trans. Gayatri Chakravorty Spivak (Baltimore: Johns Hopkins University Press, 1997), 145. The idea of supplementarity is discussed throughout *Of Grammatology*; I refer to Derrida's formulations in section 1 of Part II, ". . . That Dangerous Supplement . . ."

79. Andrew Kirkman describes the mindset that used secular tunes for *cantus firmi* in sacred masses: "potentially spiritual content inhered already in the secular entity, awaiting, as it were, the appropriate context or mindset to activate its higher, spiritual meaning." *The Cultural Life of the Early Polyphonic Mass: Medieval Context to Modern Revival* (Cambridge: Cambridge University Press, 2010), 44. Beat Kümin also illuminates the proximity of churches and pubs, and thus of sacred and profane space, in "Sacred Church and Worldly Tavern: Reassessing an Early Modern Divide," in *Sacred Space in Early Modern Europe*, eds. Will Coster and Andrew Spicer (Cambridge: Cambridge University Press, 2005), 17–38.

ments of seeming harmony and use the affective power of music to build a sense of social solidarity, even in the absence of doctrinal consensus.

Staging Harmony with "Te Deum"

Like *Wisdom*, the Digby *Mary Magdalene* synthesizes the bodily and spiritual powers of music by staging song as affective, grounded in the body, and resonant with otherworldly figures. In the final moments of the play, singing angels and a participatory "Te Deum" call on the affective and social powers of music to recall the emotional and socializing capacities of Christian religion. Staging the feeling, at least, of harmony, the play's final moments set the confessional identities of Christian East Anglians against the religious alterity of the Saracen/pagans that were portrayed in the play's Marseilles scenes.

Mary Magdalene's final moments bring angels to the stage to display reverence to the soul as well as the body of this former whore after her death. An angel descends in order to bring Mary to heaven, and he hints at his ability to do what angels do best (at least in every extent cycle drama and countless stone and glass versions in medieval churches) when he praises Jesus as "O thou osanna, angellys song!" (l. 2013). Angels' musical abilities need no introduction, and their singing constitutes the most famous and analyzed music of medieval drama. Mary is assumed into the clouds twelve lines after her first upward journey to receive the manna, this time not in silence but accompanied by what was likely sublimely beautiful singing and playing: "*Here shall she be halsyd [hauled up] wyth angellys wyth reverent song. Asumpta est Maria in nubibus. Celi gaudent, angeli laudantes felium Dei, et dicit Mari [Mary is taken up into the clouds, the Heavens rejoice, the Angels praising the son of God, and Mary says]*" (l. 2030 s.d.).[80] The moment echoes cycle drama assumption plays for the Blessed Virgin Mary, who receives glorious musical treatment in, for example, the East Anglian N-Town Mary play. Such inter-theatrical resonances would likely have enhanced the emotional impact, pleasing those in the audience who, as was typical in East Anglia, followed the cult of Mary Magdalene, recalcitrant sinner and hero of the common [wo]man. Considerable resources would have gone into not only the technical feats of having angels haul the Mary actor upward but also the rehearsal of voices and instruments so that the actors were best able to approximate celestial sounds. While the theatrical representations of angel song were likely powerful emotional

---

80. The angels likely perform another scene-stealing song seventeen lines before the play's ending, when the stage direction reads: *"Gaudent in celis [They rejoice in heaven]"* (l. 2122 s.d.).

experiences for audiences, the play returns to human music—and the sounds of the church—for its finale.

The play concludes with the singing of the "Te Deum." A hermit in the wilderness, a character who administered the Eucharist to Mary in a previous scene, invites any clerks present to join in song:

> Now, frendys, thus endyth thys matere—
> To blysse bring tho that byn here!
> Now, clerkys, wyth voycycs cler,
> "*Te Deum lavdamus*" lett us syng! (ll. 2136–39)

Even clerks with little formal musical training would have been able to improvise harmonies and sing along at this moment.[81] But a number of audience members—not just clerks but choirboys and laymen and women—would have been able to join in at this moment, because the "Te Deum" was so well known and oft-performed.[82] Using the tune to conclude a play is typical of late medieval East Anglian drama: both *Castle of Perseverance* and the Croxton *Play of the Sacrament* end with communal singing of "Te Deums."[83]

As with *Wisdom*, *Mary Magdalene*'s conclusion invites multiple doctrinal interpretations. Theresa Coletti argues that "granting the play's transgression of official religion and ecclesiastic authority," the text of the saint play "unequivocally reinforces traditional late medieval religious culture."[84] However, we have seen that the musical moments in *Mary Magdalene* indicate rather that the play invites contemplation of the ways in which religious liturgy and

---

81. Evidence for the late medieval clerks' ability to improvise chants according to well-known rules can be found in Nicholas Temperley, *The Music of the English Parish Church* (Cambridge: Cambridge University Press, 1979), 7–10.

82. As Rastall explains, "to a church-going nation this means business as usual, even if not in a church building." He also says that "*Te deum* was so well known that it is difficult to imagine a medieval audience not joining in," *The Heaven Singing*, 374, 373. Christopher Marsh talks about the makeup of pre-Reformation church choirs in wealthy areas like East Anglia. Liturgical music would be sung by the parish priest as well as parish clerk, chantry priests, choirboys, and English laymen who were invited to join choirs. *Music and Society*, 394–95.

83. David Coleman describes the ending of the Croxton play as the "*communitas* of sacramental worship" in a "closing ritual of recuperation" that means that "Lollard heresy and doubt have been formally acknowledged and triumphantly resolved." *Drama and the Sacraments* (Basingstoke, UK: Palgrave Macmillan, 2007), 28. But the play argues for this so forcefully, Coleman suggests, because such an orthodox understanding of sacraments was not universally accepted, 16–24. Vincent Gillespie calls the moment in the Digby *Mary Magdalene* a "para-liturgical moment of unity between cast and audience" in "Venus in Sackcloth: The Digby *Mary Magdalene* and *Wisdom* Fragment," in *The Oxford Handbook of Tudor Drama*, eds. Thomas Betteridge and Greg Walker (Oxford: Oxford University Press, 2012), 86.

84. Coletti, *Mary Magdalene and the Drama of Saints*, 149.

sacrament create and sustain a community that is internally heterogeneous, but at the same time unified in its Christianity. The play's use of a woman preacher as protagonist as well as its final non-clerical presentation of the "Te Deums" cannot merely be "granted." The fact that a hermit actor, not a priest, leads the "Te Deum" destabilizes the official discourse of the Church, and questions priestly authority.

Wycliffite writings often assert that priest-like authority is given to *all* believers, man and woman (like Mary), lay and clerical: "þer shulde be bot oo degre aloone of prestehod in þe chirche of God, and every good man is a prest and haþ power to preche þe worde of God."[85] In a typical Wycliffite formulation, costume and worldly powers do not grant spiritual authority: "crounne and cloth maken no prest, ne þe emperours bischop wiþ his wordis, but power þat crist ȝyueþ [gives]."[86] By having the non-sacerdotal hermit lead the conclusion of *Mary Magdalene*, which is a celebration of a woman priest, the play thus uses a beloved orthodox musical ritual from the official Church to suggest the more Wycliffite idea that power comes through faith, not position or rank in the church.

But while the "Te Deum" performs religious functions, it performs social ones as well. The tune pervaded late medieval services: it concluded Sunday Matins, third nocturnes, and night offices on Sundays and feast days.[87] At the same time, it was also sung when soldiers returned from war or when propitious military news was received: for example, "Te Deums" were sung at York Minster in 1487 when word came that Henry VII had defeated rebel Lambert Simnel.[88] The singing of the familiar "Te Deum" would have been so expected, so reminiscent of daily East Anglian life that it might not have offended even the most anti-sacramental among the audience. In the way that an unpatriotic American or Brit still often manages to join in with "The Star-Spangled Banner" or "God Save the Queen," the "Te Deum" is joyful and innocuous enough to invite participation from audience members who contemplated any mixture of confessional standpoints that would be found in fifteenth-century East Anglia.[89] The play capitalizes on the social function

---

85. From "The Sixteen points," quoted in Hudson, *Selections from English Wycliffite Writings*, 19, ll.16–18.

86. From the Ashburnham MS "De Papa," in Matthew, *English Works of Wyclif*, 467.

87. Thomas Heffernan, "The Liturgy and the Literature of Saints' Lives," in Heffernan and Matter, *The Liturgy of the Medieval Church*, 81; Ilnitchi, "Music and the Liturgy," in Heffernan and Matter, *The Liturgy of the Medieval Church*, 595.

88. Bernard, *The Late Medieval English Church*, 24.

89. Heather S. Mitchell-Buck has recently argued that the play would have had political and religious relevance in the early years of Elizabeth's reign if it were, as has been argued, performed at Chelmsford in 1562. Mitchell-Buck suggests that the play seems "uniquely suited to such a mixed,

of musical, participatory rituals: their emotional charge, the way they force participants into a shared acoustic moment they create together. Many ritual and social theorists—Victor Turner, Max Gluckman, and, to an extent, Pierre Bourdieu—have described the way that participatory rituals may create the experience of solidarity even in the absence of real consensus.[90] In David Kertzer's words, "the greater the divisiveness in society, the greater the need for compensatory ritual to hold the society together."[91] Cognitive scientists and psychologists have also proven that ritual aids in the production and transmission of social conformity, and studies have verified music's particular role in creating cohesion among diverse people.[92]

Indeed, the "Te Deum" itself has a long history of association with social harmony. An apocryphal but widely known story relates that on the first meeting of Ambrose and Augustine, spontaneous "Te Deums" were "sung together everywhere." Ambrose certainly saw music as important to Christians' sense of collective identity, writing of psalm singing that it "joins those with differences, unites those at odds and reconciles those who have been offended, for who will not concede to him with whom one sings to God in one voice? It is after all a great bond of unity for the full number of people to join in one chorus."[93] This statement was echoed by many defenders of music for generations to come. There are several accounts of "sublime de-

---

post-Reformation audience, one well aware that the Crown's attempts at religious unification over the past thirty years had brought about more division than harmony. For as densely complex as the play is, it resists any attempt to locate a single political agenda at its heart." Such an argument infers that, over a half century after its first performances, the play was perhaps remembered for its ability to mean different things to different people. "Tyrants, Tudors, and the Digby *Mary Magdalen*," *Comparative Drama* 48.3 (2014): 255.

90. For a summary of Turner's *communitas*, Gluckman's rituals of rebellion, and Bourdieu's *habitas*, see David Kertzer, *Ritual, Politics, and Power* (New Haven, CT: Yale University Press, 1988), 4, 6.

91. Kertzer, *Ritual, Politics, and Power*, 63. Revising Durkheim's views of the way ritual reforms a pre-existing social system, Kertzer suggests that solidarity is *produced* by ritual, and works socially and politically "even when participants interpret the rites differently. . . . Ritual is a means by which we express our social dependence; what is important in ritual is our common participation and emotional involvement, not the specific rationalizations by which we account for the rites." Ibid., 67.

92. Psychologist Matt Rossano writes about ritual's ability to transmit social norms in "The Essential Role of Ritual in the Transmission and Reinforcement of Social Norms," *Psychological Bulletin* 138 (2012): 529–49; the emotional force of synchronized group behavior is analyzed in W.H. McNeill, *Keeping Together in Time: Dance and Drill in Human History* (Cambridge, MA: Harvard University Press, 1995); and S. S. Wiltermuth and Chip Heath discuss the trust building of ritual activity in "Synchrony and Cooperation," *Psychological Science* 20 (2009): 1–5. In cognitive scientist Elizabeth Margulis's words, music shifts the attention so that there is a "sense of profundity, sacredness, or transcendence, as everyday goals are set aside, and new insights and perceptions are allowed to emerge." *On Repeat: How Music Plays the Mind* (Oxford: Oxford University Press, 2014), 57.

93. Ambrose, *Explanatio psalmorum*, ed. M. Petschenig. *Corpus Scriptorum Ecclesiasticorum Latinorum* 61 (1919) 1.9, 8. Quoted in Holsinger, *Music, Body, and Desire*, 259.

votional songs as sonorous panaceas promising a harmonious end to social dissension and signifying the musical immanence of salvation."[94]

At the same time, ritual music does not work the same way for everyone. As Kertzer explains, "the problem with seeing ritual as reflecting the social order and reinforcing social harmony by elevating society to the mystical plane is that in many societies social life is riven with conflicts. Sacralizing the conflicts would appear to do little to bring about social harmony."[95] It seems likely that ritual and music bound together the many who had some interest in creating a better church, which would have been a wide but probably not unanimous swath of the East Anglian population.

The performance of this orthodox song and its shared familiarity invite all audience members to remember their commonalities, but the commonalities that include them in shared identification are founded on the exclusion of others. The "Te Deum" constitutes a community that relies firstly on the exclusion of non-Christians, in the way that singing "The Star-Spangled Banner" affirms community by excluding those who don't know the song, that is, non-Americans. Exploring this phenomenon, Theodor Adorno writes of the way music reveals a "fractured total condition" rather than true solidarity, and that musical diversity implies, in fact, "the opposite of reconciled diversity" because musical tastes are socially conditioned rather than inherent preferences.[96] Holsinger points out that Adorno articulates the social dynamics of perceived harmony that Ambrose and others mystify, arguing that "the sense of harmonious solidarity music gives to those who sing in one chorus often founds itself upon the violent exclusion of those whose voices are silenced."[97] In the sense that *all* East Anglians are Christians able to sing along to the "Te Deum," then, this moment confirms their communal solidarity, a unification predicated on their distinction from those pagans who do not sing "Te Deum," that is, the orientalized non-English others the play caricatures.

In the context of East Anglian audience members' experiences in church, the laity's frequent inclusion in a church service via the "Te Deum" only

---

94. Holsinger, *Music, Body, and Desire*, 64.

95. Kertzer, *Ritual, Politics, and Power*, 62–63.

96. Theodor Adorno, *Introduction to the Sociology of Music*, trans. E. B. Ashton (New York: Seabury Press, 1976), 120.

97. Holsinger, *Music, Body, and Desire*, 260. Adorno's ideas about music are similar to those expressed by Fredric Jameson, who revises Durkheim's notion of "the symbolic affirmation of unity" through religion to argue that symbolic resolution through narrative is never a real resolution, but rather that "the ultimate subtext is social contradiction." Fredric Jameson, *The Political Unconscious: Narrative as Socially Symbolic Act* (Ithaca, NY: Cornell University Press, 1981), 292, 82.

offers an arbitrary, fictionalized inclusion in the ecclesiastic structure. The Church's hierarchy was still in place in fifteenth-century East Anglia, and reinforced in every ecclesiastic event. For example, only clerics were allowed into the sanctuary to witness the miracle of transubstantiation while the parishioners attempted to view the act through an opening in the choir screen. The play's theatrical representation of the Church's means of ideological dissemination calls attention to the way in which the unification of community through song masks real ecclesiastic power, a power that usually distances the laity from faith's central mysteries. The clergy's authority to be the sole distributors and leaders of sacraments, of the Word, and of liturgical music making has been called into question repeatedly throughout a play that represents a woman preacher and restages two sacraments with actors and props.[98] The final participatory moment further marginalizes clerical hierarchy by giving leadership of a community-affirming musical experience to lay actors and musicians, and it exposes episcopal authority as redundant. In this way, the singing of the "Te Deum" enacts a hybridized religious experience, a compromise of authority and lay participation. The *Mary Magdalene* playwright uses music to explore doctrinal issues, to create the feeling (if not the reality) of consensus, and to urge compromise on the matters of dispute *between* Christians; we will see that both Udall and Shakespeare use the theatrical resource that is music in similar ways. Performed when occasional heresy trials and executions tried to solidify confessional labeling, *Mary Magdalene* does the opposite, exposing the interdependence of myriad theological viewpoints and the impossibility of stable religious identity. *Wisdom* and *Mary Magdalene* stage harmony and encourage hybridized, reconciled confessional communities without constraining the diverse opinions that would later prove more fracturing.

It is in this environment of religious diversity that John Bale was born, in a coastal East Anglian hamlet in 1495. For him and for those around him as they approached the early years of England's reformations, music was a central issue. Bale, who admired Wyclif as the "morning star" of the Henrician reformation, agreed on principle, but not in practice, with the notion that

---

98. Wycliffite Walter Brut wrote, "the soul of a man and the soul of a woman are of the same special species. Therefore, since the soul of man is capable of priestly power, it follows equally that the soul of a woman is capable of the same power. . . . Nothing more is required for someone to become a priest except that he be admitted by God." " 'Respondet Waltherus Bryth': Walter Brut in Debate on Women Priests" in Barr and Hutchison, *Text and Controversy*, 230. I have not made gender central to my discussion, but others have, including Coletti and Shannon McSheffrey, *Gender and Heresy: Women and Men in Lollard Communities, 1420–1530* (Philadelphia: University of Pennsylvania Press, 1995).

music was distracting and unholy. The sixteenth century brought England a unique state religion that retained more music than its Protestant European counterparts.[99] In Bale's plays, the complexity of feelings regarding religious music in the early years of England's reformations suggests the affective origins of the retention of so much musical rite in the so-called Anglican compromise of Elizabeth's reign.

---

99. The seeming improbability of the English Reformation's music, considering the movement's affiliations with and debt to Wycliffite ideas, is indicated in statements such as Donald Smeeton's: "The Reformation is credited with fathering a whole hymnody. It is strange, therefore, to note the attitude of the Wycliffites." *Lollard Themes in the Reformation Theology of William Tyndale* (Kirksville, MO: Sixteenth Century Essays & Studies, 1986), 218.

CHAPTER 2

Musical Hypocrisy
The Plays of John Bale

> Take to ye yowre traysh, yowre ryngyng, syngyng
> and pypyng,
> So that we may have the scryptures openyng.
>
> —*King Johan*

> The yonge men in the forenone played a Tragedy of
> Gods promises in the olde lawe at market crosse with
> organe plainges and songes very aptely.
>
> —John Bale, *The Vocacyon of John Bale*

John Bale, one of the leading English polemi-
cists of the Henrican Reformation, recognized early on the constitutive role
drama could have in the spread of the new religion.[1] He and his company
were patronized by Thomas Cromwell, who was chief minister to Henry VIII
and an architect of the English Reformation in the 1530s. In 1535 Cromwell's
secretary and publicist Richard Morison had proposed that the Crown combat popish feasts and superstitious theater with a propagandistic drama that
would advance Reformation ideals:

> Howmoche better is it that those plaies shulde be forbidden and deleted
> and others dyvysed to set forthe and declare lyvely before the people
> eies the abhomynation and wickedness of the bisshop of Rome, monkes,
> ffreers, nonnes, and such like.[2]

---

1. To hear music contemporary to Bale's plays, listen, for example, to The Hilliard Ensemble, *Music for Tudor Kings: Henry VII and Henry VIII* (Musical Concepts, 2008), compact disc. *King Johan* may be heard on John Barton, *The First Stage*, Box N (Dover Publications, 1970), vinyl LP set. For the sound of traditional antiphons accompanied by an organ (similar to those used in *God's Promises*), listen to "Invitational Antiphon" on Benedictine Monks of Santo Domingo de Silos, *Silos: Their Finest Chants* (Milan Records, 2006), compact disc.

2. Morison is quoted and contextualized in Paul Whitfield White, *Theater and Reformation: Protestantism, Patronage, and Playing in Tudor England* (Cambridge: Cambridge University Press, 1993), 14.

While Morison focuses on slandering the "wickedness" of Catholicism before people's "eies," Bale's plays display a deep investment in reaching people's ears, too.

In three of his five extant plays (and there were at least nineteen more), Bale uses music to demonstrate the moral and spiritual superiority of the reformed religion compared to Catholicism. Evangelical reformers, including Bale himself, condemned Catholic worship for its vain and indulgent use of ornate, incomprehensible Latin music. In their sermons and prose tracts, some advocated for an outright ban on all music—and others for the allowance of only homophonic, unaccompanied psalm singing—but Bale's plays reveal that these stances were harder to maintain in dramatic performance. In *Three Laws*, *King Johan*, and *God's Promises*, Bale constantly shifts the way he represents music's role in the new church. In his morality drama *Three Laws*, music is used to deride "popery" (in Bale's preferred phrase) but also to restore order to the church, while *King Johan*'s anti-music stance seems to better resemble Bale's prose polemics. And in a move that one could describe as downright duplicitous when compared with his other writing on music, Bale uses traditional-sounding liturgical antiphons to structure the biblical *God's Promises*. The shifting attitudes toward music demonstrated in these plays reveal the impossibility of confessional uniformity in even the most zealous. For despite his well-earned reputation as a fanatic, Bale's plays show that he is increasingly moderate when it comes to music.[3] While Bale condemns hypocrisy so vehemently that he names a vice character after the term in *Three Laws*, we will see that Bale often displays something like hypocrisy in his use of dramatic song and dance. Paradoxically, Bale's compromises on otherwise rigid positions, adjustments in tactic, and other inconsistencies likely make his plays more successful in their aim to bring people to the new faith. In every sense "compromised," Bale's drama appeals to diverse religious perspectives, showing them to be far less incompatible than they claim to be.

---

3. Andrew Hadfield's assessment of his writing is typically dismissive: "his writing is nothing if not repetitive." *Literature, Politics, and National Identity: Reformation to Renaissance* (Cambridge: Cambridge University Press, 1994), 51. Bale has been receiving more favorable, or at least interested, attention as of late. For an overview of recent scholarship, see Mark Rankin, "Introduction: The Presence of John Bale in Tudor Historical and Literary Scholarship," *Reformation* 18.1 (2013): 21–35.

John Bale and Music's Role in the Henrican Reformations

By the late 1530s Henry had broken with Rome and dissolved the monasteries, and further ecclesiastic reforms led by Cromwell and Archbishop Thomas Cranmer were underway.[4] All these changes were happening despite the king's habitual wavering on various doctrinal matters and much popular resistance, including the 30,000-person Pilgrimage of Grace and uprisings in Somerset, Cornwall, and East Anglia.[5] The heart of the continental reformation theology adapted by Cromwell, Cranmer, and Bale emphasized three things: *sola scriptura, sola fidei, sola gratia.* That is, authority rests in the scriptures—the Word—not in a church or with a priest; salvation comes through faith and not good works; and salvation is possible only because of God's grace. These doctrinal shifts had musical consequences for church services.

Ideas about music and worship from early reformers on the Continent made their way to England. Martin Luther had thought of music as an excellent spiritual aid and only disparaged profane music. Swiss reformers took a much more austere stance, as demonstrated by Ulrich Zwingli's ban on choral and organ music in Swiss churches. His successor, Heinrich Bullinger, also rejected church music, and argued in the late 1540s that the New Testament never endorsed singing at all and neither should the church. Jean Calvin later advocated for only unison, congregational singing of metrical psalms, with no accompaniment (as opposed to the polyphonic settings definitive of much Catholic liturgical music).[6] In England, vernacular Bibles began to be required in churches around 1537, and the priority for music shifted to audibility of the Word. Polyphony was often simplified or replaced

---

4. From 1536–1540, the entire structure of medieval monasticism was destroyed. When 8–10,000 ex-religious were expelled from their cloisters, the endowments were redirected to the Crown. For a summation, see Peter Cunich, "The Dissolutions and their Aftermath," in *A Companion to Tudor Britain*, eds. Robert Tittler and Norman Jones (Oxford: Wiley-Blackwell, 2009), 221–37.

5. S. B. House offers a succinct account of this resistance and its impact on Cromwell and Bale: "Cromwell's Message to the Regulars: the Biblical Trilogy of John Bale, 1537," *Renaissance and Reformation* 26 (1991): 123–38.

6. For more on the opinions of Luther, Zwingli, Bullinger, and Calvin regarding music, and on their influence on the English church, see, for example: Jonathan Willis, "Protestant Worship and the Discourse of Music in Reformation England," in *Worship and the Parish Church in Early Modern Britain*, ed. Natalie Mears and Alec Ryrie (Surrey, UK: Ashgate, 2013), 136–40; Willis, *Church Music and Protestantism in Post-Reformation England: Discourses, Sites and Identities* (Aldershot, UK: Ashgate, 2010), 45–52; and Robin Leaver, "The Reformation and Music," in *European Music 1520–1640*, ed. James Haar (Woodbridge, UK: Boydell & Brewer, 2006), 371–400.

with homophony, or some reformers—including Bale at times—advocated for music to be eliminated from services altogether, because it encouraged vanity and distracted from sermon and scripture.[7]

It was clearly a time of great upheaval. The leading reformers, Bale among them, tended to be former friars rather than anyone who had ever identified as Wycliffite. Like Luther, they attempted to reform the traditional church from within before they broke with Catholicism in favor of the new church established under Henry's new Royal Supremacy in the late 1530s.[8] As was the case for the fifteenth century, the radical fluctuations of this period make categorical binaries like "orthodox and heretical" and "Catholic and Protestant" inaccurate, and Peter Marshall has suggested that the term "evangelical" is more relevant than the anachronistic "Protestant" for describing those who advocated for Henry's break with Rome and the adoption of Lutheran, Calvinist, and Zwinglian ideas in England's early reforming days.[9] While Bale's project was to solidify binaries, to set what he saw as the "true church" against a Pope he and many of his fellow reformers identified with the Antichrist, his musical plays expose these categories as overlapping, mutually constitutive, and in productive dialectical tension rather than diametrically opposed.

In his *Votaries*, Bale complains that the "Popes clergie . . . speciallye in the churche here of Englande" have commanded people to participate in "evensonges, howres, processions, lightes, masses, *ryngynges, syngynges, sensynges*, and the devyll and all of such hethnyshe wares."[10] The characterization of music as a clerical practice meant to dupe its congregants into blind submission is typical of reformist polemics focused on anti-ceremonialism. But while Bale toes the party line in his prose, he undermines this position when he writes for a medium that is itself performative. Theatrical performance mimics ritual performance in ways that print never can: it thus makes sense that it was through performance and not prose that Bale realized that music was an indispensable element of religious experience.

---

7. Around 1544, Thomas Cranmer sent Henry a letter explaining that music should be "as nere as may be, for every sillable, a note," a proposal that was typical. Quoted in Roger Bray, "England i, 1485–1600," in Haar, *European Music*, 497.

8. Further examples and context can be found in Peter Marshall, "The Reformation, Lollardy, and Catholicism," in *A Companion to Tudor Literature*, ed. Kent Cartwright (Oxford: Wiley-Blackwell, 2010), 21.

9. Ibid., 21. The first recorded use of "Protestant" to refer to English adherents to the reformed religion is by Thomas Becon in 1551 and, as it wasn't in common currency until Elizabeth's reign, I will thus refrain from using the term until chapter 4, when discussing the early Elizabethan years.

10. John Bale, *The Actes of Englysh voltaryes* (Antwerp: S. Mierdman, 1546). Emphases mine.

Bale's inconsistencies when it comes to music and sound expose the larger problems of English ecclesiastic reform in the sixteenth century. Nostalgia and popular opinion made an anti-music stance like Bullinger's untenable in England in actual practice. Such a view undermines the project of evangelism, for a new faith remains unattractive to most if it lacks the social, affective, and spiritual experience of music. These sentiments eventually led to an Anglican "compromise" under Elizabeth that provided a more musical worship experience than many early English evangelicals had proposed, and a more musical experience than is found in many forms of Protestantism that prevailed on the European continent. Bale's biography, while by nature unique, makes him a particularly representative product of the theatrical and religious climate of England's early sixteenth century.

Born in Suffolk in 1495, Bale spent his early childhood in East Anglia, where plays like *Wisdom* and *Mary Magdalene* were performed with frequency. The young Bale must have attended these popular theatrical events, for later he would go on to borrow forms and techniques from the drama of his childhood. While he grew up in a region swirling with Wycliffite discourse, Bale was resistant to it; when he came to Wyclif's ideas after his conversion, he regretted this early deafness to them.[11] His parents sent him to the Carmelite House in Norwich when he was twelve, where he was trained in sacred music, the antiphons and anthems and chants of Catholic rite. Writing from his Carmelite years reveals a fascination with religio-musical experience, and one of his hymns to the Virgin survives. He remained with the Norwich Carmelites until he went up to Cambridge in 1514 as a member of the order. He studied at Cambridge while (future Archbishop of Canterbury) Thomas Cranmer was a fellow there, at a time when early humanist and evangelical ideas from the continent were debated and promoted. Looking back later in life on his Cambridge years, however, Bale said that he wandered about in "blindness of mind."[12] His early work exuberantly upholds traditional practice and the ecclesiology of the Carmelite order; it is filled with devotions to the Virgin Mary and other saints, reverence for the liturgy, and formal scholarship on the history of the church.

Not only was Bale likely to have been exposed to East Anglian drama as a boy, but also the Carmelite order was well known for its dramatic productions. Thus, Bale's pre-conversion experiences shaped the reformer-

---

11. Bale ignores Wycliffites in his earliest writings, and even soon after conversion "he was scarcely aware of their importance as 'morning stars' of the faith he had recently adopted." Leslie Fairfield, *John Bale: Mythmaker for the English Reformation* (West Lafayette, IN: Purdue University Press, 1976), 40.

12. John Bale, *Catalogues*, 1:702.

playwright in his later years.[13] As an evangelical reformer, Bale perhaps recalled his own early deafness to Wycliffite ideas and Cambridge reformist and humanist thought, understanding the stubbornness of a religious subject brought up on the seductive images and sounds of the Catholic Church. As a Tudor playwright who understood the affective and pedagogical power of religious drama, Bale refashioned the morality plays of his Suffolk youth in *Three Laws* and the cycle drama that had been popular among the Northern and East Anglian Carmelites in *God's Promises*.[14]

Bale's conversion to evangelical ideas—at the behest of a Suffolk courtier—likely occurred around 1533, while he was a Carmelite Prior of the White Friars at Ipswich. Hoping to use his pulpit to spread the reformed Gospel and change the church from within, he initially stayed on as a friar even though he had repudiated the Catholic Mass, sacraments like auricular confession, and the cult of Mary and the saints. For the rest of his career, Bale was caught between external pressures—ever-changing official policies from the Crown, vocational responsibility, financial and political pressures to support and protect his family—and his internal convictions, which had gone through a deep, very personal break after almost thirty years as a Carmelite.[15] Pursuing his passion for reform, Bale left the Carmelites in 1536 and moved to London, and his career as an evangelical playwright and polemicist began.[16]

Bale's shift to radical religious politics came with significant personal risks. The consequences of his conversion and fiery promotion of reform included two exiles: the first to Wesel, Germany in 1540, after Henry VIII executed Bale's friend, patron, and protector, Thomas Cromwell, and again to Basel after the accession of Queen Mary in 1553 (Bale had been bishop of Ossory

---

13. Bale's conversion is the subject of Oliver Wort, *John Bale and Religious Conversion in Reformation England*, which analyzes Bale's autobiographical writings about his own conversion and argues for the influence of his Carmelite years on his reformed identity (London: Pickering and Chatto, 2013).

14. Peter Happé explains that Bale probably saw Norwich cycle plays while at the Carmelite house, Ipswich's plays when he was a prior, and Doncaster's (and possibly York's and Beverly's) when he was prior there; he likely also saw the continental cycles when he traveled to the Low Countries in his early years as a friar. "John Bale's Lost Mystery Cycle," *Cahiers Elizabethan* 60 (2001): 5.

15. Peter Happé pointed out that "religion is emotional and reassuring, not just didactic," before asking the provocative question: "how far could Bale convert?" "Rejecting and Preserving Bale's *John the Baptist*" (conference paper presented at International Medieval Congress, Leeds, UK, July 3, 2013).

16. In addition to writing and acting in plays and publishing ecclesiastical tracts, Bale was a leading bibliographer of English writers, a historiographer, and a biblical exegete. For recent discussion of some of Bale's non-dramatic work, see: Ruth Ahnert, *The Rise of Prison Literature in the Sixteenth Century* (Cambridge: Cambridge University Press, 2013), 173–78; Ernst Gerhardt, "No quyckar merchaundyce than lybrary bokes": John Bale's Commodification of Manuscript Culture," *Renaissance Quarterly* 60.2 (2007): 408–33; and Christopher J. Warner, "John Bale: Bibliographer between Trithemius and the Four Horsemen of the Apocalypse," *Reformation*, 18.1 (2013): 36–47.

in Kilkenny, Ireland, having returned to England during Edward's reign).[17] While most of his plays were written in the late 1530s, Bale's plays were performed in England and Ireland through the early years of Elizabeth's reign, and he had many of them printed on the continent while in exile. Bale's company, "Bale and his Felowes," toured England, and later Ireland; they played in town halls, Oxbridge colleges, cloisters, and noble households including the royal court, to audiences filled with everyone from noblemen (even monarchs) to lowly servants.[18] These diverse audiences shared the experience of self-definition in a tumultuous political climate, surrounded by myriad social and political discourses on religion.

"Bale and his Felowes" were primarily patronized by Cromwell, but they were supported by Archbishop Thomas Cranmer, too.[19] The troupe contained at least five male actors who had been musically trained, probably in the choir schools. The group likely included many more ex-friars and clerics like Bale, and as Paul Whitfield White explains, "every monk who had to participate in the divine office would have had some experience with plainsong and perhaps even with the polyphony fashionable in Tudor anthems and antiphons."[20] In three of his five extant plays—*Three Laws*, *King Johan*, and *God's Promises*—Bale utilizes his company's ability to perform musical theater filled with songs both sacred and profane. *Three Laws* reworks the Catholic morality play and reveals the undeniable debts the new religion, its drama, and its music have to traditional practices. In *King Johan*, Bale attempts to dramatize the anti-music, anti-ceremonial standpoints he upholds in nondramatic contexts, even while he relies on musical performances and a theatricality that shares much with the ceremonies he derides. In his more popular play *God's Promises*, Bale abandons the hard-line principles undermined in *King Johan* and shifts his strategy to create a compromised work that appeals to a far greater number of people. *God's Promises* proposes a new kind of ritualized music that is as at odds with Bale's polemic as it is consistent with the desire of his audiences to keep music central to religious life.

---

17. On Bale's episcopal tenure in Ossory, see Alan Fletcher, *Drama, Performance, and Polity in Post-Cromwellian Ireland* (Toronto: University of Toronto Press, 2000), 166–74.

18. White lays out the touring patterns of Bale's troupe in *Theater and Reformation*, 22–27.

19. White provides a history of Bale's company, which is the only troupe prior to Shakespeare's for which we can assign patron, playwright, and a repertory of extant plays. He thinks that it is representative of other troupes engaged in stage propaganda during the early Reformation; Bale's is one of over fifty noblemen's troupes on record. Ibid., 12–13. See also House, "Cromwell's Message to the Regulars," 123–38.

20. White, *Theater and Reformation*, 21.

Three Laws: New Uses for Old Plays

Three Laws is an apocalyptic revision of Christian history in which Infidelity and his six papal vices assault and corrupt God's Laws through three periods of history, those of Natural Law, Moses's Law, and Christ's Law. As a reworked morality play, it is the play closest to Bale's East Anglian dramatic roots. But Bale subverts the older dramatic tradition and turns the devil-animated vice figures of plays like *Wisdom* into pope-animated Catholic clerics. White calls Bale's mixture of vulgar songs and sacred rite an "original feature" of his stage polemic.[21] However, Bale's drama adapts the juxtaposition of sacred and profane used in the earlier East Anglian drama (and apparent in many facets of medieval life). The play is less than subtle when it figures the Roman Catholic Church as a corrupting force as old as time and the Pope as the Antichrist, but such blatancy is consistent with contemporary polemic, and with much of Bale's own prose.[22] The five-act play was likely written in the early 1530s when Bale was newly converted to reformed religion. As such, the play lambasts virtually every element of the Catholicism he had so recently left, from aural confession to masses for the dead to monasticism itself. However, for all that *Three Laws* rails against Roman liturgy and music, the final act sees the restoration of God's law celebrated musically, and the printed play ends with a sixty-six line macaronic "Songe upon Benedictus," based on verses from Luke. James Simpson points out Bale's debt to the pre-Reformation morality play as one of several paradoxes *Three Laws* inhabits, and I would add that his debt to the role of music in morality plays is central to that paradox.[23]

Three Laws has long and varied performance and textual histories. It reached Tudor audiences from all religious and demographic groups, through a variety of forms, and in several locations. These performance and textual histories also reveal the play's success: Bale continued to present and print it for decades. Evidence of doubling indicates that the play was performed by professional players for aristocrats and townspeople alike; and Bale prepared

---

21. Ibid., 38.

22. Bale refers to the Pope as the Antichrist in several works, even using the phrase in the title of *Yet a course at the Romyshe foxe . . . wherby wyllyam Tolwyn was than newlye professed at paules crosse openlye into* Antichristes *Romyshe relygyon . . .* (London, 1543); *The epistle exhortatorye of an Englyshe Christyane vnto his derelye beloued co[n]treye of Englande against the pompouse popyshe bysshoppes therof, as yet the true members of theyr fylthye father the great* Antichrist *of Rome* (London: Henry Stalbrydge, 1544); and *The pageant of popes. . . . In the vvhich is manifestlye shevved the beginning of* Antichriste *and increasing to his fulnesse.* (London?: 1574) (emphases mine).

23. James Simpson, "John Bale, *Three Laws*," in *The Oxford Handbook of Tudor Drama*, eds. Thomas Betteridge and Greg Walker (Oxford: Oxford University Press, 2012), 112.

a 1551 performance of *Three Laws* while Rector at Bishopstoke Hampshire, when he likely employed parishioners from the serving classes as actors. The text used for that performance probably resembled the one Bale had printed in Wesel in 1548 while in exile, which made the text widely available for reading and performance by other professional or amateur troupes.[24] *Three Laws* was performed in noble households and churches, before powerful leaders and poor parishioners. Bale himself acted in it on some occasions, as did both professional and amateur actors.[25]

Three Laws retains the festive comedic and musical elements that marked the sort of drama that had been a part of Bale's East Anglian monastic life, and a part of the cultural lives of many in his play's audiences. The seven musical moments of *Three Laws* borrow contexts from the drama of Bale's youth: as in *Wisdom* and the Digby *Mary Magdalene*, Bale's theatrical music represents the sacred, the profane, and the profaned sacred. But in *Three Laws*, the profaners are not vaguely defined devil workers or ominous caricatures of religious alterity. The lead vice, Infidelitas (Infidelity), and the other vices of *Three Laws* are very specifically "popish"; they are the leaders and workers of a *Christian* church, one with which much of Bale's theater audience still identified. The awkward and cogent specificity of Bale's vice figures and their crimes is made manifest in their perversions of traditional rituals.

The action of the second act centers on the corruption of Natural Law (the time between Adam and Moses) by two specific vices, Sodomismus (Sodomy) and Idololatria (Idolatry), both led by Infidelity. Infidelity enters singing a silly song:

> Brom, brom, brom, brom, brom [broom]
> Bye brom, bye, bye.
> Bromes for shoes and powcherynges [rings for closing a purse],
> Botes and buskyns [half boots] for new bromes.
> Brom, brom, brom. (ll. 176–180)[26]

Musically advertising his brooms, he presents himself as a street peddler. The "Brom" song title is printed in the Stationer's Register of 1563–64; broom-selling songs were a particularly popular type of street cry. Extant copies of the play print a blank stave below the words—actors could fill in the popular tune to which they wanted to set the song. The near proof of a catchy,

24. Peter Happé, "John Bale and the Practice of Drama," *Reformation* 18.1 (2013): 14.

25. For more on the play's performance history, see Peter Happé, *The Complete Plays of John Bale*, vol. 1 (Cambridge: D.S. Brewer, 1985–86), 22, and White, *Theater and Reformation*, 12.

26. Happé, *Complete Plays*, 2:72.

upbeat tune that breaks the auditory monotony of a performance that had until that point consisted only of formal dialogue about commandments is a reminder that melody and tempo are crucial dramatic forces.

The audience was likely pleased to hear a familiar song, but that familiarity quickly extends beyond traditional street culture to the audience's attachments to traditional religion. Part of Bale's theatrical project is to manufacture an anachronistic precedent for Catholic corruption. Infidelity immediately follows his song by greeting Natural Law in a way that reveals him to be a practicing Catholic:

> I wolde have brought ye the paxe,
> Or els an ymage of waxe,
> If I had knowne ye heare . . .
> I was in soch devocyon,
> I had nere broken a vayne. (ll. 184–86, 191–92)

Infidelity's status as peddler *and* Catholic implies that traditional religion profits from the selling of things: there is little difference between selling a broom or a pax (a tablet imprinted with the image of the crucifixion).[27] Infidelity's musical entrance thus not only instantly changes the play's mood and form—we are now in a musical comedy—but also renders traditional religion as popular, unserious, and seductive.

According to the doubling scheme printed in *Three Laws*, "into five personages maye the partes of thys Comedy be devyded," with the first as: "The Prolocutour, Christen Fayth, Infydelyte."[28] That Bale (who names himself Prolocutor) would have thus also cast himself as the vice, the play's lead role and by far the most musical, indicates that he must have been a talented singer and entertainer. One can speculate about where he acquired his performing chops—Carmelite drama and musical rites are certainly leading contenders—but, at any rate, no playwright would assign himself to his play's most musically and comedically challenging part if he was not confident that he would be up for the task.[29] Infidelity cajoles and teases the rather credulous Natural Law with witty, at times hilarious, verbal skill. For all of Bale's qualms

---

27. The analogy is one that Bale must have found effective, for, in his 1548 verse *An Answer to a Papistical Exhortation*, he replies to a papist attack by comparing the Pope's poetic powers to those of a peddler: "Everye pylde pedlar/Wyll be a medlar/Though ther wyttes be drowsye/And the lernynge lowsye." (Antwerp: S. Mierdman, 1548), sig. A2.

28. Happé, *Complete Plays*, 2:121.

29. James Simpson calls him "Bottom-like" in his eagerness to take the best roles, "John Bale, *Three Laws*," 119.

about the evils of secular diversions, he uses the best tricks of the entertainment trade for his own purposes.[30] But perhaps the fact that Bale cast himself as Infidelity betrays some anxiety over the vulgar role: assured of his own moral fortitude, he took on the part to prevent another actor from the dangers of acting out Infidelity's sins and then enjoying them too much.

Bale uses popular music and literary/dramatic forms with tenuous moral justification to capture his audience's attention long enough to hear his polemic message. Simpson elucidates the paradox at the heart of the play's entertaining vice sequences: "theatre of this kind deploys and repudiates theatre itself, since the middle section of the play is at once the most 'merry,' the most dramatic, and the least desirable."[31] The play *is* funny, with Infidelity vowing to keep Natural Law as far away from his professed purpose to worship God alone "as my grandma kept her cat/from lyckynge of her creame" (ll. 341–42). But when Infidelity reveals a few lines later that his strategy for doing so is to unleash Sodomy and Idolatry on mankind, the play's use of these specific vices—well-publicized, alleged Catholic sins—raises the stakes considerably and turns the subject matter gravely serious and pointedly relevant. Bale pairs these two vices to suggest that Catholicism's mutual exclusion of the sacraments of marriage and holy orders leads to clerical sodomy.[32]

When Sodomy and Infidelity enter together, Sodomy, dressed as a monk, says or sings:

Have in than, at a dash,
With *swash, myry annet swash*;
Yet maye I not be to rash
For my holy orders sake. (ll. 395–98)

The italicized words (my emphasis) may be the refrain to a popular song, one sung in the later plays *A Pore Helpe* and Nicholas Udall's *Ralph Roister Doister*.[33] Whether or not Sodomy actually sings while entering, his arrival establishes the notion that he enjoys the pleasures of vulgar music. His musical

30. Happé makes a similar point, "John Bale and the Practice of Drama," 18, as does Brian Gourley, "Carnivalising Apocalyptic History in John Bale's *King Johan* and *Three Laws*," in *Renaissance Medievalisms*, ed. Konrad Eisenbichler (Toronto: Centre for Reformation and Renaissance Studies, 2009), 175.

31. Simpson, "John Bale, *Three Laws*," 112.

32. A point also made by David Coleman, *Drama and the Sacraments* (Basingstoke, UK: Palgrave Macmillan, 2007), 48.

33. Cathleen H. Wheat, "*A Poore Help, Ralph Roister Doister,* and *Three Laws*," *Philological Quarterly* 28 (1949): 312–19.

tastes suggest that the sexual sins of monastic life—"sodomy" meant any kind of sexual depravity—are related to the monks' indulgence in profane entertainments.[34]

Bale addresses the dangerous acoustic powers of Catholicism when Sodomy's "owne swetehart of golde," the sex-changing, darkly magical Idolatry, professes her adherence to the popish faith (l. 480). In six stanzas, Idolatry mocks Catholic practice as pagan superstition: Saint Germaine keeps her chickens from harm (ll. 507–09), and a bit of sheep's dung with Saint Frances's girdle will protect from an illness, for example (ll. 539–42). But the witch-Catholic's first stanza contains the most biting satire. Read alone, these lines seem like the professions of a good Catholic:

> I never mysse but paulter [mumble]
> Our blessed ladyes psaulter
> Before saynt Savers aulter,
> With my bedes ones a daye.
> And thys is my commen cast,
> To heare Masse first or last,
> And the holy frydaye fast,
> In good tyme mowt I it saye (ll. 499–506).

Equating both idolatry and witchcraft to reading the Psalter, saying the rosary, and hearing the mass condemns contemporary practices that were still part of the lives of many in Bale's audiences.

The idea that the Church corrupts mankind by coercing congregants into hearing and reciting masses is further elaborated when Infidelity gives his instructions to Sodomy and Idolatry: he tells them how to "corrupt in man / the lawe wryt in hys hart" (ll. 654–55). Infidelity gives distinct commands to each of the vices, and to Sodomy he charges the rituals and sounds of the Roman rites. He lays particular emphasis on death rituals:

> Set thu fourth sacramentals,
> Saye dyrge, and synge for trentals,
> Stodye the Popes decretals,
> And mixt them with buggerage [buggery/sodomy]. (ll. 671–74)

---

34. The *OED* defines sodomy as "an unnatural form of sexual intercourse," and documents early uses of the word that involve women, for example, 1387 Trevisa, *Higden* (Rolls) III. 5: "Mempricius . . . forsook his wyf at the laste, and usede sodomye as a schrewe schulde."

Thus it is implied that, since the beginning of human history, an evil mixture of sacramentals (that is, ceremonies that are not sacraments such as administering holy water), dirges, requiem masses, and other Papal music have covered up unnatural sexual behavior.

While Henry's Ten Articles of 1536 aimed to get rid of "abuses . . . under the name of purgatory," the Purgatory article maintained that a Christian man should "pray for souls departed . . . and also to cause others to pray for them in masses and exequies [funeral rites], and to give alms to others to pray for them."[35] Corporate intercession for the dead was one of the most central and persistent rituals of traditional religion, and the Office for the Dead, the "Placebo" and "Dirige," Trentals, and the Requiem Mass were the most stubbornly upheld practices throughout the sixteenth-century reformations. When William Marshall issued an English Primer in 1534 that omitted the "Dirige," the outcry was so fierce that he reissued a second edition with the "Dirige" restored a year later.[36] Like many reformers, Bale saw intercession and death rituals as non-biblical and open to corruption, and he was frustrated by Henry's defense of them and their continued popularity. Bale's play suggests that these songs and prayers for the dead fall on deaf ears while financially and spiritually bankrupting the souls who perform them. Additionally, Sodomy's role in encouraging these aural death rites suggests that the desperation of the bereaved opens the door for sexual abuse by the clergy.

The end of the act dramatizes Bale's thesis for Idolatry and Sodomy, that man was first corrupted sexually, which was enabled by both the Church's performance of ritualized music and its encouragement of secular music. Infidelity calls for a group song after the three vices lay out their plans to distort Natural Law:

> To quycken our spretes amonge
> Synge now some myry songe,
> But lete it not be longe,
> Least we to moch offende. (ll. 695–98)[37]

---

35. The Ten Articles of 1536 were the first articles of faith to be adopted by the Convocation during Henry's reign, and are an intriguing and problematic mixture of reformed and traditional doctrine. Reprinted in *Religion and Society in Early Modern England: A Sourcebook*, eds. David Cressy and Lori Anne Ferrell (New York: Routledge, 1996; 2007), 25.

36. For more on traditional death rituals and the doctrine of Purgatory, see Eamon Duffy, *The Stripping of the Altars: Traditional Religion in England 1400–1580* (New Haven, CT: Yale University Press, 2005), 338–76, 382.

37. Act 3 ends much the same way, with Infidelity proposing a song at line 1219 to recreate their minds and celebrate his plans with Avarice and Ambition to corrupt Moses's Law. Act 4 does

The "merry" song is not indicated, but Infidelity's ironic suggestion that they keep it short so as not to offend *too* much implies that the actors were to sing something sufficiently bawdy, like one of the many drinking catches that remained popular throughout the sixteenth century.

The stage directions and lines following the call for this profane song, printed in Latin, translate as:

> After the song Infidelity shall say in a high/loud voice: Let us pray. Almighty and everlasting God, who has formed the laity in our image and likeness, grant, we beg, that just as we live by their sweat, so may we deserve to enjoy perpetually their wives, daughters, and maidservants. Through our lord Pope. (ll. 699–703)[38]

In this scene, profane song is immediately paired with a mock liturgical prayer that suggests, in Latin, that church officials had sexual relations with female congregants and took advantage of their authority as confessor and the relative privacy of the act of confession. The full force of the joke would have only been felt by those who understood the Latin: nobles and church officials, many monastically trained like Bale himself. For those who comprehended the joke, the accusation is harsh and lurid. Bale takes the risk of offending precisely those with the most power, but also those most able to help enforce his propaganda. The immediate juxtaposition of bawdy song and sacred prayer suggests that corruption is often achieved aurally and that Catholic monks are as depraved as those who perform lascivious songs. By linking carnal lust to aural penetration, Bale condemns Catholic monks as both sexually and spiritually threatening.

Act 3, the destruction of Moseh Lex (Moses's Law) by Avaricia (Avarice) and Ambitio (Ambition), continues to suggest sexual depravity among church leaders and in their music, beginning with Infidelity's tour-de-force reenactment of a duet of sorts between a friar and an old nun. At the top of the act, Infidelity enters in the middle of a laughing fit. Moses's Law, innocently eager to make a friend, asks Infidelity what is so funny, and Infidelity reports that the fun happened the previous night at Compline:

> In ded yester daye it was their dedycacyon,
> And thyrde in Gods name came I to se the fashyon.
> An olde fryre stode forth with spectacles on hys nose

---

not end in song, but Infidelity celebrates the burning of Christ at line 1754 by saying that He will now be able to sing and make cheer.

38. The translation is Happé's, *Complete Plays*, 2:166. The parody is also blasphemous, adapting Genesis 1:26: "And God said, 'Let us make man in our image, and after our likeness.'"

Begynnynge thys Anteme—a my fayth, I do not glose—
Lapides preciosi. (ll. 810–14)

The *Lapides preciosi* comes from the *Breviarum Romanum*'s common for the
dedication of a church. As with Infidelity's act 2 entrance, a blank stave is
given, which would allow an actor to write down the tune they sing. It is
likely that the actor sang at least a few lines from the Divine Office here. The
need for the actor playing Infidelity to sing in Latin means that any troupe
that performed this play would have cast an actor trained in liturgical music
in this part, and we know that Bale himself originated the role. Thus, the
part requires an actor to call on his memories of the liturgy to recreate in
jest what he once sang in earnest.[39]

The mockery continues when Moses's Law asks what followed the friar's
song. Infidelity explains that the nun was "Crowynge lyke a capon, and thus
began the Psalme:/ *Saepe expugnaverunt me a iuventute mea*" (ll. 818–19). Again
a blank stave is given, and the re-presented nun is to sing from Psalm 128:1;
the Latin translates to "often they have overcome me in my youth." An audience member trained in Latin would perhaps get the joke immediately, but
for the laity in the audience, Infidelity explains the salaciousness:

A symple probleme of bytcherye [lechery].
Whan the fryre begonne, afore the nonne
To synge of precyouse stones,
'From my youth,' sayt she, 'they have confort me,'—
As it had bene for the nones. (ll. 821–25)

That is, the nun had responded to the friar's reference to "precyouse stones"
by implying that there are stones—testicles—that have long brought her and
her fellow nuns comfort. Bale's inclusion of this bawdy joke not only suggests sexual encounters between monastic "celibates" and nuns (a theme that
recurs throughout several of Bale's prose tracts), but also it implies that church
ritual itself contains coded references to such improprieties. The laity may
not know what filth they hear and sing, so polluted and convoluted is the
Latin breviary.

The play's final act, a version of Revelation, features a vengeful God's
apocalyptic burning of Infidelity and the restoration of the three laws. God

---

39. Happé emphasizes that "Singers trained at choir schools would have very detailed memories
of the liturgy," *Complete Plays*, 1:24.

restores each of the three laws through verbal speech acts: three 6-line puri-
fications banish forever the offending vices in succession. The Laws' immediate reaction, the first actions of what is symbolically the new church, are
not a request to hear the Gospel, as one might anticipate in a play focused on
restoring the primacy of scripture. After an entire play that equates musical
liturgy with the devil, manipulation of the laity, and sexual depravity, Bale's
vision of a reformed religion is not one that privileges the Word to the exclusion of musical worship. Instead, once they have praised God and promised to serve the people, the Laws call for a final song:[40]

> NATURAE LEX: In rejoyce of thys, make we some melodye.
> MOSEH LEX: The name of our God to prayse and magnyfye.
> CHRISTI LEX: I assent therto, and wyll synge very gladlye.
> *Hic ad Dei gloriam cantabunt 'In exitu Israel de Aegypto,' vel aliud simile.*
> [This to the Glory of God they sing 'when Israel came out of Egypt'
> or some such song.] (ll. 1911–13)

The stage direction suggests that the three laws sing from the Psalter (this is
Psalm 113), but the exact song is left open to improvisation.

The song was likely one of Bale's own creations. The 1548 text ends with
a sixty-six line macaronic "Song upon Benedictus Compyled by Johan Bale."
There are no directions about when and how the song is to be sung, but the
words "thus endeth thys comedy concernynge thre lawes" are not printed
until after the song's text, so the song is clearly part of the play.[41] The text
comes not from the Psalms but from Luke 1:68–79, which is also used in the
canonical lauds of Roman rite; the Latin scriptural components are thus well
known and related to the theme of Psalm 113 that is suggested in the stage
directions. Bale leaves the Latin Gospel untranslated and adds lines of his own
English between the first and last lines of each verse, as in the first stanza:

> *Benedictus dominus Deus Israel*
> Whych hath overthrowne the myghty Idoll Bel,
> The false god of Rome, by poure of the Gospell,
> And hath prepared from the depe lake of hell,
> *Redemptionem plebis sue.* (ll. 1–5)

---

40. Happé points out that the Laws' lines immediately preceding this introduction to song (ll.
906–10) paraphrase the "Nunc dimittis" from the Compline service, *Complete Plays*, 2:179. Thus,
even before song is called for, Bale is creating a reformed version of Catholic rite.

41. The song is printed on pages 2:122–4 of Happé's edition.

It may be that Bale includes a capitulation to traditional religion here as a way "to sugar the pill of the new learning . . . among his spectators who might not be convinced."[42] But while it is perhaps a savvy move to include a linguistically hybridized song that enacts the heterogeneity of practices from Roman rite to evangelical anti-ceremonialism, Bale's inclusion of the song contradicts the practices for which most of his fellow reformers advocated.[43]

Musicologists have documented the extensive Edwardian reforms that stipulated severe restrictions on singing in church.[44] The song printed at the end of *Three Laws* would have been illegal under many of the Edwardian reforms enacted in the 1540s while the play continued to be performed and reprinted; only hymns of praise to God directly, and in English, were to be sung. Bale, for all his concern over the evils of confusing and manipulative Latin music, fights for the retention of *some* music in a reformed church, provided that it is scripturally based. The inconsistency between Bale's theoretical stance on music in his prose and the music he allows in practice in his performances suggests a personal inability to part entirely with the ritual elements of his formative years. Bale's internal discrepancy on this issue—as evidenced by *Three Laws'* final song—likely made this and similar plays appeal to diverse audiences.

It seems, then, that Bale was unwilling to imagine a church without music. While he remained adamant in his condemnation of extra-biblical music like funeral dirges, his plays advocate a place for some singing. Bale's Carmelite upbringing and long participation in liturgical culture may betray the purity of his *sola scriptorium* message, but his inability to condemn traditional musical practices completely kept his work and ideas persistently relevant and politically sound through much of the mid-sixteenth century, when Henry VIII and Elizabeth I (as well as the Catholic Queen Mary, of course) expressed a similar unwillingness to part with sacred music. Despite Bale's desire to uphold the binaries of Catholic and evangelical, *Three Laws* reveals an early

---

42. Thora Blatt, *The Plays of John Bale: A Study of Ideas, Techniques, and Style* (Copenhagen: C.E. Gad, 1968), 150.

43. Alan Fletcher also notes the tension between Bale's dramatic use of liturgy and his reformist principles: "Bale's abhorrence of ornate Roman liturgy is continually expressed in terms which betray his sensitivity to that liturgy's theatricality. . . . In drawing heavily not only on traditional stagecraft but on the aesthetic resources of the liturgy of the religious tradition that he had come to despise, Bale was attempting a delicate ambivalence that must, in practice, have been a difficult thing to maintain." *Drama, Performance, and Polity in Pre-Cromwellian Ireland* (Toronto: University of Toronto Press, 2000), 168.

44. See, for example, Leaver, "The Reformation and Music," 378–86; Bray, "England i, 1485–1600," 487–506; and Peter le Huray, *Music and the Reformation in England 1549–1660* (Cambridge: Cambridge University Press, 1978), 8–11.

inability to do so, at least with regards to music. In *King Johan*, Bale seems more able to maintain these binaries in the play's musical performances, but the play cannot escape the paradox that to satirize musical rite in a play is still to perform it and grant its power.

King Johan: Killing Kings and Ceremonies

Like *Three Laws*, *King Johan* engages in that typical obsession of early reformers: the search for and invention of historical precedent for their reforms.[45] Bale refashions England's thirteenth-century king into a proto-evangelical martyr, at odds with allegorical-turned-historical figures like Sedition, who becomes Archbishop Stephen Langton, and Usurped Power, revealed to be the Pope himself.[46] Bale's King Johan anachronistically rails against ceremonies of the Church and calls for attention and adherence to the Gospel alone; the play is consistent in its rendering of music as corrupt, devilish, and popish. But despite this representational consistency, the exigencies of performance necessitate that, in practice and interpretation, the play is unable to sustain a univocal attack on music.

Before his execution, King Johan describes the sounds of Catholicism—bells, singing, instrumental music—as noisy trash that prevents the aural flow of scriptural teaching:

Why, know ye it not? The prechyng of the Gospell.
Take to ye yowre traysh, yowre ryngyng, syngyng and pypyng,
So that we may have the scryptures openyng. (ll. 1391–93)[47]

The play is filled with satiric representations of this "ryngyng, syngyng, and pypyng," presented in varying degrees of correspondence with the Catholic rite. In an early analysis of the play, Edwin Miller points out that rites make up fully one-fifth of *King Johan*, which would cause Bale's propaganda to be "emotional" for an audience still invested in and practicing such ceremonies.[48] The play reacts strongly and specifically to Henry's Ten Articles of

---

45. The point is explored at some length in Fairfield, *John Bale*, 56.

46. As John Cox points out, naming the vice "Sedition" makes him the first known dramatic character to equate politics and the deceit of traditional ritual. *The Devil and the Sacred in English Drama, 1350–1642* (Cambridge: Cambridge University Press, 2000), 85.

47. Happé, *Complete Plays*, 1:65.

48. Edwin Miller, "The Roman Rite in Bale's *King Johan*," *PMLA* 64 (1949): 802–3.

1536, which upheld and protected Catholic traditional rituals, including auricular confession.

While *King Johan* has often been read as a polemic in support of Royal Supremacy, critics like David Scott Kastan and Alice Hunt have pointed out the instability of such an assertion.[49] Bale's King Johan resembles a fantasy king created by a wishful playwright more than the real King Henry. The precise performance history of *King Johan*, which only survives in manuscript, will never be known. Greg Walker argues that the play, with its direct political messages, was only meant as a specific intervention for powerful courtly audiences and was never intended for print.[50] Records show that the play was performed by Bale and His Fellows, patronized by Cromwell, at the household of Cranmer during the 1538–39 Christmas season. When performed for these chief architects of the English Reformation, Bale's tragic play warns the country's most important religious leaders of what could be at stake if the reformist cause continued to lose ground.[51] The play's political edge sharpened as the Tudor period wore on; a disillusioned Bale revised it in the late 1540s after the accession of Edward VI, and he added an epilogue in 1560, as a newly crowned Elizabeth I was confronting the consequences of Queen Mary's Catholic regime.[52] The play's primary goal was to address Henry's backsliding on reform, and, in later revisions, to warn new monarchs of the dangers of following in his overly compromising footsteps. Its most immediate audiences were the powerful ecclesiastic and governmental authorities in its many courtly performances, so it wasn't performed for wide and diverse audiences of potential converts, as *Three Laws* and *God's Promises* were.

The first musical moment in the two-act play calls for Sedition to await the entrance of his partner in crime, Dissimulation, and to, as the stage direction says, "seyng the leteny" (l. 636). Litanies are infinitely repeatable, and here the Sedition actor sings the actual litany of the saints, still protected under English law in the 1530s and early 1540s. He breaks it up with barnyard

---

49. David Scott Kastan, " 'Holy Wurdes' and 'Slypper Wit': John Bale's *King Johan* and the Poetics of Propaganda," in *Rethinking the Henrican Era: Essays on Early Tudor Texts and Contexts*, ed. Peter Herman (Urbana: University of Illinois Press, 1994), 268, 272; Alice Hunt, *The Drama of Coronation: Medieval Ceremony in Early Modern England* (Cambridge: Cambridge University Press, 2008), 100.

50. Greg Walker, *Plays of Persuasion: Drama and Politics at the Court of Henry VIII* (Cambridge: Cambridge University Press, 1991), 169–215. Peter Happé argues, however, that the play was revised for print, *John Bale* (Amherst: Twayne Publishers, 1996), 24.

51. Evidence of this performance is explained in Walker, *Plays of Persuasion*, 173, 194.

52. Paul Strohm and Jean Howard detail the historical contexts of its revision, adding that each compositional moment was "a time of some buoyancy for the reformist cause." "The Imaginary 'Commons,' " *Journal of Medieval and Early Modern Studies* 37.3 (2007): 553.

vulgarities: "Lyst, for Godes passyon! I trow her cummeth sum hoggherd / Callyng for his pygges: such a noyse I never herd!" (ll. 637–38). Once on stage, Dissimulation joins the singing, and the Latin turns parodic and is mixed with the vernacular, as praying is equated with cursing:

> DISSIMULAYCON SYNG: *Sancte Dominice, ora pro nobis.* (Pray for us, Saint Dominic)
>
> SEDICYON SYNG: *Sancte pyld monache,* I beshrow *vobis.* (Saint Bald Monk, I curse you)
>
> DISSIMULAYCON SYNG: *Sa[n]cte Francisse, ora pro nobis.* (Pray for us, Saint Francis) (ll. 639–41)

The difference between a prayer and a curse is also a matter of intent, and Bale implies here and elsewhere that whenever Catholic officiates pray, they take the Lord's name (literally) in vain.[53] Defending his decision to pray to the Church for Johan's death, Dissimulation parodies the *Libera Me*: "*Here syng this:/A Johanne Rege iniquo, libera nos, Domine*" (l. 650). The parroting of sacerdotal singing is likely to have amused those who already saw such pronouncements as mere performance, and the scene sets up Bale's play-length metaphor of Church power as stagecraft. As the preceding analysis of the Digby *Mary Magdalene* revealed, liturgical travesty is nothing new, and one of its hallmarks is a macaronic perversion of sacred language. However, as Alison Shell argues, "before the Reformation, the force of any perversion would have depended on the sanctity of the original and even reinforced it; thereafter, anti-popery would have encouraged a belief that Catholic religious language was spiritually void, and therefore wide open to occult influence."[54] The change in historical contexts between the late fifteenth century and the 1530s had reversed the edges of parody's double-edged sword.

The emptiness of ceremonial language as well as the theatricality of the Mass was "the very basis of the searching and vituperative polemics of reform," as Sarah Beckwith states.[55] Indeed, the description of priests as apish actors who trick congregants into taking bread for body was common rhetoric in early reformist prose. Beckwith sees *King Johan* as staging ritual in order to transform it into disguise: it is "an antitheatrical campaign that

53. Bale, *A Christian Exhortation unto Customable Swearers* (Antwerp: Widow of C. Ruremond, 1543). Bale suggests that the swearing of oaths is unnecessary. He is particularly critical of vows of celibacy.

54. Alison Shell, *Oral Culture and Catholicism in Early Modern England* (Cambridge: Cambridge University Press, 2007), 59.

55. Sarah Beckwith, *Signifying God: Social Relation and Symbolic Act in the York Corpus Christi Plays* (Chicago: University of Chicago Press, 2001), 59.

sought to render suspicious the entirety of Roman ceremony."[56] Beckwith focuses on attempts by Bale and other reformers to de-authorize the Eucharist as the center of ecclesiastic power "through a systematic figuration of ecclesiastical office as theater," but the play also refigures death ritual, auricular confession, and other aural and visual sacramentals, and its representation of these rituals fails to be entirely dismissive.[57] Bale exposes the theatricality of the Roman Church by turning Dissimulation into a producer of sorts who assigns parts to his cast of clerics and prelates in order to keep congregants paying hefty sums. Unsurprisingly, the first roles Dissimulation mentions are those people who sing in Latin:

> To wynne the peple I appoynt yche man his place:
> Sum to syng Latyn, and sum to ducke at grace;
> Sum to go mummyng, and sum to beare the crosse . . .
> Thowgh I seme a shepe, I can play the suttle foxe:
> I can make Latten to bryng this gere to the boxe. (ll. 698–700,
>   714–15)

Assigning roles for the lucrative production of religion, Bale's Dissimulation reveals the playwright's familiarity with the professional theater world of which he was a part. Bale combines personal experiences—his time as a Carmelite and his employment as a player/playwright—to fashion a diabolical theatrical economy for the Catholic characters in the world of the play. Doing battle with his own past as well as his ongoing theatrical career, Bale's assaults deploy the material conditions of his own early life and set a standard of reformist purity that is ultimately untenable, and unrealized in England, as doctrinal compromises eventually retained many of the traditional practices Bale's play mocks.

Bale continues to travesty his Carmelite past as more characters of ecclesiastic authority perform the liturgy. Unchanged or minimally altered quotations of the Breviary are desacralized by their theatrical context—a ritual moment is often immediately followed by the same characters performing a vulgar song and dance. The theatricality of such musical moments builds as Dissimulation and Sedition welcome Private Wealth, a cardinal of Dissimulation's own upbringing, and his friend, Usurped Power, to the stage. Their entrance, as would be typical of morality play vices, is musical:

56. Ibid., 145.
57. Ibid., 149.

Here cum in Usurpyd Powre and Private Welth, syngyng on after another.
USURPID POWRE SYNG THIS: *Super flumina Babilonis suspendimus organa*
nostra.
PRIVAT WELTH SYNG THIS: *Quomodo cantabimus canticum bonum in terra*
aliena. (ll. 764–65)

The words come almost verbatim from Psalm 136:1–4, and Sedition cor-
rectly identifies the Office of the Dead, a ritual that reformers strongly
opposed: "[b]y the mas, me thynke they are syngyng of *placebo*" (l. 766,
emphasis editorial). While Usurped Power's Latin is a direct quotation of
the Psalms ("By the waters of Babylon we hung our harps"), Private Wealth
changes one word, putting the word "bonum" (good) in for the Vulgate's
"domini" (God's). Private Wealth thus asks not "How shall we sing the *Lord's*
song in a new land," but "How shall we sing a *good* song in a new land?"
Private Wealth has presented himself and his friend as musical entertainers,
more concerned with their ability to sing good songs than with singing God's
songs. The portrayal of prelates as skilled entertainers implies that a church
so heavily invested in its musical production rewards performance skill more
than faithfulness or knowledge, breeding idleness and devilish vanity. This
concern is echoed by many sixteenth-century reformers, for example, a 1572
admonition to Parliament complains, "the cheefe chauntor, singing men,
special favourers of religion, squeaking queresters, organ players . . . etc live
in great idleness, and have their abiding . . . they came from the Pope, as oute
of the Trojan horses belly, to the destruction of Gods kingdome."[58]

Bale further dramatizes the argument that church leaders are merely good
showmen when, in one of the play's most comic physical spectacles, Private
Wealth, Usurped Power, and Dissimulation lift Sedition up in the air, and
the four burst into song. Sedition immediately complains about the ineptitude of his lifters, warning: "I wyll beshyte yow all yf ye sett me not downe
softe" (l. 804). Later, he jokes about his literal levity and calls for music:

I am so mery that we are mett, by Saynt John,
I fele not the groune that I do go uppon.
For the love of God, lett us have sum mery songe. (ll. 825–27)

The sight of three men lifting a fourth in the air would have been a memorable one, and physical comedy requires skill and practice. Thus, when

---

58. Quoted in John Milsom, "Music, Politics and Society," in Tittler and Jones, *A Companion to
Tudor Britain*, 493.

Usurped Power responds to Sedition's request for music with "Begyne thy self than, and we shall lepe in amonge" (l. 828), the verb "lepe" is likely a directive to dance. After Sedition praises the performance—"I wold ever dwell here to have such mery sporte" (l. 829)—Private Wealth reveals Usurped Power to be the Pope:

> PRIVATE WEALTH: Thow mayst have yt, man, yf thow wylt hether resorte, For the Holy Father ys as good a felowe as we.
> DISSIMULATION: The Holy Father! Why, I pray the, which is he?
> PRIVATE WEALTH: Usurpid Powre here, which thowgh he apparaunt be In this apparell, yet hathe he autoryte. (ll. 830–34)

Beckwith emphasizes the way in which disguise and spectacle (to which I would add acoustic performance) are the theatrical elements at the heart of reformist critiques of Catholic rite. For Beckwith, the disguises of Usurped Power and his friends mean that the work of the play is to uncover disguise itself, that is, to uncover "not that the actors are monks and ecclesiasts, but that the ecclesiasts are actors."[59] But it must also be noted that these uncovered actors are, in many cases, ex-friars. Their characters' point about disguise is granted extra authority by the actors' former religious positions. Bale's Fellows are powerfully able to reveal that monks and other churchmen are mere actors because they used to *be* monks and now work as actors.

By figuring the Pope as a singer and dancer in disguise, the play argues that he and all who follow him enable music both "sacred" and profane in order to corrupt souls and generate revenue. Throughout his career as a polemicist, Bale continued to express the notion that minstrel music and popish music were related, as in his *Epistle Exhortatorye* of 1544. The epistle goes so far as to imply that Catholics encouraged the profanity of minstrels and players:

> Non leave ye [Catholic prelates] unuexed and untrobled. No so moche as the poore mynstress players of interludes but ye are doyn with them. So longe as they played and sange bawdye songes blasphege God and corruptinge mennes consciences ye never blamed them but were verye well contented.[60]

Sedition, Private Wealth, and Usurped Power's songs and dances identify them as vices and thus equate the Pope's Catholicism with "corruptinge"

59. Beckwith, *Signifying God*, 152.
60. John Bale, *Epistel Exhortatorye* (London: Scoloker, 1548), Fol. 18a.

entertainments. "Bawdye songes" are an indispensable theatrical device for Bale's polemic, belying his condemnation of these entertainments in his non-dramatic writings. And, the mere performance of the musical rites acknowledges the cultural—and for some spiritual—power such sounds continue to have. He is unable fully to control an audience member's affective responses to the sounds of Catholic rite—including reactions that may undermine the music's intended dramatic point.

The play addresses not only sounds produced by the ministers of the traditional church, but also the sounds heard by them when it derides auricular confession. The issue was especially fraught when the play was composed and first performed. Henry's Ten Articles upheld the full sacrament of penance and auricular confession in no uncertain language:

> *Item*, that in no wise they do contemn this auricular confession
> which is made unto ministers of the church, but that they ought to
> repute the same as a very expedient and necessary mean, whereby
> they may require and ask this absolution at the priest's hands . . . to
> the intent they may thereby attain certain comfort and consolation
> of their consciences.[61]

Against this legal article, Bale sides with Cromwell and Cranmer in understanding auricular confession as a means of papal and episcopal domination, a way to exert undue power over the laity.[62] The early reformers—Bale, Tyndale, Cranmer, and Cromwell—continue the Wycliffite critique of auricular confession that is represented in *Wisdom*.[63]

The topic of confession arises early in act 1 when Sedition explains to King Johan that he dwells undetected in a priest's costume, hearing "ere confessyon" underneath "*benedicite*" (l. 267). The sacrament is so efficient for the Catholic vices' spying that it becomes central to their plan to take down King Johan. When Usurped Power returns (now dressed as the Pope), along

---

61. Reproduced in Cressy and Ferrell, *Religion and Society*, 21.

62. Henry's Six Articles of 1539, which were more conservative still, again defend confession: "Sixthly, that auricular confession is expedient and necessary to be retained and continued, used and frequented in the church of God." Reprinted in Cressy and Ferrell, *Religion and Society*, 26. White points out that were it not for Bale's protection from Cromwell, the play's debunking of Auricular Confession would have landed Bale in jail. *Theater and Reformation*, 21.

63. Along with Bale, Tyndale also agreed with the Wycliffites that confession had resulted in sexual abuses and that the rite itself lacked historical justification. See Donald Dean Smeeton, *Lollard Themes in the Reformation Theology of William Tyndale* (Kirksville, MO: Sixteenth Century Essays & Studies, 1986), 218.

with Private Wealth (as a Cardinal) and Sedition (as Archbishop Stephen Langton), the three chastise him for his loose lips. In what ensues, the words and gestures of confession are mocked:

> THE POPE: Ah, ye are a blabbe! I perseyve ye wyll tell all.
> I lefte ye not here to be so lyberall.
> *Knele and knoke on thi bryst.*
> DISSYMULACYON: *Mea culpa, mea culpa, gravissima mea culpa!*
> Geve me yowre blyssing *pro Deo et sancta Maria.*
> THE POPE: Thow hast my blyssyng. Aryse now and stond asyde.
> DISSYMULACYON: My skyn ys so thyke yt wyll not throw glyde.
> (ll. 1026–31)

After the three formally curse King Johan, the Pope calls for a final song "to syn[g] meryly" before they disperse, and thus ceremony is again paired with profane music (l. 1054). The satire is the sharper for its proximity to real confession. The fact that Dissimulation recites words from the actual rite— the one still prescribed by English law—boldly asserts that the current practices under Henry are sinful and ridiculous.

At the start of act 2, the priestly benefits of auricular confession to which Sedition alluded in act 1 are reaped when Nobility confesses his sins to Sedition (ll. 1148–89). Before the absolution, Sedition bribes and manipulates Nobility. He describes his power to do so as a sort of spell: "Naye, whyll I have yow here underneth *benedicite,*/In the Popes be halfe I must move other thynges to ye" (ll. 1166–67). Because he believes that Sedition's claim to papal authority is equivalent to divine authority, Nobility submits, and Sedition absolves him of all his sins. The play demonstrates how easily the manipulative spell of confession turns even the most well minded into popish puppets, and seduces them into committing treason and forfeiting their privacy by falsely authorized ceremony. Sacerdotal confession, falsely ritualized by ceremony, betrays an issue that for reformers should have been between a sinner and his or her God.[64]

Confession and absolution are again parodied when the King is stripped of his power and forced to confess to sins he did not commit (ll. 1781–85). Thus, Bale approaches the issue of auricular confession from several angles: he suggests the ceremony's manipulative power, its histrionic capacity, and its ability to assist in the usurpation of legitimate authority. While the wrong kinds of music, and too much of it, drown out the laity's ability to hear the

---

64. See Happé, *John Bale,* 29, for more on Bale's views of confession.

direct gospel truth, confessing sins one may or may not have committed into the intermediary ears of a priest—one of the few Catholic sacraments performed, in part, in the vernacular—orally releases information and personal sentiments that are used against a confessee. In Bale's formulation, popish ceremonies produce a deafening, muddled Latin clamor that keeps the people from God's clear and true Word, and then they coerce people into sharing personal and political information instead of encouraging them to pray to God directly in their own tongue, or to use their breath to spread the Gospel. While Bale's critique of auricular confession as worldly and politically motivated is pointed, David Coleman rightly argues for the irony of the scene's suggestion: the play argues that confession is corrupt because of its entanglements with politics, while the play itself has a strong political agenda.[65]

Politics and ritual continue to be entwined as the play documents King Johan's downfall. The King's dismissal of the Pope's excommunication of him echoes reformers' concerns with extra-biblical ceremony: "That sentence or curse that scriptur doth not dyrect/in my opynyon shall be of non effecte" (ll. 1432–33). King Johan's argument that ceremony is void if it is not scripturally based is undermined by theatrical context; the king *is* excommunicated.[66] As he exposes the dangers of Catholic rite, Bale also acknowledges—and replicates—its political and affective powers.

The Catholic Church's sacred music is called for right after Dissimulation hands King Johan the lethal poison.[67] Sedition had promised that Dissimulation would avoid hell after his crime because he would employ five monks to sing the mass for his soul (l. 2041). Before King Johan makes his dying speech, Sedition delivers on his promise:

> SEDICYON: I have provyded for the, by swete Saynt Powle.
> Fyve monkes that shall synge contynually for thy sowle.
> That, I warande the, thu shalt not come in helle.

---

65. Coleman, *Drama and the Sacraments*, 56.

66. Hunt, *Drama of Coronation*, 104, and Coleman, *Drama and the Sacraments*, 38, make similar points about this moment.

67. As King Johan continues to fall from power and is murdered, the vices repeatedly call for and perform celebratory music. Before he enters disguised as the monk who will poison the king, Dissimulation is heard offstage singing a secular Christmas drinking song:

Wassayle, wassayle, out of the mylke payle,
Wassayle, wassayle, as whyte as my nayle,
Wassayle, wassayle, in snowe, froste, and hayle. (ll. 2086–88)

For these depraved dissimulators, the play implies, secular holiday traditions like Wassailing are no different than performing the supposedly sacred music prescribed by the Catholic Church.

DISSYMULACYON: To sende me to heaven goo rynge the holye belle
And synge for my sowle a masse of *Scala Celi*,
That I maye clyme up aloft with Enoch and Heli.
I do not doubte it but I shall be a saynt. (ll. 2124–30)

After he duplicitously poisons his sovereign, Dissimulation feels confident in his salvation and assured of sainthood; music ameliorates the immediate effects of even the most heinous of transgressions. It is particularly apt that the Mass is for Cecilia, patron saint of church musicians and music. The sounds of Roman rite—prayers for the dead, vocalized confessions to priests, incomprehensible incantations and chants—drown out the Word and draw hearers into a false sense of eschatological security at best, and at worst cover up evil deeds.

After the dead King Johan is solemnly eulogized, a transhistorical, royal reforming figure called Imperial Majesty restores control by commanding Civil Order, Nobility, and Clergy to ensure that the Gospels reclaim their rightful place (ll. 2438–39). Imperial Majesty also plans to exile Sedition and his co-conspirators. As if on cue, Sedition stumbles on the scene, singing: "Pepe I see ye! I am glad I have spyed ye" (l. 2457). Bale draws a stave of music near the text, which demonstrates how important it was to him that his metaphorically tone-deaf vice enter singing.[68] Sedition explains that his fun-loving ways are just like those of his hero the Pope, "a trymme fellawe, a ryche fellawe, yea, and myry fellawe" (l. 2557). When asked by Imperial Majesty how Sedition proves that the Pope is a merry fellow, Sedition replies: "He hath pypes and belles, with kyrye, kyrye, kyrye" (l. 2564).

King Johan does not end in song, as *Three Laws* does, but with a solemn prayer. The final mood is one of warning, projecting the unsettled feeling that in a land that still echoes with profanities, the duplicity of sacerdotal confession, and baffling Latin rites, the job of the Reformers is far from complete. The play's message on the evils of music is consistent with Bale writing in his 1545 *Image of both Churches* that the first thing the papists did after they banished "Christ and his pure doctrin for ever" was to set up "songe in the church with the Latine service, bell ringing, and Organ playinge."[69] A savvy polemicist, Bale is unrelenting in his response to Henry's Ten Articles, exposing or fabricating the dangers of the ceremonies—death rituals and auricular confession in particular—that Henry's laws protect.

---

68. *King Johan* exists in manuscript form only, and Bale himself draws a stave of music that John Stevens transcribes for Happé's edition, 1:93. Bale's stave can be seen on page 57 of his manuscript, a facsimile of which can be found in *Kynge Johan, Materialen zue Kunde des älteren englischen Dramas*, vol. 25 (Vaduz, Germany: Kraus Reprint Ltd., 1963).

69. John Bale, *The Image of both Churches* (London: Thomas East, 1570), 79.

But while *King Johan* attempts to portray the evils of Catholicism, Bale's own political agenda undermines his critique of Catholicism's worldliness. Further, his representation of musical rite acknowledges music's cultural caché and likely works emotionally on audiences in ways that contradict the play's polemical intent. Finally, the very use of drama compromises Bale's suggestion that Catholicism is overly theatrical.

Perhaps Bale himself began to acknowledge that his anti-music, anti-ritual polemic revealed the power of musical ceremony, and shifted strategy accordingly. While *King Johan* attempts to present the consistent message that music is a corrupting force, *God's Promises*, likely written a few years later, performed far more widely, and printed for distribution, asserts an opposite thesis. If, as Beckwith claims, "the undeniable force of [Bale's] theatrical logic is the obliteration of Catholic ritual and ceremony," in *God's Promises* Bale reconstructs and re-forms ceremony from the ruins, fashioning a new ritualized music for the reformed church.[70]

God's Promises: Musical Compromise

God's Promises is the first of three surviving plays, along with *Johan Baptystes Preachynge* and *The Temptation of our Lord*, comprising Bale's biblical cycle. After a *Praefatorio* spoken by Bale himself ("Baleus Prolocutor"), the play is divided into seven short and formal acts, each of which features a biblical story in which one man interacts with God and is granted a promise. That promise is celebrated, in each act, with a musical antiphon printed in both Latin and English.[71] In order, they tell of God's promises to Adam, Noah, Abraham, Moses, David, Isaiah, and finally John the Baptist, creating a segue into *Johan Baptystes Preachynge*. One actor plays God throughout and a second plays all of the other characters. *God's Promises* simultaneously refashions traditional cycle drama and liturgical music to appeal to its audiences, and it suggests a compromised (in both senses of the word) acoustic experience for reformed religion.[72] Whereas *King Johan* makes specific anti-sacramental arguments to a specific audience, the printed and more widely performed *God's Promises* changes its tactics completely and introduces a re-formed musical rite that reveals its debts to traditional religion.

---

70. Beckwith, *Signifying God*, 152.

71. As Edwin Miller points out, this formal and repetitive structure would call to mind Corpus Christi prophet plays as well as traditional liturgy for its first audiences, "The Antiphons in Bale's Cycle of Christ," *Studies in Philology* 48.3 (1951): 633.

72. On Bale's exposure and debt to cycle drama, see Happé, "Bale's Lost Mystery Cycle," 5.

The play has received relatively little critical attention, and that attention has often been harsh: it is "hard to imagine a less attractive way to win converts," writes Lois Potter, and Cathy Shrank comments that "Bale chooses to tell, not show," deliberately emphasizing word over spectacle.[73] Both critics underestimate the vital role *God's Promises'* antiphons play in making God's represented Word attractive to the unconverted.[74] Indeed, the play privileges the Word over visual spectacle, but it does so by giving music a prominent theatrical and devotional role. The esteem that sacred music is given in the play is a radical departure from the perverted liturgy and the profane songs of *Three Laws* and *King Johan*, and the anti-music wrath of many of Bale's prose tracts. *God's Promises* offers a reformist, sacred musical alternative to the Catholic rites Bale hated. While Bale thoroughly discards some central ritual practices—auricular confession, offices for the dead—his music for antiphonal worship, the anthems that were musically central to English services throughout the sixteenth century, changes Catholic liturgical practice very little.

By the time he wrote *God's Promises*, Bale and Cromwell had realized that drama was an effective tool for converting practitioners of traditional religion to the new faith. S. B. House explains how *God's Promises*, along with *Johan Baptystes Preachyng* and *The Temptation of our Lord*, were played to conservative towns and monasteries, and their inclusion of so much music was likely one reason Cromwell and Bale thought they would be effective.[75] The evangelicals of the 1530s had realized that they needed to appropriate popular cycle and morality dramas to their own uses rather than simply try to suppress them, and John Milsom explains that a similar move was simultaneously made for music: "the potential harnessing of popular song was recognized by religious reformers in England."[76] Around the time Bale was touring the country with this play, Miles Coverdale attempted to leverage music's popularity by writing and publishing metrical psalms that he imagined could be sung by plowman and spinning lady alike.[77] Bale's musicality within his drama is thus of a piece with larger reformist strategies, but the kind of

73. Lois Potter, *The Revels History of Drama in English 1500–1576* (London: Methuen, 1980), 180; Cathy Shrank, "John Bale and reconfiguring the 'medieval' in Reformation England," in *Reading the Medieval in Early Modern England*, eds. Gordon McMullan and David Matthews (Cambridge: Cambridge University Press, 2007), 185.

74. Andrew Taylor points this out in "The Reformation of History in John Bale's Biblical Dramas," in *English Historical Drama, 1500–1660: Forms Outside the Canon*, eds. Teresa Grant and Barbara Ravelhofer (Basingstoke, UK: Palgrave Macmillan, 2007), 69.

75. House, "Cromwell's Message to the Regulars," 123–38.

76. John Milsom, "Music, Politics and Society," 495.

77. Miles Coverdale, *Goostly psalms and spiritual songes* (London, 1535).

music he uses—antiphons accompanied by organ—is far more traditional than the unaccompanied psalm singing Coverdale was trying (with little success at the time) to popularize.

The play, along with *Johan Baptystes Preachyng* and *The Temptation of our Lord*, went through multiple printings by at least 1578. It began as an eleven-play cycle, and then Bale first printed the three surviving plays while in exile in 1547. There is evidence of a parish performance of the longer cycle at St. Stephen's Church near Canterbury on September 8, 1538, and it is likely that the plays were seen by aristocrats, monastics, and students in its tour of conservative priories and country houses in conservative Norfolk, Leicester, and Shrewsbury.[78] Bale records a detailed account of the three-play version's disastrous performances in Kilkenny, Ireland, on the day of Mary's 1553 accession, while he was Bishop of Ossory (he had to leave Ireland for fear of execution, so outraged were the Irish church and government authorities).[79]

God's Promises was performed over a period of at least fifteen years, often in regions resistant to Cromwellian and later Edwardian liturgical reforms (both in England and later in Ireland). Knowing that the anti-liturgical parodies of *Three Laws* and *King Johan* would be counterproductive, Bale fashioned a play with frequent musical liturgical moments. While the play's music, and its surprising use of the Latin Vulgate instead of the English Bible, have been seen by critics as gestures to win over conservative audiences, I think that Bale's play also reveals the author's own ambivalence about music's role in spiritual life.

While he rails against it in other contexts, Bale relies on the Roman Breviary for the music of *God's Promises*. Antiphons are a common element of traditional liturgy; a soloist sings and the choir responds. The song at the end of act 1 is typical of all seven acts, a form that deviates little from antiphons in Catholic services. Adam ends his soliloquy with a call for song: "I have it in faythe and therfor I wyll synge/Thys Antheme to hym that my salvacyon shall brynge" (ll. 177–78). Below that final line is printed the stage direction:

Tunc sonora voce, provolutis genibus Antiphonam incipit,
O Sapientia, quam prosequetur chorus cum organis, eo interim exeunte.
Vel sub eodem tono poterit sic Anglice cantari:

---

78. House, "Cromwell's Message to the Regulars," 125, and Greg Walker, *The Politics of Performance in Early Renaissance Drama* (Cambridge: Cambridge University Press, 1998), 45.

79. For a summary of evidence regarding the St. Stephen's performance, see White, *Theater and Reformation*, 30–31; and Gourley, "Carnivalising Apocalyptic History," 171. Performance records of the Irish performance may be found in E. K. Chambers, *The Mediaeval Stage*, vol. 2 (Oxford: Oxford University Press, 1903), 446–48.

[Then on bended knee he begins in a loud voice the anthem,
O Wisdom, which the Chorus takes up, with an organ accompani-
    ment, as he goes out. Or with the same accompaniment it could
    be sung in English, thus:]
O eternal Sapyence, that procedest from the mouthe of the hyghest,
    reachynge fourth with a great power from the begynnynge to the
    ende, with heavenlye swetnesse dysposynge all creatures, come
    now and enstruct us the true waye of thy godlye prudence.
    (ll. 179–82)[80]

Adam replicates the traditional liturgical gesture of kneeling and is accompanied by an organ, as per liturgical practice. It is also crucial that while English is given as an alternative, the primary stage direction is in Latin and
initially calls for Latin singing. The singing actor is likely to have been monastically trained (or trained in a university), and he uses those skills to reproduce music reminiscent of traditional practice.

The actor playing Adam has a particularly taxing job: while the directions of Adam's song are that it be sung in a "loud" voice, Abraham is to
sing in a "high" voice, Moses "clearly," David "melodiously," and John the
Baptist "resoundingly."[81] That Bale paid enough attention to a singer's timbre
and tone to include such various and detailed directives again reveals the
playwright's keen musical ear. Such descriptors indicate that Bale developed
a semiotics of voicing to create character: a clear-voiced Moses, a high-
pitched Abraham, and a confident-sounding John the Baptist convey distinct meanings through their singing that cannot be conveyed through spoken
word. An actor would not have had time to change costumes between acts,
so the play experiments with the power of sound alone to enhance character and meaning. Moving beyond the good and evil auralities of morality
plays, Bale employs a more dramatically subtle way to use theatrical music.

The play is less innovative, though, in its use of the antiphons themselves,
and their lack of revision from the Breviary is inconsistent with Bale's commitment to the vernacular and to liturgical reform. The antiphons all come
from the sequence intended to follow the *Magnificat* each day of Advent (December 17–23): they are unchanged except for their order. While an English translation is printed as an alternative, it is just that. Peter le Huray
explains that changes to England's liturgy did not begin until 1537 when

---

80. Happé, *Complete Plays*, 2:8.
81. Abraham's voice is to be *"alta volce"* (423 s.d.), Moses's is *"clara"* (551 s.d.), David's is *"car-
nora"* (677 s.d.), and John's is *"resona"* (942 s.d.).

Henry began to take an interest in the Lutherans, and the full English Litany was not printed until 1544.[82] Those facts help explain Bale's antiphonal format at the time of composition in the 1530s: the inclusion of *any* English seems forward thinking in that context, and the use of the organ merely expected. Cranmer worked on the English litany with Henry until the king's death in 1547, and within six months of Edward's coronation, Latin processions were entirely outlawed. Records show that liturgical music in places like Canterbury, York, and Windsor were restricted and often replaced with speaking.[83] Many reformers advocated a banishment of all instruments, which only competed with the sound of the Word. Against the tide of mid-century reform, *God's Promises* was performed with organs in 1553. If Bale has a pattern of "assimilation and rejection," antiphons are part of that assimilation.[84] One can see this use of music as an example of how Bale "drew on his Carmelite devotion in developing a reformed identity," as Oliver Wort puts it.[85]

Bale details the 1553 performance in Ireland in his *Vocacyon of Johan Bale*; it was staged to protest Mary I's accession. He explains that on August 20 of that year, "was the Ladye Marye with us at Kylkennye proclaimed Quene of Englande/Fraune and Irelande." He complains about the "processions/musters and disgysinges" of the priests in their costumes.[86] Bale writes that he took Christ's testament in his hand and marched to the market cross with "the people in great nombre folowinge," where, clad in a Geneva gown instead of the expected (Catholic) cope and crozier, he preached amidst the chaos about the prelates' vain pageants for the queen.[87] Bale sees no irony, though, when he explains his company's equally theatrical response: "The yonge men in the forenone played a Tragedy of Gods promises in the olde lawe at market crosse with organe plainges and songes very aptely. In the afternone agayne they played a Commedie of sanct Johan Baptistes preachinges of Christes baptisynge and of his temptacion in the wildernesse to the small contentacion of the prestes and other papistes there."[88] Soon after these performances, Bale learned that several prelates in Kilkenny had plans "to

---

82. Le Huray, *Music and the Reformation*, 4.

83. Ibid., 7–8. For more on the phasing out of organs under Edward, see, for example, Dominic Gwynn, "The Classical British Organ 1500–1660," *The Tracker* 52.4 (2008): 18–23.

84. Happé, "Rejecting and Preserving Bale's John the *Baptist*."

85. Wort, *John Bale and Religious Conversion*, 18, and 71–94.

86. John Bale, *The Vocacyon of Johan Bale*, eds. Peter Happé and John N. King (Binghamton, NY: Renaissance English Text Society, 1990), 58.

87. Discussed in Alexandra Johnston, "Tudor Drama, Theatre and Society," in Tittler and Jones, *A Companion to Tudor Britain*, 431.

88. Bale, *The Vocacyon of Johan Bale*, 58. Bale's description of his actors as "yonge" has been interpreted to imply that choirboys, who would have been good singers, certainly, were used in this performance. For more, see Paul Whitfield White, "Reforming Mysteries' End: A New Look at

slea" him, and he fled Ireland for the continent, where he spent his second exile, lasting throughout the Marian regime.

The Kilkenny religious authorities' unfavorable response to the play is not likely to have been a result of the play's music, which would have pleased a largely Catholic audience. It is unclear whether the words were sung in Latin or English, but the use of the portative organ is apparent.[89] Mid-century reformist prescriptions regarding the use of church music, if any was allowed, were clear. Following Calvin, songs were to be sung in the vernacular and they were to be strictly scriptural, with the congregation singing in unison and in a restrained, thoughtful style. Each syllable was to only receive one sung note for the sake of clarity, and no instruments were to be used. Bale's persistent use of the organ and his possible retention of Latin violate the prescriptions of his fellow reformers. The antiphons do not just demonstrate a commitment to vernacular worship, as Shrank argues, but also negotiate a startling compromise between traditional and reformed religious perspectives.[90] Thus, for all his reputation as an unwavering polemical hothead for reform, Bale combines a reformist theology with Catholic-leaning liturgical music. Because of their call and response format, antiphons quote the Bible while encouraging communal *listening* to the Word as well as singing; it is perhaps for this reason that Bale's reformed aurality retained the practice.

While a few scholars have examined the way *God's Promises* refigures the biblical narratives of the Corpus Christi cycles, not even Beckwith addresses the degree to which *God's Promises* might refashion what she calls the sacramentality of Corpus Christi theater.[91] Beckwith claims that for Corpus Christi drama, the theatricalization of the liturgy does not empty out liturgy's content, but rather "may be a way of examining the very conditions under which it can be efficacious."[92] To this I add that Bale's biblical drama, with its embedded liturgical performances, does not just tell the stories of the Bible, but it also contextualizes them in a reformed liturgical framework.

Protestant Intervention in English Provincial Drama," *Journal of Medieval and Early Modern Studies* 29.1 (Winter 1999): 133.

89. Happé explains that a similar organ is described in the Norwich Grocers' book recording organs bought in 1534, *Complete Plays*, 2:128.

90. Shrank, "John Bale and reconfiguring the 'medieval,' " 185.

91. For a compelling treatment of Bale's plays as reformed cycle drama, demonstrating the Bible as a point of consensus between Catholics and reformers, see White, "Reforming Mysteries' End," 121–87.

92. Beckwith, *Signifying God*, 115. Beckwith suggests that "much of [Bale's] dramatic work is an attempt to replace and supersede the civic Corpus Christi dramas," but leaves *God's Promises* out of her analysis of Bale, 148.

Bale's play demonstrates that musical ritual grounded in clear scriptural understanding is consistent with the principles of reform. And while Calvin and Coverdale's advocacy of vernacular psalms maintained a similar view, Bale's music in *God's Promises* acknowledges its debts to traditional religious and theatrical practice, rather than pretending to break from them entirely. English Catholicism's most communal expression of biblical understanding, of sacrament, and of theater—the Corpus Christi plays—provides a model for Bale to present a religious experience that is not unlike the participatory narratives of civic drama.

While musicologists cite Bale's prose as an example of anti-music vitriol, even his most spiteful condemnations of music betray his attachments.[93] In his *Image of both Churches*, a 1544 commentary on Revelation, he writes of the music of the popish devils: "The mery noyes of them that play upon harpes, lutes and fidels, the swéet voice of musicians that sing with virginals, vials and chimes, the armony of them that pipe in recorders, flutes, and drums, and the shirle showt of trumpets, waits, & shawmes, shall no more be heard in thée to the delight of men."[94] So detailed a list could not be produced by someone lacking in musical experience and interest. His modifiers for this music—"mery," "swéet"—suggest regret: he does not seem to describe Satanic singing.

Elsewhere in the same text, Bale outlines a new type of music: "And swéetly they uttered with their voyces a song that séemed all newe, before the seat of the Lorde, before the foure beastes, & before the auncient elders. This song is the word of the Lorde, all new both to the good and to the faythfull it renueth in the spirit of their mynds, provoking them to do on a new man in Christ."[95] The songs of *God's Promises* are songs of the new learning: biblical songs of praise to be sung, eventually, in clear and loud English and that reflect the spirituality of the believer in direct, personal communion with God. While Bale may have aspired to that ideal, in practice he was only able to produce a musical alternative that parrots the old faith's sounds almost exactly. John Craig has written about how acoustic experience recreated the church's affective power once evangelical iconoclasm had stripped it bare visually: "If sacred space existed for English Protestants, it was found preeminently in the place and sounds of worship, as the word was preached,

---

93. See, for example, Willis, *Church Music and Protestantism*, 523, and le Huray, *Music and the Reformation*, 23.

94. Bale, *The Image of both Churches*, 336.

95. Ibid., 243.

the Sacraments administered, prayers prayed and psalms were sung."[96] Bale's ability to approximate an experience that was both verbally and acoustically effective prefigures later ecclesiastic developments.

There are many contradictions in the works of prior, playwright, and polemicist John Bale. He preached, played, and printed (his friend John Foxe's trifecta for disseminating reform) against a religious practice that he simultaneously reproduced, and he ultimately helped to preserve for England elements of traditional religion that continental reformers expunged. Within the context of English church history, Bale's losses of principle allow for gains in practice as, by the end of the sixteenth century, the Elizabethan Anglican Church had preserved some of the rich auralities of England's religious past, including traditional liturgical elements sung in English.[97] The ultimate failure (in England's official church) of the Cromwellian agenda and Bullinger's anti-music stance reveal the complexities of Tudor people's attachments to music, a subject on which it seems that even the staunchly reformist were willing to risk hypocrisy. Bale's story points to the ways in which polemical viewpoints are often compromised in expression, and the way hypocrisy might paradoxically promote something like tolerance.

Bale's influence can certainly be seen in an Edwardian play like Lewis Wager's *The Life and Repentaunce of Marie Magdalene*, where the vice Infidelity enters singing a medley of Catholic liturgical phrases:

With heigh down down and downe a down a,
Salvator mundi Domine, Kyrieleyson,
Ite Missa est, with pipe up *Alleluya.*
Sed libera nos a malo, and so let us be at one. (ll. 87–90)[98]

This version of a vice named "Infidelity" replicates Bale's use of liturgical music to signal Catholic corruption, mocking the ceremonies newly made illegal by Edward in 1550, in order to correct the popish backsliding of Henry VIII's later years. But while Bale's legacy is apparent in this and other reformist dramas, Bale's musical-dramatic techniques also rework their precedents. John Watkins suggests that the view that reforms squelched native medieval

96. John Craig, "Psalms, groans, and dog whippers: the soundscape of worship in the English parish church, 1547–1642," in *Sacred Space in Early Modern Europe*, eds. Will Coster and Andrew Spicer (Cambridge: Cambridge University Press, 2005), 106.

97. See, for example, Francis Higman, "Music," in *The Reformation World*, ed. Andrew Pettegree (London: Routledge, 2000), 495–501.

98. Lewis Wager, "The Life and Repentaunce of Mary Magdalene," in *Reformation Biblical Drama in England*, ed. Paul Whitfield White (New York: Garland Publishing, 1992).

traditions—both theatrical and religious—"underestimates the extent to which the reformers refashioned themselves as heirs to long-standing traditions of medieval dissent."[99] Without question, Bale's dramatic strategies, including especially the ambivalent use of music, owe something to "medieval" dramas like *Wisdom* and the Digby *Mary Magdalene*.

Soon after Bale's controversial performance of *God's Promises* for Queen Mary's accession, Nicholas Udall took up the form of the political morality play to present *Respublica* before the new Catholic monarch. He, too, urged a religio-political model that eventually failed, but his use of music in that play, and in his comedy *Ralph Roister Doister*—which includes a liturgical parody along the lines of the Digby *Mary Magdalene* and *King Johan*—owes much to Bale, a playwright with whom Udall had likely worked in the 1530s.[100] But while Bale had fled to the continent under Mary, the cagier Udall remained to write plays for her, demonstrating a religio-political identity even more dissembling and flexible than Bale's.

99. John Watkins, "Moralities, Interludes, and Protestant Drama," in *The Cambridge History of Medieval English Literature*, ed. David Wallace (Cambridge: Cambridge University Press, 1999), 787.

100. Many critics have compared *Three Laws* and *King Johan* to Udall's *Respublica*, including Tom Betteridge, "Staging Reformation Authority: John Bale's *King Johan* and Nicholas Udall's *Respublica*," *Reformation and Renaissance Review* 3 (2000): 34–58, and Howard and Strohm, "The Imaginary 'Commons.'"

CHAPTER 3

Learning to Sing
The Plays of Nicholas Udall

Come on, ye shall Learne to solfe [sing]: Reformacion.

—*Respublica*

DOBINET: Cal ye these your frends?
ROISTER: Sing on, and no mo words make.

—*Ralph Roister Doister*

When she acceded to the throne in 1553, the
Catholic Mary Tudor hoped to reverse the damage her reformist brother
Edward VI had done to church music in his preceding six-year reign.[1] Contemporary records indicate that on the reading of the proclamation that
Mary was the new Queen: "suddenly a great number of bells was heard ringing. . . . And shortly after the proclamation, various Lords of the Council
went to St. Paul's . . . and had there sung the 'Te Deum laudamus,' playing
organs and thanking the Almighty . . . which displays were not customary
with them and had altogether been put aside of late."[2] There are multiple
accounts of nationwide singing, bell-ringing, and organ playing to celebrate
the proclamation and accession of Mary I, and a "Vox Patris Caelestis" for
six voices was composed for her coronation.[3] In late 1553 such music had

---

1. For music definitively composed during the early part of Mary's reign, listen to tracks 19, 20, and 21 from disc 2, the *Missa Puer Natus Est Nobis*, on Tallis Scholars, *Christmas With the Tallis Scholars*, dir. Peter Phillips (Gimell, 2003), 2 compact discs. Other examples of mid-sixteenth-century music both sacred and profane can be heard on *Tudor Age Music* (Griffin, 2010), compact disc. *Ralph Roister Doister* can be heard on John Barton, *The First Stage*, Box N (Dover Publications, 1970), vinyl LP set.

2. *The Accession and Coronation and Marriage of Mary Tudor as Related in Four Manuscripts of the Escorial*, trans. C.V. Malfatti (Barcelona: C.V. Malfatti, 1956), 20.

3. Henry Machyn writes of "Te Deums," bells, and organs throughout London in *The Diary of Henry Machyn, Citizen and Merchant-Taylor of London from AD 1550 to AD 1563* (J.G. Nichols. Lon-

not been heard publicly in England for several years, as Edward VI's reign had drastically changed the sounds of English religious experience in official churches. In the early months of her reign, Mary was still deciding exactly what form England's newly revived Catholicism would take and, in particular, how the Church's musical rituals would sound.

While some historians have read the celebrations of Mary's accession and coronation as a demonstration of the people's enthusiasm for the return to traditional religion (and certainly some staunch Catholics took her triumph over the evangelical Jane Grey as a sign of God's favor), most people had more complicated views.[4] Some reformists vehemently opposed the new Queen, like Bale, who staged sartorial and theatrical protests on accession day. But Alice Hunt is right to point out that the notion that most others rejoiced at the return of "Catholicism" implies a polarization of political and religious identities, and "this polarization does not properly account for figures that migrated successfully from one regime to another."[5] The playwright Nicholas Udall was one such migratory figure: he composed reformist plays for Henry VIII and Edward VI before likely writing *Ralph Roister Doister* and *Respublica* to be performed at court during the first year of Mary's reign.[6]

---

don: Camden Society, 1848), 37. Richard Taverner writes about ringing of bells and other mirth throughout England and Wales in *An Oration gradulatory made upon the joyfull proclayming of the moste noble Princes Quene Mary Quene of Englande* (London, 1553), A2r-v.

4. For example, Eamon Duffy, "The Conservative Voices in the English Reformation," in *Christianity and Community in the West: Essays for John Bossy*, ed. Simon Ditchfield (Burlington, VT: Ashgate, 2001): 87–90, and Christopher Haigh, *English Reformations: Religion, Politics, and Society under the Tudors* (Oxford: Oxford University Press, 1993), 203–18. One such example of a traditionalist taking Mary's coronation as a sign of God's favor is John Christopherson, *An exhortation to all menne to take hede and beware of rebellion wherein are set forth the causes* (London, 1554).

5. Alice Hunt, *The Drama of Coronation: Medieval Ceremony in Early Modern England* (Cambridge: Cambridge University Press, 2008), 115.

6. *Ralph Roister Doister* was first printed in 1566, but its original performance date is a matter of debate. David Bevington proposes a performance during Mary's first year in *Tudor Drama and Politics: A Critical Approach to Topical Meaning* (Cambridge, MA: Harvard University Press, 1968), 124; he is echoed by many including Hunt, *Drama of Coronation*, 116, and Greg Walker, *The Politics of Performance in Early Renaissance Drama* (Cambridge: Cambridge University Press, 1998), 165. Some scholars, however, advocate for a 1552 date, for example, Robert Hornback, "A *Dirige* and Terence 'In the Briers': Mock-Ritual and Mock-Classicism as Iconoclastic Translation in Udall's *Ralph Roister Doister*," *Research Opportunities in Medieval and Renaissance Drama* 48 (2009), 22. As for *Respublica*, while there is no author's name on the manuscript, archival and stylistic analyses by several scholars have convincingly linked the play to Udall. See W. W. Greg, "Introduction," in *Respublica: An Interlude for Christmas 1553* (London: Early English Text Society, 1952), viii–xviii. A number of plays were performed by the Children of the Chapel Royal during Mary's first year as Queen, and *Respublica* is a Christmas play for children written by someone who is known to have had a number of plays produced that year, so "the weight of probability" is that the play was produced at court over Christmas 1553–54. Walker, *The Politics of Performance*, 171–72. See also Hunt, *Drama of Coronation*, 111–45, and Sarah Carpenter, "*Respublica*," in *The Oxford Handbook of Tudor Drama*, eds. Thomas Betteridge and Greg Walker (Oxford: Oxford University Press, 2012), 514–30.

Staged in this early Marian moment, *Respublica* directly takes up an issue of contemporary concern: in a period of so much religio-political change, who will look out for the good of the people, the "common weal" (or in Latin, the "Respublica")? *Roister Doister* also takes up this issue, if indirectly, in its exploration of social dynamics and its promotion of liturgical compromise. It was the "age of the common wealthe," and variations on the idea of the common weal/th (or the "commonitie" as it is called at the end of *Roister Doister*) pervade political tracts by both Catholics and evangelical reformers who desired a monarch to put the good of the whole people before the good of their sole person.[7] For example, John Ponet's *A shorte treatise of politike power* (London, 1556) uses the word "common wealthe" thirty-three times.[8] There were many economic and political issues facing England's first female monarch and the commonweal of her people, but no issue was more contentious than religion. Music was crucial to the changes Mary hoped to make in state religion, and to her ability to please the commonweal while she made those changes.

Mary's December 1553 proclamation forbade "interludes . . . ballads, rhymes, and other false treatises in the English tongue concerning doctrine in matters now in question and controversy touching the high points and mysteries of Christian religion," so Udall had to be careful that his play not appear controversial when it came to religious matters.[9] *Ralph Roister Doister*, an English version of traditional Roman comedy, and *Respublica*, a political morality play, are both filled with music, which is appropriate for the choirboy performers for whom they were written. While the plays do not seem to address "the high points and mysteries of Christian religion" directly, they both do so obliquely. They leverage the musical skills and religious resonances of choirboy performers to display the ways that music's social and political benefits have religious utility. *Ralph Roister Doister* presents itself from the start as frivolous mirth: music and comedy seem to keep the play light, and song and laughter are put on display as useful tools for coalescing diverse audiences, distracting subjects from more disturbing truths, and teaching children. The play's parodic Catholic liturgy is deliberately equivo-

---

7. Michael Pincombe and Cathy Shrank call the sixteenth century the "age of the common wealthe" in "Prologue" in *The Oxford Handbook of Tudor Literature*, eds. Mike Pincombe and Cathy Shrank (Oxford: Oxford University Press, 2009), 6. See also Jean Howard and Paul Strohm, "The Imaginary 'Commons,'" *Journal of Medieval and Early Modern Studies* 37.3 (2007), 551–52.

8. John Ponet, *A shorte treatise of politike* power (London, 1556). See also, for example, *Certayne questions demaunded and asked by the noble realme of Englande* (London, 1555), where the anonymous writer worries that the realm has been given over to monarchs "without the consent of her commons."

9. In *Tudor Royal Proclamations*, vol. 2, eds. Paul L. Hughes and James F. Larkin (New Haven, CT: Yale University Press, 1969), 6.

cal in its religious messages, and it demonstrates a sort of compromised musical liturgy. The music of *Respublica* enhances its allegory, and aids in the play's messages about the political utility of dissimulation.

The music and musical features of Udall's plays demonstrate the possibility of a hybridized musical liturgy for the new Marian church, one that combines elements of traditional Roman Catholic religion with those of Edward's evangelical reforms. Only a playwright as cagey and adaptable as Nicholas Udall could have suggested such a musical-religious compromise in this historical moment. Udall's caginess—his ability to be oblique, even to dissemble—is represented in the plays themselves. Such shrewdness is also a hallmark of the survival strategies employed by the many people in the mid-Tudor years that chose to adapt to a quick series of confessionally diverse monarchs rather than flee into exile.

Nicholas Udall and the Early Marian Moment

Udall's extant plays and nondramatic writings sketch out some of the complexities of navigating rapid religious changes while keeping favor with royal patrons, religious powers, and academic administrations. When Mary came to the throne, many reformers, including Bale, fled to the continent, forced into exile if they wanted to save their heads and stay faithful to their beliefs.[10] Looking at Udall's early history, one might suspect that he would have joined them: he was expelled from Oxford for his Lutheran tendencies in a 1528 heresy hunt, and in the 1530s and '40s he worked as a humanist educator and reformist playwright; like Bale, he wrote plays that were patronized by Thomas Cromwell.[11] His career as an educator and translator indicates something of his professional savvy: he was a teacher, a writer of popular Latin schoolbooks, and headmaster of Eton from 1534–1541. In 1541 he was fired from his post on charges of "buggery" (sodomy) with an older male student with whom he had also committed a robbery. But his disgrace and punishment were surprisingly short-lived, as soon afterwards he had a steady stream of commissions by the likes of Catherine Parr (Henry VIII's final,

10. For more on Marian exiles, see Haigh, *English Reformations*, 190–97, and Perez Zagorin, *Ways of Lying: Dissimulation, Persecution, and Conformity in Early Modern Europe* (Cambridge, MA: Harvard University Press, 1990), 108–223.

11. For a discussion of his early drama and the complexities of Udall's religious identity, see Robert Hornback, "Lost Conventions of Godly Comedy in Udall's *Thersites*," *Studies in English Literature, 1500–1900* 47.2 (2007): 281–303. For an outline of Nicholas Udall's biography and output, see William L. Edgerton, *Nicholas Udall* (New York: Twayne Publishers, 1965).

and reformist, wife).[12] He also translated humanist texts written by the moderate Catholic Erasmus and by the zealous Italian reformer Peter Martyr Vermigli; his affiliation with the cross-confessional humanists likely contributed to his flexibility. During Henry's reign he was hired to be then-Princess Mary's tutor, which perhaps might go some way toward explaining why she favored him as a playwright when she was Queen, writing, "our welbeloved Nicolas Udall hath at soondrie seasons convenient heretofore shewed . . . dialogues and interludes before us for our regell disport and recreacion."[13] But it is no doubt surprising that a figure with such a reformist past would not only remain to serve Mary, but become a favorite.

Udall's work and life span and transcend categories of sacred and secular, Catholic and reformist. In response to this multifariousness, critics have viewed him variously as a timeserver or as a moderate, but his slippery religious identity is consistent with the slipperiness of early Tudor religious politics, and demonstrative of the way Tudor subjects often elide categories of religious confession.[14] Many Catholics continued to participate in secret Masses under Edward's reign: several evangelicals were similarly covert under Mary. Jean Calvin and Vermigli called them "Nicodemites," those who saved their lives and residence by outwardly conforming to Catholicism (they are named after Nicodemus, who only visited Christ at night).[15] Their reasons for doing so were varied and often more political than theological; many did their duty to the Queen and the system of primogeniture which had put her in place. As one contemporary poet wrote, "And though I lik'd not the Religion/Which all her life Queen Mary had professed,/Yet in my mind that wicked Motion/Right heirs for to displace I did detest."[16]

The audiences for Udall's plays reflected the complexity of Mary's subjects. In the early years of her reign, the continued presence of members of

---

12. While buggery was punishable by death, Udall's punishment was to lose his position and be briefly imprisoned, and then to continue in a successful career. For speculation on the oddness of this situation, see Elizabeth Pittenger, " 'To Serve the Queere': Nicholas Udall, Master of Revels," in *Queering the Renaissance*, ed. Jonathan Goldberg (Durham, NC: Duke University Press, 1994), 165 and Edgerton, *Nicholas Udall*, 38.

13. Albert Feuillerat, ed. *Documents Relating to the Revels at Court in the Time of King Edward VI and Queen Mary: The Loseley MSS* (Vaduz: Kraus Reprint, 1963), 159–60. Evidence for Udall's involvement in the 1554–55 Christmas season can be found in W. R. Streitberger, *Court Revels, 1485–1559* (Toronto: University of Toronto Press, 1994), 212.

14. William Peery argues that Udall was a "timeserver" in "Udall as Timeserver I," *Notes and Queries* 194.6 (1949): 119–21, and "Udall as Timeserver II," *Notes and Queries* 194.7 (1949): 138–41. Edgerton, however, views him rather as a moderate: "The Apostasy of Nicholas Udall," *Notes and Queries* 195 (1950): 223–26.

15. For more on religious dissimulators including Nicodemites, see Zagorin, *Ways of Lying*.

16. From "The Legend of Sir Nicholas Throgmorton," quoted in Anna Whitelock, *Mary Tudor: Princess, Bastard, Queen* (New York: Random House, 2009), 188.

Edward's court meant that many committed evangelicals were in attendance at court performances. Several historians warn against thinking of members of Mary's court, and of England as a whole, in terms of categorical Catholics who supported the Queen and evangelical reformers who opposed her.[17] Not only were such categories of identification not available in the 1550s, but also the retention of Edwardian advisors in Mary's court and the ability of people like Udall to serve successive but religiously different Tudor monarchs suggests "a more nuanced and complex mix of loyalties."[18] The nuances of that mix of loyalties were often evident when it came to the role of music in Mary's new church.

Since Henry's dissolution of the monasteries and choir schools, church music had been largely defunded. Edward's *Book of Common Prayer* and a series of injunctions banned organs and replaced polyphony and instrumental music in parishes with unaccompanied Psalms sung by the congregation in English.[19] While Mary was eager to return to the Latin musical polyphony of the pre-Reformation church, official changes to church doctrine came more slowly. Nicholas Temperley explains that "there was a period of more than eighteen months at the beginning of Mary's reign in which it was possible to conduct worship according to the [reformist, Edwardian] 1552 prayer book, and even to hope for some compromise in the future."[20] However, in 1554, Mary's ally Cardinal Reginald Pole publicly rebuked Edward's reforms and composers such as Thomas Tallis and Christopher Tye were commissioned to write complex Latin masses. Mary began to make slow but sure progress in restoring the Catholic faith and the music of its services, even if many remained hopeful that there would someday be further compromises toward reformed services.[21]

---

17. Thomas Cranmer, for example, supported Mary's claim to the throne over Jane Grey's. See Haigh, *English Reformations*, 252–57, and Duffy, "The Conservative Voices in the English Reformation," 87–97.

18. Hunt, *Drama of Coronation*, 115–16.

19. Duffy summarizes: "The most devastating impact had probably been in music, since the heavy emphasis of reformed Protestantism on the intelligibility of the written or spoken word in worship left no place for Latin word-setting and elaborate polyphony," *Fires of Faith: Catholic England under Mary Tudor* (New Haven, CT: Yale University Press, 2009), 3. See also Peter le Huray, *Music and the Reformation in England* (Cambridge: Cambridge University Press, 1967), 9–29; and Kenneth Fincham and Nicholas Tyacke, *Altars Restored: The Changing Face of English Religious Worship, 1547–c. 1700* (Oxford: Oxford University Press, 2007), 2, 64.

20. Nicholas Temperley, *The Music of the English Parish Church* (Cambridge: Cambridge University Press, 1979), 27.

21. Roger Bray, "England i, 1485–1600," in *European Music 1520–1640*, ed. James Haar (Woodbridge, UK: Boydell & Brewer, 2006), 488–96. Duffy also explains how the strategy of Mary and Cardinal Pole was to focus on the aesthetics of Catholic worship in order to bring the English back to traditional religion in *Fires of Faith*, 531–32. Doctrinal flexibility is seen in many composers: the

Crucial to the delivery of this new music were choirboys, who needed to be trained in the new liturgy. Early Tudor choirboy actors performed in their schools and at court, and also in cathedrals and chapels; these spaces overlapped with the playwrights' careers as educators, courtiers, scholars, and priests.[22] In Greg Walker's words, the drama of playwrights like Udall "lived in the spaces in which the real events which they allegorized also took place, and it drew rhetorical and symbolic strength from that fact."[23]

As religious singers, players, and students, these choirboy performers inhabit and symbolize the domains of religion, music, drama, and education, and thus help to expose how the controversies regarding each subject are related and mutually constitutive. The choirboys' education taught them the music of the new church, and they used their musical skills to perform sacred and profane music in their dramas. These young singers who performed before Mary were given audience at court by the most powerful decision makers in the land, and they were a reminder of the changes afoot in terms of musical liturgy.[24] Taking the socializing force of music, the musical education of children, liturgical change, and dissimulation as both direct and implied topics, *Respublica* and *Ralph Roister Doister* demonstrate and urge the sort of variegated religious policy that seemed possible only at the start of Mary's reign.

---

reformist Tallis composed Latin masses for Mary before writing his more famous English anthems for Elizabeth; his protégé, William Byrd, was a staunch Catholic who wrote both Catholic masses and English anthems during the reign of Elizabeth.

22. Jeanne McCarthy, "'The Sanctuary is Become a Plaiers stage': Chapel Stagings and Tudor Secular Drama," *Medieval and Renaissance Drama in England* 21 (2008): 56–86. For more on the use of chapels, churches, and cathedrals as playing spaces, see also Paul Whitfield White, *Theater and Reformation: Protestantism, Patronage, and Playing in Tudor England* (Cambridge: Cambridge University Press, 1993), 130–62.

23. Walker, *The Politics of Performance*, 1. Suzanne Westfall articulates the way in which both royal and non-royal aristocratic household chapels allowed for theatrical experimentations and the addressing of politically charged religious issues: "religious ensembles functioning under the protection of secular patrons, the great household Chapels could afford, both financially and politically, to experiment with styles and themes that their unprotected brethren could not." *Patrons and Performance: Early Tudor Household Revels* (Oxford: Clarendon Press, 1990), 31.

24. For more on Tudor child performers, see Reaveley Gair, *The Children of Paul's: the Story of a Theatre Company, 1553–1608* (Cambridge: Cambridge University Press, 1982); Edel Lamb, *Performing Childhood in Early Modern Theater: The Children's Playing Companies, 1599–1613* (New York: Palgrave Macmillan, 2009); and Michael Shapiro, "Early Boy Companies and Their Acting Venues," in *The Oxford Handbook of Early Modern Theater*, ed. Richard Dutton (Oxford: Oxford University Press, 2011), 121–35.

Socializing with Music in *Ralph Roister Doister*

While most other late medieval and early Tudor plays use the singing of profane song primarily to denote idle characters, the non-religious music in *Ralph Roister Doister* has a more complex multivalence. Silly songs connote distraction and idle merriment in early scenes, but popular music is eventually shown to be an effective socializing force. The idea that music should bring about social harmony is consistent with humanist education, and it has religious repercussions. Music is sung or discussed at length in nine scenes in *Roister Doister*; it is integral to the play's structure, to its plot, and to the characterizations of everyone from Ralph (as a "roister," he is a loud braggart) to the servants.

Spurred on by his manipulative, freeloading companion Matthew Merygreke, the (mock) hero Ralph spends the course of the play unsuccessfully trying to woo the widow Christian Custance, often by means of music. Custance inconveniently finds Ralph despicable and is also engaged to one Gawayn Goodluck. For Ralph, music is a deeply emotional experience, tied closely to his several failed attempts at courtship. As his servant Dobinet explains:

> With every woman is he in some loves pang,
> Then up to our lute at midnight, twangledome twang . . .
> Of Songs and Balades also he is a maker,
> And that can he finely doe as Jacke Raker . . . [25]
> Yet must we sing them, as good stuff I undertake,
> As for such a pen man is well fittyng to make.
> Ah for these long nights, heyhow, when will it be day?
> I feare ere I come she will be wowed away.
> Then when aunswere is made that it may not bee,
> O death why commest thou not? By and by (saith he) (2.1.19–20,
>   27–28, 31–36)[26]

As Dobinet's description implies, Ralph's musical attempts often have the opposite of their intended effect: he marks himself as an inept suitor and an antisocial nuisance with his songwriting, which he forces his embarrassed servants to perform. But while the play uses music—or specifically *bad* music

---

25. A common nickname for one who writes bad verse.

26. Quotations and line numbers come from Nicholas Udall, "Royster Doyster," in *Tudor Plays: An Anthology of Early English Drama*, ed. Edmund Creeth (New York: Anchor Books, 1966), 215–314.

and descriptions of it—to set up Ralph's antisocial qualities and exclusion from his community, other music is used throughout the play to designate social concord and incorporation into community. These moments are relevant to the play's trajectory toward social reconciliation, and they are important inasmuch as they highlight the musical education of the choirboy performers.

The play's prologue on the merits of mirth marks it a Roman comedy, and implies that the play will not touch the religious controversies Mary had forbade discussion of in her proclamation. But as Peter Happé points out, there's no such thing as merely providing laughter in Tudor drama:

> To induce laughter implies entertainment. . . . Because dramatic form embodies many voices and the dramatist can exploit the unfolding of the plot to reveal shifts of meaning and emphasis, it was ideal for manipulating such divisions as well as for reflecting or obtaining the hoped-for support of the monarch.[27]

Happé focuses on issues of plot, and indeed *Ralph Roister Doister*'s use of tropes from Roman farce makes the play seem like mere comic mirth. But even more than the plot, it is music that allows for the "manipulating" of divisions. Specifically, Udall's use of music allows for nonverbal engagement with issues regarding religious liturgical music. The fact that the performers were boys—seemingly innocent of adult religio-political machination and too young to have been fully inculcated to Edwardian Reformism—makes the plays seem particularly unlikely to touch on Christian controversy.[28] Their boyishness allows Udall to (re)present religious music more explicitly than he might have done for adult performers.

After its prologue, the play proper begins with Merygreke's solo singing on entrance, which at once associates him with wily vice figures likes those in *Wisdom* and *Three Laws*. But while Merygreke's lone singing and Ralph's inept wooing songs set them both apart from the wider community, the communal music-making done by the play's servants demonstrates music's socializing properties, enacting points made on the subject in contemporary discourse.

---

27. Peter Happé, "Laughter in the Court: Four Tudor Comedies (1518–1585), from Skelton to Lyly," *Tudor Theater* 6 (2002): 12–13.

28. Ejner Jensen discusses the disguise inherent in the acting of boy players in "The Boy Actors: Plays and Playing," *Research Opportunities in Renaissance Drama* 18 (1975): 6–7, and Jeanne McCarthy discusses the "ill-fitting mask" of the boy player who plays against type and its political advantages in "Disciplining 'Unexpert People': Children's Dramatic Practices and Page/Stage Tensions in Early English Theatre," *The International Shakespeare Yearbook* 10 (2010): 153.

In an early scene, Custance's servants Tibet Talkapace, Madge Mumblec-rust, and Annot Alyface join in song, presumably in three-part harmony. Annot proposes that singing while working will make the time pass more quickly for them, and they interrupt their singing to complain about their work: "this sleeve is not willying to be sewed I trowe," comments Tibet (1.3.56). When singing the final refrain, the servants articulate their decision to give up their work entirely:

> *They sing the fourth tyme.*
> Pipe Mery Annot. etc.
> Trilla. Trilla. Trillarie.
> When Tibet, when Annot, when Margerie.
> I will not, I can not, no more can I.
> Then give we all over, and there let it lye.
> *Lette hir caste down hir worke.* (1.3.72 s.d.–77 s.d.)

While music has brought the women into literal harmony, it has also distracted them from their spinning work and led to idleness. The dramatic tradition that equates singing with idleness—used by evangelical playwrights like Bale—is indicative of feelings many reformers had regarding music.[29] Some of Mary's evangelical advisors might have found that this early scene confirmed their fears about music's dangerous frivolity.

The idleness continues in the following scene, when Merygreke, Ralph, and his servants and hired musicians head to Custance's house to serenade her, only to be intercepted by Custance's old servant and go-between Madge Mumblecrust. Unable to play for Custance herself, Ralph and Merygreke decide to not waste the hired musicians, so they have those musicians accompany them on a couple songs. They sing the ridiculous "Whoso to Marry a Minion Wyfe," the lyrics of which are printed along with those of other songs in an appendix at the end of the unique copy of the play, and Madge bawdily dances along (1.3.112 s.d., appendix.1–12). The music and musical discourse of the play's opening scenes demonstrate Ralph's social ineptitude, and seem to accede to concerns about music's distracting and seductive capacities as voiced by its detractors.

Udall, however, would have known that his royal patron Mary was fond of and skilled in music, which she enjoyed in non-religious (or less religious)

---

29. See, for example, Maura Giles-Watson, "The Singing 'Vice': Music and Mischief in Early English Drama," *Early Theater* 12.2 (2009): 57–90.

contexts.[30] The play goes on to demonstrate that, in many other circumstances, music could productively unite people rather than alienate, annoy, or distract them. And indeed, Ralph's inept singing has already likely united the audience in laughter, proving that, as the prologue professes, "Mirth increaseth amitie" (l. 10). Even though the servants stopped working and Ralph and Merygreke were unsuccessful in their mission, music ameliorates otherwise frustrating situations in both cases. By dramatizing music's social properties, Udall's comedy appeals to the Queen's love of music even while seeming to please his former constituency, the reformers who used music to represent vanity and idleness. Various viewpoints on music are entertained, so that the play satisfies a broader spectrum of the audience. As the play progresses, it seems to advocate more cogently for music's role in constructing social concord.

In a later scene, music spreads the sort of goodwill beneficial to the "common weal," and also appeases the lower classes. In act 2, scene 3, Ralph's servant Dobinet is stranded at Custance's house while he awaits a response from Custance. Custance's lone male servant, Tom Trupenie, asks Tibet and Annot: "Shall we sing a fitte to welcome our friende . . . ?" (2.3.53). Dobinet is then welcomed into the household by joining Tom, Tibet, and Annot in a song about music's ability to inspire people, as the refrain says, "lovingly to agree."

Music's capacity to incorporate new members into the community is a reminder of the Tudor pedagogical tradition that uses music to educate boys about social harmony, because musical harmony requires the suppression of the ego for the common good.[31] Music's defenders frequently praise song as a form of social harmony, pointing to singing as a shared and unified moment for listeners or a moment of cooperation for singers. For these educators, musical training creates subjects better able to serve the common good. For example, Sir Thomas Elyot tells tutors to "commende the perfecte understanding of musicke, declaring howe necessary it is for the better attaynynge

---

30. Mary was an accomplished player of the virginals and her mother even told her to take comfort in music when she was distraught. Dietrich Helms, "Henry VIII's Book: Teaching Music to Royal Children," *The Musical Quarterly* 92.1–2 (2009): 129–31, and Linda Austern, "Women's Musical Voices in Sixteenth-Century England," *Early Modern Women: An Interdisciplinary Journal* 3 (2008): 136–37.

31. See, for example, Jonathan Willis, *Church Music and Protestantism in Post-Reformation England: Discourses, Sites and Identities* (Aldershot, UK: Ashgate, 2010), 205–35, and "'By These Means the Sacred Discourses Sink More Deeply into the Minds of Men': Music and Education in Elizabethan England," *History* 94.3 (2009): 294–309.

the knowledge of a publicke weale."[32] There is a related tradition of celebrating music for its ability to promote egalitarian feelings, temporarily
transforming a household (like Ralph's or Custance's, or even Mary's) into
a unified whole: music "joyneth and accordeth diverse thinges that seeme
contrary, and maketh the high sound to accord with the low."[33] The servants thus not only enact music's ability to be welcoming, but also remind
the upper classes that music can placate the discontented, in this case, servants who don't want to spin and do their master's wooing errands. The
trajectory of the play's first several songs, then, moves music from a solitary
activity for a wayfarer, to idle and distracting entertainment, to a social activity bringing new acquaintances together in literal and figurative harmony.

While this singing has social consequences, it has political and religious
import, too. Social concord promotes goodwill among the commonweal,
which would have been a particularly important goal for Mary's government
in its contentious early years. The three- and four-part harmonies of the servants' songs highlight the way in which the musical talents of choirboys
across the country could be put to better use under Mary's religion than
under her brother's. While some polyphonic compositions were written
under Edward, polyphonic singing in choir schools had diminished considerably. In fact, composers who wrote masses during Mary's reign often wrote
them for only four parts to account for the fact that the cutbacks in choral
provisions from Edward's reign had not been fully repaired.[34] The theatrical,
harmonious singing of the boys here is an embodied metaphor that reminds
Mary of the fact that these choirboys, like her Children of the Chapel, were
being trained to restore complex harmonies for church services.[35] Records

---

32. Sir Thomas Elyot, *The Boke named The Governour* (1531), 28. He is echoed by Roger Ascham
in *Toxophilus* (London, 1545), fol. 9, and Richard Mulcaster, *Positions wherein those primitive circumstances be examined, which are necessary for the training up of children* (London, 1581), fol. 36–38.

33. Stephen Batman, *Batman upon Bartholome, his Booke De Proprietatibus Rerum* (London, 1582),
424. See also Christopher Marsh, *Music and Society in Early Modern England* (Cambridge: Cambridge University Press, 2011), 58, for more examples.

34. Roger Bray, "Sacred Music to Latin Texts," in *Music in Britain: The Sixteenth Century*, ed.
Roger Bray (Oxford: Blackwell, 1995), 79.

35. Robin A. Leaver explains that Henrican polyphonic masses were used under the 1548 prayer
book, but were forbidden under the 1552 prayer book, in "The Reformation and Music," in Haar,
European Music 1520–1640, 382–83. The debate during Edward's reign was whether to simplify
music into unified melodies to be sung by congregations, or to eradicate it altogether. Reformers
like Edward's chaplains William Turner and Thomas Becon rail against Catholic music in, respectively, *A Worke entytled Of ye Olde God & the Newe* (1534) and *Jewel of Joye* (1553). Daniel Bennett
Page writes about how the polyphonic style of composers like Tallis and Tye became the "explicit
emblem" of the Queen's restoration of Catholicism, "Uniform and Catholic: Church Music in the
Reign of Mary Tudor (1553–58)" (PhD diss., Brandeis University, 1996), 125.

indicate that Mary financially rewarded the dean of St. Paul's choir school for training their choristers to sing Catholic liturgy; she would have been pleased by the ability of young singers to perform the kind of music she was keen to reinstate nationwide.[36]

Not only does the boys' singing remind Mary of the musical skills they have learned already, but also it is a reminder that they were likely employed to share musical training with others.[37] The performing choirboys in Udall's *Roister Doister* would have reminded Mary that choirs outside of court were also being trained to sing counterpoint and polyphony. Pedagogy itself— the musical education of the boy performers—is thus an implicit theme of the play that the career educator Udall presented. The opening scenes of *Ralph Roister Doister* demonstrate that musical skills can bring people together and quiet their discontent as easily as they can reduce productivity; promoting music seems worth the risk. While the play's first two acts only imply that the choirboys' musical skills will be useful in spreading the music of the Catholic liturgy, the middle of the play turns more explicitly to the singing of religious music.

Ralph's Fake Funeral

We have seen the various uses to which theatrical parody of musical ritual is put in both the Digby *Mary Magdalene*, when it invites both Wycliffite and traditional responses, and *King Johan*, when it attempts to critique the emptiness of Catholic rite. While Bale surely did not intend for parody's interpretive openness to undermine his polemic, Udall exploits the slipperiness of this musical theatrical technique. The musical parody in *Ralph Roister Doister* demonstrates to Mary how the continued cultural caché of Catholic rites will allow them to be resurrected easily, while at the same time the play mocks them as laughable entertainment in a way that the evangelical reformers in her court would have enjoyed. While the scene allows for various interpretations, it also calls to mind liturgical compromises recently made by the Queen, suggesting that such compromises could help reconcile the audience's ideological diversity on such issues.

Ralph almost makes good on his frequent promise to die from the pain caused by Custance's rejection in the third act. With the help of Merygreke

---

36. Reavley Gair, "The Conditions of Appointment for Masters of Choristers at Paul's (1553–1613)," *Notes and Queries* 27, no. 2 (1980): 117.

37. See also Page, "Uniform and Catholic," 131.

and his servants, he stages a mock funeral with music from Catholic rites for the dead. As the scene begins, Merygreke returns with the news that Custance has rejected Ralph's love yet again, and the two have the following exchange:

> ROISTER: Well, what should I now doe?
> MERYGREKE: In faith, I cannot tell.
> ROISTER: I will go home and die.
> MERYGREKE: Then shall I bidde toll the bell?
> ROISTER: No.
> MERYGREKE: God have mercie on your soule, ah good gentleman
> [. . .] How feele your soule to God?
> ROISTER: I am nigh gone.
> MERYGREKE: And shall we hence straight?
> ROISTER: Yea.
> MERYGREKE: *Placebo dilexi.*
> Maister Royster Doyster will straight go home and die.
> (3.3.47–49, 52–54)

Merygreke then begins to intone an entire funeral sequence for Ralph, who periodically interrupts the ritual, usually to agree that it is warranted: "Heigh how, alas, the pangs of death my hearte do break" (3.3.55). Merygreke begins with the "Placebo dilexi," which is the start of Vespers in the Catholic Sarum Rite's Office of the Dead. He moves on to the "Nequando," an antiphon from the Burial Service, then to the "Dirige" and several other antiphons, including the Office's "Requiem aeternum." Edward's final prayer book had eliminated the processional and the Office of the Dead, and Merygreke's liturgy—in Latin with English commentary—quotes directly from all parts of the newly restored Catholic funeral and burial rites.[38] As critics of *Roister Doister* have pointed out, the play re-presents Catholic ceremony almost verbatim, and that fact coupled with the play's likely performance context makes this parody a particularly complicated interpretive crux.[39]

---

38. On changes to the 1552 Burial of the Dead, see Brian Cummings, *The Book of Common Prayer: the Texts of 1549, 1559, and 1662* (Oxford: Oxford World Classics, 2013), 742, and Duffy, *Fires of Faith*, 537. David Cressy also describes how funeral rites reformed under Henry and Edward were restored under Mary in *Birth, Marriage, and Death: Ritual, Religion, and the Life-Cycle in Tudor and Stuart England* (Oxford: Oxford University Press, 1997), 398.

39. Edward Shephard Miller's "*Roister Doister*'s 'Funeralls,'" *Studies in Philology* 43.1 (1946): 42–58, explains the reproduction of the rites. Bevington, in *Tudor Drama and Politics*, 124, and Tobias Doring in *Performances of Mourning in Shakespearean Theater and Early Modern Culture* (Basingstoke, UK: Palgrave Macmillan, 2006), 167–68, both remark on the oddness of the ritual's fidelity to actual rite.

As is argued in the previous chapter, the contradictions in Bale's prose polemics and dramas with regards to music reveal the reluctance with which even the most zealous of reformers parted with musical rites. Where Bale's contradictions might be seen as unintentional hypocrisy, Udall's writing reveals more calculated shifts in perspective. Gaining favor with Mary while Bale was in exile, Udall was far cagier in his use of theatricalized music, intentionally invoking the sort of *aporia* that likely saved his life.

By juxtaposing the solemnity of the religious text and the frivolity of Ralph's love life, the mock funeral calls attention to itself as ironic comedy. But when Bale and other polemical evangelical playwrights parodied Catholic rites in the 1530s and '40s, they decimated them in the process and reduced the rites to scatological gibberish instead of re-quoting them verbatim as Udall does.[40] By having young choirboys intone the rites anew, *Roister Doister*'s funeral demonstrates the resilience of traditional religious musical forms.

Many auditors—including Mary herself—who advocated for a return to complex Latin liturgical choir music could hear in the citation of this music an acknowledgment of the cultural relevance the rites continued to have. Ralph and Merygreke are negative exempla: Merygreke a freeloader who uses his wits and his singing to charm and deceive, Ralph a dolt whose musical forays alienate his beloved and annoy his servants. The fact that they are mocking the funeral rites, then, could be interpreted as another example of antisocial musical behavior. The joke is on Ralph, who looks silly for taking part in such a ritual while still alive. He, not the rite, comes off looking foolish. That is, the faithful citation of the musical rites may prove that these extra-theatrical rituals survived and held their own against misuse by the idiotic Merygreke and Ralph. Udall thus massages the inter-theatrical resonances of parodic rite and the interpretive openness of sound and comedy to signal several meanings at once, nodding to his former constituency of reformers while not offending his Queen.

On the other hand, the scene obliquely comments on changing doctrinal policies without causing offense to members of the court who were less fond of such changes, as all is part of a comedic farce. To those reformers who held onto hope that Mary's church would retain some of the vernacular and participatory elements for which the reformers had advocated, a theatricalized funeral mass in any form could be heard as ridiculous, a mockery of musical rites no longer relevant except in entertainment. Because the moment's resonances with plays like *King Johan*—which clearly intends to de-

---

40. For more on the tradition of anti-Catholic ritual mockery, see Allison Shell, *Oral Culture and Catholicism in Early Modern England* (Cambridge: Cambridge University Press, 2007), 59–67.

ride Catholic rite—would support this interpretation, recent theatrical history could color the moment in a reformist light for some.

In a conservative reading of the funeral mass parody, then, the scene models the rites that will soon be restored so fully that even idiots will know them. In a reformist interpretation, the parody mirrors the emptiness of the rites themselves, which have lost so much efficacy that they are merely a comic theatrical trick.[41] This feature of parody—its double-edged voice— is exactly what makes this scene work so well in Udall's comedy. By gently parodying an issue of great contention between reformers and Catholics, Udall has it several ways. Not only does he send varying messages to audience members of different strokes, he also pushes both resistant, reformist courtiers and the Catholic Queen toward a middle ground. Reminding reformers that even a return to Catholic rites allows for parody, reminding Mary that even parody allows for a return to Catholic rites, the play urges against extremism.

The moment also indirectly advocates for moderation in that it calls to mind recent events. The performance of a funeral for a (fake) boy corpse at this moment reminds audiences of a recent real funeral: that of Edward VI in August 1553. Windsor Herald Charles Wriothesley's account of the events explains how Mary arranged her brother's funeral and burial: "The 9th of August, in the afternoone, the Quene helde an obsequy for the Kinge within the church in the Tower, her Grace beinge present, and had a solemne dirige songe in Latine. The morrow . . . the Quenes highness had a solemne masse of Requiem songe within the chappell in the Tower for the Kinge."[42] This private Mass had public consequences: not only was it documented, it was also replicated throughout the country.[43] That is, Mary orchestrated a nationwide Catholic funeral to mark the death of her brother, in whose reign those very funeral rites had been abolished.[44]

However, the day after Mary heard her "private" Latin Requiem Mass, Edward was buried in the Abbey in a reformed service conducted by Thomas Cranmer. The Queen had thus agreed to a compromise, a two-part burial that included both a traditional requiem and reformed rites from the 1552

---

41. The language of "models" and "mirrors" is inspired by Don Handelman, *Models and Mirrors: Towards an Anthropology of Public Events* (New York: Berghahn Books, 1998), 49 and passim.

42. Charles Wriothesley, *A Chronicle of England During the Reigns of the Tudors*, ed. William Douglas Hamilton (London: Camden Society, 1875), 96.

43. Hunt also comments on the public nature of Mary's private funeral Mass for Edward in *Drama of Coronation*, 130.

44. See also Eamon Duffy, *The Stripping of the Altars: Traditional Religion in England 1400–1580* (New Haven, CT: Yale University Press, 2005), 527; Hunt, *Drama of Coronation*, 130; and Page, "Uniform and Catholic," xii.

Book of Common Prayer.[45] Wriothesley's account indicates that the burial "was all in Englishe, without any copes or vestments, but onely surplus, accordinge to the Booke of Common Prayer last sett forth by Act of Parliament."[46] Thus, while historians tend to remember Mary for promoting Catholic funeral (and coronation) activities, it seems that at the very start of her reign she was open to the idea of mixing conventional Catholic and reformist elements in religious rites, allowing the sort of denominational hybridity usually associated with the reign of her younger sister, Elizabeth I.

Udall's mock funeral enacts a similar compromise. While there is fidelity to the words of the Catholic rites, reformist thought is represented, too. Early in the funeral sequence, Merygreke comments in Latin and English on the kind of service he will conduct: "*Dirige*. He will go darklyng to his grave,/ *Neque lux, neque crux, neque* mourners, *neque* clinke" (3.3.58–9). That is, Merygreke says Ralph will be buried without the usual props and actors of a Catholic requiem: without candles (lux), without a crucifix (crux), without mourners, and without the traditional passing bells (clinke). This macaronic language mirrors reformist language about eschewing popish props for funerals. For example, when Matthew Parker wrote to John Foxe about the burial of the Duchess of Norfolk, he assured him that "all things were done honourably, *sine crux, sine lux et non sine* tinkling."[47] Indeed, candles, crucifixes, and bells were objects of scorn for most reformers. While Merygreke is being somewhat silly here—they necessarily will not have these elements because they are in a house and not a church in the play's reality—he also suggests that they conduct a sort of hybridized rite, one combining Catholic musical liturgy with some reformist restraint. Merygreke's funeral sequence thus mirrors the compromised funeral sequence Mary had just orchestrated for her brother. By parodying it (and doing so gently, without outright mocking of either the Catholic format or the reformist exclusion of props), Udall's play reifies the hybridity of mid-century perspectives on the funeral rite. The play makes it seem as though this kind of funeral sequence that draws from both Catholic and reformist practice could become the new standard; the mirror of Edward's funeral becomes a model for the future.

While the mock service never uses candles or crucifixes (or traditional vestments, as Wroithesley had indicated was also the case with Edward's

---

45. Whitelock, *Mary Tudor*, 198.

46. Wriothesley, *A Chronicle of England*, 97.

47. John Strype, *Annals of the Reformation and Establishment of Religion and Other Various Happy Occurrences in the Church of England* (London: Edward Symon, 1735), vol. 2, 45. Farmer points out this connection in *The Dramatic Writings of Nicholas Udall*, ed. John S. Farmer (London: Early English Drama Society, 1906), 136.

burial), Merygreke changes his mind at the end of the service and *does* call for bells, which he orders Ralph's servants to ring:

Pray for the late maister Royster Doysters soule,
And come forth parish Clarke, let the passing bell toll.
Ad servos militis [to the soldier's servants]. Pray for your mayster sirs, and
for hym ring a peale:
He was your right good maister while he was in heale.
The Peale of belles rong by the parish clark, and Roister Doister's foure men.
The First Bell A Triple
When dyed he? When dyed he?
The Seconde.
We have hym, We have hym.
The Thirde.
Roister Doyster, Roister Doyster.
The Fourth Bell.
He commeth, He commeth.
The Freate Bell.
Our owne, Our owne. (3.3.81–84, Appendix.24–28)[48]

The props here must be real handbells, and they were probably brought into the court performance from the chapel or cathedral in which the choirboys usually performed, or else borrowed from the nearby Chapel Royal. That Merygreke changes course to make the funeral sequence end with this traditional musical practice is politically important. Bells have their own contentious history in the sixteenth century, and were one musical element that by the end of the sixteenth century had survived even the harshest iconoclasm. Edward had banned all bells except one to signal the beginning of a sermon, and many sixteenth-century evangelicals had requested burial without bells.[49] While many bells were too large to destroy, many handbells, being so small, were demolished under Edward. In her first year, Mary required

---

48. The direction *"ut infra,"* referring to the bell passage that is printed with the other songs at the end of the quarto, comes before these lines, but I agree with Scheurwegh's assessment that the bell pealing sequence likely follows these lines that clearly cue it. "Ralph Roister Doister," reprinted in *Materials for the Study of the Old English Drama* 16, ed. G. Scheurwegh (Vaduz: Kraus Reprint Ltd., 1963), 102, n. 990.

49. Cressy quotes the dean of Wells, who ordered communities to "abstain from such unmeasurable ringing for dead persons at their burials." *Birth, Marriage, and Death,* 422. See also Marsh, *Music and Society,* 454–501, and his essay "'At it ding dong': Recreation and Religion in the English Belfry, 1580–1640," in *Worship and the Parish Church in Early Modern Britain,* eds. Natalie Mears and Alec Ryrie (Surrey, UK: Ashgate, 2013), 151–53.

parish churches to buy several kinds of service bells, including handbells for funerals.[50] The repurchasing of bells was expensive for churches, but the process of fundraising and rebuilding was underway the year *Roister Doister* was likely performed. The props used for this play would thus either be new bells or bells that had been preserved during Edward's reign. By staging the traditional practice of summoning prayers for the dead through the playing of handbells, even in jest, the moment reminds Mary of the funeral bells' nationwide resurrection. While iconoclasts had destroyed many small bells, their reintroduction was popular with *almost* everyone, and Udall's inclusion of funeral bells finds a common ground between the majority and all but the most radical, a common ground that would lead to the retention of funeral bells in the Elizabethan Settlement.

Roister Doister's mock funeral thus implies religious toleration in its interpretive ambiguity. At this midpoint in the play, however, Ralph is still a social outcast and a failed suitor. Later in the scene, Ralph joins his men in a song about being "married a Sunday." In a reading of this song's potential religious politics, Carla Mazzio points out that Ralph turns the word "married" to "marieb" (a couple times, so it seems to not be an error), changes "by God" to "by gosse," and commits other linguistic faux pas, which "further thematize his compromised relation to a spiritual community." She also suggests that the song's six repetitions of Sunday "may at least hint at the association of immoderate rhyme . . . linked to the Catholic liturgy."[51] Thus, song links social and religious communities: Ralph is shown to be inept in both, and he stands in opposition to the socialized harmonies of proper courtship and respectful religious behavior. But the play eventually incorporates Ralph into the wider community in a scene that models the way music can be used to express forgiveness of wrongdoers, and celebrate new alliances despite social or religious differences.

"Sing on, and no mo words make"

The play's concluding moments use music to smooth over hard feelings among opponents: music is used to create the sensation of social harmony. After Roister Doister has been defeated in a mock battle, and the much-

---

50. Marsh, *Music and Society*, 459; Duffy, *Fires of Faith*, 545.
51. Carla Mazzio, *The Inarticulate Renaissance: Language Trouble in an Age of Eloquence* (Philadelphia: University of Pennsylvania Press, 2009), 64.

besieged Custance has been reunited with her Gawayn, he attempts to heal hard feelings with the man who won Custance by calling for a song. A prayer for the Queen immediately follows, which was perhaps also sung.

Gawayn is something of a fuddy-duddy, arguing against music and sport in a way that recalls, most recently, the attacks on music by ardent anti-music reformers like Bale who had exiled themselves under Mary. But when the play ends, Gawayn's protestations turn to expressions of regret, and he is reminded that "melodie" is, in fact, something he once enjoyed:

> ROISTER: I wyll be as good friends with them as ere I was.
> MERYGREKE: Then let me fet[ch] your quier that we may have a song.
> ROISTER: Goe.
> GAWAYN: I have hearde no melodie all this yeare long.
> MERYGREKE: Come on sirs quickly.
> ROISTER: Sing on sirs for my frends sake.
> DOBINET: Cal ye these your frends?
> ROISTER: Sing on, and no mo words make.
> *Here they sing.*
> GAWAYN: The Lord preserve our most noble Queene of renowne
> And hir vertues rewarde with the heavenly crowne. (5.6.41–47)

We do not know what song was sung here, or if the song was in fact the prayer for the Queen, led by the newly reconciled Gawayn (the prayer continues, with the other characters speaking or singing, for ten more lines). Whether there was just a sung prayer, a song and then a spoken prayer, or a song and then a sung prayer, a representative of a more extremist anti-music position has chosen to join in harmony with the group, praising the new Queen.[52] Rather than answering Dobinet's question—"Cal ye these your friends?"—Ralph starts a song, letting music symbolize harmony even when there has been no real reconciliation, or even conversation.

Musical harmony seems community-forming not only for the way, as humanists said, it briefly subsumes the individual into the larger whole, but also because, as the Marian administration emphasized, it was symbolic of the community's oneness. Even Mary's advisors admitted that music's affective and social powers would aid in the spread of their religion, and Udall dramatizes music's ability to symbolize unity.[53] In the final line of the prayer, the entire

---

52. In Mazzio's words, the ending "privileges musical harmony over the play's verbal and textual ambiguities," ibid., 76.

53. See, for example, Duffy, *Fires of Faith*, 545.

company pleads: "God graunt the nobilitie hir [the Queen] to serve and love,/With all the whole commontie as doth them behove" (5.6.2013–14). At a time when Cranmer had been imprisoned but the heresy burnings had not yet begun (they started in 1555), Udall's play pleads with the Queen to choose toleration and the needs of the "commontie" over univocal fanaticism. It reminds her that something as simple as music might be a persuasive ameliorator, creating moments that *feel* harmonious even as that feeling may mask irreconcilable differences.

While the play's music tries to suggest social and spiritual harmonizing, at least on the surface, Mazzio reads defiance into many of the songs. She senses resistance on the part of Custance, who may be left out of the final song, and complaint from the servants, who sing of their tedious lives in the song for which Ralph calls, a song that might briefly appease them but does not change their subordinate positions.[54] Music is palliative, not curative: Udall seems aware of both its usefulness and its limitations. To join hands and sing a song feels unifying in the moment, but is at best a temporary fix to more complex societal ills and tensions. While Udall's play may present a model of compromise, the strains of resistance at which the play subtly hints will prove to be more fracturing than flexible. In Mary's reign, at least, theatrical-musical advocacy did not result in much real conciliation.

Ralph Roister Doister exhibits that comedy and music are useful tools of social control: their interpretive looseness makes them able to please diverse audiences, and they unify people—temporarily—in shared laughter and harmony. Udall's musical theater is the antithesis of the kind of performances Mary would authorize later in her reign, for while musical drama like his choirboy plays resolves binaries, symbolizes unity, and exposes the complex variances in everyone, the theater of the scaffold enforces confessional labels, symbolizes irreconcilable difference, and insinuates that subjects may be uniformly condemnable. That is, if musical comedies optimistically overlook the real differences between people to stage the feeling of harmony, executions cynically overlook the real similarities between people to stage the feeling of discord. So, even if the unities that theater stages are lies, they still urge an abeyance of violence that has political import.

While Udall's play ultimately failed to move Mary toward the social compromises it enacts, theatrical indeterminacy at least saved his own head. In *Respublica*, Udall shows how the benign deceits of music and theater can be put to use in political and educational spheres.

---

54. Mazzio, *Inarticulate Renaissance*, 79.

Allegory and Song in *Respublica*

If *Ralph Roister Doister* focuses on music's social usefulness and only hints at its political utility, *Respublica* directly confronts political issues. It is a play about leadership and the way a monarch's decisions affect the populace, and in it music becomes a political tool, one that allows leaders and the subjects who must please them to mean many things at once. While critics of the play have noted its cagey indeterminacy on, for example, leadership, economics, and the nature of truth, it is also worth noting that the play leverages the hermeneutic flexibility of music and of allegory to signify in multiple ways about religion, and to demonstrate the related usefulness of multivocality and dissimulation.[55]

Respublica is a political morality play that begins with the central titular figure, a woman who represents the whole state of England, left destitute after the disastrous decisions of previous leaders. Respublica stands for the common weal of the state, which her name Latinizes, so the play participates in contemporary discussions about to what extent Mary will serve the common good of her people.[56] The play's engagement with political and economic issues is clear. Advised by a cadre of disguised vices instead of a legitimate council, Respublica makes bad decisions that bankrupt the state and send the "People" (a character in the play) into poverty. These vices call to mind the specific advisors who essentially ran the government under the Edwardian minority, but they also expose the dangers of poor advising more generally. The play's lead vice, Avarice, disguises himself as Policy and renames his minions—named in the dramatis personae as the "gallaunts" Insolence, Oppression, and Adulation—as Authority, Reformation, and Honesty, respectively. The vices work to keep Respublica in the dark about People's plight, and are thwarted by the arrival of Misericordia, Veritas, Justicia, and Pax. These daughters of God uncover the truth about the State's dire straits and corrupt advisors, but order is restored only when the goddess

---

55. Sarah Carpenter says the play "reinforces our understanding of the flexible and subtle ability of Tudor court dramatists . . . to compose plays which can at the same time support and critique prevailing rulers and governments." "*Respublica*," 518. Kirk M. Fabel argues for the play saying two things simultaneously about economic matters in "Questions of Numismatic and Linguistic Signification in the Reign of Mary Tudor," *Studies in English Literature* 32.2 (1997): 239, and Hunt points out the ambiguity of truth in the play in *Drama of Coronation*, 145.

56. The phrase "Respublica" is first found in 1460, according to the *OED*, and the *OED*'s next recorded use is in this play. It is clearly synonymous with the "common weal," and the character Respublica calls herself this many times throughout the play, as in 2.2.530: "what common weale shall then bee so happie as I?"

Nemesis arrives to judge the corrupt vices.[57] She punishes all of them except Adulation, who freely confesses his sins and is absolved and allowed to serve the State going forward.

Many plays were performed during Mary's first Christmas season by the Gentlemen and Children of the Chapel Royal, and *Respublica* was most likely written for and performed by the Chapel's choirboy Children. Most critics assert that *Respublica* "eschews the violence of religious controversy," but I argue that the play obliquely but crucially addresses matters related to church politics as well as church doctrine, urging moderation and religious tolerance.[58] The choirboy performers are crucial to the play's meanings. To make the play seem like mere entertainment, the boys sing throughout; they cut political tensions by turning to the distractions of musical comedy used in plays like *Ralph Roister Doister*. But, as with that play, *Respublica* highlights the way in which the musical talent of choirboys will be put to better use under Mary's religion than it had been in her brother's. Music is thus both a cloak and a symbol: its comedic valences mask the play from the "controversy touching the high points and mysteries of Christian religion," in the Marian Proclamation's language, while its performance by choirboys becomes symbolic of access to those very mysteries. So, while Daniel Bennett Page argues that the theatrical nature of the Chapel Royal's liturgies is clarified by the Chapel's performance of actual theater in plays like *Respublica*, I would also add that the religious nature of these plays is clarified by the fact that the performers deliver polyphony reminiscent of Catholic liturgy to the Queen and her court.[59]

Udall knew how to use the multivalence of allegorical symbolism and music to his strategic advantage when presenting topical matters before an audience of such confessional and political diversity. *Respublica*, the prologue boy explains, is told "not as by plaine storye,/but as yt were in figure by an allegorye" (prologue ll. 17–18).[60] The boy then goes on to explain exactly how the allegory works—how the vices conceal their identities and how the re-

---

57. A Nemesis, in classical mythology, is the goddess of vengeance who reverses fortune and punishes wrongdoing—the *OED*'s first citation of this use of the word is in fact Udall in his 1542 translation of Erasmus.

58. Peter Happé, "Introduction," *Tudor Interludes* (New York: Penguin Books, 1972), 27. Similar arguments about the play avoiding religious matters are found in Hunt, *Drama of Coronation*, 141, and Jacqueline Vanhoutte, *Strange Communion: Motherland and Masculinity in Tudor Plays, Pamphlets, and Politics* (Newark: University of Delaware Press, 2003), 68, 73. Walker, however, points out that "the play is shot through with detailed references to ecclesiastical issues and policies," *The Politics of Performance*, 185, 187.

59. Page, "Uniform and Catholic," 111.

60. All quotations come from *Respublica: An Interlude for Christmas 1553*, ed. W. W. Greg (London: Early English Text Society, 1952). I follow Greg's orthography but occasionally re-punctuate his lines for clarity.

storative Nemesis character at the play's end is Mary herself—and he emphasizes the pervading presence of dissimulation.[61] The playwright is thus on
record asserting that the salvific Nemesis is Mary, but it is hard not to see
the besieged Respublica as, at the very least, a warning figure for the female
monarch.[62] While some may argue that allegory—with its bald-faced character (mis)naming and predictable plotlines—is the least subtle of dramatic
forms, it is also heavily symbolic, and modern theories of religion, politics,
and narrative have shown us how symbolism is able to project feelings of
resolution while maintaining contradictions.[63]

Respublica reveals that the allegorical symbolism and symbolic music of
political drama and Catholic ritual work to suggest unity precisely because
they appeal to divergent beliefs at the same time.[64] If, as David Kertzer argues, symbols gain their ritual and political power from their condensation
of meaning, their mulitvocality, and their ambiguity, *Respublica* uses symbolism to appeal variously to the Queen and to other audience members with
whom the Queen does not agree on political and religious matters.[65] So, for
example, using Kertzer's formula, a symbol like the character Avarice *con-
denses* several associations with greed into one character, resulting in an interpretive synthesis that would be individual to each audience member. Thus,
the character Avarice simultaneously calls to mind different avaricious hyp-
ocrites across the confessional and political spectrums. Kertzer explains that
the variety of possible meanings—the symbol's *multivocality*—is a way in
which symbols "build unity in the absence of real consensus"; we have
seen how music has similar capabilities. It is thus the *ambiguity* of symbols, and
of music, that give them their political power.

---

61. The players thank God "that he hath sent Marye our Soveraigne and Quene/to reforme
thabuses which hithertoo hath been . . . She is oure most wise and most worthie Nemesis/Of
whome our plaie meneth tamende that is amysse" (prologue ll. 49–50, 53–54).

62. See also Hunt, *Drama of Coronation*, 141, for this argument, and Jane Griffiths, "Counterfet
Countenance: (Mis)representation and the Challenge to Allegory in Sixteenth-Century Morality
Plays," *Yearbook of English Studies* 38, no. 1/2 (2008): 22.

63. See, for example, Fredric Jameson's critiques of Durkheim in *The Political Unconscious: Narrative as a Socially Symbolic Act* (Ithaca, NY: Cornell University Press, 1981), 293. He says that "Durkheim's view of religion (which we have expanded to include cultural activity generally) as a
symbolic affirmation of human relationships" is unrigorous and in the end "false and ideological."
For Jameson, the ultimate subtext to narrative and symbolism is social contradiction, and the sec-
ondary subtext is ideological, 82–83.

64. Duffy writes of the ways that participation in Catholic symbolic ritual could be community
forming, *Fires of Faith*, 531, 532. Cardinal Pole, Mary's chief political advisor, explained that "participation in Catholic ceremony was symbolic of acceptance of the grace of God in the Church,
and of attentiveness to the truths of God here proclaimed" (ibid., 531).

65. David Kertzer lays these three categories out in *Ritual, Politics and Power* (New Haven, CT:
Yale University Press, 1988), 11.

Further, as with *Ralph Roister Doister*, the play's topical matter is presented by children, which diminishes its political charge. The prologue boy asks: "but shall boyes (saith some nowe) of suche highe mattiers plaie?" (prologue l. 39). While he answers himself by citing Jesus's preference for children, the real answer is surely that the boys' obvious dissimilarity to anything like a greedy political advisor makes them especially suitable for the symbolic roles.[66] Looking nothing like that which they represent, the boys' ambiguity as symbols is amplified, and the audience's interpretations can be especially varied.

Like Merygreke or the vices of *Wisdom* or *Three Laws*, Adulation, Insolence, and Oppression enter singing; the singing is again shorthand for the mischief of such characters. The stage direction records no specific song, but the boys could have sung any song they knew well, and they could have sung for as long as they wanted.[67] At the same time it was a theatrical mainstay, recreational singing continued to be criticized both when represented in drama and when performed on its own, and such critiques were usually animated by religious politics. Writing in 1554, John Christopherson discusses the sinister bond between actors and singers in his Catholic polemic:

> At which tyme also the devil, for the better furtheraunce of heresy piked out two sorts of people. . . . that is to say, minstrels and players of enterludes. The one to singe pestilente and abhominable songes, and the other to set forth openly before mens eyes the wicked blasphemye, that they had contrived for the defacing of all rites, ceremonies, and all the whole order, used in the administration of the blessid Sacramentes.[68]

Mary's patronage of drama indicates that she did not entirely agree that minstrels and interlude players had both been equally responsible for the defacement of Catholic rite, but Udall's play for child actors takes special care to discourage Christopherson's line of thinking. Whereas the minstrels and interlude players to which Christopherson took offence were knowing adults, the young players of *Respublica* change the nature of the game. One key here is that, as Maura Giles-Watson explains for all vice characters, "the Vice simultaneously foregrounds his performative identity and his musical and acting skills."[69] And instead of gaining their musical skills from working as lurid

---

66. Carpenter makes a similar point, "*Respublica*," 519.

67. Richard Southern suggests that they might have begun their singing outside the hall and continued for as long as it took them to enter the place, giving them a goodly amount of time to impress the audience with their voices. *The Staging of Plays Before Shakespeare*. (New York: Theatre Arts Books, 1973), 377.

68. Christopherson, *An exhortation to all menne to take hede and beware*, C3v.

69. Giles-Watson, "The Singing 'Vice,'" 61.

entertainers, the musical skills of the choirboy actors come from training for Chapel services. As such, the quality of their angelic voices could please those in the audience who advocated for the return to polyphony and counterpoint in church services. While Mary and others could have been pleased by a reminder that these boys were capable of this musical skill, for those with more evangelical perspectives who were familiar with plays like Bale's, the vocalization of a complex song by four vices might come as no surprise.

Additionally, the vices' banter after their singing questions music's spiritual effectiveness in a way that evangelicals might have applauded:

> ADULACION: Oh noble Insolence if I coulde sing as well
>   I wolde looke in heaven emonge Angells to dwell.
> INSOLENCE: Sing? Howe doo I sing, but as other manye doe?
> ADULACION: Yes, an Angels voice ye have to herken unto.
> INSOLENCE: Yea, but what availeth that to highe dignitiee?
> OPPRESSION: By his armes not a whitte, as farre as I can see.
> INSOLENCE: Or what helpeth that thinge, to sett a man a lofte?
> OPPRESSION: By his woundes not a strawe, so have I told yowe ofte.
>   (1.2.123–30)

That is, Adulation longs to sing like an angel, like his friend Insolence, but Insolence and Oppression assure Adulation that good singing grants one nothing when it comes to dignity among men, and will be equally useless when it comes to eschatological reckoning. For some in the audience, the notion that music (or any kind of performance, or deed) could aid one in their journey to heaven was one of the causes for reform in the first place. At the same time, it is *vices* who sing and say these things, and if one really believes that the vices symbolize the corrupt and radical advisors to Edward VI, the critique could be dismissed as self-negating. The voicing of these perspectives grants them continued legitimacy, and the fact that it is boys who represent vices makes this multivalence particularly flexible.

The way one interprets the allegorical vices is important when they break into harmony, as they do in acts 2 and 3.[70] After Respublica reveals that their inequity has been caught out, they highlight their musical skill when they discuss pitch before singing a song:

> ADULACION: She is gonne.
> AVARICE: Well then sirs lett us make no delaye
>   But abowte our markett departe eche manne his waye.

---

70. They sing at 2.3.589–97 and 3.6.887–97.

ADULACION: Naie first lett us sing a song to lighten our hartes.

AVARICE: Than are ye like for me to sing but of three partes.

Canne Avarice harte bee sett on a merie pynne [proper pitch]

And see no gaine no profitte att all coming in?

INSOLENCE: We shall have enoughe to drive awaie all sorowe.

AVARICE: Than sing wee on bowne viage [bon voyage], and Saincte George the[e] borowe [save].

Cantent, Bring ye to me and I to ye, et cetera *et sic exeant.*

(2.3.590–97 s.d.)

Insolence's point that their music should "drive awaie all sorowe" echoes praise of music's emotional benefits as expressed in many humanist defenses of music, and the vice's cooperative singing models the sort of cooperation music educators praised. Many evangelicals, even if they wanted to reduce the amount of singing in the church and simplify its deliverance, praised the benefits of worldly music in enhancing education, and the metrical Psalms produced under Edward were an attempt at a spiritual music that prioritized the Word and unified congregants. And as Hyun-Ah Kim argues, evangelical emphasis on music's ability to convey words intelligibly was aligned and associated with humanist enthusiasm for rhetorical force in oral delivery.[71] It is thus true that both evangelical and Catholic leaders were interested in teaching children to sing the songs of their faith, and no one would have been more aware of that than a humanist teacher like Udall. By using choirboys to sing polyphony, the music calls to mind the sounds of the new Catholic church; by expressing evangelical hopes for musical education, the music dramatizes a position with which many reformists agreed. But by finding this common ground in the singing of *vices*, *Respublica* exposes the hypocrisy inherent on both sides: Catholic liturgical music sounds like the "sinful" music it sets itself against, and music's social properties, so praised by many reformers, could just as easily soothe or unify a pack of sinners. Clearly, the role of music in training children in the new faith mattered, and *Respublica* also explicitly addresses the role of musical education in promoting social and political harmony.

Learning to Re-Form

When Avarice renames his gallants, the scene discloses the extent to which both reformers and traditionalists had high hopes for (re)forming religious

---

71. Hyun-Ah Kim, *Humanism and the Reform of Sacred Music in Early Modern England* (Aldershot, UK: Ashgate, 2008), 10.

subjects through musical education; despite the illusion of binary opposition, there were many commonalities. When Adulation cannot remember Avarice's new name, Adulation tries to use music as an educational tool to reinforce the new titles:

> AVARICE: And what callest thow hym [Oppression] here?
> ADULACION: Dyffamacion.
> AVARICE: I told the he shoulde be called Reformacion.
> ADULACION: Veraye well.
> AVARICE: What ys he nowe?
> ADULACION: Deformacion. . . .
> AVARICE: Come on, ye shall Learne to solfe [sing]: Reformacion.
>   Sing on now. Re.
> ADULACION: Re.
> AVARICE: Refor.
> ADULACION: Reformacion. (1.4.405–7, 410–11)

Christopher Warley suggests that this moment is whole-heartedly for Mary's benefit: "the joke, playing to the newly Catholic court, is that from the point of view of official Marian England, the Reformation is a 'Dyffamacion' and a 'Deformacion,' and the vices are the embodiments of the hypocrisy of evangelical reformers."[72] The lame puns on "defamation" and "de-formation" do imply that the players have fun at the expense of the word "reformation," but the moment has more valences than just jokey puns for Mary.

Adulation, the one vice who will eventually be redeemed, has trouble learning the word "Reformation." Perhaps he is not as stupid as he seems, for even as it signals the generic re-forming of a nation, this word is probably distasteful to the Queen (the word "reformation" had been used to describe evangelical efforts since at least 1531). Adulation suggests that he is reluctant to sing and remember so repugnant a word as "Reformation," but since he is the flatterer, it is possible that he pretends to not know the word in order to please. Cloaked in so much disguise and delivered by innocent boys who know little of such matters, the moment speaks many things at once.

The age of the boy actors makes it crucial that the moment uses music as a pedagogical tool. Avarice wants Adulation to learn to *sing* the word Reformation, building it syllable by syllable in a literal re-form-a-tion of the word itself, beginning with the solfège syllable "re" (as will be discussed in the next chapter, solfège is the use of "do re mi" syllables to teach singing).

---

72. Christopher Warley, "Reforming the Reformers: Robert Crowley and Nicholas Udall," in Pincombe and Shrank, *The Oxford Handbook of Tudor Literature*, 286.

The pedagogical and musical resonances of this repeat-after-me singing suggest that even the most reluctant student is able to (re)learn religious music, and to (re)learn the proper political stances on religious doctrines when educated musically.[73] So, while the moment on one level mocks the word and concept of "reformation," it also suggests the ways in which songs and religio-political positions are constantly re-formed and re-taught, baffling the young, and perhaps the old, too. But since musical education was so central to humanist and reform programs, the moment can be read more cynically, too. Any young person can be formed and re-formed by the ideology imposed on them, and what they learn from one religion often needs only to be renamed in order to be applicable in another. Given what we know about the way melody travelled across devotional lines, and moved from profane ballads to holy psalms, we can see that music was part of an endless re-branding process not dissimilar to the gallants taking on new identities. But while these disguises and the inherent similarities seem to expose the hypocrisy of maintaining that pure confessional identities are possible (enough so to be tried and punished by death), the play ultimately suggests that embracing one's inner complexity leads to something like toleration of others' contradictory religio-political subjectivities.

Urging Harmony

In the resolution of Udall's political play, the allegorical figures enact a model for an ideal commonwealth based on compromise and mercy, using music to highlight the relationship between social, political, and religious concord. Part of this resolution is the forgiveness and incorporation of Adulation (alias Honesty), the gallant who best emulates the political and social expediency of dissimulating flattery. The four vices are not caught out by the Four Daughters of God until the play's final act, the ten scenes of which also include the restoration of order by Nemesis.

Misericordia, the daughter of God who represents Mercy, fills the act's first scene with a soliloquy on how God's mercy will always exceed man's.[74]

---

73. In Page's words, "Before the Reformation, training in counterpoint, chant, and organ playing was crucial to the Chapel Gentlemen's preparation and their education of the Children. The reconstruction of this musical culture under Mary ensured the education of another generation of young musicians in this tradition." "Uniform and Catholic," 131.

74. For a discussion of the way the play scripts female authority, see Lynn Forest-Hill, "Maidens and Matrons: The Theatricality of Gender in the Tudor Interludes," in *Interludes and Early Modern*

Her contrasting of man's unwillingness to forget the wrongs of others with God's unending mercy gives both an explanation for and criticism of Marian policies that might penalize evangelicals:

> Scarce anie emendes maie mannes eagrenesses appeace,
> Yea and thoughe he forgeve, he wil not soone forgetter:
> Towardes true penitens gods wrathe foorthwith doothe cease,
> And he their past sinnes, behind his backe dooeth sett. (5.1.1173–76)

Living up to their names, the four sisters pledge to mercifully "temper the vigoure" of punishment (Misericordia), but also to reveal the truth (Veritas), redress wrongs (Justicia), and bring flourishing peace when "th'uncurable is clene cutte awaie" (Pax) (5.4.1416, 1417). Careful not to use the word "Reformation" to describe this cleansing and rebuilding, Veritas promises: "The blysfull renovacion ye shall reign in/muste from hensfoorthe nowe immediatelye begynne" (5.4.1429–30). The scene concludes with the four sisters joining in song, "renovating"—or counter-reforming, one could say— the sounds of the four singing vices.[75] While the sound of choirboy actors singing the profane songs of the previous acts was a reminder of the newly-crucial singing abilities of these youngsters, a religious song sung by the four boys playing the sisters would have been significantly more evocative of their roles in the restoration of the Sarum Rite.

Theatrical juxtaposition again reveals the kinship between songs labeled godly or profane. The stage direction does not call for a song from the Latin liturgy, but rather for the unidentified "Mercye of God." This implies that the song sung here could have been in English, and may have even been the Anglicized conclusion of the "Te Deum" found in Edward's 1552 *Book of Common Prayer*. It is thus possible that the suggestion lobbies Mary to keep the musical rites in English, at least some of the time, and urges a compromised approach to religious music.

Avarice puns on the idea of the kinship between sacred and profane music when brought to judgment before Nemesis. All three gallants deny responsibility for Respublica's downfall, and blame everything on Avarice. Avarice, in turn, fabricates a story that passes the buck back to the three of them (5.10.1832). He saves his most withering condemnation for Adulation:

Society: Studies in Gender, Power, and Theatricality, eds. Peter Happé and Wim Hüsken (Amsterdam: Rodopi, 2006), 57.

75. The stage direction reads: "*Cantent, the Mercye of god et cetera, et exeant*" (5.4.1430 s.d.).

Flatterye gotte his thrifte, by counterfaicte honestie
Ye by those tenne bones, I bydde hym use modestie
Therefore spare not hym he will ner come to goode passe
But I maie welbe mended by the marie masse. (5.10.1852–55)

That is, Avarice does not want Adulation to receive mercy, and he might meanwhile convert to that religion he recently robbed, and be saved by "the marie masse." In "marie," there is the three-way pun on the Blessed Virgin Mary, the Queen Mary, and the word "merry," as heard in and descriptive of many of the vice's songs.[76] Such wordplay suggests that Avarice is saying what Nemesis wants to hear, but does not truly understand (or care) about the difference between sacred and profane music. But while Avarice attempts to flatter Nemesis, his defense is rejected. Only one gallant is crafty enough to be granted a reprieve and, fittingly, that is Adulation.

After hearing the vices' defenses, Nemesis and the four sisters turn their thoughts to a philosophical quandary: Misericordia and Justicia wonder how mercy and justice could coexist, and Nemesis responds by urging the sort of temperance that an audience member might have desired from their Queen:

Ladies we have harde all your descrete advises
And eche one shall have some parte of youre devises
Neither all nor none, shall taste of severitee
But as theye are nowe knowen throughe ladie veritee
So shall theye receyve oure mercie or our Ire,
As the wealthe of Respublica shall best require. (5.10.1872–77)

A policy that "neither all nor none should taste of severitee" would give both hope and fear to any wrongdoer, and would have seemed a plausible path for Mary to take in the moderate days of December 1553. That Mercy is only given to the flatterer who was ironically renamed "Honesty" raises the question of whether or not Adulation has really changed his tune. In an earlier scene, Adulation—who had for most of the play been the song leader— indicates that he is in the process of reforming himself when he resists Avarice's suggestion that they sing:

---

76. For example, Adulation says, "Canne Avarice harte bee sett on a merie pynne . . ." (3.3.593); and later, "[Music] prolongeth the life of manne to bee merye" (3.6.894); and sings the song "I wilbe merie while I maie" (5.9.1662).

ADULACION: But what remedie therewhile?
AVARICE: Feith all wilbe nawght.
ADULACION: Tell us what to doo . . .
AVARICE: Nowe sing a song, honestie.
ADULACION: I am past singing now.
AVARICE: Yes, one song honestie.
    Haye, haie, haie, haie,
    I wilbe merie while I mae. (1.8.1656–58, 1559–62)

Adulation's grumpy "I am past singing now" could suggest that, as he matures into the figure who will be forgiven in the end, he sheds the frivolity of his profane ditties; he starts to be "renovated." At the same time, though, he has proven his ability to shape-shift, to play the role. Are learning the right music and learning the right words (he promises Nemesis to "ever change my wicked mynde" [l. 1881]) all that are necessary to serve a new master? That question begs the further quandary: if Adulation now *pretends* to be honest but does indeed serve the commonweal, can he be a good subject even if he is still an unchanged flatterer in his heart? We can address these questions and their implications for the Marian years by looking at the career of Udall himself.

Dissimulation in Tudor England

Because Adulation is the music-lover among the vices and the character that gives up profane song when he begins to acknowledge his errors, the play connects the necessary act of dissimulation to the socializing force of harmony. While music does not actually prolong life (as Adulation suggests early on), or cure all social wrongs, it does offer a figuratively multivocal symbol of literally multivocal cooperation. After Avarice is sent off to be tortured and Oppression and Insolence are jailed to await trial, Pax calls for the song that will end the play:

PAX: Now leat us all togither bothe with harte and voice
    In god and in Quene Marie mooste joyfullie rejoyce.
VERITEE: Praying that hir Reigne mooste graciouslye begonne
    Maie long yeares endure as hithertoo yt hath doone.
MISACORDIA: Praie wee forre hir Counsaile to have long life and healthe.
JUSTICIA: Theire soveraigne to serve.
PAX: And to mainteine Comonwealthe.

OMNES: Amen
   Cantent, et Exeant.
   Finis. (5.10.1932–37)

Presumably, Adulation joins Respublica, Nemesis, People, and the four daughters in this final song, which was likely something like a "Te Deum," that ever-popular Catholic-Latin song of thanksgiving that permeated Mary's rise to the throne a few months before the play's performance. As performative ritual, the song "builds political solidarity in the absence of consensus," in Kertzer's words, and it points to the diversity of voices needed to create beautiful music.[77] Such an appeal toward solidarity within the commonwealth was consistent with the desires of people of all confessional dispositions. In 1556 John Ponet instructed: "Next unto God men ought to love their countrey, and the hole common wealthe before any membre of it."[78] The end of the play thus publicly implores Mary to consider the diverse needs of everyone in the audience; it does so by prematurely celebrating political solidarity in music.

Again, that these singing characters are choirboys—choristers now perhaps even singing from the Chapel's repertoire for this final song—assures Mary that the young are learning the musical rites of her religion, even while the play's plot suggests that harmonious concord from adults is more hard won. By 1555 Mary would burn reformist martyrs at the stake. One of those martyrs was Nicholas Ridley, who had attacked Mary's Catholicism precisely for *not* including the commoners of the commonwealth: in the popish Mass, "the commen people are utterly ignorant, what their preestes doo, or what they goo abowte."[79] At this hopeful moment in Mary's reign, Udall's play uses music to advocate for Misericordia to temper Justicia. That Mary's reign was later unable to find lasting Pax suggests that Veritas is slippery, and that honesty may only ever be a disguise.

It is perhaps unsurprising that a few critics have seen in the character of Adulation a model for Udall himself: Udall the flatterer, Udall the dissimulator, Udall the Nicodemite.[80] In his book on early modern religious dis-

---

77. Kertzer, *Ritual, Politics and Power*, 11.

78. Ponet, *A shorte treatise of politike power*, 31.

79. Nicholas Ridley, *Certen godly, learned, and comfortable conferences, betwene the two Reverende father and holy Martyrs of Christe, d. Nicolas Rydley late Bysshoppe of London and M. Hughe Latymer Someyme Bysshoppe of Worscester during the time of their emprysonmentes* (London, 1556), 6r.

80. For example, Thomas Betteridge, "Staging Reformation Authority: John Bale's *King Johan* and Nicholas Udall's *Respublica*," *Reformation and Renaissance Review* 3 (2000), 55, and Howard B. Norland, *Drama in Early Tudor Britain 1485–1558* (Lincoln: University of Nebraska Press, 1995), 278.

simulation, Perez Zagorin explains that Mary's reign featured widespread dissimulation, as subjects professed the old religion but often secretly practiced and believed parts of reformist doctrine. These accommodators included Marian administrators as prominent as Cardinal Reginald Pole, who had formerly worked for reform and then persecuted reformers when he served Mary.[81] While committed reformers like Bale and Peter Martyr maintained that "true" Christians could never attend Mass, the majority of English folk were content to save their heads and homes by doing so, and many did not see traditional and reformist doctrines as mutually exclusive. While those who attended state-required Masses while secretly practicing reformed religion (and those who did the opposite in Elizabeth's reign) were called Nicodemites, there is a sense to which everyone is bound to be inconsistent in the practice of faith. But when an absolutist like Mary Tudor displays duplicity in her actions, the dissimulation is marked.

Mary herself had indeed been a dissimulator: in the words of the Proclamation she had issued a few months before the play's performance: "her majesty, being presently by the only goodness of God settled in her just possession of the imperial crown of this realm . . . cannot now *hide* that religion which God and the world knoweth she hath ever professed from her infancy hitherto."[82] She not only hid her religious feelings to survive, but she was not ashamed to admit it. In fact, the cultivation of dishonesty was likely a part of her education. Two widely circulated and translated early modern writers explained that dissimulation could be a necessity: Erasmus calls manners a "cloak" in 1530, while Castiglione's 1528 *Book of the Courtier* suggests that "honest dissimulation" is a tool for social survival.[83] By featuring the forgiveness of Adulation, then, *Respublica* asserts the pragmatic necessity of lying and hiding, the near-impossibility of "true honesty," and the socializing need for forgiveness. It seems as though Mary was increasingly able to shift or sublimate her religious convictions in the years before her accession. After resolutely hating Anne Boleyn, she reconciled with her father and the evangelical Jane Seymour, and toward the end of Henry's life she came to find common ground with him on matters of doctrine.[84] That is, Mary understood the slipperiness of identity, hiding or professing her personal faith depending on

---

81. Zagorin, *Ways of Lying,* 108.

82. "Offering freedom of conscience; Prohibiting religious controversy, unlicensed plays, and printing," from 18 August 1553. Reprinted in *Tudor Royal Proclamations,* vol. 2, 5, emphasis mine.

83. Desiderius Erasmus, *De ciuilitate morum puerilium (Manners for Children)* (1532); Baldesar Castiglione, *The Book of the Courtier,* trans. Charles S. Singleton (Garden City, NY: Anchor Books, 1959).

84. See for example Judith M. Richards, *Mary Tudor* (London: Routledge, 2008), 188.

her political position, and befriending and collaborating with people whose religious views she opposed.

Her father's last (and reformist) wife, Catherine Parr, was so influential with the Princess Mary that in 1545 she persuaded her to translate Erasmus's paraphrase of the Gospel of St. John into English.[85] Mary needed a Latin tutor to help her with this project, and hired one Nicholas Udall. She never finished it herself, but when Udall published his own version in 1548, he dedicated it to her in acknowledgment of their early work on it together. Perhaps Udall taught Mary about timeserving; perhaps he learned from her model. In any case, Udall seems to have been optimistic about people's ability to adapt to doctrinal vagrancies.

During Edward's reign, around the time Udall was finishing the Erasmus paraphrase, Edwardian authorities employed him as a public spokesman for the new State religion. When a group of Catholic rebels in Devonshire and Cornwall argued that they did not want to use the reformed Christmas service and preferred to "have our old service of matins, mass, evensong, and procession in Latin, not in English, as it was before," Udall responded. Arguing for the power of acclimation, he wrote them:

> after ye shall have well used it one Christmas, ye shall find such sweetness and ghostly comfort in it, that all days of your life after ye will curse, abhor, detest, and defy all such pernicious ringleaders of mischief as will attempt or entice you to make any more such midsummer games as ye have now at this present time played.[86]

One must wonder if Udall himself found it so easy to get used to religious change, or if he thought these Cornwall residents would be equally willing under Mary to change back again to that which they were to "curse, abhor, detest, and defy" under Edward's law.

Udall's confidence in people's ability to change their minds, his own shape-shifting, and his relationship with Mary led him to urge religious compromise on matters musical and doctrinal in *Respublica* and *Ralph Roister Doister*. Why Mary later eschewed an evenhanded position for her Catholic militancy is open for debate. But in 1553, Udall found a way to use the resources of music and theater to urge compromise in a time of religious uncertainty.

---

85. David Loades, "The Personal Religion of Mary I," in *The Church of Mary Tudor*, eds. Eamon Duffy and David Loades (Aldershot, UK: Ashgate, 2006), 13.
86. Reprinted in Doring, *Performances of Mourning*, 170.

Comedy, music, and allegory are polyvalent theatrical devices that invite multifarious responses even as they expose the internal contradictions that are inherent to everyone. Udall was able to please his audiences enough to serve four consecutive and confessionally oppositional monarchs, and he likely did so by lying or, at least, underplaying many of his ideas.[87] But even if comedy is a cheap fix and musical concord only masks real disagreements, and even if the things people say and do are as scripted and rehearsed as a theatrical performance, it is perhaps through feigning harmony together that people can best serve the commonweal.

When, a mere five years after Mary's accession, her younger and reformist sister took the throne, the religio-political poles were reversed. While the Elizabethan reign is most associated with the professional theater of its later years, the more polemical court, household, and educational drama of the 1560s and 1570s made crucial contributions to musical and religious discourse in a time when such issues were as fraught as they were during the Marian years.

---

87. It is beyond the scope of this chapter to explore the less pleasant aspects of some of Udall's dissimulating. In addition to his expulsion on grounds of buggery, there is reason to think that he was a notorious flogger as a teacher, and perhaps abused his students in other ways, too. The occlusion of his sexual desires and his ability to receive relatively minimal punishment for his wrongdoings is consistent with his religious shape-shifting, if far more morally problematic. See Pittenger, " 'To Serve the Queere,' " 162–89; and Alan Stewart, *Close Readers: Humanism and Sodomy in Early Modern England* (Princeton, NJ: Princeton University Press, 1997), 100–21. Holsinger's argument that corporeal punishment played an important role in musical pedagogy is also provocative in this context. *Music, Body, and Desire in Medieval Culture: Hildegard of Bingen to Chaucer* (Palo Alto, CA: Stanford University Press, 2001), 269–70.

CHAPTER 4

Propaganda and Psalms
Early Elizabethan Drama

> O that mens lippes were so opened, that theyr
> mouthes myght shewe prays of God. Yee wold God
> that . . . pure carters and plow men other thynge to
> whistle upon, save psalmes, hymns, and soch godly
> songes as David is occupied with all.
>
> —Miles Coverdale, *Goostly psalmes and spirituall songes*
>
> Yet with a joyful hart to God a Psalme I meane to sing.
>
> —*Cambises*

Once she was Queen, Elizabeth I and her
council wasted little time in composing an Act of Uniformity, but it had to
pass in Parliament.[1] It did so narrowly—by three votes—establishing the
Church of England by "the merest whisker."[2] While the new prayer book
was more flexible and "Popish" than many reformers had hoped it would
be, the Act did end legal Catholic worship in June 1559: Mass was abolished,
the litany was required to be in English, and the cults of saints and of the
dead as well as images and vestments were outlawed.[3] The next task was to

---

1. The "Congregational rendition of Psalm 29 to the 'Low Dutch' Tune," on the CD accompanying Christopher Marsh, *Music and Society in Early Modern England* (Cambridge: Cambridge University Press, 2011), is the best place to hear an approximation of what metrical psalms, the subject of much of this chapter, sounded like in church; the Dufay Collective renders all the note values equal, and has a parish clerk "line out" the congregation by informing them of the words they are to sing (ibid., 553). I am grateful to Christopher Marsh for alerting me to the recording *Salm, vol. 1: Gaelic Psalms from the Hebrides of Scotland* (Celtic America LLC, 2005), compact disc, which he reckons may also approximate the kind of sound that was heard in early modern parishes.

2. Christopher Haigh, *English Reformations: Religion, Politics, and Society under the Tudors* (Oxford: Clarendon Press, 1993), 241.

3. Eamon Duffy, *The Stripping of the Altars: Traditional Religion in England 1400–1580* (New Haven, CT: Yale University Press, 2005), 573. For more on the complex religious politics of the Elizabethan Settlement, see, for example, Norman Jones, "Religious Settlements," in *A Companion to Tudor Britain*, eds. Robert Tittler and Norman Jones (Oxford: Wiley-Blackwell, 2009), 238–53;

unify the nation in this "new" and contentious religion, itself a revision of Edwardian Protestantism. Two of the tools for promoting this early Elizabethan religious agenda were plays and the congregational singing of metrical psalms in churches.[4] Morality plays written and performed during the first two decades of Elizabeth's reign (and before the rise of the public theaters and subsequent skepticism regarding drama's ability to aid in spiritual matters) take up this proselytizing agenda, and they represent and examine the role music may or may not have in spreading the new faith, often exposing inconsistencies and discrepancies in doctrine and practice. From the optimistic endorsements of psalms in *Cambises* and *Patient and Meek Grissill*, to explorations of music's ability or failure to mediate between principles of Calvinism, conversion, and education in *The Trial of Treasure*; *Like Will to Like, Quoth the Devil*; and *The Longer Thou Livest, the More Fool Thou Art*, to an attempt at social and theological conciliation in *Misogonus*, plays of the 1560s and '70s reveal that, as the early years of Elizabeth's reign wore on, the role of music in religious life was increasingly fraught. Examining the music of these plays reveals how both drama and music became increasingly compromised tools of propaganda.

Psalms and Propaganda in Early Elizabethan England

To understand how drama and music promoted, undermined, and complicated the early Elizabethan religious agenda, it is useful to first lay out some aspects of that agenda that drama and music addressed. Six goals on which I will focus are the new church's aspirations to: form new religious identities among subjects (conversion); create the feeling of social and spiritual harmony among people (unification); demonize Catholic practice as backwards, evil, and anti-social (defamation); establish doctrinal continuity with Edward's reign in an effort to undermine and forget the "damage" done under Mary; spread various theological ideas learned on the continent by ministers newly returned from exile, including Calvinist concepts; and educate children in

and Peter Marshall, "Confessionalization, Confessionalism, and Confusion in the English Reformation," in *Reforming Reformation*, ed. Thomas F. Mayer (Surrey, UK: Ashgate, 2012), 43–64.

4. On the rise of metrical psalms in relation to the early Elizabethan church, see, for example, Beth Quitslund, *The Reformation in Rhyme: Sternhold, Hopkins and the English Metrical Psalter, 1547–1603* (Aldershot, UK: Ashgate, 2008); Robin A. Leaver, *Goostly Psalmes and Spirituall Songes: English and Dutch Metrical Psalms from Coverdale to Utenhove, 1535–66* (Oxford: Oxford University Press, 1987); Jonathan Willis, *Church Music and Protestantism in Post-Reformation England: Discourses, Sites and Identities* (Aldershot, UK: Ashgate, 2010); and Christopher Marsh, *Music and Society*, 391–448.

the new faith.[5] Music was central to all of these goals. It could form or strengthen a sense of religious identity through repeated singing both in public and in private devotion, aid in the memorization of doctrinal propaganda, and educate people in the new faith; it was also crucial to creating the feeling of harmony through unified singing, establishing itself as an alternative to Catholic ecclesiastical music and as continuous with music composed during Edward's reign. It was additionally hoped that psalm singing would keep people's voices and ears engaged in holy rather than wanton music. As we will see, early Elizabethan plays often attempt to uphold these goals and music's role in their promotion, but they also—intentionally or not—expose the contradictions between these aims and music's usefulness in spreading the new religion.

Elizabeth's Royal Injunctions of 1559, and in particular their 49th article, clarified the use of music in churches, ordering that "no alteration be made of such assignments of lyvynge, as heretofore hath ben appointed to the use of syngyng or musicke in the Churche." It ordered that songs be "modeste and destyncte," and "playnelye understanded, as if it were read without singing." While catering to the desire for understandable, plain music, the article also expressed the more moderate sentiment that such music could bring comfort and "delyte," and gives the vague directive that "the best sorte of melodye and musicke that maye be convenientlye devised" should be used.[6] Because "best" could be so widely interpreted, the injunctions left the door open for a variety of church music, from polyphonic choruses sung by trained choirs in the Chapel Royal with organ accompaniment to the unaccompanied singing of metrical psalms by entire congregations, which became the most popular form of music in most parishes.[7]

A number of theologians affected England's debates over music's proper role in church. Influenced by Heinrich Bullinger, the extreme no-music view peaked in England under Edward VI, with the publication of vitriol by John Bale and others. Responding to continental views learned in exile, many early Elizabethan ministers came to something of a compromise by endorsing the unison congregational singing of metrical psalms, which was the preferred form of music for Jean Calvin, who wrote in his preface to the 1542

---

5. Jonathan Willis lays out the first three of these goals in "Protestant Worship and the Discourse of Music in Reformation England," in *Worship and the Parish Church in Early Modern Britain*, eds. Natalie Mears and Alec Ryrie (Surrey, UK: Ashgate, 2013), 201.

6. Church of England, *Injunctions geven by the Quenes Majestie* (1559), C4r–C4v.

7. Willis explains that these injunctions "meant that the same religious message could be packaged in a number of different ways, and so be made palatable to individuals of divergent religious inclinations." *Church Music and Protestantism*, 62.

Genevan Psalter that singing had the "force and vigor to move and inflame the hearts of men to invoke and praise God with more vehement and ardent zeal."[8]

Miles Coverdale had compiled his *Goostly psalmes and spirituall songes* in 1535 in hopes that psalm singing would supplant profane balladry, and be as popular in England as it was among Lutherans on the continent, but it never fully caught on in Henry's increasingly traditional Church of England. Thomas Sternhold published a version of singable psalms in 1549 that was never incorporated into the Edwardian church. These psalms became popular among reformers in exile under Mary, and were republished as Thomas Sternhold and John Hopkins's *Psalmes of David in Englishe metre* in 1560, and then as the immensely popular *Whole Booke of Psalmes* starting in 1562, establishing a sense of continuity with Edward's reign. Their popularity is evident by the fact that 220,000 copies of the *Whole Booke* had been produced by the end of Elizabeth's reign, one for every eighteen inhabitants of England and Wales.[9] They were sung in both private and public contexts: people intoned them at home for private devotion and sang them in unison with their church congregations.[10] Humanist scholars defended the edifying and moralizing power of teaching everyone to sing, and although the music of these books was initially disparaged for slowness and monotony, it is clear from their fairly quick popularity that most people grew to enjoy the tunes. In addition to a few new compositions, the books drew on melodies borrowed from: the Latin liturgy; the German Lutheran, French Huguenot, and Swiss Calvinist versions of the psalms; and a range of profane dance and ballad tunes.

Plays written by self-identified Protestant preachers and educators comment on music's ability to convert, unify, and educate a population. The Anglican "Compromise" did not please everyone, and while psalms were popular, they were not universally embraced. In the early years of Elizabeth's long reign, further alterations to state religion seemed possible, as some reformers resisted conforming to the 1559 settlement on the grounds that it was too popish, and some crypto-Catholics plotted to dethrone the Queen

---

8. Jean Calvin, "1542 Preface to the Genevan Psalter," quoted in Charles Garside Jr., "Calvin's Preface to the Psalter: A Reappraisal," *The Musical Quarterly* 37 (1951): 568. In Willis's words, "while Mary restored traditional musical forms in the short term, it was the experience of exile, together with the influence of Calvin and Bucer, that in the long run helped save English church music from Bullingerian austerity." *Church Music and Protestantism*, 55.

9. Quitslund, *Reformation in Rhyme*, 242.

10. See, for example, Nicholas Temperley, " 'If any of you be mery let hym synge psalmes': the Culture of Psalms in Church and Home," in *"Noyses, sounds, and sweet aires": Music in Early Modern England*, ed. Jessie Ann Owens (Washington, DC: The Folger Shakespeare Library, 2006), 90–100.

and destroy any agents of the new Protestantism.[11] During this unsettled time, both plays and metrical psalms were praised by some for their instructional potential while others worried that music and drama could be sources of corruption rather than moral guides against it. The plays discussed below dramatize many of the contentious issues regarding the role of music in the new church. In doing so, they explore the nuances of the church's evangelical agenda, considering the effectiveness of music in personal devotion, the close relationship between metrical psalms and profane ballads, and tensions between Calvinist doctrine, conversion, and humanist education.

Singing Subjects in *Cambises* and *Patient and Meek Grissill*

In the first few years of Elizabeth's reign, two plays were performed before her court that promoted music as an effective way to solidify and express religious identity, and even to petition God for comfort and aid in times of oppression. *Cambises* and *Patient and Meek Grissill*—which toured to other venues in addition to playing at court—train audiences to be wary of worldly music that may be used to mask political and moral corruption, a skill that would seem particularly relevant in the years just following Mary's reign. In order to combat the evils of repressive and manipulative leaders and husbands, the plays' female characters sing psalms or psalm-like songs.[12] While *Grissill* exposes the fact that profane melodies are often used for religious purposes, both plays present the non-ecclesiastic, private singing of religious music promoted by the Elizabethan church as an effective way to petition God in musical prayer.

---

11. Haigh, *English Reformations*, 252; Peter Holmes, *Resistance and Compromise: The Political Thought of Elizabethan Catholics* (Cambridge: Cambridge University Press, 1982), 12. Such plots came to a head with the Northern Revolt of 1569, when Catholics in Northern towns tore up Protestant prayer books in about seventy churches and restored the Mass for a while in several of them. While fifty priests and 220 laymen were called before church courts about the uprising, the ultimate failure of the rebellion was reflective both of the Queen's power and the fact that most crypto-Catholics were politically loyal to her despite religious differences (not unlike the many reformers who had been politically loyal to Mary).

12. It is beyond the scope of this chapter to discuss the gender implications of these female characters' psalm singing in depth, but much has been written on the importance of the psalter to premodern and early modern women. See, for example, Linda Phyllis Austern, " 'For Musicke is the Handmaid of the Lord': Women, Psalms, and Domestic Music-Making in Early Modern England," in *Psalms in the Early Modern World*, eds. Linda Phyllis Austern, Kari Boyd McBride, and David L. Orvis (Aldershot, UK: Ashgate, 2011): 77–114.

Both *Cambises* and *Grissill* were written by playwrights who supported the Elizabethan government's desire to unify England as a Protestant nation. Thomas Preston's *A Lamentable Tragedy Mixed ful of pleasant mirth, conteyning the life of Cambises, King of Persia* was likely acted at court between 1559 and 61.[13] Preston was an evangelical Protestant, a Cambridge academic who wrote anti-Catholic ballads. The play may have been performed by Leicester's Men, known anti-Catholic players patronized by Elizabeth's then-favorite minister Robert Dudley. Around the same time that *Cambises* played at court, a group of choirboys from St. Paul's likely presented *The Comedy of Patient and Meek Grissill* before Elizabeth; it was written by John Phillip, an organ master at Paul's.[14] Early scenes in both plays use music to set up the moral and political trials facing the virtuous women central to the play's conflicts. Both plays juxtapose worldly and spiritual music in attempts to contrast vain, indulgent music—profane ballads, courtship songs and dances, the trumpet blasts and drumbeats of war—with the simplicity and sincerity of unaccompanied psalmody. In *Grissill*, Phillip experiments with the frequent practice of contrafactum (putting news words to an old tune, in particular, setting religious songs to profane tunes) to suggest that it is intention—not melody—that gives music the power to corrupt and deceive or to petition God and heal the soul. In *Cambises*, the King's abuses of political and domestic power are rendered musically, and the sounds of corruption are only overthrown by the spiritual effectiveness of his maligned Queen's psalm singing.

Grissill relates the familiar Griselda story of a lowborn woman's wifely obedience to an aristocratic, tyrannical husband and her Job-like patience throughout his abuse and neglect. In the play, the use of profane melodies taken from popular ballads underwrite the spiritual power of the psalm-like

---

13. *Cambises* has received much derision for this title, including by Shakespeare in *1 Henry IV*, but it is an apt descriptor. E. K. Chambers suggests it was performed for the Elizabethan court during the 1560–61 Christmas season, *The Elizabethan Stage* (Oxford: Clarendon Press, 1923): vol 4, 79. For evidence supporting its courtly performance in 1559–61, see Eugene D. Hill, "The First Elizabethan Tragedy: A Contextual Reading of 'Cambises,'" *Studies in Philology* 89.4 (1992): 404–33; and Robert Carl Johnson, "Introduction," in *A Critical Edition of Thomas Preston's* Cambises, ed. Robert Carl Johnson. *Elizabethan & Renaissance Studies* 23 (Salzburg: Institut für Englische Sprache und Literatur, 1975), 29.

14. Evidence for these probable performances can be found in Henry Machyn's diary records, when he says that on 5 August 1559 it was played before Elizabeth at Nonsuch by the children of St. Paul's and "master Phelypes and master Haywod." Critics agree that even if it was not performed on this exact occasion, it was likely performed by the boys on another occasion at court. Faith Gildenhuys, "Introduction," in *A Gathering of Griseldas: Three Sixteenth-Century Texts*, ed. Faith Gildenhuys (Ottawa: Dovehouse Editions, 1996), 46; David Bevington, *From Mankind to Marlowe: Growth of Structure in the Popular Drama of Tudor England* (Cambridge, MA: Harvard University Press, 1962), 62.

songs that pervade the play, showing the more Godly uses to which memorable harmonies and other musical charms may be put. The particular choices of melody Phillip pairs with his lyrics reveals the effectiveness of the standard practice of setting metrical psalms to myriad extant melodies, some of which were profane.[15] Listening to these performances, Elizabeth and her advisors would hear a demonstration of the way melodies carry devotional lyrics into deeper affective registers, which were crucial to music's usefulness as propaganda. Those involved with early Elizabethan campaigns to enforce the new Protestantism needed to assure skeptics that their congregational psalm singing would be as emotionally and spiritually powerful as the traditional music to which many held strong attachments. They realized music was essential to the affective power of the new faith, and thus to the success of converting the masses. Effective propaganda tends to work on the emotions, an idea iterated in Calvin's statement (which is echoed, too, in Theodore de Beze's preface to his French metrical psalms) that "singing has the power to enflame the hearts of men."[16] The St. Paul's organ master dramatizes this point about the new church music's affective force and suggests that borrowing melodies that people know and love only makes church music more learnable and emotionally powerful for parishioners.

Phillip clearly cared enough about melody to want his musical choices documented in the printed text; other early modern playwrights tended to leave such decisions to the actors. His use of these tunes indicates perhaps that his choirboys knew them already and were demonstrating their applicability to more spiritual lyrics. Christopher Marsh has shown how remnants of Marian church choirs may have played a part in the dissemination of psalm tunes, because statutes and financial records leave traces of parish clerks, "singinge boyes," and choir school children leading congregational songs.[17] So it is likely that a few years after Mary's death, when the kinds of choirboys who performed in plays like *Respublica* were still boys, the rigorous Catholic

---

15. See, for example, Linda Austern, Kari Boyd McBride, and David L. Orvis, "Introduction," in Austern, McBride, and Orvis, *Psalms in the Early Modern World*, 18; and Nicholas Temperley, *The Music of the English Parish Church* (Cambridge: Cambridge University Press, 1979), 66. Christopher Marsh has recently called that claim into question, citing, for example, remarks by a Kentish vicar and by Mistress Ford in *Merry Wives of Windsor* disparaging the singing of psalms to Greensleeves. But it seems to me that the fact that the practice was derided in the 1590s makes it *more* likely that it was practiced, and maybe with more fervor, in the 1560s and 1570s, when Protestant officials were desperate for this new music to take hold with the populace. *Music and Society*, 420.

16. Calvin, "1542 Preface to the Genevan Psalter," 568. De Beze, *Les pseaumes mis en rhyme francoise* (Lyons, 1563), A4r. Quoted in Andrew Pettegree, *Reformation and the Culture of Persuasion* (Cambridge: Cambridge University Press, 2005), 42.

17. Marsh, *Music and Society*, 425.

music training they had received was leveraged to help teach and spread the new melodies of Protestantism.

Grissill is first introduced to the audience by singing "The Song of Patient Grissill" at the start of act 2; music is used to demonstrate her piety:

> God by his providence divine,
> Hath formed me of climy clay.
> Then why should I in aught repine,
> Or seek his will to disobey?
> Be it far from me to do such ill
> As to contend against his will.
> Sing danderly distaff, and danderly,
> Ye virgins all come learn of me. (ll. 214–21)

No melody is given for this song, but a few things are worth noting. All six verses of the song are in long meter (when every line is tetrameter) and are eight lines long. While common meter (that is, alternating tetrameter and trimeter) would come to dominate metrical psalmody by the end of the sixteenth century, long meter was frequently used for psalms, including in the 1573 version of the Sternhold and Hopkins *Whole Booke of Psalms*.[18] Sternhold and Hopkins's eight-line melodies dominated metrical psalms until the closing decades of the sixteenth century, when they were replaced with four-line tunes.[19] Around 1559, when *Grissill* was performed, eight-line stanzas in long meter sounded like many of the newly popular metrical psalms. Grissill's song could have been set to something that was already a psalm tune, or to one of the many ballad tunes and dances that were recycled into psalm tunes. This song, unlike the music of earlier Tudor dramas, is not a bawdy ditty sung by a fool or vice, nor is it a representation of liturgical music. This is a moral expression of faith and devotion in English, sung by a poor woman at work. It is the dramatic realization of Coverdale's 1535 desire that his metrical psalms would supplant profane ditties so women "spynnynge at the wheles, had none other songes to passe theyr tyme withall . . . they shulde be better occupied, then with hey nony nony, hey troly poly, & soch lyke fantasies."[20]

---

18. Ibid., 408. An example of an early modern long meter psalm tune that is still used today is the Doxology ("Praise God from whom all blessings flow").

19. Ibid., 412.

20. Miles Coverdale, *Goostly psalmes and spirituall songes drawen out of the holy Scripture, for the comforte and consolaycon of soch as love to rejoyce in God and his Worde* (London, 1535), 2v.

But while music may aid in devotion, Phillip also demonstrates that it can lead its listeners astray when sung with ill intent and to profane lyrics. When Grissill meets the classist, demeaning Marquis Gauthier, music is used to stage a powerful man's manipulation of a relatively helpless woman. Unlike most Tudor plays, *Grissill* provides both lengthy lyrics for the songs and, in most cases, the melody to which the lyrics are to be sung. In scene 7, Grissill has just been betrothed to Gauthier, and he calls for all to "sound up [their] instruments" so that, "in token of victory," he can sing a song with his lady (ll. 820, 821).[21] Taken out of context, the song's lyrics seem loving, but audience members familiar with this well-known story know that she will soon suffer emotional abuse. Further, the text indicates that the song is sung "to the tune of Malkin." The Malkin tune—Malkin is a version of the name "Matilda"—was musical shorthand for a lower class woman.[22] Grissill and Gauthier are thus singing love lyrics to a melody that points out Grissill's lower class, the very thing Gauthier will exploit later in the play. The melody makes meaning in the dramatic context, giving an acoustic clue to Grissill's upcoming misfortunes and reminding audiences to be suspicious of any kind words from the Marquis, who is using music to conceal his contempt. The combination of the Marquis's malevolence and the profanity of love lyrics demonstrate music's ability to deceive and seduce when misused. But, while the Malkin melody here underscores the dangers of profane music, such tunes are paired with devotional and petitionary lyrics elsewhere to suggest the importance of words and intent over the aesthetic trappings of melody.

When Grissill learns of her mother's death in scene 4, she enters singing "to the tune of Damon & Pythias," a song that begins:

Can my poor heart be still,
Can I possess sweet peace,
When Jove hath given Parchas the charge
My blissful joys to cease? (ll. 489–92)

"Damon and Pythias" was a popular ballad about male friendship.[23] Its tune is found in one of the few extant Elizabethan broadside ballads containing music, a broadside from 1568, and it is also used in Richard Edward's 1564–65 play

---

21. All quotations from "The Comedy of Patient and Meek Grissill," in Gildenhuys, *Gathering of Griseldas*, 75–152. The text is not on EEBO, and no early spelling edition is easily accessible.

22. Gildenhuys, *Gathering of Griseldas*, 204, n. 61. Charles Walter Roberts, "An Edition of John Phillip's *Commodye of Pacient and Meek Grissill*" (PhD diss., University of Illinois, 1938), 396.

23. Gildenhuys, *Gathering of Griseldas*, 203, n. 53; Peter Happé, *Song in Morality Plays and Interludes* (Exeter, UK: Short Run Press, 1991), 17.

about the classical friends, *Damon and Pithias*.[24] Ballads in the sixteenth century were written in all kinds of meter, and Phillip chose one in short meter (tetrameter, tetrameter, trimeter, tetrameter) which, along with long and common meters, was used in psalm tunes. The song is not an actual psalm, but it ends with eschatological hopes: the grieving Grissill imagines her mother "in endless bliss, where Christ our Lamb/Doth her revive again" (ll. 514–15). Functionally, then, the song brings spiritual comfort, like "an hymn or suchlike song" in the words of the 1559 royal injunctions permitting such music.

At the emotional low point of the play, when Gauthier sends Grissill back to her father, Grissill takes comfort in devotional music that sounds very much like a psalm. The stage direction indicates that this return to her lower class origins is represented by acoustically and visually echoing her opening scene: the character Diligence is to "let Grissill sing some song, and sit spinning" (l. 1811 s.d.). The melody indicated in this case is "A Song for Grissill." The song sung here was likely the sixteenth-century ballad "The Ballet intituled the sonnge of pacyente Gressell unto hyr mate," which would be perfectly suited, it would seem.[25] Or, perhaps because of its association with the play, this melody became the "Grissill" tune for a few decades; melodies were often renamed under similar circumstances.

The song is written in that most popular meter for psalm tunes, common meter. It functions as a spiritual salve for Grissill's woes:

How greatly am I bound to praise
My God, that sits in throne,
Which hath assuaged by Providence,
My anguish and my moan. (ll. 1812–15)

Thus, Phillip and his choirboys recontextualize ballad and dance tunes in a dramatic play that represents spiritual crises for its female protagonist. Grissill is comforted through songs that remind her of devotion and faith, songs that function in the way psalm compilers hoped their tunes would. The performing choirboys—who, as discussed in the previous chapter, occupy the overlapping domains of the church, dramatic playing company, and court—sing

24. Claude Simpson, *The British Broadside Ballad and Its Music* (New Brunswick, NJ: Rutgers University Press, 1966), 157–59.

25. Gildenhuys, *Gathering of Griseldas*, 206. This sixteenth-century ballad should not be confused with the later "A most excellent and vertuous Ballad of the patient Grissill," which wasn't printed until the seventeenth century. Several versions of it can be found on EBBA, http://ebba.english.ucsb .edu/search_combined/?ss=grisel.

new devotional lyrics to old tunes. Mimicking contrafactum, the newly ubiquitous practice of resetting psalms to a variety of melodies, the music of *Grissill* shows that the effectiveness of psalms for the formation of reformed religious subjects—in both private and public singing—comes from how easily they are learned and remembered. The ease with which they are remembered is a result of their borrowing of melodies from popular culture, a principle that Luther had articulated decades earlier. In fact, Luther and his successors were happy to acknowledge this as deliberate strategy. In the words of the 1575 preface to *Bohemian Brethren*: "our singers took up [secular melodies] intentionally, in order that the people be attracted to a grasp of truth more easily through familiar sounds."[26]

In England, Miles Coverdale's hope in 1535 had been that "mens lippes [would be] so opened, that theyr mouthes myght shewe prays of God. Yee wold God that . . . pure carters and plow men other thynge to whistle upon, save psalmes, hymns, and soch godly songes as David is occupied with all."[27] And it was perhaps the use of familiar melody that helped these hopes finally become at least partially realized in the early years of Elizabeth's reign: John Jewel wrote in 1560, "You may now sometimes see at Paul's Cross after the service, six thousand persons, old and young, of both sexes, all singing together and praising God."[28] *Grissill* discloses the kinship of psalms with popular song, assuring the Queen that psalm singing is a convincing and valuable tool for spreading the new doctrine and uniting people in the feeling of social harmony.

Cambises also demonstrates the effectiveness of psalm singing, demonstrating its usefulness for another woman in distress at the end of a play full of abuses of musical (and otherwise) power. *Cambises* is a violent play showing the tyranny often bred by royal succession, as well as the nightmares resulting from an heirless monarch. After initially heeding good counsel, King Cambises is quickly corrupted by bad advice and his own evil. He starts a war, kills a boy for sport, and has his brother and then his new wife murdered before himself dying from a hunting accident. The king's violent behaviors are accompanied by music, suggesting the dangerous potential of worldly music. These moments all employ instruments, which many Protestant evangelicals saw as extraneous and vain compared to the human voice.

---

26. Quoted in Rebecca Wagner Oettinger, *Music as Propaganda in the German Reformation* (Aldershot, UK: Ashgate, 2001), 5.

27. Coverdale, *Goostly psalmes and spirituall songes*, 2r–v.

28. John Jewel, "Letter to Peter Martyr, 5 March 1560," in *Zurich Letters*, ed. Hastings Robinson (Cambridge, 1842), 71.

In the play's first two scenes, music is used to both call for war and cynically expose war's social malfeasance. The opening scene is the only moment in which King Cambises is reasonable: he listens to a character named "Counsel" on the matter of whom to appoint as judge, and prepares to go to war with Egypt (as Persian kings were wont to do). At the end of the scene, the eager King calls for acoustic representation of his martial plan: "Strike up your drummes us to rejoyce, to hear the warlike sound" (1.111). In early modern texts, plays, and ballads, drums signified courage.[29] The actions of the King and his soldiers, however, are shown to be anything but courageous, suggesting a discrepancy between what instruments purport to connote and a reality they might silence.

When the play introduces the King's ill-advising vice and his minions in the next scene, the vices enter singing, setting up inter-theatrical resonances with characters from *Wisdom*'s Lucifer to *Respublica*'s gallants (2.159 s.d.). No song is indicated, but the first line following the song makes a crucial point about war. Huf says:

Gogs flesh and his wounds these warres rejoyce my hart:
By his wounds I hope to doo wel for my parte.
By Gogs hart the world shall go evil if I doo not shift:
At some olde Carles [countryman's] bouget [wallet] I mean for to lift.
    (2.160–63)

Huf's confessions predict both Shakespeare's pickpocketing Autolycus and Brecht's war-profiteering Mother Courage, and establish that a seemingly sound royal action, starting a war, has consequences for non-royal people who may be robbed blind, if not killed, by crafty opportunists like Huf. The double-edged quality of this war—its ambidexterity—is rendered musically. Those noble-sounding drums from the opening scene are replaced with the pointless singing of war profiteers, who then get into fistfights and sword brawls with Ambidexter, aurally mocking the idea of noble, purposeful violence. The drums are thus an empty signifier, stirring up feelings of courage and pride to conceal the moral bankruptcy of the King and his war.

The contemporary connotations of instruments are again dramatically leveraged when the play introduces trumpets. The King's bad deeds are called out by the character Shame, who speaks of the King's shamelessness in words and also enters with a "trump [trumpet] black" (4.340 s.d.). Trumpets sound

---

29. Marsh, *Music and Society*, 55, 159.

of power: town waits (musician-guards employed by cities) heralded monar-
chical proclamations with trumpets, and military trumpeters were crucial in
battle. Bruce Smith writes of how brass instruments created an "aura" of
sound, defining a "power scene" by the process of metonymy.[30] Evoking
the sounds of power for a corrupt monarch reveals the sense to which these
loud instruments were used to augment the influence of such rulers. But
while it sounds of earthly power—and abuses of that power—the trumpet
also sounds of the Last Judgment.[31] Shame exploits the trumpet's many valences to show how an instrument used to hail the royalty may also be used
to judge their misdeeds: "As *Fame* dooth sound the royall trump of worthy
men and trim:/So *Shame* dooth blowe with strained blast, the trump of shame
on him" (4.351–52). Power and judgment are both sounded by the same instrument, so that which indexes earthly power is used to demonstrate that
venal kings will also face eschatological reckoning. Dermot Cavanagh writes
of the way that the violence in *Cambises* exceeds its conceivable mission to
lead by negative exemplum, for at first the goal seems to be "to deepen grati-
tude for the benefit deriving from Elizabeth's accession and to stress the
importance of continuing its continuity."[32] But, because Cambises inherited
his throne through succession as surely as did the Tudor monarchs, the play
shows that "succession can result in a monarch who derogates from all great
responsibilities," and that succession under sovereignty "does indeed appear
to be a tragedy waiting to happen."[33]

If *Cambises* at once praises the English Queen for not being like the Persian King and warns audiences of the tyranny absolute monarchy can breed,
we can see that music is a crucial theatrical resource for projecting these dual
valences: the sounds of power can mask evil intent on earth even while they
remind audiences that tyrants will also face eternal judgment. Shakespeare
uses music similarly in *Henry V*, when the King calls for "Non Nobis" and
"Te Deum" to bury the French dead. While those liturgical songs presumably express humility and thanksgiving, the English soldiers are in fact using
harmony and righteous sentiment to blanket the slaughter they have just
committed. But while Shakespeare has a more cynical use of the popular

30. Bruce Smith, *The Acoustic World of Early Modern England: Attending to the O-Factor* (Chicago:
University of Chicago Press, 1999), 243.

31. Ibid., 130, 159. *Wisdom* also makes use of this double valence, when Mynde says, "Ande
here mentrellys be convenient,/For trumpys shulde blow to the judgement!/Off batell also yt ys on
instrument,/Gevynge comfort to fight" (ll. 700–4).

32. Dermot Cavanagh, "Political Tragedy in the 1560s: *Cambises* and *Gorboduc*," in *The Oxford
Handbook of Tudor Literature*, eds. Mike Pincombe and Cathy Shrank (Oxford: Oxford University
Press, 2009), 490.

33. Ibid., 491, 499.

"Non Nobis" psalm in his 1599 play, Preston presents psalms more optimistically at the end of his play.

Cambises depicts the way that music can aid in political tyranny, and like *Grissill* it also discloses music's ability to aid in more domestic and sexual affairs. Cambises uses song and dance to muffle the violence of his kidnapping and then forced marriage of the Lady who becomes his Queen. The play's ninth scene demonstrates how easily the sounds of courtship can turn into the sounds of coercion. At the start, a Lord suggests to a Lady that they take a romantic walk among flowers and fields where:

> The chirping birds whose plesant tunes, therin shall hear record
> That our great joy we shall it finde, in feeld to walke a brode.
> On Lute and Cittern there to play a heavenly hermony:
> Our eares shall heare, hart to content, our sports to beautify.
>   (9.865–68)

The Lady agrees to this plan, and the stage direction indicates that they "heer trace up and down playing" on their instruments (9.870 s.d.). Music is thus used to indicate the beauty of nature, heaven, and love; the "heavenly harmony" the Lord and Lady make with their lute and cittern symbolizes their love and oneness with nature. This pastoral bliss is interrupted by the entrance of the King, who immediately spots the Lady and decides he must have her. The Lady kindly declines, but the King prevails and takes her against her will. His exit line evokes the sounds of the scene's opening, but with a sinister twist: "Come on my Lords with gladsome harts, let us rejoice with glee:/ Your Musick showe to joy this deed, at the request of me" (9.935–36). The scene divulges the way the music of courtship can signify love but not realize it, for the King's music has instead manipulated perceptions and obscured a forceful abduction with sounds of mirth.

The marriage and banquet of the King and his new Queen in scene 10 furthers the notion that music can obscure immoral and unjust social situations, and musically ties the King's mistreatment of the Lady to the play's politics. Ambidexter tells the audience that the wedding festivities will include jousting and masking and "such dauncing, such singing, with musicall hermony" (10.944). When the King and Queen themselves enter, the King calls for music and Ambidexter tells him what he will get:

> KING: Me think mine eares dooth wish the sound, of musicks hermony: Heer for to play before my grace, in place I would them spy.
> *Play at banquet.*

AMBIDEXTER: They be at hand Sir with stick and fidle:
They can play a new daunce called hey didle didle. (10.1014–17)

None of this is unusual—weddings usually involve dancing. Fiddle music and dancing signify mirth, but the audience knows that they are empty signs in this instance—there is no real joy for the Queen. The dance's function as amusement—the fact that it is being performed on stage in an entertaining production number—is at odds with its narrative function, acoustically creating dramatic irony. Moments later, the King rashly decides to have the new Queen murdered to punish a perceived slight.[34] The fiddle songs and dancing of the wedding have not corrupted anyone—the King was already evil—but this courtly music did nothing to build social harmony or concord, as some, like Thomas Elyot in *The Boke of the Governor*, propose it might.[35] Music has given the outward sign of comity and political integrity, but in reality the concord is as ephemeral as the sound of dance music at a wedding.

The final scenes of *Cambises* are also a form of dramatic propaganda, in this case advocating for the psalms as a particularly effective way to petition God even in the darkest times. At the King's behest, the Queen's executioners Murder and Crueltie arrive to kill her, but before they can do so, the Queen has a request, the granting of which concludes the play's penultimate scene:

QUEENE: Yet before I dye some Psalme to God let me sing.
BOTHE [MURDERERS]: We be content to permit you that thing.
QUEENE: Farwel you Ladyes of the Court, with all your masking hew:
    I doo forsake thee brodered gardes, and all the facions new.
    The Court and all the courtly train, wherein I had delight:
    I banished am from happy sporte and all by spightful spight.
    Yet with a joyful hart to God a Psalme I meane to sing:
    Forgiving all men and the king, of eche kinde of thing.
    Sing and exeunt. (10.1119–26)

In one of the few explicit references to psalm singing in extent drama from this period, the play's most sympathetic character eschews secular mirth and other company for the solo singing of a psalm of forgiveness. In the very early

---

34. Immediately after the dance, the King tells his new Queen the story of young lions at court, and how a stronger lion cub helped his weaker brother rather than killing him. The Queen bursts into tears, pointing out that these lions have behaved more nobly than the fratricidal King. Hearing her analogy as betrayal, the King immediately curses her and sends Ambidexter to fetch murderers to kill her.

35. For Thomas Elyot, musical education promoted "the better attaynynge the knowledge of a publike weale: whiche . . . is made of an ordre of astates and degrees, and, by reason thereof, conteineth in it a perfect harmony." *The Boke named the Governer* (London, 1537), 23r.

years of Queen Elizabeth's reign, then, Preston's play demonstrates that the prayerful singing of a psalm could petition God more effectively than a sacrament performed in a church. For rather than needing a priest to grant her satisfaction and last rites—as a Catholic character would have needed in this moment—this Queen's personal faith, as expressed through psalm singing, brings joy and forgiveness in her final hour. She therefore sounds like one of Foxe's martyrs, singing psalms at the stake as many had done between 1534 and 1559.[36] These "Tower psalmists," along with the Marian exiles who had sung metrical psalms on the continent and brought them back to England under Elizabeth, are the historical contexts of the church music newly in vogue, authorized by the new Queen.

Additionally, the psalm is the most musically simple of the play's songs. Its single melodic line is sung by a solo singer, with no instrumental accompaniment. Since Elizabeth's Chapel Royal hosted far more elaborate choral services than anywhere else, and those services were often sung by choirboys, the play is obliquely making a point that the court's other musical indulgences are at best extraneous and at worst vain displays of worldly power, especially compared to the sincere psalmody that was beginning to be sung all over England in parishes.[37] The following and final scene demonstrates that the psalm did more than comfort the Queen.

Following the Queen's implied murder, the King enters, bleeding from his side because of a hunting accident. Even he recognizes this mortal wound as "A just reward for my misdeeds" (11.1166), and so the immediate effect of the Queen's psalm, it seems, is retribution against her enemy. The play markets psalms as righteous devotion that can petition God to effect divine retribution, a feature that Protestants who were exiled or persecuted under Mary (including the Queen herself) might find particularly attractive. A converted Ambidexter even refers to Mary's chief minister (or tormentor, as many would have it):

What a King was he that hath used such tiranny?
He was a king to Bishop *Bonner*, I think verely,

---

36. Hill, "The First Elizabethan Tragedy," 41.

37. While people in the parishes tended to sing unaccompanied songs, polyphonic choruses were sung by trained choirs in the Chapel Royal with organ accompaniment. John Milsom speculates that the Chapel Royal's elaborate music and choirboy performances were maintained for political reasons, making the chapel a "status symbol, projecting an image that would impress even visiting Catholic dignitaries." Indeed, visitors from abroad did often remark on the Roman-ness of the Queen's services, but her employment of composers like Thomas Tallis could have been aesthetically and devotionally motivated as well as politically savvy. Milsom, "Music, Politics and Society," in Tittler and Jones, *A Companion to Tudor Britain*, 498.

For bothe their delights was to shed blood:

But never intended to doo any good (11.1141–44).

Psalms are an effective salve to the hurt caused by tyrants, be they Cambises or Mary; they have power in times of conflict. Preston reminds Elizabeth, and in other performance contexts, regular folk, that metrical psalms are not earthly indulgences like battle drums, trumpet blasts, courtship melodies, or dancing, all of which can conceal corruption and evil. Strengthened by the "lamentable tragedy" of Mary's reign, psalms were a "pleasant mirth" with real spiritual power.

Cambises was a hugely popular play that arguably helped condition later audiences for Elizabethan tragedy. Its representation of the power of psalms may have helped further the acceptance of this crucial musical form. The singing of psalms by women in both *Cambises* and *Grissill* calls to mind a longer tradition of portraying female musical piety on stage: Penny Granger has drawn attention to the Virgin Mary's psalm singing in the East Anglian N-Town plays, the performances of which were contemporary with not only *Wisdom* and the Digby *Mary Magdalene*, but also these Elizabethan plays, as they were performed until the 1570s.[38] Singing psalms in Latin and English and both alone and in groups, the N-Town Mary's musical devotion, Granger argues, instructs spectators on how to use psalms in public and private devotion. *Cambises* and *Grissill* function similarly—adult and child actors indoctrinate audience members from the Queen to commoners on how and why they should sing psalms. If psalms are a tool of emotional propaganda, these plays are an advertisement for their effectiveness.

Both *Grissill* and *Cambises* reveal that music itself is a dynamic and unstable signifier, capable of inspiring or aiding in violence and the seizure of women against their will. While both plays uphold solo devotional singing as the spiritual and moral opposite of such musical abuses, both profane song and dance and psalms share the properties inherent to music. That the plays' sacred and profane musical moments are all sensual as well as emotional, and presumably also socially unifying in their own ways, could lead audience members to question the ways in which psalm singing, too, is able to coerce its listeners and singers. While Phillip and Preston do not set up this problem in their plays' narratives, the fact that devotional music gains its power from the very properties that make worldly music problematic becomes a

---

38. Penny Granger, "Reading her Psalter: The Virgin Mary in the N-Town Play," in Austern, McBride, Orvis, *Psalms in the Early Modern World*, 61–76.

more pronounced source of anxiety in later plays. *Grissill* and *Cambises* follow Calvin and de Beze in advocating for the singing of spiritual music to "enflame the hearts of men," leading or compelling them into a feeling of harmony with God and each other. The plays try to testify to the compatibility of psalm singing with the new Elizabethan religion. While they were being performed at court, other plays grappling with music's role in Elizabeth's new church were being performed around the country. Morality plays from this period—like *The Trial of Treasure* and *Like Will to Like, Quoth the Devil*—reconfigure the Protestant morality play in attempts to yet again demonstrate the virtues of spiritual music and the vices of sensual and profane song and dance. But in a more theologically complex climate, as we shall see, they weren't entirely successful at picking up where the drama of the early sixteenth century left off.

Morality Plays and Reprobates in *Trial of Treasure* and *Like Will to Like*

One of the ways that the ministers, writers, and artists of early Elizabethan England sought to establish continuity with the pre-Marian years of reform was to write and produce Protestant morality plays in the style of those written by Bale and others in the first half of the sixteenth century. The genre—with its popish villains and musical depictions of virtues and vices—was in fact more popular than ever before in the early years of Elizabeth's reign.[39] But popular understanding of theology had changed: ministers returning from their Marian exiles in Geneva brought with them ideas that were heavily influenced by Calvin, and passed versions of these points on to their congregants. Calvin's clarification on double predestination—that is, that if the Elect are predestined to Salvation (as is described by both Paul and Augustine) then the reprobate must also be doomed for damnation and thus irredeemable—wreaks havoc on the older morality play storylines because it makes temptation and conversion beside the point.[40] The morality plays *Trial of Treasure* and *Like Will to Like, Quoth the Devil*, both written by

---

39. As Kent Cartwright explains, 5% of extant late medieval interludes are morality plays, compared with 25% of early Elizabethan (1558–1576) plays. "Humanist Reading and Interpretation in Early Elizabethan Morality Drama," *Allegorica* 28 (2012): 9.

40. The doctrine of Predestination is upheld by Paul in Romans (8:29–30) and Augustine in his letter to the Pelagians. Calvin's chief contribution to the conversation was to clarify it and add that if some are predestined to be Elect, others must be predestined to be Reprobate.

preacher-playwrights, reveal the way the morality plot and Calvinist doctrine are at odds, and how music mediates between the strict binaries that some religious polemicists sought so fervently to uphold.

Morality plays share with the popular psalm collections a desire to praise virtue and give a morally sound alternative to vice, so it is no surprise that they dialogize the early Elizabethan version of conversations on music's capacities for good and evil. As Jonathan Willis summarizes, there were two competing discourses on music in Elizabethan England: "the first states that music could be a carnal, venal, and corrupting force. The second states that music could be a divine gift capable of lifting the soul to otherwise inaccessible states of holy contemplation, forging religious community, and providing comfort and solace to the weak, embattled, and otherwise distressed."[41] Sternhold and Hopkins's title for the *Whole Booke* explains that the psalms are for "laying aparte all ungodly songes and ballades, which tend only to the nourishing of vice, and corrupting of youth."[42] This aim echoes Henry VIII's *Advancement of True Religion*, which permitted "songes, plaies, and enterludes" only if they were produced for "the rebuking and reproaching of vices and setting forth of vertue," a sentiment expressed by all three of his monarchial children, too.[43] Plays from the 1560s like *Trial of Treasure* and *Like Will to Like, Quoth the Devil* support this moral aim, but they do so by representing both godly music, particularly psalms, *and* the "ungodly songes and ballades" that psalms were meant to replace. The psalms presented by the plays' virtuous characters are the plays' musical combat against vice and popery; however, the Calvinist doctrine of double predestination would hold that these songs can only be signs of Elect status rather than tools for conversion. These doctrinal complexities alter the dramatic and musical meanings of the morality play genre.

The repetitiveness of these forms is part of why they have been scorned in retrospect. But repetition and recycling of older materials have their own aesthetic functions: the familiarity of music gives it its affective power, and the continuity of morality play plots give them the patina of pre-Marian authority.[44]

---

41. Willis, "Protestant Worship and the Discourse of Music," 147.

42. The entire title reads: *The whole booke of Psalmes collected into Englysh metre by T. Starnhold, I. Hopkins, & others, conferred with the Ebrue, with apt notes to synge the[m] with al; faithfully perused and alowed according to thordre appointed in the Quenes Maiesties injunctions; very mete to be used of all sortes of people privately for their solace & comfort, laying apart all ungodly songes and ballades, which tende only to the norishing of vyce, and corrupting of youth* (London, 1562).

43. A. Luders, et al., eds. *Statutes of the Realm, vol. 3* (London, 1810–28), 894.

44. Cognitive scientist Elizabeth Hellmuth Margulis analyzes the repetitive nature of music—both the way people tolerate hearing songs over and over, and the way that individual songs repeat melodies—two features of music that are demonstrated to almost an extreme degree in metrical

Kurt Schreyer's argument that we can think of later Elizabethan drama and reformation discourse as a palimpsest that bears the accretion of early dramas and the practices of the traditional church makes sense here, too.[45] *Trial of Treasure* and *Like Will* overwrite the Catholic and early reformist morality dramas of the fifteenth and early sixteenth centuries, taking up the musical valences for virtue and vice that those plays codified. The palimpsestic nature of these later morality plays both enhances and undermines their effectiveness as religious propaganda: the plays express continuity not only with reformist plays and continental Protestantism, but also with traditional dramatic traditions and practices. Metrical psalms rework old materials in a way similar to morality plays, building their own palimpsest out of verses from the Old Testament and tunes that are from both continental Protestant and traditional liturgical sources. Thus, both morality plays and psalms are built on traditions with which they seek to establish continuity, and also on traditions from which they would like to project a complete departure.

Trial of Treasure and *Like Will* use music to establish the concupiscence and popery of the vices at the center of their plots, and then use psalms or psalm-like music to depict the plays' virtuous, Elect characters as the moral inverse of the Reprobate vices. While the plays attempt to contain their meanings to dogmatic binaries between the saved and the damned, the meaning of music, with its interpretive flexibility, can exceed the received wisdom of the morality plot's simplicity. *The Trial of Treasure* is usually attributed to preacher-playwright William Wager, possible son of Lewis Wager.[46] It focuses on the vanity of material pleasures, and its goal is to show that pleasures of wealth, lechery, and vain indulgences like music—all signified in the character Lust and his vile mentor, Inclination—need to be shunned for the restraint and godliness exemplified by Just. In *Like Will to Like, Quoth the Devil*, by preacher-playwright Ulpian Fulwell, the devil commissions Nichol Newfangle to tempt men with vain new fashions, which is easily done with Tom

---

psalmody. She argues, "Music's function is obviously not to convey information, and its repetitive nature seems to be bound up with this other function—a function that might best be described as aesthetic." *On Repeat: How Music Plays the Mind* (Oxford: Oxford University Press, 2014), 14.

45. In Kurt Schreyer's words, "As the Christian church in England was reformed, its sacraments and rituals were re-formed as well. Resinscribed, not erased, late medieval sacraments form the palimpsestic subtext . . . of later early modern discourses." *Shakespeare's Medieval Craft: Remnants of the Mysteries on the London Stage* (Ithaca, NY: Cornell University Press, 2014), 33.

46. This attribution is based on the many passages it shares with William Wager's play *Enough is as Good as a Feast*. It was probably first performed around 1567, the year it was printed. For another reading of power and religious politics in this play, see David Bevington, "Staging the Reformation: Power and Theatricality in the Plays of William Wager," in *Interludes and Early Modern Society: Studies in Gender, Power, and Theatricality*, eds. Peter Happé and Wim Hüsken (Amsterdam: Rodopi Press, 2007), 353–80.

Tosspot and Rafe Roister, but which is unsuccessful with those named Honor or Severity. Both plays are written for five actors according to their given doubling schemes, and all five actors sing multiple songs in both plays, many of them singing as singing vices *and* singing virtues.

Trial's Lust enters "like a gallaunt, singing this song: Hey howe care away let the world passe/For I am as lusty as ever I was" (ll. 62–63).[47] He explains why he sings: "What the Devill ailed me to singe this/I crie you mercy by my faith for entring" (ll. 66–67). With the archaic "ail," he means that the devil causes his behavior, and in apologizing "by my faith," he uses a popish oath; his statuses as reprobate, Catholic, and traditional dramatic vice are thus conflated.[48] In *Like Will*, the opening scene features Lucifer himself convincing Nichol Newfangle to act on his behalf, so that later when Nichol brings out his gittern in order to sweep Tom Collier up in a song and dance, it is clear that the devil is behind it all (ll. 177–88 s.d.).[49] Nichol also joins up with the drunkard Haunce, who swears and prays with Roman Catholic language when he is sober enough to speak at all. The vices and fools of both plays are embodiments of concupiscence, the tendency toward enjoying sins in this world that will preclude them from going to heaven in the next.[50] In the world of double predestination, these characters are hopeless reprobates, picked out by the devil and destined to remain sinful and also Catholic. The plays' conflation of the worldly and the popish suggests that there are two kinds of behaviors that mark reprobation: earthly vanity and Catholicism. The songs do not seduce an everyman to sin, as they do in *Wisdom*, and there is no hope for redemption or conversion, as there was for Adulation in *Respublica*. The songs are rather indexes of the characters' internal and unchangeable state of reprobation.

Both plays are invested in making the sounds of reprobation entertaining and memorable. For example, in one of the few stage directions in early English drama that gives an acting note, the printer of *Trial of Treasure* indicates that Lust's song with Sturdiness should be done "braggingly." There is also

---

47. Quotations and line numbers come from *The Trial of Treasure*, ed. Peter Happé (Scarborough, UK: Malone Society Reprints, 2010). The play can also be found on EEBO: *A new and mery enterlude, called the triall of treasure* (London, 1567), http://eebo.chadwyck.com.

48. *OED*, "Ail" (v.) definition 2.c.

49. Ulpian Fulwell, *A pleasant enterlude, intituled, Like will to like quoth the Deuill to the collier . . .* (1587). Line numbers come from Ulpian Fulwell, "Like Will to Like Quoth the Devil," in *Two Moral Interludes*, ed. Peter Happé (Oxford: Malone Society Reprints, 1991), 49–108.

50. Similar points are made by P.K. Ayers, "The Protestant Morality Play and the Problems of Dramatic Structure," *Essays in Theatre* 2 (1984): 98, and David Coleman, *Drama and the Sacraments* (Basingstoke, UK: Palgrave Macmillan, 2007), 85.

attention to musical harmony. One of the play's five actors is a boy—he first appears as Elation, adding vocal diversity to two songs that he sings with Greedy Gut and Inclination. In the second song, Inclination even makes a musical pun to announce that he will sing treble in their harmony: "Yes I will sing the trouble with all my hart" (l. 399). In *Like Will*, the printer is so invested in the melody of Nichol's singing that there is a musical staff on which are written the notes for his opening ditty, "Trim marchandice, trim trim." According to the stage directions, he is to "sing as oft as he thinketh good," while "going about the place shewing [his bag of items] to the audience" (ll. 895–96 s.d.).

Robert C. Jones argues that the obvious sinfulness of the vices in later moralities (as opposed to the everyman of earlier plays) pushed audiences to disassociate with the vices.[51] It is possible that these plays allowed audiences to rehearse shutting their ears to sin, but, as with earlier morality plays, they hear the actual songs, and possibly quite enjoy them. The theatrical power of these scenes in earlier moralities comes from the way that they put audiences on edge with the feeling that they are hearing sounds that might endanger their souls, and certainly many audience members may have had that concern in 1567, too. However, for audience members who had absorbed Calvinist doctrines of double predestination, they would understand that their fates were already written, so the songs pose no real threat. Rather, they make one question whether or not they are doomed for the same fate as Lust and Nichol, or if they are destined to be saved like Just and Virtuous Living. The questions become epistemological. Instead of wondering if music is damning them or not, audiences might rather wonder if it can assist them in determining the state of their soul. Enjoyment of the vices' music is less a falling into temptation than a potential signal that one's soul has already been doomed.

The plays must also allow audiences to hear the sounds of the Elect—to have the opportunity to guess that they are perhaps in deeper resonance with those virtuous songs and thus destined for salvation themselves. The doubling schemes of both plays indicate that the same actor-singers play both kinds of characters, and thus intone both kinds of songs. The boy who played Elation in *Trial* comes back as the female Trust, who sings with Just and Contention, played by the actors who played Greedy Gut and Sturdiness, respectively. When God's Promise, Honor, and Virtuous Living sing in *Like*

---

51. Robert C. Jones, "Dangerous Sport: the Audience's Engagement with Vice in the Moral Interludes," *Renaissance Drama* 6 (1973): 47, 61.

Will, they have also appeared as vices.[52] The logic of this doubling is that the old and sinful can be replaced by the new and virtuous. This point is crucial to the rhetoric of conversion and social harmony, two important tactics for promoting the Elizabethan church. However, conversion and social harmony are incompatible with the logic of double predestination that is upheld by the plays' plots. The musical performances of these plays thus undermine the narrative in ways that encourage some ideological compromise that would be useful in these early Elizabethan years. This compromise is furthered by the probable melodies used in the songs of virtue.

Just, Contention, and Trust's first song expresses the joy of being assured in one's Elected status (far easier for allegorically named dramatic characters than actual people):

> So happy is the state of those
> That walke upright and juste,
> That thou Lorde doest thy face disclose
> By perfect hope and truste. (ll. 649–52)

The song is in common meter, making its melody interchangeable with metrical psalms, and with popular ballads. For their final song, Contention leaves little doubt as to their preferred kind of music:

> A psalme of thankesgeving first let us sing,
> To the laude and prayse of the immortall kinge.
> *Here if you wil: sing the man is blest*
> *that feareth God. &c.* (ll. 770–74).

This is the only song in *Trial* that does not supply lyrics, and "if you wil" probably indicates that whichever troupe later performs the play from this printed edition may sing "The Man is Blest" as the first company had done, or another psalm of their choice. The words "The Man is Blest that feareth God" open Psalm 112 as printed in Francis Seager's 1553 *Certayne Psalmes select out of the Psalter of David*.[53] Produced right before Edward's death and Mary's accession, the book was not as popular as the *Whole Booke of Psalms*, but it was still in circulation in the 1560s. Psalm 1 in Sternhold and Hopkins's

---

52. The printed doubling scheme in *Like Will* is not actually workable, as several characters who are onstage at the same time, including Virtuous Living and God's Promise, are played by the same character, but presumably any small company would have doubled vices and virtues.

53. F[rancys] S[eager], *Certayne Psalmes select out of the Psalter of David, and drawen into Englyshe Metre, with Notes to every Psalme in iiij parts to Syne, by F. S.* (London, 1553), A14v.

Whole Booke of Psalms begins similarly, and is also in common meter: "The man is blest that hath not bent/to wicked rede his eares."[54] Both of these psalms are possibly parodied in a contemporary ballad called "the Man ys blest that lyves in rest."[55] The interchangeability of melody and meter in these two popular psalms and a contemporary ballad helps demonstrate the crucial point that in the 1560s, many melodies were used for both sacred and profane purposes; the fact that audiences could have likely sung along only reinforces that point through participation.

Part of the early Elizabethan religious agenda was to set up strict dichotomies between Reformed and Catholic, the Elect and the Reprobate, the sacred and the profane. Calvin and his English followers wanted all churches to do away with all popish music, and Calvin advocated for congressional psalm singing—the kind represented at the end of *Trial*—as the antithesis of all that is vain and popish. The dramatic juxtaposition of myriad kinds of music in these plays discloses that they are intricately related rather than diametrically opposed, a point underscored, too, by the use of the same bodies and voices to perform them. Like *Wisdom*, these plays musically express the dialectic of music's sensuality and spirituality, while also holding up the ever-shifting dialectics of orthodoxy and heterodoxy.

Much of the music of early Elizabethan Protestant morality plays relies on and engages with profane balladry, while in the context of an originally "Catholic" dramatic form. This music enacts the phenomena Peter Lake describes wherein the traditional forms left behind after the reformations' "narrative forms and expectations, images and tropes" are appropriated by the "protestant godly . . . for their own evangelical purposes." In Lake's analysis (speaking primarily of its seventeenth-century manifestations), these appropriations accentuate "what revisionists took to be the most counter-intuitive and off-putting of their doctrines—predestination and providence."[56] These early Elizabethan plays, I suggest, reveal the way particularly theatrical and musical forms that bear the traces of the traditional past are strained by new doctrine.

The plays' presentation of virtuous music invites response from all kinds of souls; it aurally sounds of spiritual conversion, even if such a message con-

---

54. Sternhold and Hopkins, *The whole booke of Psalmes*, C1r.

55. Peter J. Seng, *Tudor Songs and Ballads from MS Cotton Vespasian A-25* (Cambridge, MA: Harvard University Press, 1978), 35–36. This ballad is possibly related to one entered in the stationer's register in 1559. Hyder Rollins, "Analytical Index to the Ballad-Entries in the Registers of the Company of Stationers of London," *Studies in Philology* 21 (1924): 258.

56. Peter Lake summarizes his earlier work this way in *The Antichrist's Lewd Hat: Protestants, Papists, and Players in Post-Reformation England* (New Haven, CT: Yale University Press, 2002), xvi–xvii.

tradicts the plot. The logics of palimpsestic accretion and of conversion may
be at odds with the doctrine of double predestination, but they are consistent with contemporary humanist teachings.[57] I turn now to explore the
ways morality plays performed a few years later variously attempt to resolve
the tension between the ideals of a humanistic education and Calvinist reprobation by looking at the more overtly pedagogical *The Longer Thou Livest*
and *Misogonus*.

Learning to Sing: *The Longer Thou Livest* and *Misogonus*

If *Trial of Treasure* and *Like Will* expose that the doctrine of double predestination conflicts with contemporary humanists' confidence in education and
moral conversion, the later plays *The Longer Thou Livest, the More Fool Thou
Art* and *Misogonus* take this issue head on in morality plays focused on youth.
The plays are experimental, coming to different conclusions about the unsettled situation arising from competing discourses about music, religion, and
education. Kent Cartwright explains how late moralities like *Longer* are characteristic of early Elizabethan humanist habits of thought: the tensions between predestination and Protestant educational theories create a world in
which "knowledge [is] not stable or universal but cumulative and dynamic,"
and folly itself becomes ambiguous.[58] William Wager's *The Longer Thou Livest*, from the late 1560s, suggests that if reprobates are unchangeable, as was
the case in *Trial of Treasure* (likely an earlier Wager play), then attempts to
teach them anything are futile. But whereas *Longer* ends in irresolution and
a failed pedagogical agenda, the late 1570s play *Misogonus* attempts to reconcile official Elizabethan religion with educational ideals by acknowledging
the "new" religion's debt to the Catholic and the profane.[59] While *Longer*
emphasizes a clean break with the popish past, *Misogonus* stresses continuity.

---

57. Cartwright argues that in *Like Will*, the "opposing themes of Calvinist reprobation and humanist amelioration negate each other almost willy-nilly." "Humanist Reading and Interpretation," 12.

58. Ibid., 16. Janette Dillon and P. K. Ayers discuss similar ideas in Dillon, *Language and Stage in
Medieval and Renaissance Drama* (Cambridge: Cambridge University Press, 1998), 132, and Ayers,
"The Protestant Morality Play," 102.

59. *The Longer Thou Livest*, printed in 1569, has had its composition and initial performance
dated between 1559 and 1569. Martin Wiggins convincingly argues for 1569 in *British Drama
1533–1642*, vol. 1 (Oxford: Oxford University Press, 2012), 41. *Misogonus* was printed in 1577 and
likely performed around that time. The names Anthony Rudd, Laurentius Bariona, and Thomas
Rychardes appear on the title page, and the group of them possibly first wrote the play for performance at Trinity College, Cambridge. Lester Barber, "Introduction," 7–27.

In the late sixteenth century, education was musical, and music was educative; music's edifying capacity is likely the very reason it remained central
to both churches and schools. Religious leaders and humanist educators alike
cited music's pedagogic powers, including its ability to teach and spread the
Protestant doctrine to young and old. For reformer John Jewel, music an-
noyed both "mass-priests" and the devil "for they perceive that by these
means the sacred discourses sink more deeply into the minds of men, and that
their kingdom is weakened and shaken at almost every note."[60] Richard
Hooker wrote of how psalm singing teaches godliness to the young: "To
this purpose were those harmonious tunes of Psalms divised for us; that they
which are either in years but young, or touching perfection of Vertue, as yet
not grown to ripeness, might, when they think they sing, learn."[61] Musical
education received much praise from humanist pedagogues, too. In educator Roger Asham's debate about education, *Toxophilus*, the debaters agree that
"some musike is fit for lerning," while Richard Mulcaster finds music "still
one of the principles" that is "best fit" for training up youth.[62] *Longer* and
Misogonus both address the issue of musical education directly, having the
central characters partake in solfège, that is, the "do re mi" syllables assigned
to a scale's notes for the purpose (then and now) of teaching sight-singing and
intervals.[63] But while music was lauded in Protestant and humanist discourse,
Catholics had used and continued to use music pedagogically, too. In *Longer*
and *Misogonus*, anxiety over this fact is dramatized by having the young fools
in both plays swear Catholic oaths and partake in or comment on the traditional saunce bell rituals, thus demonstrating the specific dangers of Catholic
music in a young person's education (the saunce bell was the bell rung to
signal that a Catholic Mass was about to begin).

Both *Longer* and *Misogonus* tell the stories of foolish boys who ignore the
reformist, educative efforts of teachers, godly figures, and, in the case of
Misogonus, a pious father. As we have seen with morality plays, the fools are
characterized by their indulgence in pleasures of the flesh and their affinity

60. John Jewel, "Letter to Peter Martyr," 71. Quoted in John Craig, "Psalms, groans, and dog
whippers: the soundscape of worship in the English parish church, 1547–1642," in *Sacred Space in
Early Modern Europe*, eds. Will Coster and Andrew Spicer (Cambridge: Cambridge University Press,
2005), 108.

61. Richard Hooker, *The works of Mr. Richard Hooker (that learned and judicious divine), in eight
books of ecclesiastical polity* . . . (London, 1566), 184.

62. Roger Ascham, *Toxophilus the schole of shootinge contayned in tvvo bookes* (1545), 9r; Richard
Mulcaster, *Positions vvherin those primitiue circumstances be examined, which are necessary for the training vp
of children* (1581), E36v.

63. The practice dates back to at least the 11th century. Solfège is also represented in the contemporary hybrid morality play *King Darius*. "King Darius," in *Early English Dramatists: Anonymous
Plays*, ed. John. S. Farmer (London: Early English Drama Society, 1904), 66.

for music. *Longer's* Moros first enters "synging the foote of many Songes, as fooles were wont," and breaks into a medley of the openings from six different profane ballads before Discipline asks if he is "ashamed/thus vainly the time to spende" (ll. 70–104).[64] Moros is not ashamed, in fact he asserts that his mother "taught me these and many other," making the point that his parents and the musical education they provided him have doomed him (l. 117). He sings and dances his way through the rest of the play.[65] Misogonus also expresses a love for drunken and lascivious dancing, at one point joining in a four-part song to demonstrate his carelessness (2.1.140).[66] Moros and Misogonus thus behave much like younger versions of Lust and Nichol, but while Moros will suffer a fate similar to theirs, Misogonus eventually adopts of life of virtue.

The wider implications of Moros and Misogonus's musical educations differ, too. In *Longer*, the scene featuring solfège comes after Moros's vice-ridden friends Idleness, Wrath, and Incontinence tell him that feasting, drinking, and ample women are waiting for them at a house of entertainment. After learning this good news, Moros says, "before you go, let us have a song;/I can retche up to sing sol, fa, and past" (ll. 884–85).[67] Moros wants to pick a starting note that will suit the vocal ranges of his friends, who could care less about such things:

> IDLENESS: Thou hast songes good stoare sing one,
>   And we three the foote will beare.
> MOROS: Let me study it will come anone,
>   Pepe la, la, la, it is too hye there,
>   So, ho, ho, and that is to lowe.
>   Soll, soll, fa, fa, and that is to flatte,
>   Re, re, re, by and by you shall knowe,
>   My, my, my, how saye you to that.

---

64. William Wager, *A very mery and pythie commedie, called the longer thou livest, the more foole thou art* (London, 1569). Line numbers come from Wager, "*The Longer Thou Livest*," in *The Longer Thou Livest and Enough Is as Good as a Feast*, ed. R. Mark Benbow (Lincoln: University of Nebraska Press, 1967), 1–78.

65. Moros also sings, joined by vice figures, at l. 898 (as will be discussed), and at l. 1512. He talks about how often he sings and dances at ll. 145, 320, and 403. The character Pleasure explains that fools like Moros "love alway" with "lusty girls to sing and dance" (ll. 809, 811).

66. All quotations from *Misogonus*, ed. Lester Barber. The play is not on EEBO and there are no readily available original spelling editions. Misogonus says he wants to dance a "Scottish" jig with a prostitute at 2.1.102, and his father reports on his tendency to sing "some song" at 1.1.190.

67. Angela Heetderks explains that "retch" would pun on the verb that means to cough up phlegm to an early modern audience. She also points out that Moros inverts the notes here, for "fa" is lower than "so," not higher. "Witty Fools and Foolish Wits: Performing Cognitive Disability in English Literature, c. 1380–c.1602" (PhD diss., University of Michigan, 2014), 137, 138.

IDLENESS: Care not for the true [pitch] but what is thy song,
No remedie thou must first beginne.
INCONTINENCE: I will be gone if you tarry long,
Whan we knowe how, we shall come in. (ll. 886–97)

Angela Heetderks illuminates how Moros's use of the solfège indicates that he gets it wrong: he mixes nonsense syllables with real ones, and he is out of order in his scale.[68] It is likely, Heetderks also suggests, that Moros is using the newly current fasola sofège system rather than the medieval syllables.[69] This system is printed in the 1570 *Whole Booke of Psalmes*, indicating its likely popularity in the late 1560s with Protestants eager to teach sight-singing skills to congregations.[70] Heetderks argues that Moros's failure to comprehend sofège indicates that his musical education has failed him both cognitively and morally.[71] I would argue further that Moros's inability to master the simple system of sight-singing that psalm compilers hoped would teach the necessary musical skills to the congregants indicates that spiritual education fails reprobates. This exposes but offers no solution to the problem of what to do with immoral youth if, as the doctrine of double predestination dictates, they are beyond redemption. The play expresses its skepticism with regards to music's ability to effect spiritual change. Against humanist discourse to the contrary, Moros's failures suggest that religion and morality can't be taught.

In *Misogonus*, the titular fool is a more reluctant singer, but his conversation with his fellow fool Cacurgus and his servants Orgalus and Oenophilus before they too have a pre-whoring song reveals that he has musical training. Cacurgus begins with solfège:

CACURGUS: Fa, fa, fa, sol, sol, sol. Cods! That's too low.
La, la, la, me, me, re. By th' mass, that's as high.
MISOGONUS: Take heed, sir, you go not too low for the crow.
CACURGUS: Take heed, sir, you go not too high for the pie.
ORGALUS: None of us, to tell the truth, can sing well mean.
Too high or too low we sing, every one. (2.1.127–32)

Cacurgus, exasperated by this banter and everyone's inability to sing in the middle, takes on the role of master, evoking the educational contexts in which the young men apparently learned their musical skills and vocabulary:

---

68. Ibid., 136–40.
69. The fasola system names the seven notes: "fa, sol, la, fa, sol, la, mi," and, in the sixteenth century, came to replace the medieval six-note scale of "ut, re, mi, fa, sol, la." Ibid., 139.
70. Ibid., 139.
71. Ibid., 140 and passim.

Well then, because you take me for your dean [master],
I'll appoint thy parts myself, by Saint John.
You shall sing the false kind [falsetto]. I mean, you now what.
And thou'st bear the bass because thou art rusty.
The counterfeit tenor [countertenor] is yours, by your lot.
Myself will sing the treble, and that very trusty. (2.1.133–38)

It is clear that singing too high or too low provokes insults: the servant who
is assigned falsetto lacks masculinity, while the bass is less than musically gifted,
growling the easier vocal line at the bottom. Misogonus is presumably the
countertenor to Cacurgus's treble, indicating that the two upper class fools
have the most musical ability. The quartet sings "Sing care away, with sport
and play" to the popular tune "Heart's Ease," and they sing for a long time—
the lyrics go on for 34 lines (2.1.139–79 s.d.).[72] Both the dialogue and the
lengthy musical demonstration show that Misogonus only uses his musical
training for idle and sensual purposes. But while Moros's musical education
ultimately does nothing to redeem him, Misogonus's salvation is indebted to
music.

Crucially, both characters demonstrate that they have learned music from
the traditional church. While in *Longer* this fact is used to further demonize
popish influences, *Misogonus* acknowledges the way these older forms have
enabled the musical practices of the new church. Moros errs in his solfège,
but he demonstrates that he can sing. The four-part song he sings with his
three friends, "I have pretty tytmouse," twice associates the sounds of traditional religion with profane songs like the one they are singing. In the second stanza, the singers ask for "Christmasseale [ale]/In the honour of saint
Steven" (ll. 904–05). And stanza three makes a familiar connection between
birds and church choirs, singing of "Robyn readbrest with his noates/Singing
a lofte in the quere" (ll. 906–07). As in *Trial*, reprobation, vice, and popery
are musically conflated.

In a youth play performed less than a decade after the Marian monarchy,
Moros explains after his song that "this song learned I of my dame" (l. 916).
If Moros's mother was a lover of profane songs and a Catholic, this implies
that another consequence of music's pedagogical utility is that it can be used
to proliferate vanity and Catholicism from generation to generation. Discipline directly asks Moros if his foolishness was from "the best lessons of [his]
Parents" (l. 163), and Moros responds by referring to Catholic musical practice: "No, forsooth, I can ring the saunce bell/And fetch fier when they go to

---

72. "Heart's Ease" is also mentioned, for example, in *Romeo and Juliet* (4.5.102).

Mattins" (ll. 164–65). Moros's proud reporting of his participation in this
ritual, and in his parents' attendance at matins, gives Discipline all the information he needs to conclude: "Better it were to have no education/Then to be
instructed in any part of idolatry;/For there is no part without abominacion/
But all together full of sectes and heresie" (ll. 166–69). Educational projects fail Moros—his prior education has only deepened his vices, and he is
beyond redemption. The play ends with Moros riding off stage on the back
of Confusion, who promises to take him to the devil. Many critics have noted
that the play thus ends with equivocation—either education is potentially
salvific, and characters like Discipline had a purpose that failed in this case, or
no worldly activity can even make a difference to predestined reprobates.[73]
Either reading is deeply skeptical of education—it is either nearly impossible or actually impossible to convert a vice-ridden, popish reprobate into a
virtuous, Protestant believer. But while Wager's play reinforces such binaries
and sets up Elizabethan religion as a firm break with Mary's Catholicism and
a stark contrast to anything profane, *Misogonus* acknowledges the way the
new religion is written on and indebted to the old; in Schreyer's terms, it
exposes the palimpsestic nature of reformed religion.

At first glance, the priestly Sir John with whom Misogonus gambles is a
stereotype of a corrupt, hypocritical priest.[74] While Sir John, Misogonus,
Cacurgus, and Orgalus are gambling, a bell sounds, and Cacurgus identifies
it: "By Saint Sunday, methinks I hear the sauce bell go dingdong./Oh, Sir
John, by th'matins, you must out for't, wrangler" (2.2.209–10). Sir John, who
is losing the game, will not leave. John's clerk enters the scene in search of
his boss, and John's directions contradict *Longer*'s claims that Catholic learning is worse than no learning. So that he can continue gambling, John instructs the clerk on how to lead the service himself: "Faith, Jack, it's no matter
an all thy lessons be lacking./Say a Magnificat nunc dimittis and even end
with the Creed" (2.2.242–43). E.S. Miller's research on this confusing in-
struction reveals that Sir John has prescribed a hybrid rite, blending the Canticle of the Blessed Virgin Mary and the Canticle of Simeon-the-Magnificat
from Vespers with the *Nunc Dimittis* from the *Brevarium Romanum*. That is,
the priest is combining two offices that had been separate services in the

---

73. Dillon, *Language and Stage*, 140. Ineke Murakami also discusses the play's ambiguity, which he
sees as socio-economic, in "William Wager: Monstrous Ambition and the Public Weal," in *Moral
Play and Counterpublic: Transformations in Moral Drama, 1465–1599* (New York: Routledge, 2010),
45–72.

74. Sir John as Catholic parody is discussed by Alan R. Young, *The English Prodigal Son Plays: A
theatrical fashion of the sixteenth and seventeenth centuries* (Salzburg: Institut für Anglistik ind Amerikanistk Universität, 1979), 125.

Catholic Breviary. In the new English prayer books, though, these two canticles, whose titles are printed in Latin even though the prayers are in English, were placed in the same service. As Miller explains, "by splicing two Latin rubrics of the new evening service, he is carrying ad absurdum the tendency of the Prayer Book to abridge and combine Roman rites."[75] The moment thus simultaneously parodies the Anglican service *and* old Catholic offices (as well as the nonchalant priests who administer them). At the same time, the moment is a reminder that the new faith's liturgy shares much—and is built on—the old faith.

The turning point is when, in the middle of the play, the despair of Misogonus's father Philogonus has reached its apex and he has nothing to do but sing of his woes alone to his God; it is worth pointing out that, consistent with Calvin's recommendations, Elizabethan religion stressed the importance of private prayer. Sending his friend away so he can be alone, Philogonus explains, "My grief here to the Lord in a doleful ditty will I vow" (2.2.413). In Elizabethan contexts, "Ditty" often refers to a song using contrafactum, and indeed his song, "O mighty Jove some pity take," is to be sung "to the tune of Labondolose Hoto" (2.2.415 s.d.).[76] This tune, as Hyder Edward Rollins points out, is also known as "Labandala Shot," which can be heard on the English Broadside Ballad Archive.[77] It is indeed a doleful tune, performed slowly in a minor key; it was also hugely popular and later parodied in Ben Jonson's *Eastward Ho!* The distraught father's prayerful lament uses the same musical technique—contrafactum—that is so often employed by the church, and indeed, the tune is in eight-lined long meter stanzas, making it melodically applicable to metrical psalms. While Philogonus does not sing a psalm, the lyrics to his long, metrical lament mimic in their intent the ever-popular penitential psalms, that grouping of psalms that, as Clare King'oo says, "survived the mid-sixteenth c. as a unit."[78] Philogonus sings: "My sins I willingly confess," and repeatedly confesses that he is to blame for his son's state; he is without hope "except though succours to me at need" (2.2.427, 425). King'oo has pointed out the way in which penitential psalms—which were often part of private devotion in Elizabethan England—were used to combat and replace the traditional sacrament of

---

75. E. S. Miller, " 'Magnificat Nunc Dimittis' in *Misogonus*," *Modern Language Notes* 60.1 (1945): 46.

76. Christopher R. Wilson and Michela Calore, *Music in Shakespeare: A Dictionary* (London: Continuum, 2007), 139.

77. Hyder Edward Rollins, "The Date, Author, and Contents of a Handfull of Pleasant Delights," *Journal of English and Germanic Philology* 18.1 (1919): 57–58. It can be heard on EBBA at http://ebba.english.ucsb.edu/ballad/32522/player.

78. Clare Costley King'oo, *Miserere Mei: The Penitential Psalms in Late Medieval and Early Modern England* (Notre Dame, IN: University of Notre Dame Press, 2012), 2.

penance.[79] Philogonus does not need a confessor to air his sins, and he needs no mediator for his petitions to reach God. Combining a popular tune with sincere contrition, Philogonus's long song turns the tide for his son: the father's prayers are answered and Misogonus, who for most of the play looked just like the irredeemable reprobates of other Elizabethan moralities, vows to pursue only "godliness and learning." The play thus joins *Grissill* and *Cambises* in demonstrating the effectiveness of privately sung prayer, paying close attention to the arbitrary rules by which church leaders decide what music is most powerful, for psalms are closely related to ballads and their performances often benefit from Catholic musical training.

By the time Misogonus converts to a life of piety, the play has demonstrated that the music of the new faith relies on Catholic liturgy and ballads and dances, that which is rejected as "reprobate" in earlier plays. Thus, rather than denying the music of the past and the music of the street, *Misogonus* incorporates them in ways consistent with musical practice. In Robin Leaver's words, "Much of the music of the Reformation was thus a synthesis of continuity from the past with the discontinuity of the present."[80] *Misogonus* acknowledges the palimpsestic nature of music, liturgy, and its own dramatic genre. In taking a less than absolutist stance on issues of election and reprobation, it acknowledges the hybridity and flexibility of church doctrine, too.

Scholars of psalm culture have shown that these songs floated between people across and among confessional divides, synthesizing categories of sacred and profane.[81] The very late Protestant morality play *Misogonus*—defying the logic of double predestination to promote the view that *anyone* can eventually benefit from "godliness and learning"—demonstrates that the impact of reformed practices comes not from their rejection of traditional and profane musics, but rather from their incorporation of them. It is important to note, however, that while the popularity of the Elizabethan church's music may have, in a congregational setting, produced the feeling of harmony, not everyone was convinced. In Willis's words, "music created a sense of social harmony, but also reinforced difference and separation through both condemning and expressing minority values."[82] William Byrd's

---

79. Ibid., 132–50.

80. Robin Leaver, "The Reformation and Music," in *European Music 1520–1640*, ed. James Haar (Woodbridge, UK: Boydell & Brewer, 2006), 372.

81. In one summation, psalms "were passed from generation to generation within and sometimes between specific denominations to the point that male and female musicians of every Jewish, Orthodox Christian, Roman Catholic, and Protestant practice created works that often dissolved the boundaries between the past and present, the living and the dead, and even the sacred and the secular." Austern et al., "Introduction," 24.

82. Willis, *Church Music and Protestantism*, 235.

continued compositions of Latin motets are one example of the ways in which crypto-Catholics strengthened their own recusant communities through music.

The plays discussed here demonstrate an optimistic (re)introduction of metrical psalms to English religious life (*Cambises* and *Grissill*), skepticism as to the effectiveness of music's power to educate, convert, and save (*Trial, Like Will,* and *Longer*), and a moderate compromise in synthesizing musical forms to suggest that no one is beyond hope (*Misogonus*). Many well may have felt unified by the singing of psalms in the way described in the anonymous *Praise of Musicke*: feeling that they were singing with "one voice of the whole church," in music that was "a restrainer of the perturbations and rage of our cogitations . . . making friendship, bridging those to concord which were at variance, and a reconciler of utter enemies."[83] But more hard-line believers on both sides of the "great muddled middle" who were appeased by the Elizabethan Settlement continued to reject those harmonies. By the time Marlowe radically rewrote the morality play in the 1580s, the "perturbations and rage of our cogitations" had for many become more of a cacophony than a harmony.

---

83. *The Praise of Musicke* (Oxford, 1585), 120v–121r.

CHAPTER 5

Sound Effects

Doctor Faustus

A sound Magician is a mighty God.

—*Doctor Faustus*

When Faustus tells himself to "begin thine incantations," he chooses a word that shares etymological roots with "enchantment" and "charm," both of which stem from the Latin *cantare*, to sing (1.3.5).[1] Language fossilizes the conceptual links between magic, music, and religion, and we can see traces of these connections in the fact that the word "enchantment" was most frequently used in early modern England to talk about magic, devils, Catholics, and music.[2] As critics have long noted, magic,

---

1. I quote directly from the A-text, Christopher Marlowe, *The Tragicall History of D. Faustus* (London, 1604), and the B-text, *The Tragicall History of the Life and Death of Doctor Faustus* (London, 1616), both reprinted in facsimile (Menston, UK: Scolar Press Limited, 1970). Line numbers (as well as act divisions) refer to *Doctor Faustus: A- and B-texts*, eds. David Bevington and Eric Rasmussen (Manchester, UK: Manchester University Press, 1993). Recordings relevant to this chapter include those of "Kemp's Jig" and "Pealing Bells" from the CD accompanying Christopher Marsh, *Music and Society in Early Modern England* (Cambridge: Cambridge University Press, 2011). Other contemporary music, including a Gallyard and several sacred songs, may be heard on Rose Consort of Viols and Catherine King, *Elizabethan Songs and Consort Music* (Naxos, 1999), compact disc. Music may also be heard in the Globe Theatre on Screen *Doctor Faustus*, directed by Jules Maxwell (Kultur Video, 2013), DVD (and on the Globe's streaming video service).

2. William Barlow writes about working "gaynst the devils enchauntment" in his *Rede me and be nott wrothe for I saye no thynge but trothe* (Strasbourg: Johann Schott, 1528), 64v. The 1561 printing of Calvin's *Institutes* calls on magical and Catholic valences both: "It is certaine that their [Catholics'] eyes were only deceived with the enchantment of the Magicians," *Institute of Christian Religion* (London: Reinolde Wolfe & Richarde Harison, 1561), 128. Christopher Wilson and Michela Calore also describe the word "charm" as "the practice of chanting or reciting verse with magic power,

devils, and cultural remnants of Catholicism all pervade *Doctor Faustus*. The play also stages the connections between these entities, connections that echo the concerns of late sixteenth-century evangelical reformers who branded Catholic practices as theatrical, magical, and, crucially for our purposes, overly musical. Their arguments were staged in polemical early Elizabethan plays like those discussed in the previous chapter, but by the 1580s, hard-line reformers had abandoned drama as a tool for religious propaganda. Reworking elements of outmoded Protestant morality plays, Marlowe's play stages not Catholic-coded vices but real devils, not magic-like tricks, but actual magic. In taking polemical connections between Catholicism, magic, and music to their logical extremes, *Doctor Faustus* parodies the religious logic behind such associations, undermining the very notion of religious certainty.

In fact, the play questions almost all forms of certainty; for while Faustus desires to be resolved of all ambiguities, he is only faced with more equivocality. While Faustus "bids adieu" to logic, medicine, law, and divinity in the play's first scene, the sensual pleasures, natural magical arts, and necromancy he embraces instead present him with little material gain and just as much uncertainty. Richard Halpern has pointed out that *Doctor Faustus* exposes the emptiness of those who say that they have knowledge, dramatizing Francis Bacon's suggestion that books contain nothing but endless repetitions and that on examining them, one "will pass from admiration of the variety to astonishment at the poverty and scantiness of the subjects which till now have occupied and possessed the minds of men."[3] While Halpern argues that Marlowe's trajectory out of religious and scientific uncertainty and into another way of knowing is aesthetic, I see it as specifically theatrical. More precisely, I argue that *Doctor Faustus* exposes music, magic, and religion as culturally interdependent and all reliant on the human-produced theatricality of sound to give them the illusion of divine or magical power and authority, and that this illusion masks their inability to make real truth claims. Performance itself grants power, authority, and pleasure.

Throughout the play, sound and music are central to Faustus's desires and frustrations. The play stages a series of epistemic crises, and shows how music and sound signify the controversies waged over ambiguous and unprovable declarations of doctrine and theology. After outlining the contours of the musical, magical, and religious controversies of the late sixteenth century,

---

going back to the fourteenth century." *Music in Shakespeare: A Dictionary* (London: Continuum, 2007), 93.

3. Richard Halpern, "Marlowe's Theater of the Night: Marlowe's Faustus and Capital," *English Literary History* 71.2 (2004): 481. He quotes from Francis Bacon, *The New Organon* 1, sec. 86 in *Bacon, Selected Philosophical Works*, ed. Rose-Mary Sargent (Indianapolis: Hackett, 1999), 121.

this chapter presents six types of sound or music in the play that demonstrate that the real power of religion is theatrical. One of the first things Faustus embraces is sensual pleasures, and Marlowe pushes the morality play tradition of equating music with vice to its logical extreme, exposing the absurdity of attributing otherworldly power to earthly sensations like music. Secondly, while earthly sensation provides Faustus with little real gain, the natural magic he hopes to practice comes up empty when it comes to obtaining actual knowledge: engagement with the people and arts of ancient Greece and Pythagorean musical theory brings him little real understanding. Thirdly, Faustus's experiments in the dark arts of necromancy are equally inconclusive; in his attempts to conjure and chant, he evokes the long history that associates Catholic liturgy with magical incantations, assailing the provability of both. While the first three sections of this chapter detail the material and epistemic failures of sensual pleasure, natural magic, and necromancy, in my fourth section I explore the Pope's excommunication ritual as revelatory of the social and political power of religion's sound effects. This is followed by an exploration of the sound effects of heaven and hell at the end of the play, effects that reveal how eschatology, particularly the concepts of heaven and hell, are reliant on theatrical tricks. The final section describes the play's one surety, examining how the bell-ringing accompanying Faustus's final moment pits the surety of death against the uncertainty of claims for divine understanding.

Magical, Musical, and Religious Controversies in the Late Sixteenth Century

Contemporary critics have noted *Doctor Faustus*'s engagement with the two professions remonstrated by late sixteenth-century reforming polemicists: the player and the magician.[4] But these dogmatists were often equally concerned about the evils of profane music and dancing, and some continued to protest overly indulgent church music. And while public theaters were representing music and magic on the stage, debates raged on about the dangers of music, magic, and the theater itself.

---

4. See, for example, Sara Munson Deats, " 'Mark this show': Magic and Theater in Marlowe's *Doctor Faustus,*" in *Placing the Plays of Christopher Marlowe: Fresh Cultural Contexts,* eds. Sara Munson Deats and Robert A. Logan (Aldershot, UK: Ashgate, 2008), 13. In order to avoid the imprecise term "Puritan," I will be referring to the non-conforming radical Protestants I cite—those who advocated for little or no music or ceremony in the church and railed against theatrical and musical entertainment—as "reforming polemicists."

Following in the footsteps of Bullinger, many non-conforming reform-ists of the late sixteenth century continued to object to all or most types of music, concerned about its affective powers and abilities to seduce people into sin. At the same time, the Queen herself and her many more moderate subjects took part in a variety of musical rites in church services: the ser-vices of the Chapel Royal featured ornate polyphony while unaccompanied metrical psalms filled most parishes. Treatises and sermons filled with many defenses of music, and there were also many who defended and supported the theater as well as the study of natural magic. And while debates raged in public about the role of music in the church and the dangers or merits of actors and magicians, recusant Catholics continued to worship in enclaves all around England, becoming the very models of iniquity for the perceived theatricality, musicality, and superstitious sorcery of their faith.

By the 1580s it had been more than a generation since 1559, when the sensuousness—visual, olfactory, and aural—of most official Christian wor-ship was diminished in comparison with the traditional rites briefly restored under Mary.[5] Richard Baines's accusatory statements about Marlowe's reli-gious opinions—the famous Baines Note—hints that perhaps Marlowe himself found delight in old and clandestine ceremonies. The playwright is alleged to have said, "if there be any god or any good Religion, then it is in the papistes because the service of god is performed with more ceremonies, as Elevation of the mass, organs, singing men, Shaven Crownes, &cta. That all protestantes are Hypocriticall asses."[6] The use of those "organs" and "singing men" continued to be a contentious issue in the 1580s.

When thinking about music's potential spiritual and moralizing power, defenders like John Taverner thought that music "should have power to ex-orcize & chase away evill spiritts, yet itt seemes that itt had a gift beyond this, to attract the good."[7] While moderates like Richard Hooker and Taverner advocated for music in the church, almost any indulgence in music's de-lights brought on the vitriol of reforming polemicists. Some advocated for a complete avoidance of music—including in church ceremony—though not

5. For detailed analyses of the historical issues, see Matthew Milner, *The Senses and the English Reformation* (Surrey, UK: Ashgate, 2011). For a longer discussion of these issues with regard to con-temporary drama, see Jennifer Waldron, *Reformations of the Body: Idolatry, Sacrifice, and Early Modern Theater* (New York: Palgrave Macmillan, 2013).

6. BL Harleian MSS 6848 (1592). Reprinted in Constance Kuriyama, *Christopher Marlowe: A Renaissance Life* (Ithaca, NY: Cornell University Press, 2002), 219.

7. John Taverner, "Praelections musical in aedibus Greshamensibus" (1610/11) MS 2329, Sloane Collection, British Library, 23v. Thomas Wright echoes this idea that music makes good men better in *The Passions of the Minde in Generall (1604)*, ed. Thomas O. Sloan (Urbana: University of Illinois Press, 1971), 163–71.

all non-conforming reformists hated all music.[8] For many evangelical non-conformists, music needed to be purely scriptural and linguistic—most music was "feeding the eares" rather than "edifying the minde" for preacher William Perkins.[9]

At the same time that the wrong kinds, or all kinds, of church music inspired such vitriol, the music of the theater also came under attack by anti-theatrical evangelicals. The popular phrase "chaste ears" was used to describe what needed to be preserved against the dangerous aural penetrations of the theater and "popery"—it is found in the Geneva Bible, and in several sermons and treatises.[10] For nonconformists like John Northbrooke, no place assaults the ears' chastity more than the theater: "Thou beholdest thee in an open theatre, a place where the soule of the wise is snared & condemned: in those places (sayth he) thou . . . hearest spurciloquia, filthie speaches . . . where thou shalt by hearing divelishe and filthie songs hurte thy *chaste eares*."[11] Stephen Gosson worries about people who "delight beeing moved with varietie of shewes, of eventes, of musicke, the longer we gaze, the more we crave," and William Prynne also rails against "ravishing musicke" in both theater and church.[12]

While they were attacking theatrical sounds, evangelicals were also concerned about the popularity of natural magic, a field of study that used and explored the power of sound. In the sixteenth century a transformation of sacred and secular spaces coincided with rapid developments in natural magic and related scientific fields. Penelope Gouk and others have shown the many intersections between music and magic, dating back to Platonic and Aristotelian conceptions of the celestial spheres and their earthly effects, including the production of certain musical pitches.[13] There were two kinds of

---

8. For more on the topic, see Percy Scholes, *The Puritans and Music: In England and New England* (1934; repr., Oxford: Clarendon Press, 1969). For more on no-music sects, including General Baptists and antecedents of the Quakers, see Marsh, *Music and Society*, 394, and Jonathan Willis, *Church Music and Protestantism in Post-Reformation England: Discourses, Sites and Identities* (Aldershot, UK: Ashgate, 2010), 72.

9. Quoted in Milner, *The Senses and the English Reformation*, 297.

10. From Ezek. 23:8: "The holy ghost useth these tearmes which seeme straunge to chaste eares to cause this wicked vi[c]e of idolatrie." *The Bible and Holy Scriptures conteyned in the Olde and Newe Testament* (Geneva, 1561). A search for "chaste eares" on EEBO Text Creation Partnership (TCP) yields 65 texts using the phrase.

11. John Northbrooke, *Spiritus est vicarious* (London, 1577), 61.

12. Stephen Gosson, *Playes Confuted in Five Actions* (London, 1582), 51r; William Prynne, *Histrio-Mastix* (London, 1633), 375.

13. Penelope Gouk, *Music, Science and Natural Magic in Seventeenth-Century England* (New Haven, CT: Yale University Press, 1999), 12. See also John Haines, "Why Music and Magic in the Middle Ages?" *Magic, Ritual, and Witchcraft* 5.2 (2010): 149–72; Gary Tomlinson, *Music in Renaissance Magic: Toward a Historiography of Others* (Chicago: University of Chicago Press, 1993); and Linda Austern,

sixteenth-century magic: natural magic, a systematic, universal philosophy of word and man, the knowledge of which helped unite him with God's divine mysteries, and black magic (far more powerful in reputation than practice), a witchcraft that supposedly gathered power not from the natural world but from the devil.[14] Natural magic had been recently popularized by Heinrich Cornelius Agrippa (German, 1486–1535) and John Dee (English, 1527–1609), who suggested that knowledge of the occult (that is, hidden) properties of the world and universe could be used to achieve a state of divinity.[15] Agrippa and Dee used the late antique writings of the pseudo-historical Hermes Trismegistus as well as the work of Marsilio Ficino (Italian, 1433–1499) and Giovanni Pico della Mirandola (Italian, 1463–1494) to propose that personal transcendence and access to God could be achieved through knowledge of the natural world and its correlation to heavenly spheres. While many understood a separation between natural magic and the sorcery of black magic, the practice (or rumors of the practice) of either kind of magic were held in suspicion by many.

Reformist polemicists often linked magical practices of any kind with popery, branding them as dangerous abominations. Miracles of the old religion—healing ceremonies, transubstantiation, and other transformations that gleaned their power from incantation—were disregarded as magic tricks. These miracles were at best futile superstitions, and at worst demonstrations of devilish necromancy. Arthur Marotti writes about the effects of the 1582 publication of Catholic martyr Edward Campion's biography, *A true reporte of the death & martyrdome of M. Campion Jesuite and preiste*, by Thomas Alfried. The account includes reports of miracles, including the martyr's ability to lift his body up while burning to death; these reported miracles gave hope and inspiration to underground Catholics and fueled the fire for the vehemently anti-Catholic.[16] *Doctor Faustus* calls on all of these discourses regarding the joys and dangers of music, magic, and the theater in

---

"Nature, Culture, Myth, and the Musician in Early Modern England," *Journal of the American Musicological Society* 51.1 (1998): 1–47.

14. In Thomas Elyot's 1538 dictionary, he explains that "Magike . . . is in two sortes, one is the secret knowledge of the naturall qualities and hydde operations and causes of thynges, and that is called Magia naturalis, naturall magike: Another is superstitious & devillishe, called witche crafte, sorcery or other lyke detestable names, whiche is unlofull by the lawes of god and man." *The dictionary of syr Thomas Eliot knight* (London, 1538).

15. See Andrew Duxfield, "Doctor Faustus and Renaissance Hermeticism," in *Doctor Faustus: A Critical Guide,* ed. Sara Munson Deats (London: Continuum, 2010), 197.

16. Arthur Marotti, *Religious Ideology & Cultural Fantasy: Catholic and Anti-Catholic Discourses in Early Modern England* (Notre Dame, IN: University of Notre Dame Press, 2005), 14.

performing the connections between such things. Throughout the play, the sounds of sensual pleasure, traditional religion, and magic demonstrate the cultural interdependence of competing ways of understanding divine order, and the absurdity of claiming moral superiority for any one of them.

Ravishing Sounds and Dancing Devils

The ontological status of the theater—its actual performance of the sounds and spectacles that delight, damn, and accompany death—gives Marlowe's versions of the Faust legend entirely new powers over printed works such as the *English Faust Book* that he adapts in the course of writing his play. To describe Faustus's sensual desires, Marlowe's characters echo the language of music's detractors and defenders: the play thus calls into question what precisely makes music so powerful over one's body and exposes accusations against music and theater as logically absurd.[17]

Doctor Faustus frequently uses four words that were contemporaneously associated with the sensuality of music, theater, and church ceremony; those words are: "ravishing," "sweet," and the oft-paired terms "delight" and "pleasure." They can all be found, for example, in Northbrooke's dialogue about music's dangerous ability to captivate one's senses and reason:

YOVTH.
Why doth Musicke so rapte and *ravishe* men in a maner wholy?
AGE.
The reason is playne. For there are certaine *pleasures*, which onely fill the outwarde senses: and there are others also, which pertaine only to the mynde or reason. But Musick is a delectation so put in the middest, that both by the *sweetnesse* of the soundes it moveth the senses, and by the artificiousnesse of the number and proportions, it *deliteth* reason it selfe.[18]

Age's admission of music's power even as he later professes that God desires "Nor string of Musicke very *sweete*/Except the heart conjoyne and meete" betrays the ambivalence many staunch evangelicals—following in

---

17. In Chloe Preedy's words, Faustus's desire to be sensually ravished echoes "Protestant accusations that Catholic rituals seduced the senses rather than appealing to the rational mind." *Marlowe's Literary Scepticism: Politic Religion and Post-Reformation Polemic* (London: Arden Shakespeare, 2012), 37.

18. Northbrooke, *Spiritus est vicarious*, 81. Emphasis mine here and below.

the footsteps of centuries of Christian writings that worried about music's sensuality—had regarding music's role in the church.[19] These four words were used by music's detractors and defendants to articulate the sensual force of sound, and they are used to describe Faustus's seduction into magical arts, the shows he enjoys and performs, and even his hopes for salvation. Using the same musically coded diction to describe magic, performance, and salvation reveals that connections between magical arts, theater, and religious doctrine are grounded in contested and unverifiable claims on sensory experience.

As he describes the effects of magic and music, Faustus often describes himself as "ravished." In the first scene, he twice says that he is ravished by magic, which is appropriate given that treatises on natural magic attest to the power of sound and music in ordering the universe (1.1.6, 1.1.112). When he later describes ancient music as the "ravishing sound of melodious harp," the word is more precisely used to signify the enrapturing, captivating power of sounds and sights of spectacles (2.3.29). This connotation is echoed in the B-text when the astounded Emperor says, "pardon me, my thoughts are so ravished" after the appearance of Alexander and his paramour (B 4.1.105). Focusing primarily on visual spectacle, Erika Lin explains that the word "ravish" was often used to show that "spectacle engenders involuntary disturbance of the physiological, emotional, and social realms," a valence heightened by the fact that the word also refers to rape or the violent seizure of goods.[20] At the same time, "ravish" was often used to explain the power of music to affect the emotions, to overwhelm one with passion. In the eighth sonnet of *The Passionate Pilgrim*, John Dowland's lute playing is praised because it "doth ravish human sense," while an early modern account of hearing angels' song describes the way their music "ravish'd the hearts of those stood by/so sweet the Musick did abound."[21]

That music or magic's possession over one's body should be accompanied by a loss of reason was precisely the source of anxiety for evangelical nonconformists, even as it was a reason for praise from others. The play's use of the term to describe possession by forces that ultimately damn Faustus seem to articulate evangelical concerns for music, but the play's own musical performances would thus endanger audiences by that logic. And the play, no less than the Baines Note, is well aware that sensory ravishment is in fact crucial to the power of religion; John Donne later performs this conflation

---

19. Ibid., 84.

20. Erika Lin, *Shakespeare and the Materiality of Performance* (New York: Palgrave, 2012), 121.

21. *The Passionate Pilgrim,* Sonnet 8, quoted in Wilson and Calore, *Music in Shakespeare*, 357; *Diary of Samuel Pepys*, eds. R.C. Latham and W. Mathews (London: HarperCollins, 1995), vol. 4, 186.

of the sensory and spiritual when he asks God that he be not "ever chast, except you ravish mee."[22]

In its frequent use of the term "sweet," the play divulges that the promise of musical delight brings people to religion as surely as it seduces Faustus to magic. "Sweet" is employed twenty-three times in the A-text, with four additional uses in the B-text. The chorus describes a "sweet" delight in theology as well as "sweet" magic, which Faustus "preferres before his chiefest blisse" (prologue ll.18, 26, 27); he also says in his opening speech that he is ravished by "*sweete* Analytikes" (1.1.6). He calls Mephistopheles "sweet" five times, but also uses the word to describe the Old Man, who himself uses it twice to explain the sweetness of salvation. The word was frequently used in the Elizabethan era to express the concord and harmony created by music, and indeed, the play provides more examples of acoustic pleasure than olfactory or gustatory delight.[23] "Sweet" is used in *Doctor Faustus* to describe both the magic and the sensuousness that damns, as well as the "Saviour sweete" that might be redemptive.

In a similar vein, Lin has explained the repeated uses of the words "pleasure" and "delight" to describe early modern spectacles, and how in their historical context these terms "signal complex cultural attitudes toward spectacle as both healthful and dangerous, both stimulating and seductive."[24] Falsely associated with promiscuity or "light-ness," the word "de-light" (which actually derives from the Latin delicere, "to entice") had sexual connotations, as did, and still does, the word "pleasure."[25] The A- and B-texts' frequent uses of both words almost always refer to the sensual indulgences Faustus hopes to or does gain through his magic, which is also described as a "delight" in the prologue. In the B-text, Faustus clarifies that pleasure and delight are what he most desires: "Sweete Mephosto, thou *pleasest* me./ Whilst I am here on earth: Let me be cloyd/With all things that *delight* the heart of man" (3.1.57–59).[26] But, these pleasures and delights are often musical, and the words resonate with musical discourses both defending and disparaging music. For early modern music defenders like Hooker, music is

---

22. John Donne, "Sonnet X," in *Poems, by J.D. With elegies on the authors death* (London: 1633), 38.

23. Faustus also delights in visual and somatosensory pleasures, which are less frequently referred to as "sweet." "Pleasing to the ear" is a definition of "sweet" used as early as 900, according to the *OED*, which lists this as definition 4a. See also Wilson and Calore, *Music in Shakespeare*, 412.

24. Lin, *Shakespeare and the Materiality of Performance*, 109.

25. Ibid., 115.

26. Additionally, he studies magic for "a world of profit and *delight*," on his travels he goes "past with *delight* the stately towne of Trier," and he tells the Emperor and the Duchess that he will "de-light" them (l. 1.55, 3.1.2, 4.1.91). In the play's final scene, Faustus explains that he is damned for "vaine pleasure (5.2.41)" or for his "store of pleasure."

that "wherein we *delight*," and it is thus a sign of God's providence that that which causes sensual pleasure also benefits the soul.[27] The mixed connotations of these words are revelatory of early modern confusion regarding when sensual pleasures are damning and when they are holy, how one is to know the difference, and what it means that heaven promises the very delights people are meant to eschew or restrict while on earth.

We have seen in the previous chapters how music itself indexes vice in morality plays, and *Doctor Faustus* engages this theatrical tradition of equating music and vice even as it echoes contemporary discourse condemning music. Matthew Milner summarizes the ways in which that discourse recalls the binaries of morality plays: "The dangers of sensation were so severe for nonconformists because of their stress on the utter corruption of human rational capabilities and robust belief in the lack of free will within the traditional binary ethical framework of vice and virtue."[28] Marlowe's play tests this extremist viewpoint, asking if sensation can corrupt the imperfect, doomed soul. For while it demonstrates the power of what antitheatricalists called "filthie songs" to ravish a soul like Faustus's, such songs and speeches are also heard by the audience, theoretically damaging their "chaste ears" in the same way they damage any theater-goers', according to the likes of Northbrooke and Prynne. So either sound has the power that these nonconformists say it does, and therefore the audiences are also damned by listening to the sounds they cannot but choose to hear (one can shut their eyes, not their ears), or *Doctor Faustus* is exposing the ridiculousness of such claims.[29]

The play also inherits the recent Protestant morality play tradition of associating profane, devilish music with Catholicism. The association of devils with Catholics was quite common in sixteenth-century plays, treatises, and ballads. By the 1580s, then, the devil-priest-player idea was already more of a cliché than a fresh metaphor. Thus, the rather ridiculous request of

---

27. Hooker writes, "O the wise conceit of that Heavenly Teacher, which both by his skill found out a way, that doing those things wherein we *delight*, we may also learn that whereby we profit!" *The works of Mr. Richard Hooker (that learned and judicious divine), in eight books of ecclesiastical polity compleated out of his own manuscripts, never before published: with an account of his life and death* (London, 1566), 38. The anonymous *Praise of Musicke* also uses the word to defend music: "Now although there be none but few men so senselesse & blockish by nature, or of disposition so pevish, & waiward, that taking no *delight* in Musick themselves . . . I trust that these men will reforme their opinions from thinking so basely of it, or refraine their tounges from inveighing so bitterly against it." *Praise of Musicke* (Oxford: 1585), 90.

28. Milner, *The Senses and the English Reformation*, 338.

29. Jennifer Waldron makes a similar version of this point: "Rather than pitting theatrical experience against religious doctrine, that is, Marlowe causes the two to converge with particular force through his attention to the bodies of actors and the bodily sense of audiences." *Reformations of the Body*, 92.

Faustus's that Mephistopheles reappear as a devil neither invents nor even reiterates anti-Catholic sentiment; Mephistopheles's costume just as easily parodies the reformers who continued to make the by-then hackneyed association. The meta-theatricality of this re-presented theatrical metaphor demonstrates that the casting of priests as devils is itself a show; *Doctor Faustus* stages the conflation of conjured devil, friar, and actor while making obscure how and why such a creature should appear. The play thus makes the logic behind such associations of priests, devils, and actors seem faulty.

Mephistopheles further plays with the connection between theater and devils when he summons not Catholic-coded agents of the devil (like Lust in *Trial of Treasure*, say) but actual devils. The dancing devils bring together the Protestant morality play conflation of devils and Catholic priests and the diction of the anti-music and anti-theatrical crowd regarding song and dance. Their musicality calls on contemporary associations of music with devils.[30] After "*homo fuge*" appears in blood on Faustus's arm when he signs the deed of gift, Mephistopheles distracts Faustus by bringing him a group of dancing devils: "Ill fetch him somewhat to *delight* his minde," he says, and the stage direction indicates that he re-enters "with divels, giving crownes and rich apparell to Faustus, and daunce, and then depart" (2.1.81–2.1.81 s.d.). When Faustus asks "what means this shew?," the word "delight" is repeated in explanation: "Nothing, Faustus, but to *delight* thy minde withall" (2.1.83, 84).[31] As with the profane dancing of *Wisdom*, the dancing devils both present action that is part of the play's narrative, and at the same time create a live spectacle. In Lin's words, "as the onstage spectator, Faustus is in a position that mirrors that of the actual playgoer. The spectacle that seduces him is the very one that theater audiences have paid to see."[32] The multi-functionality of the scene as both narrative element and dangerous entertainment is not produced by visuals alone. The sounds of this dance—the music that accompanies the movement—also connote both pleasure in entertainment and perilous lasciviousness.

It matters, too, that staged music in Marlowe's theater is not made by clerics or schoolboys but by professional actors and musicians. The devil's song might well have been played by the town waits—those musical city guards who played fairs, processions, and dances and were often hired by late

---

30. In Marsh's words, "Music could form a sympathetic channel linking human and God, but it could also operate as a sonic signpost to the devil's realm." *Music and Society*, 48.

31. The stage direction for the show itself reads: "*Enter with divels, giving crownes and rich apparell to Faustus, and daunce, and then depart*" (2.1.81 s.d.).

32. Lin, *Shakespeare and the Materiality of Performance*, 123.

sixteenth-century theater companies.[33] The waits could play jigs on their loud shawms (or hautboys, an early version of the oboe), and in dramatic performance they would have likely played a familiar tune—something they had played on other occasions, too. Thus, the devil's dance would have sounded and felt very much like the entertainments popularly enjoyed in early modern England. While that could identify extra-theatrical music as dangerous, the fact that the devil's dance could have been played by performers recognizable to audience members as city musicians equally signals the absurdity of equating harmless and pervasive entertainments with the devil.

The "delight" that is the devil's dance awakens dangerous sexual urges in Faustus and, according to reformist prudes, dance is dangerous because of its wantonness. The popularity of dance music made it a frequent target for anti-entertainment polemicists. Northbrooke rails: "What newe kinde of daunces, and newe devised gestures the people have decised, and daylye doe devise, it will grieve chaste eares to heare it, good eyes to see it, or tongue to utter it."[34] Christopher Marsh catalogues the abuses hurled at dance music: it was "filthy," "lewd," "wanton," "fleshly," and "lascivious," a "form of spiritual whoredom."[35] In the play, the clown Robin directly associates dance with lust and wantonness. He hopes to use magic to create music that will have precisely the effects Northbrooke warns against: "now wil I make al the maidens in our parish dance at my pleasure starke naked before me" (2.2.4–5). In addition to its associations with lust, dance was also called "devilish," "wicked," and "heathen," and it was thought by some to be one of Satan's agents of seduction: "a libertie to wantonnesse, a friende to wickednesse, a provocation to fleshlye lust, [and an] enimie to chastity."[36] Thus, dances performed by actual devils exemplify and perform contemporary objections to dance.

The music accompanying the dancing devils stages the frequent conflation of the theatrical and the ceremonial. In Northbrooke's attack on church music, for example, he says that "christian people doe runne unto the Churche, as to a Stage playe, where they may be *delighted* with pyping and singing (and doe thereby absent themselves from hearing the worde of God preached) in this case we must rather abstaine from a thing not necessarie,

---

33. See, for example, Marsh, *Music and Society*, 115–30.
34. Northbrooke, *Spiritus est vicarious*, 141.
35. Marsh, *Music and Society*, 357.
36. Ibid., 358; Northbrooke, *Spiritus est vicarious*, 135. As Heather Hirschfeld puts it, the devils' dance and the pageant of the seven deadly sins establish the play's startling pattern that, "rather than Faustus going to hell, hell comes to Faustus." *The End of Satisfaction: Drama and Repentance in the Age of Shakespeare* (Ithaca, NY: Cornell University Press, 2014), 57.

than to suffer their *pleasures* to be cockered with the destruction of their soules."[37] Thus, Mephistopheles's plans to "delight" Faustus may for some audience members corroborate Northbrooke's concern about all types of musical pleasure: its inherent theatricality and its ability to drown out the "worde of God preached" will destroy the soul of the listener. However, the scene's performance *in* a theater necessarily destabilizes the Puritans' concern, for either the playwright and actors do not fear hell, or the notion that the music in church and theater can destroy souls is demonstrably ludicrous. Marlowe is perhaps at his most subversive when the play's action suggests an agreement with the anti-conformists' bizarre claims about devil-priests and devil-playhouses: "Stage playes," says William Prynne, "are the very Devils own peculiar pompes, Play-houses his Synagogues; Players, his professed Masse-priests and Choirsters; Play haunters his devoted servants."[38] *Performing* the overlap between ceremony and theater, *Doctor Faustus* suggests that no one can know for sure the dangers of either type of performance. The audience is trapped in an interpretive crux, and the only way out is to annihilate the notion that any one belief system can prove itself with certainty.

Homer's Song, Natural Magic, and Faustus's Shows

In addition to dancing devils, Mephistopheles has entertained Faustus with music of the ancient world (2.3.31). When Faustus turns into the producer rather than the auditor of musical spectacle, he too calls on classical precedent. The play's many references to ancient Greeks resonate with Pythagorean and Platonic musical theories that inform natural magic, and they are reminders of pre-Christian precedent for the study and use of music's power. While Faustus turns to natural magic as a source of knowledge early in the play, it is revealed to him to be as empty of surety as any other belief system.

When Faustus recalls the music that keeps him from either despairing or repenting, he highlights Mephistopheles's participation in resurrecting classical sounds for him:

My hearts so hardned I cannot repent,
Scarse can I name salvation, faith, or heaven,
But feareful ecchoes thunders in mine eares,

---

37. Northbrooke, *Spiritus est vicarious*, 85. Emphases mine.
38. Prynne, *Histrio-Mastix*, 529.

Faustus, thou art damn'd . . .
And long ere this I should have slaine my selfe,
Had not swéete pleasure conquerd déepe dispaire.
Have not I made blinde *Homer* sing to me,
Of *Alexanders* love, and *Enons* death,
And hath not he that build the walles of *Thebes*,
With ravishing sound of his melodious harp
Made musicke with my *Mephastophilis*,
Why should I dye then, or basely dispaire? (2.3.18–21, 24–32)

In one of many analyses of the play's meta-theatricality, Halpern points out that Mephistopheles is often a purveyor of visual special effects.[39] But Mephistopheles is equally devoted to entertaining Faustus with music, a theatrical trick Faustus learns to use, too. In this speech, the memory of music's "sweete pleasures" keeps Faustus from despairing—as music defenders confident in music's cheering properties hoped it would—but music also prevents him from repenting his sins, as music detractors warned. In hearing the magically resurrected sounds of Homer and Amphion, Faustus implies that he has heard Homer himself sing his famous epics, and he cites a favorite Renaissance illustration of the power of music from Ovid. In the *Metamorphoses*, Amphion, the ruler of Thebes, was such a skilled harpist that his music moved the stones themselves to build a protective wall.

For early modern music theorists, classical music was thought to have been far more moving than any sounds produced in their own time. John Taverner writes that in the times of the classical Greeks, "Homers verses were anciently sung in their theatres by certaine men with wands or rods in their hand whoe were thereupon called Homerists. . . . fore a Poet & a musician were in effect both one," and "the musicke of their Theaters . . . were among them esteemed as part of their Religion or Divine Service."[40] Faustus is thus invigorated by the music from a time when music held nearly unquestioned spiritual power, a time when theaters were sacred. Taking pleasure in these pre-Christian sounds of power and beauty, he is able to eschew—at least for a time—concerns about how any "sweet Saviour" or minister of the church might view his delights. It is thus not surprising that he is happy to resurrect the classical Alexander, or that his final request is to behold Helen of Troy.

Faustus also invokes ancient Greece when he inquires about the nature of the universe, and this inquiry brings together centuries-old affiliations be-

---

39. Halpern, "Marlowe's Theater of the Night," 459.
40. Taverner, "Praelections musical," 62r, 64v.

tween music and magic.[41] Faustus associates himself with natural magicians like Agrippa and Dee and their desires to understand in Thomas Elyot's words, the "hydde operations and causes of thynges"; he even expresses a desire to be "as cunning as Agrippa was" (1.1.119). Early modern defenders of religious music share with natural magicians a use of classical precedent to authorize the notion that music is able to connect heaven and earth. Agrippa writes that "nothing is more efficacious in natural magic than the hymns of Orpheus if they are presented with appropriate harmonies, careful attention, and apt ceremonies known to the wise."[42] In the anonymous *In Praise of Musicke* (1585), music's abilities to divide soul from body and lift "up [man's] cogitations above himselfe" are attributed in part to the fact that music "is ancient and of great continuance . . . it was translated from the religions of the heathen, which in hymnes and songes, yeelded all reverence and honor to their gods of wood & stone."[43] Faustus connects his desire to understand music's heavenly resonances with the classical past, for it is the memory of creating music with the resurrected Homer that makes Faustus curious about the production of sound. The association is made most clear in the B-text, where Faustus's question to Mephistopheles reads: "Speake, are there many Spheares above the Moone?" (B 2.3.33). But rather than answer this or any of Faustus's questions about the nature of the universe, Mephistopheles gives him stock or sarcastic answers, and then distracts him with conjured delights.

Thus, Faustus's bargain does not grant him a greater understanding of the universe, let alone the ability to use such knowledge to meet his own ends. Faustus gives up on Agrippa and his early magician heroes, learning virtually nothing of their arts, and instead relies on Mephistopheles's unexplained tricks. The wonder of the ancient world and the theories of natural magic become, to Faustus, nothing more than empty signs of an authority he never really gains. In a play that begins with a quest for knowledge, the ability to know anything for certain is repeatedly denied.

But, while he has not learned anything about the universe from Mephistopheles, Faustus *has* learned how to put on a good show, and his shows often recall and resurrect ancient Greece, giving them the patina of authority in the absence of real knowledge. In the A-text, Faustus's show for the Holy Roman Emperor is staged as a simple show-and-tell: Mephistopheles appears on stage escorting Alexander the Great and his paramour, who are inspected to Charles's satisfaction. In the B-text, however, the scene expands to include

---

41. See, for example, Haines, "Why Music and Magic?," 163–64.
42. Elyot, *The dictionary of syr Thomas Eliot knight*. Trans. Tomlinson, in *Music in Renaissance Magic*, 63. Agrippa uses Pico, *Conclusiones sive theses DCCCC*, 80. Agrippa's Latin is printed by Tomlinson, 256.
43. *Praise of Musicke*, 152.

a musical dumb show. The dumb show resembles the sort of neoclassical drama popular in England during the 1560s, '70s, and '80s, plays like Thomas Norton and Thomas Sackville's *Gorboduc* (1561). Lacking the ability to produce dialogue, Faustus creates a ravishing show by using music—the very thing that had ravished him—to delight his royal patron. The Emperor is heralded by a sennet (as in *Cambises*, the *sound* of power), and Faustus calls attention to the trumpet's ritualistic significance when he sets the scene for the arrival of the classical paragon of military and political might:[44]

> Mephosto away.
> And with a solemne noyse of trumpets sound,
> Present before this royall Emperour,
> Great Alexander and his beauteous Paramour. (B 4.1.80–83)

Faustus has become a consummate showman, calling for the sounds that will flatter both living and dead emperors. His calling for these sounds—usually a given in a royal entrance—focuses attention on their theatricality. They are the acoustic signal of power, but can easily be replicated by any actor— or devil.

The show itself begins with the "solemn" (that is, ceremonious) music of the trumpet, which apparently accompanies the entire dumb show:

> Senit. Enter at one the Emperour Alexander, at the other, Darius; they meete, Darius is throwne down, Alexander kils him; takes off his Crowne, and offering to goe out, his Paramour meetes him, he embraceth her, and, sets Darius Crowne upon her head; and coming backe, both salute the Emperour, who leaving his State, offers to embrace them, which Faustus seeing, suddenly staies him. Then trumpets cease, and Musicke sounds. (B 4.1.102 s.d.)

The Emperor is so enamored with the show that he tries to join it, and Faustus, the magician turned theatrical producer, changes the acoustics from blaring trumpets to something more melodic, "musicke" to which the actors can continue to move about the stage in a formalized procession. Faustus must warn the Emperor that these are shades rather than Alexander and his paramour themselves: "My gracious Lord, you doe forget your selfe,/These are but shadoes, not substantiall" (4.1.103–4). Anticipating Shakespeare's

---

44. Militaristic sounds are parodied soon after this scene in the B-text, when a devil's drumming accompanies Mephistopheles and Faustus's ambush of Benvolio's army: "Faustus strikes the dore, and enter a devill playing on a Drum, after him another bearing an Ensigne: and divers with weapons, Mephostophilis with fire-workes; they set upon the Souldiers and drive them out" (B 4.3.105 s.d.).

Puck, Faustus reminds the Emperor that this musical dumb show was a magical conjuring.[45] Faustus's real music, real actors, but fake Greeks remind the audience of the insubstantiality of the theater itself: the actors playing Alexander and his paramour are actual flesh and blood, they are no more resurrected Greeks than the Emperor's conjured spirits are in the reality of the play.

The Emperor, however, demonstrates that there is visual and acoustic power in such shadows, that is, in magical, theatrical, and religious imagining: "O pardon me, my thoughts are so ravished/With sight of this renowned Emperour,/That in mine armes I would have compast him" (B 4.1.105–7). The word "ravished" points again to aural pleasure as well as visual, and to the fact that the scene's sensual power comes in part from its musical accompaniment. If ceremonial and theatrical musics—the kinds hated by Prynne and Stubbes and Northbrooke and Gosson—peaked in classical Greece, they must be the most ravishing and dangerous of all. In fact, anti-music polemicists Henry Smith and John Udall both tried to undermine music's role in religion by attacking the classical discourses that attributed power and comfort to it.[46]

At the same time, in pulling out all the theatrical and musical stops for the Emperor's classical resurrection show, Faustus evokes the ancient traditions that undergird natural magicians' interest in music as well as defenses of music made by all but the staunchest detractors (even Northbrooke admits that music delights reason by its "number and proportions"). That he does not have a better understanding of musical power than the Emperor or anyone else suggests that real knowledge and power are bluffs, fictions perpetuated by a good show.

And while Faustus becomes a great showman himself, his final request is to be an audience member for one more show. The meta-theatrical conjuring of Helen, accompanied by music (in both texts), again associates the theater with magic. As with the Emperor's dumb show, Faustus demands sonic control so that the music and the spectacle of her supposedly peerless beauty can be most effective: "Be silent then, for danger is in words/*Musicke sounds, and Helen passeth over the Stage*" (5.1.25–5.1.25 s.d.). A boy actor would have played Helen, and again music is used to distract the auditor from potential

---

45. "If we shadowes have offended,/Thinke but this (and all is mended)/That you have but slumbered heere/While these visions did appeare./And this weake and idle theame,/No more yeelding but a dreame." *A Midsummer Night's Dream* (Epilogue 1–6).

46. Henry Smith, *The sermons of Maister Henrie Smith gathered into one volume* (1593), 149; John Udall, *A commentarie upon the Lamentations of Ieremy* (1593), 14. See also Willis, *Church Music and Protestantism*, 72.

disappointment, in case the boy did not have a face that could launch a thousand ships.

The conjuring of Helen is another act of theatrical imagination, and its tonal accompaniment reinforces the sense to which this beauty, like the she-devil "wife" presented in act 2, scene 1, is at root a demon's trick. If a popular tune were played at this moment, perhaps a well-known dance song, the moment would suggest Helen's tawdry similarity to any seductive woman, or boy for that matter. If the musicians played a more slow and mysterious melody, possibly in a minor key, the music would enhance the unreality of the trick. Either a popular or odd tune would in different ways call attention to the trickiness of the moment, to the fakeness of Faustus's show. Though he calls her "heavenly Helen," Faustus forsakes heaven's ravishing harmony for a purely sexual ravishment. The power of music to captivate Faustus and enhance this lewd scene points simultaneously to music's sexual connotations and its use in moments signifying transcendent joy, including spiritual rapture. If music's affective and sensual effects can be put to such divergent ends, claims for music's powers over people are man-made constructions, their authority supported only by the mechanisms of show business.

Incantations

While Faustus associates himself early on with natural magicians like Agrippa, he also aligns himself with the dark art of necromancy, the forbidden and feared type of magical demonology involving the revival of dead beings and the conjuring of spirits. "He surffets upon cursed Negromancy," the chorus says, and after he bids divinity adieu, Faustus valorizes the dark art as a new form of bliss: "These Metaphisickes of Magicians/And Negromantike bookes are heavenly" (prologue 25; 1.1.51–52). While Faustus's engagement with natural magic led him to his ultimately futile questions about speculative music, in his attempts at necromancy he tries to harness the occult force of sound to conjure a demon out of nothing.

When it comes to incantation, as John Haines explains, there is a close relationship between traditional Christian liturgy and magic.[47] The work of Haines on music and magic in the Middle Ages as well as Gary Tomlinson's work on music and early modern magic highlight the sense to which the supposed incarnational power of a spell or Mass is not only in its words, but in its sounds. Haines describes incantation as a repertoire of sound that is

---

47. Haines, "Why Music and Magic?," 153–58.

between recitation and song, and when we listen to Faustus's incantations for their acoustic properties (as opposed to or in addition to their linguistic ones), we hear the ways in which Faustus's chants resonate with anxieties expressed in both anti-Catholic and anti-magic discourses about the power of sound over people's minds and bodies.

When the audience first encounters Faustus, they hear him telling himself to "Settle thy studies *Faustus*, and beginne/To sound the deapth of that thou wilt professe" (1.1.1–2). He is thus reminding himself that his journey of study, magic, and conquest will involve both listening and sounding forth. Using the now-obscure sense of the verb "sound" as "to penetrate" in order to describe sinking to his soul's depths, Faustus puns on the fact that he will *make* "sound" when he "profess[es]."[48] Faustus's proclamation to sound the depths of his magic is consistent with a notion shared by Renaissance magicians that language is more potent when sounded than when written. The notion that words have acoustic power can be understood as similar to the perlocutionary forces associated with speech acts.[49] For Agrippa, spoken words have the power to alter people and things: "Words therefore constitute a most fitting bond between the speaker and the listener and carry with them not only the meaning but even the force of the speaker, transmitting and bearing a certain energy to the listener with such strength that not only he but other bodies and even inanimate things are altered."[50] That "certain energy," with its power to alter other beings and things, is exactly what Faustus seeks to understand and harness.

Faustus's incantations at the beginning of the play not only resonate with Catholic liturgical practice, as many critics have pointed out, but also with magical treatises on the power of sound.[51] His ritual is in Latin, the language used for many ancient and contemporary magical treatises as well as the

---

48. He also anticipates the sense of sounding as inquiry developed centuries later: the *OED*'s first cited use of the word "sound" as making inquiry or investigating is Thomas Jefferson in 1793: "They have sent commissioners to England to sound for peace."

49. Speech acts, which have the power to constitute a material reality, are famously defined by J. L. Austin in *How to do Things with Words* (Cambridge: Cambridge University Press, 1962; 1975). For recent work on how speech-act theory illuminates this scene, see Andrew Sofer, *Dark Matter: Invisibility in Drama, Theater, and Performance* (Ann Arbor: University of Michigan Press, 2013), 16–37, and Eric Byville, "How to Do Witchcraft with Speech Acts," *Comparative Drama* 45.2 (2011): 1–33.

50. All Agrippa is from *De occulta philosophia libra tres* (Cologne, 1533). Translated in Gary Tomlinson, *Music in Renaissance Magic*, 59–60. For Agrippa and others, writing mediates and thus diminishes the idea: voice is more powerful in part because it is closer to thought than written word.

51. See, for example, John Parker, *Aesthetics of Antichrist: From Christian Drama to Christopher Marlowe* (Ithaca, NY: Cornell University Press, 2007), 236–43; Waldron, *Reformations of the Body*, 90–97; and Preedy, *Marlowe's Literary Scepticism*, 34–37. Recent productions also stress Catholicism in this moment, including the 2011 productions at the London Globe and Manchester Exchange.

Catholic Mass. He enters the scene "to conjure" and describes his actions as "incantations" (1.3.1 s.d., 1.3.5). Andrew Sofer explains that the incantations here are performative, using the occult force of words to alter reality, and Jay Zysk illuminates the way that Faustus's bodily gestures and Latin language harness Eucharistic power.[52] Certainly, Faustus's words sound like priestly Latin, yet the musicality of his spells is the quality that most resembles the incantatory qualities of the Catholic Mass.

Part of the occult force of Faustus's spells comes from the extra-verbal sounds of chanting; the Faustus actor could even intone rhythm and timbre that sound like the Mass. The Mass—like magic or theater—promises to make something out of nothing. Indeed, Catholic belief in the miracle of ordinary bread turning into the substance of Christ's Body became the basis of associating Catholics with dark magical arts like necromancy. Faustus's Latin incantation conjures not a body out of bread, but a body out of thin air. Sounds make conjuring work for both Catholic priests and magicians: the melodies and words of the Mass and spells have perlocutionary force. In the case of both sound and word, the indecipherability of the sounds—in Latin, obscured by music—led to their suspiciousness for objectors. Zysk also limns a formal relation between mass books and magic books, which contribute to "the blurred distinction between satanic and sacramental conjuration."[53]

But the musicality of the moment also had demonic connotations. While Ficino had speculated in the fifteenth century that magical song had a relationship to demons, he was echoing centuries of tradition that ascribed evil magical powers to music.[54] Isidore of Seville's seventh-century *Etymologies*, for example, warns that magicians "cause much destruction through the violence of song," and that witch's incantations are a "harmful art."[55] While incantations were long associated with evil witchcraft, chanting was also central to salubrious ceremonies that were rooted in antique theories of the music of the spheres and were often performed by lower clerical orders in rites unsanctioned by the church but nonetheless popular throughout the Middle Ages.[56] So, when sixteenth-century evangelicals associate magic and Catholicism, their accusations are grounded in centuries of conflating and

---

52. Sofer, *Dark Matter*, 18–22; Jay Zysk, "The Last Temptation of Faustus: Contested Rites and Eucharistic Representation in *Doctor Faustus*," *Journal of Medieval and Early Modern Studies* 43:2 (2013): 335–67.

53. Zysk, "The Last Temptation of Faustus," 339.

54. Haines, "Why Music and Magic?," 172, and Tomlinson, *Music in Renaissance Magic*, 101–44.

55. Quoted in Haines, "Why Music and Magic?," 156.

56. Richard Kieckhefer, *Magic in the Middle Ages* (Cambridge: Cambridge University Press, 1989), 153–56.

confusing authorized church rites, rogue spells incanted by lower clerics in desperate hopes of medical success, and the legends of witchcraft and demonology. In the sixteenth century, as Jennifer Waldron points out, an incantation like Faustus's could be heard as a kind of "devil's sacrament," an inverted ritual calling on long associations of witchcraft and Catholicism and believed by many to be of real danger.[57]

These magical, folk, and religious traditions are con-fused and mutually constitutive, having in common the notion that words carry more power when incanted than they do when spoken. When Faustus decides to "trie the Uttermost Magicke can perform," he is not clear at all on where, exactly, the acoustic powers originate, or why they seem to have been able to conjure a devil (1.3.15). The audience does not know how this dark magic works, either, and that uncertainty mimics the questions invoked by the sensory betrayal of the Mass: does transformation occur because of priestly intent, does the chanting that voices those words have hidden powers? The pitches and words of liturgical chants were often little changed when performed in non-authorized ritual incantations, and it is thus likely that Faustus's incantations sound simultaneously of Catholic liturgy, unauthorized healing ceremonies, and of the vaguely defined necromantic arts that were more derided and feared than actually practiced.[58]

When the chanting does result in the appearance of a demon, of course, the demon explains that he has arrived *not* because of Faustus's "conjuring speeches," but rather because of Faustus's intention: "That was the cause, but yet *per accidens*" (1.3.46, 47; "*per accidens*" designates an extraneous or nonessential circumstance). The feeling of danger provoked by Faustus comes from the fact that his incantations invoke dangerous, forbidden Catholic and magical sounds. However, according to Mephistopheles (who as a demon may or may not be trustworthy), the sounds of chanting that were so crucial to authorizing the spectacle of the Mass, and so derided by those who feared such incantations as sorcery, are incidental. These sounds have social and political power because of these associations, but they do not, according to Mephistopheles, have occult force. The play leaves uncertain the question of how Mephistopheles could conjure a devil merely by "intent," but it shows that the words and music of chants are unable to conjure bodies out of thin air *or* bread; the chants of necromancy or Catholicism contain no secret

---

57. Waldron, *Reformations of the Body*, 95. Relatedly, Alison Shell has shown how liturgical travesties like the Black Mass "encouraged a belief that Catholic religious language was spiritually void, and therefore wide open to occult influence." Alison Shell, *Oral Culture and Catholicism in Early Modern England* (Cambridge: Cambridge University Press, 2007), 59.

58. Haines, "Why Magic and Music?," 169.

power or wisdom except the power and wisdom of being immensely useful stage tricks.

Communion and Ex-communion

The idea that religion no less than magic uses incantational sounds to bolster legitimacy in the face of unverifiable claims to divine (or magical) knowledge is explored again when Faustus travels to Rome. As in other parodies of religious rite we have seen, Marlowe exploits the multifariousness of the form to create interpretive ambiguity. But rather than suggesting community by exposing religio-musical common ground, as parodies in *Mary Magdalene* and *Ralph Roister Doister* do, the parodic excommunication of *Doctor Faustus* reveals that the sounds of religion are performative tactics that have real social and political effects—they form communities by means of inclusion and exclusion. Divinity and magic are unknowable—perhaps even fictional—but the effects of performances done in their name are very real.

Faustus's actions against the Pope simultaneously resemble those of a Protestant hero and a dark magician, and the Pope and his cardinals' response sounds at once "orthodox" in its exclusion of evil spirits and comically derisive of Catholic rites. Thus, as soon as one interpretation of the scene's religious implications develops, it is undermined by actions that would be condemned by the doctrinal standpoint enabling that interpretation.

Several critics have pointed out the sense to which Faustus becomes a Protestant hero in the scene at the Pope's court: Chloe Preedy describes him as an English Protestant who, on going to Rome, would, in evangelical Anthony Munday's words, "tell the Pope of his lascivious and unchristian life."[59] But whatever satisfaction could be won by evangelicals from seeing the Pope and Cardinals suffer is countered by the fact that Faustus is using dark magic for his pope-baiting practice.

Faustus uses performative sounds to torment the Roman authorities, and the Pope and his cardinals counter with the sounds of the excommunication

---

59. Quoted in Preedy, *Marlowe's Literary Scepticism*, 170. See also John Parker, "Faustus, Confession, and the Sins of Omission," *English Literary History* 80.1 (2013): 40–42; Brett Foster, "Hell is Discovered: The Roman Destination of Doctor Faustus," in *Christopher Marlowe the Craftsman: Lives, Stage, and Page*, eds. Sarah K. Scott and Michael Stapleton (Surrey, UK: Ashgate, 2010), 196. Paul Whitfield White goes so far as to say that Puritans in the audience would have applauded the scene, though one might wonder exactly how many "Puritans" went to *Doctor Faustus*. "Marlowe and the Politics of Religion," in *Cambridge Companion to Christopher Marlowe*, ed. Patrick Cheney (Cambridge: Cambridge University Press, 2004), 81.

ritual. Faustus deliberately recalls the props and sounds of traditional religion when he invites the Roman authorities to curse him:

> . . . bell, booke, and candle, candle, booke, and bell,
> Forward and backward, to curse *Faustus* to hell.
> Anon you shal heare a hogge grunt, a calfe bleate, and an asse braye,
> Because it is S. *Peters* holy day. (3.1.184–87)

While many read sarcasm into Faustus's lines, the narrative fact of the play is that Faustus *is* cursed to hell (just as Bale's King Johan really is excommunicated in the world of that play)—the ritual Faustus calls for, and receives, is redundant by the play's internal logic. At the same time, the absurdity of the situation—and later the staginess of hell—theatrically expose the narratives of damnation and salvation as well as rites of exclusion and inclusion as performative, and even arbitrary.

The sung dirge performed by the Friars quotes the *Maledicate Dominus* ("may God curse him") from the Roman excommunication service:

> *Enter all the Friers to sing the Dirge.*
> Come brethren, lets about our businesse with good devotion.
> *Sing this.*
> Cursed be hee that stole away his holiness meate from the table.
> *Maledicate Dominus.*
> Cursed be hee that stroke his holinesse a blowe on the face. *Maledicate*
>   *Dominus.*
> Cursed be he that tooke Frier *Sandelo* a blow on the pate. *male, &c.*
> Cursed be he that disturbeth our holy Dirge. *male, &c.*
> Cursed be he that tooke away his holinesse wine.
> *Maledicate Dominus.*
> *Et omnes sanctis Amen.* (3.2.87 s.d.–100)

While some critics argue that the dirge demonstrates that Catholicism has no power, others contend that many audience members might well have thought that the rites were actually working.[60] Critical divide on the issue likely parallels a multiplicity of interpretations for contemporary audiences,

---

60. Thomas Healy argues that the exorcism shows that Catholicism is defunct, "*Doctor Faustus*," in Cheney, *Cambridge Companion to Christopher Marlowe*, 185. On the other hand, Foster asks, "Are papal curses somehow efficacious, and does Marlowe mischievously imply it? There is no reason to believe that early audiences entirely wrote off as silly or ineffective the highly controversial acts of exorcism or papal excommunication at the episode's end." "Hell is Discovered," 197.

too. The indeterminacy of the rites' power comes from the very debates of Europe's Reformations, but it is too simplistic to say that "Catholics" would see them as effective, "Protestants" as ineffective. Firstly, of course, audiences were not neatly divided between these categories, and many who outwardly conformed to Elizabethan Protestantism continued to believe in some—if not all—Catholic practices. Moreover, confessional purity is impossible even for the most zealous. But, in addition, the emotional effects of musical rites likely cross any confessional divide.

In the 1580s the sung, Latin *Maledicate Dominus* would not be heard anywhere else—at least publicly—but on the stage. The Friars sing a song to the tune of real rites, tunes sung in England as recently as the 1550s for official use, and long a part of England's ecclesiastic structures. Heard decades later, sounds resembling the liturgical chants of one's youth make listeners recall details of their past as well as the emotions they had once felt. So, while the English words of the rite are comic, the musical sounds could override the theatrical context for audience members of a certain age. In Andy Wood's words, the reformers attempted to "sweep away the signifiers of an earlier culture" in their assault on local memory; this theatrical moment reanimates a musical signifier, complexly representing it in a parodic, theatrical context.[61] Before the complexity of parody could be intellectually processed, the melody likely produced a more emotional response. Born in 1527, Roger Martin recalled in 1590 the church music of his youth; on Palm Sunday a singing procession reached the Lady's Chapel "at which time a boy with a thing in his hand pointed to it, signifying a prophet as I think, sang, standing on the turret . . . and then all did kneel down, and then rising up went and met the sacrament, and so then went singing together into the church."[62] The tunes sung by the Friars—as well as the scene's Latinity and the actual props of bell, book, and candle (at least specified for use in the B-text, and possibly Marian remnants)—could evoke nostalgia as specific as Martin's (B 3.3.94 s.d.). So, while divinity is inconclusive, the social resonances of these nostalgic rites give them real power, including the power to remind people of former feelings of belonging or exclusion with regard to their past experiences in church. The fact that their affective response and their intellectual one might well be at odds in this moment would destabilize doctrinal inter-

---

61. Andy Wood, *The Memory of the People: Custom and Popular Sense of the Past in Early Modern England* (Cambridge: Cambridge University Press, 2013), 92. Steven Mullaney also writes of reform's assault on memory in the introduction to *The Reformations of Emotion in the Age of Shakespeare* (Chicago: University of Chicago Press, 2015).

62. Roger Martin, "Memories of Long Melford," in *Early Modern Catholicism: An Anthology of Primary Sources*, ed. Robert S. Miola (Oxford: Oxford University Press, 2007), 310–11.

pretation, instead calling attention to the actual way religious music's effects have been constructed socially. An audience member might feel wonder at the sound of the rites even while they know that they should be, according to the play's logic, written off as silly.

The difference between parody and reverence—in Marlowe's play and in all representation—is not always distinct.[63] In a *New York Times* review for the 2011 musical *The Book of Mormon*, an irreverent send-up of the modern-day LDS church and its ecclesiastic history, Ben Brantley describes the complex relationship between represented ritual, parody, and (musical) theater:

> But a major point of 'The Book of Mormon' is that when looked at from a certain angle, all the forms of mythology and ritual that allow us to walk through the shadows of daily life and earth are, on some level, absurd; that's what makes them so valiant and glorious. And by the way, that includes the religion of the musical, which lends ecstatic shape and symmetry to a world that often feels overwhelmingly formless.[64]

Sounding not unlike the Baines Note, Brantley points to the popular power of illogical religious ceremonies.[65] Mocking prelates (or Mormons) on the stage suggests that the blend of absurdity and meaning in the church is not unlike the chicanery of the theater. Even meaningless ceremonies create order; they always have.

As John Parker argues, the "Protestant hero" of this anti-Catholic scene, Faustus, points to the way that, at least for reformers, "the old religion . . . was as demonic and lacking in substance as the commercial theater."[66] But, at the same time, the realities of performance implicate all involved: those in the audience of *Doctor Faustus* cannot deny their participation in the derided art form of Elizabethan commercial drama. Following the radical reformist logic that profane music corrupts one's soul, that friars are devils in disguise, that popish rites are at worst occult and at best empty and ripe for parody, allows one to believe in the plot of *Doctor Faustus*. But that same set of beliefs condemns an audience member to being present at the devil's playhouse,

---

63. Suzan Last says that the play's comic elements are parodic but not satiric, and that parody is "warmer" than satire. "Marlowe's Literary Double Agency: *Doctor Faustus* as a Subversive Comedy of Error," *Renaissance and Reformation* 25 (2000): 24.

64. Ben Brantley, "Missionary Men with Confidence in Sunshine," *New York Times*, March 25, 2011, sec. C.

65. In David Coleman's words, at the least the Baines Note tells us that "the Marlovian interest in ritual and religious ceremony was perceived by his contemporaries, and that it was a potentially controversial and subversive mode of dramaturgy." *Drama and the Sacraments* (Basingstoke, UK: Palgrave Macmillan, 2007), 99.

66. Parker, *Aesthetics of Antichrist*, 242.

which in turn exposes the absurdity of those beliefs. Doctrinal surety is revealed as impossible, but (as with the *The Book of Mormon*), the powerful *effects* of belief are on full display. If the thesis of *Mormon* is something like "religious truth is improvable, but religious belief can sometimes prevent people from doing awful things to each other," the thesis of *Doctor Faustus* is "religious truth is improvable, but religious belief can sometimes allow people to terrify each other." And that which allows religion to invoke emotional nostalgia, to create communities and exclude undesirables, and to terrify believers into preferred behavior is a form of musical theater. Exposing the deceptions of religion by using performance itself, Marlowe's play upholds only performance as that which lends shape and meaning to the world.

Sounds of Heaven and Hell

It is in the doctrine of Last Things—death, judgment, heaven, hell—that religion matters most. Marlowe stages eschatological anxiety in the final scenes of *Doctor Faustus*, using acoustics to demonstrate that the uncertainty of sound's power is linked to the uncertainty of the afterlife. *Doctor Faustus* represents the sounds of heaven (in the B-text) and of hell, unearthly sounds not accessible to human ears and thus unknowable by any on earth.

Doctor Faustus's final act begins with the question of judgment, and as has been often discussed, it pits Calvinist doctrines of double predestination against the more Catholic hope of redemption through the confession of sins, making it famously uncertain if the Good Angel's pleas for last minute repentance would, if taken, redeem Faustus's soul.[67] The B-text dramatizes the centrality of sound in one's salvation or damnation, adding a final return of the Good and Bad Angels. They enter and emphasize the importance of listening to the right sounds:

> Good Angel: Oh Faustus, if thou hadst given eare to me,
>   Innumerable joyes had followed thee.
> But thou didst love the world.

---

67. For an account of critical responses to the predestination versus free will question in *Doctor Faustus*, see Bruce Brandt, "The Critical Backstory," in Deats, *Doctor Faustus: A Critical Guide*, 32–33, and Kristen Poole, "*Dr. Faustus* and Reformation Theology," in *Early Modern English Drama: A Critical Companion*, eds. Garrett Sullivan Jr., Patrick Cheney, and Andrew Hadfield (Oxford: Oxford University Press, 2000), 96–107. Alan Sinfield suggests that Faustus is predestined to hell, but that the play condemns the God who sends him there, and several others suggest that the play is deliberately ambiguous, *Literature in Protestant England, 1560–1660* (London: Croom Helm, 1983).

BAD ANGEL: Gave ear to me,
    And now must taste hels paines perpetually. (B 5.104–8)

Faustus's twenty-four years of musical and other delights have, according to the Bad Angel, damned Faustus; his ears were the opposite of chaste. The "innumerable joyes" he forfeits by giving ear to the sounds of the world, however, are described in terms used to describe the very sounds that damned Faustus. That is, heaven's joys are awkwardly similar to earthly joys—indeed, it is often the sensuality of heaven that entices zealots who force themselves to eschew worldly pleasures.

The afterlife can only ever be described and performed with the resources of the world, but the resources of the world—including those of the theater—can and do have power. The power of music and sound—the power to corrupt one with sensual pleasures, to express prayer to God or confess and absolve sins, to turn bread into body and thin air into devils—has been rendered indeterminable by the competing discourses of music's detractors and defenders, natural magicians, and church doctrines represented by the play. But, as no one knows better than a man of the theater, music and sound have affective and associative power, a power that comes from its players and not necessarily from God or the spheres.

In the B-text, heaven's joys are not only described but also witnessed, only to be withdrawn. Within the narrative context, the dramatic representation of heaven is ironic—it is at this point impossible for Faustus to be saved. The stage directions and the Good Angel's speech indicate the stagecraft:

Musicke while the Throne descends.
GOOD ANGEL: O thou hast lost celestiall happinesse,
Pleasures unspeakeable, blisse without end.
Hadst thou affected sweet divinite,
Hell, or the Divell, had had no power on thee.
Hadst thou kept on that way, Faustus behold,
In what resplendent glory thou hadst set
In yonder throne, like those bright shining Saints,
And triumph over hell, that hast thou lost. (B 5.2.112 s.d.–20)

David Bevington and Eric Rasmussen explain that the throne would have been let down from above by means of a winch, cord, and pulleys, and that Faustus and the audience would see the gilded throne surrounded by saints, who were either painted or portrayed by mute actors.[68] The scene also calls

---

68. Bevington and Rasmussen, *Doctor Faustus*, 46.

on the long theatrical tradition of representing heaven by means of music; the effect is seen in *Mary Magdalene* when Mary ascends into heaven. But whereas the aural and visual representations of heaven are most often staged in the context of a character's triumphant ascension, *Doctor Faustus*'s staged heaven tantalizes Faustus with what he will never have, beginning his torture. The man who has throughout the play been able to conjure and listen to music at will is, for the first time, unable to control sound. He hears sounds he will never hear again—and this is unusual, for heaven's harmonies are presumably reserved for the saved, and never would be heard by the living, especially the damned living. But this is the theater, and the sounds are not *really* from heaven: they're produced by hired musicians who are trying to sound heavenly. The music gives the Faustus actor and the audience a shared acoustic experience of approximated heavenly music, but the actuality of such songs is no more proved than the possibility of a resurrected Helen.

The performed music may not live up to the sublime beauty that would make a virtuous life worthwhile. In theatrical representation, staging heaven's music may support or undermine the play's plot, depending on an audience member's willingness to suspend disbelief. It may be, for example, that, as Steven Justice has claimed for medieval belief in transubstantiation, doubt itself is constitutive of belief, and theatrical testing strengthens one's convictions in an actual heaven.[69] But the performativity of religious belief is nonetheless held up for inspection.

This test of credulity at the final moment is consistent with the play's continued meta-theatrical examination of the theatrics of religious belief. Christians of all denominations hoped for angels' song at their deaths; heaven's music transcends earthly debates about ecclesiastic, profane, and magical music on earth. Believers of various confessional identities in the audience would have in common a desire for this music at the end of life, but its ironic representation may cause them to wonder about their access to such music.

The trope of hearing angels' song at one's death was not only a theatrical tradition. In the late sixteenth century, many people expected to hear singing angels beginning at the moment of their deaths. When Sir Philip Sidney died in 1586, he called for earthly music "to fashion and enfranchise his heavenly soul unto that everlasting harmony of angels, whereof these concords were a kinde of terrestriall echo."[70] The staged music of *Doctor Faustus*, in Thomas Wright's words, should "resembleth in a certain manner the voyces &

69. Steven Justice, "Eucharistic Miracle and Eucharistic Doubt," *Journal of Medieval and Early Modern Studies* 42.2 (2012): 311 and passim.

70. Fulke Greville, *The Life of the Renowned Sir Philip Sidney* (London, 1651), 159.

Harmonye of Heaven."[71] Hooker explains that humans can, at times, experience music on earth that provides a sort of out-of-body experience if it sounds like the music of heaven: "there is also that carrieth as it were into extasies, filling the minde with an heavenly joy, and for the time, in a manner, severing it from the body: So that although we lay altogether aside the consideration of Ditty or Matter, the very Harmony of sounds being framed in due sort, and carried from the Ear to the Spiritual faculties of our Souls."[72] Hooker makes it clear that it is musical notes, not words, that can provide the experience of heaven on earth to a living listener, addressing detractors who saw music as only serviceable inasmuch as it is a vehicle for the Word. So, the representation of heavenly, presumably wordless music could provide an experience like the one Hooker describes, taking the audience out of themselves with its musical sublimity. Such transcendence—which any music lover knows to be possible, at least metaphorically—contradicts the reformist notions of the vanity of earthly harmonies. The theater cannot stage the kind of angel-made song reformers believed in—humans must perform it. Its power and beauty in a dramatic performance tests the powers of representation and anti-music stances at the same time, suggesting that it is likely people—not God or the devil or the heavenly spheres—that causes music to have such affective power.

The far more overwhelming extraterrestrial sounds in *Doctor Faustus*, though, come from hell. Heather Hirschfeld has shown how the entire play can be seen as reworking the *Harrowing of Hell* drama from the mystery cycles, and at the very least it is possible to see how the play borrows from that tradition's theatricality.[73] Seventeenth-century accounts of Restoration performances of *Doctor Faustus* attest to the play's potential to be sonically overwhelming (as well as to its ability to generically transform). "None made such a great noise as his comedy of *Doctor Faustus* with his devils and suchlike tragical sport, which pleased much the humors of the vulgar," writes William Winstanley in 1687.[74] The B-text especially lays the foundation for a noisy play. Faustus's final descent into the hellmouth is likely the loudest moment. As soon as the Good Angel finishes his speech about Faustus's lack of access to heaven's joys, the stage direction reads: "Hell is discovered"

---

71. Wright, *Passions of the Minde*, 206.

72. Hooker, *The Works of Mr. Richard Hooker*, 184.

73. Hirschfeld, *The End of Satisfaction*, 39–57. See also Kurt Schreyer's argument that the opening peals of thunder and the Porter's speech in *Macbeth* recall the soundscapes of the *Harrowing of Hell* pageants. *Shakespeare's Medieval Craft: Remnants of the Mysteries on the London Stage* (Ithaca, NY: Cornell University Press, 2014), 139.

74. William Winstanley, *The Lives of the most famous English poets* (London, 1687), 134. Edward Philips gives a similar account in *Theatrum Poetareum* (London, 1633).

(B 5.2.120 s.d.). Likely, a curtain was drawn to reveal a gaping hellmouth, and out of this jaw came violent noises representing Faustus's future torments.

In staging the discordant sounds of hell—the actual existence of which is untestable—the play ironically presents one of the chief fears used to control religious behavior and morality. Re-staging hell in this deeply destabilizing play calls attention to its theatrical power, while giving little eschatological clarification. Though the epistemology of the power of religious and magical sounds and the actual existence of what they represent is rendered insecure, the final nonverbal sounds of the play borrow their acoustic force from religion to emphasize the surety of the one certain last thing: death.

". . . it tolls for thee"

Faustus's final monologue is accompanied by bells, the tolling of which signals the certainty of death, echoing the bell-ringing rituals that by the 1580s had been used by Catholics for centuries and withstood several attacks by evangelicals in order to remain central to parish life in the Elizabethan church. As is discussed in chapter 3, the religious usage of bells survived the sixteenth century despite attempts to eliminate them and restrictions on their use under Edward VI. In the 1580s passing bells continued to mark the presence of dying souls in a parish, and bells rung for burials. While reformers had tried to limit the use of bells, and using them to mark burials was still contentious, for most early moderns bells resonated deeply and prompted reflection and devotion.[75] Early reformer John Hooper writes of them that "some think that the sound hath power in the soul of men."[76]

While doctrines of salvation and damnation would continue to be contested, there was one certainty on which all could agree. And the terrifying certainty of death is what ultimately grants power to competing truth claims about the uncertainty of what comes after death. There are many reasons that this sound might have such a powerful effect on people, but as its performance in Marlowe's play suggests, it may be one of religion's many acoustic tricks. Whereas the otherworldly sounds of heaven and hell signify great unknowns, the sounds of earthly bells signal the known that animates belief in those unknowns. The sound of bells in Faustus's final hour marks

---

75. Milner, *The Senses and the English Reformation*, 298.
76. John Hooper, "Answer to the Bishop of Winchester's Book," in *Early Writings of John Hooper*, ed. S. Carr (Cambridge: Cambridge University Press, 1843), 97.

the certainty of death against the uncertainty of his many failed epistemic projects.

Brian Walsh writes about how the play's final moment—when three spaced out bells mark the passing of Faustus's final hour in the space of fifty lines—startles the audience into "collective attentiveness."[77] Through the loudness of these recognizable sounds, and the suspense of the drama, "Marlowe creates the conditions for collective contemplation of a universal anxiety over damnation."[78] The phenomenological experience of hearing these bells aligns the audience with Faustus's awareness of his impending doom: it sounds of both passing time and death ritual. Writes John Donne, "[n]ow, this Bell tolling softly for another, saies to me, Thou must die."[79] The bells of the play would remind audiences of their final hour, though it is established social practice and the facts of biology that make this association chilling, not necessarily any special power bells have in and of themselves.

While his death is rendered in acoustic surety, Faustus does not know where to assign agency for his impending doom: to his parents (and by extension, the creator of his prenatal soul), to himself, or to the Devil:

Curst be the parents that ingendered me:
No Faustus, curse thy selfe, curse *Lucifer*,
That hath deprived thée of the joyes of heaven:
    The clocke striketh twelve.
O it strikes, it strikes, now body turn to ayre,
Or *Lucifer* will béare thee quick to hel:
    Thunder and lightning.
Oh soul, be changed into little water drops,
And fal into the *Ocean*, nere be found:
My God, my God, looke not so fierce on me:
Enter divels. (5.2.113–20 s.d.)

The clock bells and the sound of thunder accelerate Faustus's descent, acoustically assuring him and the audience of his upcoming destruction. Faustus,

---

77. Brian Walsh, "Marlowe and the Elizabethan Theatre Audience," in *Christopher Marlowe in Context*, eds. Emily C. Bartels and Emma Smith (Cambridge: Cambridge University Press, 2013), 75.

78. Ibid., 76.

79. John Donne, *Devotions* (London, 1624), 410.

like Shakespeare's Richard II who also hears discordant sounds before his death, wasted time, and now doth time waste him.[80]

Faustus's final indecision about whom to curse for his destruction iterates the play's central, horrible unknowable: we do not know what dooms or saves us anymore than we know whether we are destined for heaven, hell, or neither. Do our choices and deeds damn or redeem us, or has God already chosen our fate? But it's not just Faustus's words—and the pressure of the angels and Old Man—that raise the questions, as many critics have discussed. Hearing a sound that signals the related phenomena of time passing and traditional death practices would remind audiences simultaneously of mortality and the recent religious contentiousness of death practices. Death is certain; the exact nature of the afterlife echoes with the horrors of bottomless uncertainty.

In the theater, bells are sound effects, used to manipulate and to scare audiences. Marlowe uses them, too, in *Massacre at Paris*, where they accompany the brutal slaughter of Huguenots in the name of religion.[81] In both plays, Marlowe uses sounds with spiritual valences—Catholic, Protestant, classically philosophical-magical—to dramatize recent slaughters made in the name of religion and to represent a world from legend in which devils carry sinners off to hell. Is it surprising, *Massacre at Paris* asks, that fear and uncertainty about such questions leads to the political, destructive uses of religion? And is it plausible, *Doctor Faustus* asks, that indulgence in the pleasures of music, magic, and the theater itself should send a man to hell? Marlowe exposes religious logic to parody, contestation, and ridicule, undermining the very controversies for which countless had died.

Raising serious questions about spirituality and sonic efficacy, Marlowe exposes sound as a tool of theatrical power, one gaining its strength through social and political performance, not through gods or heavenly spheres or the devil. It is not, as critics have pointed out, that *Doctor Faustus* presents an atheistic worldview.[82] Rather, the play presents the folly of religious certainty by presenting competing truth claims. Music's powerful role in religion, the danger of being ravished by sensuous sounds, the science of celestial harmonies—all of these issues were debated because people wanted to pre-

---

80. Before his death, Richard hears music outside his prison cell: "Musicke do I heare?/Ha, ha? Keepe time: How sowre sweete Musicke is,/When time is broke/ . . . I wasted Time, and now doth Time waste me" (5.4.45–47, 54).

81. The end of scene 6 indicates that the theater would echo with the sounds: "the ordinance being shot of, the bell tolles" (6.61 s.d.). Christopher Marlowe, "Massacre at Paris," in *The Complete Works of Christopher Marlowe*, vol. 5, ed. Edward Esche (Oxford: Clarendon Press, 1998), 317–62.

82. White, "Marlowe and the Politics of Religion," 86; Gillian Woods, "Marlowe and Religion," in Bartels and Smith, *Christopher Marlowe in Context*, 230.

dict the movement of the soul after death. Marlowe's play unveils how religious powers, ceremonial music, and magic—all contested enchantments—are mutually constitutive and lacking in individual authority. Like Mephistopheles, actors, magicians, and priests borrow each other's acoustic tricks, but if these sounds are damning, then all attending the theater are also damned. Hard-line religious ideologies are necessarily compromised, reliant on other viewpoints to have power or even make sense. Thus, these viewpoints are inherently hypocritical in any form that does not admit to their contingency.

The real power of religion is all too terrestrial in *Doctor Faustus*. Sensual dances, chants, excommunication rituals, death rites, heavenly harmonies, bells: these sounds certainly have social and political power, and Marlowe experiments with the powers of music, theater, and liturgy in exploiting sound for his own dramatic ends. Those who made and debated sounds in early modern England achieved great ends—religious reforms, publication, popular success—but do these sounds matter beyond the sublunar world? Marlowe's play exposes that philosophical and theological knowledge is only ever "seeming," that competing claims to truth only make sense in terms of each other, and gain their power through performance.

If the epistemic failures and performative successes of religion anticipate Macbeth's nihilistic "Tale/Told by an Ideot, full of sound and fury/Signifying nothing," Shakespeare asserts a different conclusion in two of his final plays (5.5.26–28). Avowing that human artistic power—including theatrical power—can do more than deceive or mask a lack of divine order, the diverse sounds of *The Tempest* and *The Winter's Tale* lead not to unresolved discord, but to the fragile harmonies of reconciled communities.

Chapter 6

Arts to Enchant

The Tempest and *The Winter's Tale*

If this be Magick, let it be an Art
Lawfull as Eating.

—*The Winter's Tale*

Art is magic delivered from the lie of being the truth.

—Theodor Adorno

When it comes to religious, musical, and the-
atrical life in early modern England, 1611 was an important year.[1] In the year
that the *King James Bible* was first printed, William Byrd, that great composer
of both Catholic and Anglican church music, published his last and most
diverse songbook, *Psalms, Songs, and Sonnets*, while the King's Men presented
The Winter's Tale and *The Tempest*.[2] That these religious, theatrical, and musical achievements should so concur may be mere coincidence, but they were
shaped by similar forces. The subtitle of Byrd's final songbook even employs
the same phrase the publisher used to describe Shakespeare's comedies in a
preface to a 1609 quarto of *Troilus and Cressida*: Byrd promotes his songs as
"some solemn, some joyful, *framed to the life* of the words."[3] Turning the

---

1. To hear the music discussed in this chapter, listen to the CD accompanying Ross Duffin's
Shakespeare's Songbook (New York: W. W. Norton & Company, 2004); the CD accompanying
Christopher Marsh, *Music and Society in Early Modern England* (Cambridge: Cambridge University
Press, 2011), which includes recordings of ballads, knells, and psalm singing; the recordings of ballads found on EBBA at www.ebba.english.ucsb.edu; and any recordings of William Byrd's music,
for example, The Tallis Scholars, *The Tallis Scholars Sing William Byrd* (Gimell, 2007), 2 compact discs,
and Ensemble Plus Ultra, *William Byrd: Gradualia (1607)* (Musica Omnia, 2008), compact disc.

2. Simon Forman saw a performance of *The Winter's Tale* on May 15, 1611, and it was performed at court on November 5, 1611; *The Tempest* was performed at court on November 1, 1611.

3. Kerry McCarthy, *Byrd* (Oxford: Oxford University Press, 2013), 208. Emphasis mine.

phrase back to Shakespeare, the sacred and profane music of two of the playwright's final three single-authored plays can be similarly described.

The topic of Shakespeare's religious ambiguity has been a major interest in the early twenty-first century, but while most critics explore the issue by studying his plays' texts and visual spectacles, I argue that the religious diversity—even inclusiveness—that many see as characteristic of these plays is most perfectly rendered musically, where the metaphorical power of social concord and the persistent idea of universal harmony lend extra charge to performed songs.[4] In the aftermath of the Gunpowder Plot and in the context of ongoing attempts by the clergy and laity to compromise regarding the use of music in the early Jacobean church, the harmonies of *The Tempest* and *The Winter's Tale* resonate with the urgency of religious and social cooperation.

Like *Doctor Faustus*, these two plays represent music as both a speculative and practical art with myriad potentials for use and abuse. And, again like Marlowe's play, they ultimately suggest that the real power of music comes not so much from unexplained sources as from human performance and human myth making. But in Shakespeare's late plays, the human element of music—its capacity for artistry and cooperation—makes it capable of not only deception and coercion, but also reconciliation.[5] In these plays, it is revealed that while theater gets sacramental power from religious allusion, the church likewise gains authority from theatrical techniques. Whereas this kinship between stage and church seems to be a source of disdainful skepticism for Marlowe, Shakespeare's representation of the human-made commonalities between theatrical and religious narrative, masques, and musical deceptions is rather a cause for cautious celebration. In *The Tempest*, Shakespeare warns against the abuses of music's vaguely defined but commonly believed magical and spiritual powers, yet stages a model of artistic and social harmony reliant on the yielding of authority and the acquisition of real empathy. In *The Winter's Tale*, Leontes's perversion of practical and speculative music is of a piece with his tyrannical delusions, pernicious fallacies that can only be righted by Autolycus's deceptive and lecherous songs, the

---

4. For a recent survey of Shakespeare and religion studies, see David Scott Kastan, *A Will to Believe: Shakespeare and Religion* (Oxford: Oxford University Press, 2014), 8–11. See also Alison Shell, *Shakespeare and Religion* (London: Arden, 2010). I agree with Maurice Hunt's assertion that Shakespeare was preoccupied "with resolving, or harmonizing, conflicting points of view." *Shakespeare's Religious Allusiveness: Its Play and Tolerance* (Aldershot, UK: Ashgate, 2004), 239.

5. In privileging artistic power in these plays, this part of my argument is in line with, for example, Richard McCoy's *Faith in Shakespeare* (Oxford: Oxford University Press, 2013) and Gillian Wood's *Shakespeare's Unreformed Fictions* (Oxford: Oxford University Press, 2013).

shepherds' dances, and the staged musical magic of Hermione's resurrection. While music and art thus appear as deceptive and distracting as any puritanical treatise might claim, *The Winter's Tale* clarifies this perspective to suggest that the inherently deceptive qualities of art and religious experience make them paradoxically best able to inspire penance and forgiveness.

Situating the music of *The Winter's Tale* and *The Tempest* in early Jacobean religious and social contexts—which include the rising popularity of the masque, the growing field of scientific acoustics, and reforming polemicists' continued opposition to papist liturgy, music, and theater—helps one hear how the plays' musical moments call for religious and artistic liberty. Censorship of controversial religious material—long promoted and enforced by law starting in 1606—encouraged Shakespeare "to use indirection and ambiguity in handling both general and specifically topical religious subject matter."[6] Accordingly, the classicized *Winter's Tale* and fantastical *Tempest* prove more open in arrangement and oblique in topic than any of the plays discussed in previous chapters of this book.

Both plays were written after the King's Men had taken over the former Dominican priory Blackfriars, a unique acoustical space that included a "new music consort [that] brought the largest single alteration to the King's Men's practices."[7] Indeed, the King's Men began to pay their band in 1609, and the consort's skilled instrumentalists became the highest paid production personnel.[8] The success of this "more fully articulated field of sound" led the company to retrofit their outdoor venue, the Globe, with a curtained music room above the stage.[9] Stage music and song soon became "what differentiated the King's Men at the Globe from other amphitheater companies."[10] While most of Shakespeare's plays are highly musical, later plays capitalized

---

6. Arthur Marotti, "Shakespeare and Catholicism," in *Theater and Religion: Lancastrian Shakespeare*, ed. Richard Dutton, Alison Findlay, and Richard Wilson (Manchester, UK: Manchester University Press, 2003), 219. In 1606 Parliament passed "an act to restrain the abuses of players," outlawing any use of the names God, Christ, the Holy Ghost, or any member of the Trinity on the stage. Andrew Gurr, *The Shakespearean Stage 1574–1642* (Cambridge: Cambridge University Press, 1970), 54.

7. Andrew Gurr, *The Shakespearian Playing Companies* (Oxford: Clarendon Press, 1996), 368.

8. See, for example, Marsh, *Music and Society*, 132.

9. This is the phrase Bruce Smith uses to describe the acoustic changes in Shakespeare's plays after the move to Blackfriars, in *The Acoustic World of Early Modern England: Attending to the O-Factor* (Chicago: University of Chicago Press, 1999), 221.

10. Gurr, *The Shakespearian Playing Companies*, 368. On the performance of music and the importance of sound on the Shakespearean stage, see especially, Joseph Ortiz, *Broken Harmony: Shakespeare and the Politics of Music* (Ithaca, NY: Cornell University Press, 2011); Erin Minear, *Reverberating Song in Shakespeare and Milton* (Aldershot, UK: Ashgate, 2011); David Lindley, *Shakespeare and Music: Arden Critical Companions* (London: Arden, 2006); and Wes Folkerth, *The Sound of Shakespeare* (London: Routledge, 2002).

on the musical sophistication afforded by these changes to the company's consort and venue.

Whether the plays were performed in public or private, their audiences were religiously diverse. Blackfriars provided a particularly interesting audience of known Catholic recusants, and indeed this enclave of "cultural inclusiveness" emerged as London's most fashionable center for Masses, which were held in another part of the building.[11] As with any of the periods studied in this book, there were those who were labeled as recusant Catholics (or Papists), discontented Puritans, or conforming Anglicans, but everyone was influenced by the doctrinal mix of England's early seventeenth century. "Puritans," as they were called by their contemporaries (though that unitary term obscures a great deal of confessional diversity), became more and more shrill in their disparagement of all or most music, including that of the professional theater. Many such nonconforming reformers enjoyed music in private, but "public worship was another matter entirely."[12] To counter such attacks, more defenses of music were copiously written, printed, and even sung by everyone from church leaders to anonymous ballad-writers.[13]

As has been discussed in the previous two chapters, liturgical music in the parishes had been transformed into unaccompanied psalm singing: the "bare ruined choirs" of Shakespeare's sonnet 73 were aural as well as architectural losses.[14] The writer of the "Treatise on Church Music" from around 1610 blames Elizabeth for the fact that she restricted, "if not wholly supprest,"

---

11. Richard Wilson, *Secret Shakespeare: Studies in theater, religion, and resistance* (Manchester, UK: Manchester University Press, 2004), 266. For more on the vitality of early modern English Catholicism, see, for example, Alison Shell, *Oral Culture and Catholicism in Early Modern England* (Cambridge: Cambridge University Press, 2007); Ronald Corthell, Frances Dolan, Christopher Highley, and Arthur Marotti, eds. *Catholic Culture in Early Modern England* (Notre Dame, IN: University of Notre Dame Press, 2007); and Arthur Marotti, *Religious Ideology and Cultural Fantasy: Catholic and Anti-Catholic Discourses in Early Modern England* (Notre Dame, IN: University of Notre Dame Press, 2005). While scholars such as Wilson and Velma Bourgeois Richmond (in *Shakespeare, Catholicism, and Romance* [New York: Continuum, 2000]) are interested in "proving" Shakespeare's Catholic ties, most scholars agree with Alison Shell's sentiment that "the sympathetic recollection of medieval religion seems to have been possible for both Catholics and conformists, and does not necessarily betoken sympathy for the new Catholicism." *Shakespeare and Religion* (London: Arden, 2010), 16.

12. Jonathan Willis, "Protestant Worship and the Discourse of Music in Reformation England," in *Worship and the Parish Church in Early Modern Britain*, eds. Natalie Mears and Alec Ryrie (Surrey, UK: Ashgate, 2013), 133. Willis gives the example of Andrew Willet, who played the organ alone but railed against the use of instruments and polyphonic song in churches.

13. For an account of early modern defenses and denigrations of music, see Marsh, *Music and Society*, 71–106.

14. See Eamon Duffy's essay on this sonnet's Catholic resonances, "Bare ruined choirs: remembering Catholicism in Shakespeare's England," in *Theatre and Religion: Lancastrian Shakespeare*, eds. Richard Dutton, Alison Findlay, and Richard Wilson (Manchester, UK: Manchester University Press, 2003), 1–39.

singing stipends, indicating that this had led to "decay of Musick." The result of this defunding of national religious music was, according to this writer, that "the estimacion & reputacion of songe in Churches (except Geneva psalmes) was in short tyme in no regard (nay in detestacion) with the Comon people. Thus the estimacion of singing [was] diminished in the myndes almost of all men (which was one speciall policye of these pretented reformers)."[15] Indeed, congregational singing of metrical psalms had been the primary music of the parish throughout Elizabeth's reign. But even as parish music was unprofessional and unadorned, Elizabeth I employed such musical luminaries as Byrd and Thomas Tallis to compose for the choirs and musicians of her Chapel Royal. By the time James I became king, then, there were several polyphonic anthems being sung in some cathedrals; so, while there continued to be a nostalgia for a musical culture eroded by the reformations, elite religious spaces featured a robust musical program employing the finest composers, choristers, and organists. Musical tolerance and diversity had become something of a luxury item, a prerogative of the royal household.

Historians have traditionally described the religious transformations of the English Reformations as a time when music, liturgy, and preaching were in an antagonistic relationship, and in which preaching won out over word-obscuring polyphonic singing and instrumental music; indeed, the *Treatise on Church Music* writer laments the way church musicians lost their "lyvinges . . . or els [were] at least to putt the reverence to preaching onlye."[16] While there was certainly hearty debate about the proper role of church music; the social, political, and legal ramifications of creating and consuming such music; and the censorship of art in conflict with official policies, recent work by musicologists and historians has shown that the early seventeenth century was marked by efforts on the parts of many to reconcile the different spiritual modes of preaching and song. Peter McCullough argues that in the sermons and writings of some churchmen who were working while Shakespeare composed these late plays, one finds "the integration of music, liturgy, and sermon in a brief period of pre–Civil War English church history when it seemed the three might coexist rather than be conceived of as mutually exclusive."[17] I believe that it is in this spirit of finding amicable coexistence

---

15. "Treatise on Church Music" (1610?), MS 18 B XIX, Royal Collection, British Library, 5v.

16. Ibid., 5v.

17. Peter McCullough, "Music Reconciled to Preaching: A Jacobean Moment?," in Mears and Ryrie, *Worship and the Parish Church*, 116. See also John Craig, "Psalms, groans, and dog whippers: the soundscape of worship in the English parish church, 1547–1642," in *Sacred Space in Early Modern Europe*, eds. Will Coster and Andrew Spicer (Cambridge: Cambridge University Press, 2005), 104–23.

between word, art, and ritual that *The Tempest* and *The Winter's Tale* were written. In these plays, Shakespeare represents the various practical musics sounding throughout England even as he makes this music evoke divine, magical, and heavenly sources. But, in such highly meta-theatrical plays, as we will see, the real power and enchantment of music ultimately comes not from speculations about extraterrestrial resonances, but rather from the earthly, practical performances of human players.

Ariel's Enchanting Songs

If *Doctor Faustus* links the magician, the priest, and the player to expose how the only provable powers—including acoustic powers—of magic and religion are mere stagecraft, *The Tempest* creates the same links, but rather concludes that such artistry can attend genuine productive power.[18] The play's soundscape—its performed songs and acoustic effects and its musical metaphors and allusions—reveals music to be an agent of deception and coercion, one that allows the magician-director Prospero to trick or enslave Caliban, Ariel, and the shipwrecked lords. Yet, as the play progresses, it suggests that the very properties of music that give it these maleficent powers are the same properties that can bring about and signify forgiveness and reconciliation. That which gives music power in the world of *The Tempest* and the world of the seventeenth-century church are the same: human authority, human artfulness, human capacities for emotion. Thus, when Prospero listens to others rather than drowning out all sounds but his own, music and all its deceptive charms move him and others to the empathy needed to form a tenuous harmony. *The Tempest*, like *Doctor Faustus*, swirls with many discourses—magical, religious, and scientific—that seemingly ascribe the authority of music to higher powers. However, the play ultimately suggests that music's most compelling powers come from human skill and cooperation.

Most of the play's songs are performed by Ariel, who embodies not only magical and religious claims to music's potency, but also the theatrical power of music. Both captive and capturer, Ariel performs Prospero's bidding for

---

18. For an influential discussion of the theatricality of Prospero's magic, see Alvin Kernan, *The Playwright as Magician: Shakespeare's Image of the Poet in the English Public Theater* (New Haven, CT: Yale University Press, 1979), 156–59. For Prospero as priest, see, for example, Todd Edmundson, "Prospero's Exile and the Tempest of the English Reformation," *Religion and the Arts* 14 (2010): 252–66.

all but his final song. That is, Ariel is servant-church musician-actor to the play's master-priest-stage director. But while Prospero has Ariel use the power of music to deceive and coerce the island's inhabitants and visitors, the social powers of Ariel's acoustic deceptions are, in the end, salubrious to both the play's human characters and his magical self.

Ariel's non-human status is part of what invites diverse and meta-theatrical interpretations of the music the actor playing Ariel performs. He is defined in the First Folio's dramatis personae as "an ayrie spirit." The phrase is practically tautologous; "spirit" could mean any airy, immaterial being, as in the Middle English *Cloud of Unknowing*, which explains that "the devil is a spirit & of his owne kynde. He hath no body."[19] Because an audience can't quite know—either in performance or in reading—what Ariel's (non)body is supposed to look like when it is not shape-shifting into various gendered forms at Prospero's behest, Ariel's unknowable form is one of the ways the play limits an audience's ability to assign singular, definitive religious, political, magical, or social meanings to his music.

The sounds of the play's opening trick, the tempest Ariel conjures and conducts, are powered by magic in the play's plot, but by apparent stagecraft in the world of the theater; this is the case for all of Ariel's acoustic deceits and songs. Right away, then, the force of magic is of a piece with the tricks of theater: the no-doubt impressive drumming noises that create the acoustic effects of a storm in the Globe or Blackfriars create theatrical magic.[20] The storm at first appears to the audience (and to the lords and mariners) as a natural phenomenon, perhaps created by a God who may or may not answer their prayers to end it (1.1.50, 52). The Boatswain's sarcastic suggestion that the councilor Gonzalo "command these Elements to silence, and worke the peace of the present" (1.1.21–22) prefigures the revelation in the next scene that the storm *has* been commanded by an authority figure. But revealing that Prospero's authority and Ariel's magic have orchestrated the rather unnatural storm begins the play's meta-theatrical exploration of the staging of acoustic deceit.

The storm rages on through most of act 1, scene 2, and the unheard command between Prospero and Ariel is likely a direction to end the storm:

---

19. *The Cloud of Unknowing*, trans. A.C. Spearing (London: Penguin Books, 2002), 80. Shakespeare uses the word to mean an incorporeal being, a person's ghost, the Holy Spirit, an actor, sperm, and a spiritual essence. R. Chris Hassel Jr., *Shakespeare's Religious Language: A Dictionary* (New York: Continuum, 2005), 340. For more on the etymology of these terms and how they give a contemporary actor liberty to create a character, see my "Ariel's Liberty," *Shakespeare Bulletin* 26.1 (2008): 23–42.

20. Lindley, *Shakespeare and Music*, 97.

Enter Ariel, like a water-Nymph

PROSPERO: Fine apparision: my queint Ariel,
    Hearke in thine ear.
ARIEL: My Lord, it shall be done. (1.2.317 s.d.–19)[21]

Ariel performs this task musically, simultaneously calming both the seas and the stranded Ferdinand as he sings "Come Unto These Yellow Sands."

This opening song refers to the musical sounds of both the Church and ideas of natural magic; it also calls to mind early modern perspectives on the socializing potential of non-religious music and dance. The lost son reports after hearing the tune: "This Musicke crept by me upon the waters/Allaying both their fury, and my passion/With it's sweet ayre" (1.2.392–94). By simultaneously allaying the water's fury and Ferdinand's passion, Ariel's music seems to demonstrate the ancient notion that music's socializing and curative properties flow from a profound resonance with the order of the natural universe.[22] By 1611, the word and concept of "sympathy" referred to both occult sympathies between different ontological states, like between music and the natural world, and also social accord, that is, sympathetic harmony between people. Ariel's song seems to create sympathy with both nature and Ferdinand, dramatizing an explanation for music's power found in defenses of music. The anonymous *Praise of Musicke*, for example, suggests that a personified Nature used music to create the world, explaining that:

To prove this looke upon the frame, & workmanship of the whole worlde, whether there be not above, an harmony between the spheares, beneath a simbolisme between the elements. Looke upon a man, whom the Philosophers termed a litle world, whether the parts accord not one to the other by consent and unity. And who can blame nature in any reason for using her owne invention?[23]

---

21. Quotations again come from the Norton *First Folio Facsimile*, with line numbers from *The Tempest: Arden Shakespeare*, eds. Virginia Mason Vaughan and Alden T. Vaughan (London: Arden, 1999).

22. Linda Austern summarizes: "music was a physical force of nature with evident influence on visible and invisible bodies," and its effects to this end were studied by philosophers, musicians, physicians, and occult practitioners alike. Austern, "'Tis Nature's Voice': Music, Natural Philosophy and the Hidden World in Seventeenth-Century England," in *Music Theory and Natural Order from the Renaissance to the Early Twentieth Century*, eds. Suzannah Clark and Alexander Rehding (Cambridge: Cambridge University Press, 2001), 30. For more on *The Tempest*'s magical discourses, see also Gareth Roberts, "'An Art Lawful as Eating'?: Magic in *The Tempest* and *The Winter's Tale*," in *Shakespeare's Late Plays: New Readings*, eds. Jennifer Richard and James Knowles (Edinburgh: Edinburgh University Press, 1999), 124–44; and Ian McAdam, "Magic and Gender in Late Shakespeare," in *Late Shakespeare 1608–1613*, eds. Andrew J. Power and Rory Loughnane (Cambridge: Cambridge University Press, 2013), 243–61.

23. *The Praise of Musicke* (Oxenford: Joseph Barnes, 1586), 2–3.

The notion that the world reflects the "harmony between the spheares" and that humans are microcosms of this system informs Ferdinand's understanding of music's ameliorating effects; this was a central tenet of natural magic, scientific discourse on acoustics, and many religious defenses of music, which ascribed these correspondences to God's design.

Just as this first song evokes natural magic, scientific discourse, and religious defenses of music, the words of Ariel's sea-calming song metaphorically order a more mundane partner dance between wave and sand:

> Come unto these yellow sands
> And then take hands;
> Curtsied when you have, and kist
> The wilde waves whist;
> Foote it featly here, and there, and sweete Sprights beare the burden.
>   (1.2.376–80)

As the Arden 3 editors explain, the kissing refers to a customary country dance directive for couples to kiss on certain beats, and "foot it featly" means "dance skillfully." Some early moderns thought that dance steps were analogous to the movement of the celestial spheres, thus tying the song further to the music of the spheres that undergirds natural magic. For poet John Davies, "dauncing" began "when the first seedes whereof the earth did spring," so that

> . . . Natures mighty King,
> [Did] leave their first disordered combating;
> And in a daunce such measure to observe,
> As all the world their motion should observe."[24]

Several early modern Christians, often humanists, proposed that partner dancing was an ideal model of social concord. Thomas Elyot's educational *The Boke Named the Governour*, for example, explains that man and woman dancing together "betokeneth concord" as in a marriage, implying that perhaps Ariel's courtship dance between land and sea previews Ferdinand's marital accord with Miranda.[25] But the music at this early stage remains a deception: Prospero has his own motives for calming the sea and the man.

---

24. John Davies, *Orchestra or a Poeme of da;ncing Judicially proving the true observation of time and measure* (London, 1596), A5v.

25. Thomas Elyot, *The Boke named the Governer* (London, 1531), 1.235.

However, the ruse's emotional effect—the calming of Ferdinand—is authentic within the play's story (as will be his bond with Miranda). Ferdinand's uninformed explanation of music's emotional power calls extraterrestrial acoustic authority into question, for the audience knows that in the world of the play, the song is a magic trick ordered by a human (and in the world of the theater, a performance by an actor). Music's ability to calm people in moments of agitation and to evoke emotional paternal bonds comes from its performance and human connection more than unexplained, speculative magic.

In calling to mind ancient musical theories, natural magic, the Gospels, and social dancing, the sounds of "Come Unto These Yellow Sands" present Ferdinand with a puzzle, and the audience with a complex web of signification. That puzzle is instantiated and augmented by the crux that is the Ariel actor's non-mimetic body.[26] The Ariel actor's body is not imitating a human character's body, as is the case for most actors who enact human characters, but rather his body stands in for a spirit whose form(s) an audience must imagine. This paradox is manifest in the stage direction before he enters singing "Come unto these yellow sands": "*Enter Ferdinand & Ariel, invisible playing & singing*" (1.2.375 s.d.). So, the body of the actor playing Ariel produces sounds that are audible to humans (both the play's characters and the audience) but these sounds are signifiers for which audience interpretation is less or differently guided than it is for the bodies and voices of most other characters.

The spiritual or magical underpinnings of "Come Unto These Yellow Sands" are as Protean and invisible as Ariel himself, and because an audience cannot fully comprehend what sort of being he represents, definitive interpretations of the song's allusions and metaphors become impossible. What is clear is that Ariel's music and lyrics are for human benefit, as he translates his spirit world into the tones and words that Ferdinand and the audience can understand. Deliberately elusive and allusive, music demonstrates a sympathetic collaboration between different ways of understanding the world and its workings, none of which can be proved or disproved. The only certainty, as in *Doctor Faustus*, is that the man-made theater—its actors and its musicians—is able to create the acoustic effects that have real power on humans. As we have seen expressed throughout this book, one of the

---

26. Leslie Wade Soule describes the "non-mimetic function" of the actor, enacting his presence and skills rather than imitating a character, in *Actor as Anti-Character: Dionysius, the Devil, and the Boy Rosalind* (Westport, CT: Greenwood Press, 2000), 3.

key sources of music's influence is that its evocation of ambiguous spiritual dimensions can be used both to mislead and to compel its listeners; to elevate and to capture them; to evoke genuine experience and to intimate a false reality.

Ariel's next song uses the ambitious notion of music's supernatural power to authorize a lie, but it is nonetheless a lie that produces real affective and social effects in the world of the play. "Full Fathom Five," the ditty that "remember[s Ferdinand's] drown'd father" is, according to its onstage auditor, "no mortall business, nor no sound/that the earth owes" (1.2.406–7). It is wrong about the business of mortality, lying about the death of Alonso. While the song is often read allegorically—as prefiguring Alonso's "sea change" later in the play—it is also a necessary lie, for Prospero cannot manipulate Ferdinand without him thinking that his father has died.[27] The falsely elegiac song thus demonstrates the power of suggestion, the ability of music to deepen one's agitated mood rather than to calm it, as the previous song had done.[28] John Bodenham's poem "Of Paine" (1600) describes this phenomenon: "Sad musicke to sad passions, addes more paine."[29] While "Come Unto These Yellow Sands" had the effect of "allaying" Ferdinand's worry, "Full Fathom Five" schizophrenically undoes that work by using music to further his lonely melancholy.

The lying words of "Full Fathom Five" have clear religious echoes when the "dead" father is aurally memorialized:

ARIEL: *Sea Nimphs hourly ring his knell.*
[SPIRITS]: Burthen: *Ding dong.*
ARIEL: *Harke now I heare them.*
[SPIRITS]: *Ding-dong bell.* (2.2.403–6)[30]

The song thus describes, then vocally simulates, the sounds of the traditional English funeral. As discussed in chapters 3 and 5, bells survived even the

---

27. Lindley also points this out in *Shakespeare and Music*, 224. For a musicological reading of Robert Johnson's musical setting as enacting an acoustic sea change, see Jacquelyn Fox-Gold, "Other Voices: The Sweet, Dangerous Air(s) of *The Tempest*," *Shakespeare Studies* 24 (1996): 241–75. The setting can be found in Duffin, *Shakespeare's Songbook*, 157–59.

28. The use of music to calm the mood of one who is upset, part of the function of "Come Unto These Yellow," can be summed up by John Playford's explanation of music as something that "gently breaths and vents the Mourners Grief." *A breefe introduction to the skill of musick for song & viol* (London, 1654), A5r.

29. In John Bodenham, *Bel-vedére, or, The Garden of the muses* (London, 1600), 206.

30. While the First Folio gives the whole of the song's last line to Ariel, I agree with the Arden 3 editors that it is likely that both "Ding dong" burdens were song by the Spirits in performance.

harshest iconoclasm, remaining central to Anglican practice. In the "Ding
Dong Bells," Ferdinand hears that the island's natural world is alive with the
sounds of the Christian church (both past and present), and echoing with
the sounds emotionally linking the play's auditors to the certainty of death,
and to each other, in their Christian communities.[31] Sounds played and
evoked thus reproduce feelings of grief in Ferdinand—feelings that allow
Prospero to manipulate him, but also that enable the son's openness to the
play's final reconciliations.

Alonso reports that Ariel's music lulled him into believing a lie, too, and
this acoustic deception is also described in terms of Christianized musical
instruments and the sounds of the natural world:

> The windes did sing it to me: and the Thunder
> (That deep and dreadfull Organ-Pipe) pronounc'd
> The name of *Prosper*: it did base my Trespasse,
> Therefore my Sonne i'th Ooze is bedded . . . (3.3.97–100)

Ascribing truth-telling power to sounds of the natural world and conflating
natural and church noises, this musical description evokes the still common
practice of Christianizing the music of the spheres: Lorenzo does the same
when describing them to Jessica in *Merchant of Venice*.[32] When seventeenth-
century pamphleteer John Taylor described church music in Germany, he
noted that the voices and instruments "all strike up together, with such a
glorious and delicious harmony, as if the Angellicall musicke of the Sphears
were descended into that earthly Tabernacle."[33] Both Ferdinand and Alonso
hear nature echo with the authority of the Church's sounds—death knells
and organ pipes—and are confident that these funereal noises betoken each
other's deaths. But they have gone astray in their hermeneutics, led by Ariel's
acoustic tricks.

---

31. "Ding Dong Bell" is a popular refrain in many early modern songs; this song re-contextualizes
that familiar burden into a funeral bell.

32. Sit Jessica, looke how the floore of heaven
Is think inlayed with patterns of bright gold,
There's not the smallest orbe which though beholdst
But in his motion like an Angell sings,
Still quiring to the young eyed Cherubins:
Such harmonie is in immortall soules. *Merchant of Venice* (5.1.63–68)

33. John Taylor, *All the Workes of John Taylor the Water Poet* (London: Spenser Society, 1869),
vol. 3, 571.

Organs, like bells, were both verbally and physically attacked throughout the sixteenth century by some reformers, though many survived through various means.[34] By 1611 both instruments symbolized the failures of anti-music Elizabethan reformations to suppress church music, and the desire on the part of many for more of such music.[35] The "Treatise on Church Music" which blames the early Elizabethan reforms for music's erosion, is particularly upset about the taking down of organs:

> not so fewe as an 100 paire of Organs were pulled downe (and many of them sold and imploide to make pewter dishes) in such places where musick was used. Then divers preachers being sett a worke by the humors of these aforesayd reformers, people from the reverent use of service in songe, affirmminge it to be nothing but an unnessisary pypinge, and minstrellie.[36]

Recalling these religio-musical sounds of decades past, but doing so in musics that are literally false, *The Tempest* asserts the continued cultural salience of traditional religious music while questioning religious music's ability to provide clearly interpretable messages. The seemingly natural and religious sounds of thunder and organ pipe evoke, but do not prove, the existence of higher powers. They do so by provoking Alonso's associations with the sounds of the church and theories of natural magic and science—associations audience members likely shared. These associations lead Alonso to the humbling, and ultimately productive, feeling of repentance.

The Tempest stages music's potency, revealing its potentially dangerous affective forces. Music can be used for good or ill in the play, but sometimes its good effects, as in the music Ferdinand and Alonso hear, come from its ability to manipulate emotions. While the affective force of music is redeemed in their cases, the play does not unambiguously endorse music's power over people. *The Tempest* balances music's role in aiding reconciliatory harmonies with demonstrations of music's hand in not only deceiving but also oppressing others, a function that is particularly on display in the music Caliban experiences and reports.

---

34. See, for example, Dominic Gwynn, "The Classical British Organ 1500–1660," *The Tracker* 52, no. 4 (2008): 18–23; and Marsh, *Music and Society*, 396–401.

35. Regarding bells, organs, and choirs—all of which were defunded to varying degrees but ultimately survived into the seventeenth century—McCullough writes, "There was very close to the surface of religious culture in London, even in the musically silent parish churches, a sympathy for church music on the part of many." "Music Reconciled to Preaching," 111.

36. "Treatise on Church Music," 5v.

Caliban's Liberty

While it is by now a commonplace to read Caliban as a victim of colonial oppression, it is important to note the role music has in his enslavement.[37] Prospero controls Caliban in part through wielding musical authority to subdue him. His most famous and beautiful speech describes the sounds that have coerced him into an aural addiction:

> Be not affeard, the Isle is full of noyses,
> Sounds, and sweet aires that give delight and hurt not:
> Sometimes a thousand twangling Instruments
> Will hum about mine eares; and sometime voices,
> That if I then had wak'd after long sleepe,
> Will make me sleepe again, and then in dreaming,
> The clouds methought would open, and shew riches
> Ready to drop upon me, that when I wak'd
> I cri'de to dreame againe. (3.2.135–44)

The island's mysterious ambient sounds, despite Caliban's assertion of their benignancy, enforce his imprisonment. While the mysteriously-sourced sounds of instruments and musical "aires" of *The Tempest* dramatize *musica mundana* (universal and philosophical harmony), the "literal manifestations of cosmic music prove wonderful, haunting, and profoundly disturbing."[38] Indeed, the wonders of Ariel's mysterious musical enchantments are tempered by the way music subjugates Caliban—for while the musical deceptions played on Ferdinand and Alonso end up having munificent effects, the songs affecting Caliban are never redeemed. The way music manipulates Caliban demonstrates that on Prospero's island, music controlled by his authority is utilized to subdue his subjects. Caliban's performed music includes a parody of musical liberation that, while prefiguring Ariel's real musical liberation at the play's end, also reveals music's most disturbing capabilities.

---

37. For an overview of (post-)colonial approaches in criticism and performance, see Trevor R. Griffiths, " 'This Island's Mine': Caliban and Colonialism," in *Critical Essays on Shakespeare's Tempest*, eds. Alden T. Vaughan and Virginia Mason Vaughan (London: Bloomsbury Arden, 2014), 130–51. See also Brian C. Lockey, "Empire," in *The Oxford Handbook of Shakespeare*, ed. Arthur Kinney (Oxford: Oxford University Press, 2012), 618–22; Julia Reinhard Lupton, "Creature Caliban," *Shakespeare Quarterly* 51.1 (2000): 1–23; and Ania Loomba and Martin Orkin, eds. *Post-Colonial Shakespeares* (London: Routledge, 1998).

38. Minear, *Reverberating Song*, 145.

Prospero and Ariel's musical power over others is demonstrated in Stephano, Trinculo, and Caliban's drunken singing. At the start of their first scene together, Trinculo fearfully refers to the brewing storm as something he hears "sing i'th' wind," an echo of the winds Alonso heard (2.2.19–20). Stephano, on his entrance, then combats the sounds of Ariel's next storm with his own drunken singing:

I shall no more to sea, to sea, here shall I dye ashore.
This is a very scurvy tune to sing at a mans
Funerall: well, here's my comfort. *Drinkes. Sings.* (2.2.41–44)

Stephano thus offers a profane and land-locked perversion of the funeral tune "Full Fathom Five." In stark contrast to Ariel's controlled, accompanied melodies (likely sung by the company's finest singer), this drunken fool stumbles through a bawdy, unaccompanied ballad about a swearing girl who sleeps with tailors but not sailors (2.2.45–54). The island's sounds are lorded over by the controlling presence of Prospero, and enforced by the trained and practiced Ariel: heretofore, those are the only musical moments the play has presented. Stephano's drunken *a cappella* revelry is the first song of a man who is not beholden to anyone but himself, but his song is sung in fearful reaction to the sounds of the storm orchestrated by Prospero, so Stephano's singing is a product of acoustic manipulation.

When the scene ends with Caliban singing of his newfound freedom, the effect is ironic, for the audience knows that Stephano and Trinculo are mastering him as surely as Prospero had, and that Caliban is not really out of Prospero's grasp. David Lindley writes, "the fact that he sings of rebellion—and perhaps does so to a well-known tune—invites our participation in his sense of release."[39] If it is true (and it likely is, I think) that audience members recognized Caliban's tune, the moment's participatory element would further encourage sympathy with Caliban's delusional celebration, with his longing for freedom to create a new but human and familiar noise in a land of twanging instruments and manipulative lyrics sung by a magical spirit.

Caliban's lyrics move from defiance to self-affirmation to an order for his old master to find a new slave, and finally break into exuberant shouts:

No more dams I'le make for fish,
Nor fetch in firing, at requiring,

---

39. Lindley, *Shakespeare and Music*, 221.

Nor scrape trenchering, nor wash dish,
  Ban' ban' Cacalyban,
  Has a new Master, get a new Man.
Freedom, high-day, high-day freedome, freedome high-day,
  freedome. (2.2.176–82)

While the audience might believe there is real emancipation behind this expression of personal freedom, the next scene with the threesome will prove that this song is but a profane parody of liberation, for Prospero's lackey Ariel carefully controls the island's sounds.

On their return in act 3, scene 2, Trinculo has begun to abuse and mock Caliban, but Stephano defends his new subject enough to let him share his plans against the "tyrant" and "sorcerer" Prospero. The invisible spy Ariel joins in, repeatedly proclaiming "thou liest" in Trinculo's aped voice as Caliban speaks of Prospero's treachery. "The isle is full of noyses," but these noises are used to put Caliban in his place as a slave, be it by giving him just enough musical "delight" to ameliorate his desire to protest, or by acoustically undercutting his authority when he does rebel from his master.

The trio formulates a plan, and when they celebrate their alliance, they do so musically, echoing the conspiratorial vices in morality plays like *Respublica*. Caliban proposes a song:

Thou mak'st me merry: I am full of pleasure,
Let us be jocond. Will you troule the Catch
You taught me but whileare? (3.2.116–18)

To "troll" means to pass a part from one voice to another, as in a catch/round or in an antiphonal psalm; they are trying to harmonize. Stephano's attempt to troll the catch falters:

STEPHANO: At thy request Monster, I will do reason,
  Any reason: Come on, *Trinculo*, let us sing.
  Sings.
  Flout 'em and cout 'em: and skout 'em and flout 'em,
  Thought is free.
CALIBAN: That's not the tune.
  Ariell plaies the tune on a Tabor and Pipe.
STEPHANO: What is this same?
TRINCULO: This is the tune of our Catch, plaid by the picture of
  No-body. (3.2.119–27)

Thus, their attempt at harmony fails, with the invisible Ariel trolling the catch and the mortals' song falling apart amidst the confusion.[40] Ariel co-opts their rebellious melody, playing the tune that Caliban expects while invisible to him. Thought is clearly *not* free. Ariel, Prospero's agent, has seemingly stolen the tune right out of Stephano's head, and alone has the ability to play it in a way Caliban and Trinculo will recognize. Ariel's trolling is reminiscent of both sacred and profane musical practice, but he deprives the humans of their songful moment. Prospero's island does not allow its inhabitants to create art of their own volition.

While the music and sounds performed for Alonso and Ferdinand are deceptive yet ultimately redemptive, Caliban's music demonstrates the ways earthly authorities—including, by implication, church authorities—might claim extraterrestrial sources for their music and magic tricks, coercing listeners into submission and blind belief. The implication may be that in a society overruled by a prescriptive tyrant (Caliban is surely correct in this), music is as likely to control subjects who descend into rebellious but futile discord as it is to liberate communities and bring about concord. Until Prospero learns to listen to others and let go of this stronghold on his subjects, he will be a model of the priest-player-magician using music to manipulate others in many of the ways music's detractors feared. But, as in *The Winter's Tale*, the tyrant is redeemed, learning at the last to listen to others' sounds instead of just conjuring his own.

Prospero Stages Harmony

In the last act of the play, Prospero uses Ariel's music to literally and figuratively stage harmony, musically bringing about the play's final reconciliations. It is crucial that the scene begins with Prospero's first act of empathy in the play, the initial moment in which he questions the workings and feelings of a mind other than his own:

ARIEL: . . . if you now beheld them, your affections
    Would become tender.
PROSPERO: Dost thou thinke so, Spirit?

---

40. Catherine Dunn suggests that this moment refers to early modern musical theories that say that discordant souls cannot make concord: "For as they cannot sing individually, so they cannot sing in concert. As there is chaos in their individual lives, there will be confusion and failure in their joint conspiracy to murder Prospero," "The Function of Music in Shakespeare's Romances," *Shakespeare Quarterly* 20.4 (1969): 401.

ARIEL: Mine would, Sir, were I humane.
PROSPERO: And mine shall. (5.1.18–20)

After the non-human Ariel teaches Prospero to be human enough to care for his fellow man, Prospero decides it is time not only to rescue and reconcile with them, but also to give up his magical authority: "Goe, release them, *Ariell,*/My Charmes Ile breake, their sences Ile restore,/And they shall be themselves" (5.1.30–32). Prospero thus functions as a musician-king (in Robin Wells's phrase), one who resolves political discord through the power of solemn music.[41] He dramatizes at once Richard Hooker's metaphor of the functional state as a well-tuned instrument and Ficino's notion that the musician provides the love that links the whole universe. Indeed, the final scene of the play demonstrates a correlation between political harmony, theater, and magic, a correlation enabled by music.

Prospero tells Ariel that he requires "some heavenly Musicke," an "Ayrie-charme" that will work the sense of the Neapolitan lords (5.1.52, 54). It is unclear what this "solemne" air sounds like, but it is the last piece of music Ariel plays (without singing this time) at Prospero's behest. That it is described as "heavenly," as a final piece of "rough Magicke," and also as "the best comforter,/To an unsetled fancie" makes it resonate with Christian, magical, and humanist discourses on the spiritual efficacy and socializing powers of music (5.1.58–59). The word "heavenly" implies that the tune draws strength by mimicking the music of the spheres that was so essential to both natural magic and Christian worldviews. The word also calls to mind the heavenly noise of the angel choir. Henry Lok's religious sonnet praises the power of heavenly music to create order, and also to awaken and guide humans (like Prospero's enchanted, island-meandering lords) from metaphorical slumber and aimlessness:

Thy thundering voice and Angell Lord of long,
Had cald my soule from slumber where it lay,
The harmony of heavenly musickes song,
Hath made my wandering feete at last to stay.[42]

Referring to both harmony and angels, Lok's sonnet suggests that the celestial harmonies of the spheres as well as the voices of angels enact the speaker's transformation. The music for which Prospero calls refers to multiple musical

---

41. Robin Wells, *Elizabethan Mythologies: Studies in Poetry, Drama, and Music* (Cambridge: Cambridge University Press, 1994), 63, 66, 69.

42. Henry Lok, "Sonnet 8," in *Ecclesiastes, othervvise called The preacher . . .* (London, 1597), K3r.

theories at once, thereby eluding the notion that it is authorized by any one supernatural power.

Prospero must have Ariel help him perform his final trick: employing musical harmony to awaken and reconcile those who wronged him. Prospero orders Ariel to summon the lords and bring about the literal harmonies of the "solemne Ayre." The play thus indicates that this social harmony is in fact orchestrated—it's a magic trick, a theatrical game, a political manipulation. Like a church congregation lulled into a sense of unity by singing metrical psalms in unison, the lords are part of a unifying moment staged by an authoritarian "priest." Just as musical authority can lead to enforced bondage, it can also bring people together in ways that are at once unsettlingly coercive and ultimately socially productive.

Prospero's authority seems to be underwritten by the magical arts he has mastered, and as with *Doctor Faustus*, the real-life corollaries of his magic lie in the performance tricks of stage and church. That is, if in the play world "these our actors" are all "spirits," then in the real world those spirits are all actors (4.1.148–49). It is for this reason that Prospero's promises to break his charms (5.1.31) and drown his book (5.1.57)—to rid himself of his authority to manipulate others—are the real reconciliatory acts. In destroying the tools of his magic and later freeing his agent Ariel, Prospero has returned to the realm of the merely human, the realm that the non-human Ariel told him to pity. Abjuring his powers of manipulation, he has pledged to join the ranks of his vulnerable family. If one sees Prospero as a priest figure, he appears here to be relinquishing the mechanisms of church authority—Catholic vestments and hocus pocus "charms," but also the reformed religio-political powers of the Word in the form of a "book." Deciding to no longer rely on acoustic tricks or performances of authority, he moves away from the power of musical-magical-religious theatrics even as he demonstrates the best possible potential of such things in his final trick. *The Tempest* suggests that abjuring the assertions of extraterrestrial authority allows for an acknowledgment of the power of human achievement in creating art no less than reconciled families. The sounds of religion—with their social, political, magical, and theatrical elements—could be implicated in the play's final model of a music that can be liberating and considerate rather than intimidating and divisive.

Taken in its particular early Jacobean moment, a moment that McCullough argues featured an attempt to reconcile pulpit and choir, Prospero's move from controlling magician to humble supplicant is consistent with contemporary moves to distribute authority between congregation and ecclesiastic officials. McCullough has shown that in the early seventeenth century, preachers like Lancelot Andrewes of St. Paul's advocated for a link between sermon and music in church services.[43] In *The Tempest*, the depiction of Prospero's musical control over the island through his slave-servant Ariel, the exposure of his manipulative power, and finally the portrayal of his desire to yield that power and abase himself before others accumulate to cohere with religio-political discourse that questioned and attempted to reconcile competing claims about where ecclesiastical authority lay and was best expressed.

Lindley argues that the moment of Prospero's book drowning enacts the conflict between political and symbolic readings of music because it "echoes the way in which thinking about music in the period itself was in transition, and the understanding of the source of its effectiveness was moving from a metaphysical to a rhetorical foundation."[44] That is, Prospero moves from understanding music as a force that harnesses the occult properties of universal resonances toward an understanding of music as a more explainable acoustic phenomenon with social analogues. Indeed, early seventeenth-century thinkers like Francis Bacon were beginning to conceptualize music less as a speculative art occupied with the relationship between harmony and the cosmic order, and more as a practical, technical science learned by mastering specific skills, including the skills of playing and singing together.[45] As the seventeenth century wore on, references to "universal harmony" became increasingly rare, except in purely poetic usages.[46] Even as music was increasingly thought of by many as a practical science mastered by human musicians, defenders of music in the seventeenth century continued to write about music's ability to create social harmony.[47] The implication is that the effects of music may be humanly created—bringing a sense of unity or calm not because they resonated with heavenly angels or celestial spheres, necessarily, but because skilled, human musicians had mastered a technical art of harmony, and learned to play and sing together.

In his analysis of the way *The Tempest* presents music and magic as forms of control, Joseph Ortiz argues, "*The Tempest* presents a scathing critique of artistic power."[48] While I agree that the play exposes the mechanisms of artistic power—and, I would argue, of religious power—I do not agree that

---

43. McCullough, "Music Reconciled to Preaching," 114–17.

44. Lindley, *Shakespeare and Music*, 230.

45. See, for example, chapter 3 of Penelope Gouk, *Music, Science, and Natural Magic in Seventeenth-Century England* (New Haven, CT: Yale University Press, 1999).

46. See, for example, John Hollander, *The Untuning of the Sky: Ideas of Music in English Poetry, 1500–1700* (Princeton, NJ: Princeton University Press, 1961), 172–79, and Marsh, *Music and Society*, 35.

47. For one contemporary example, Robert Jones wrote in his 1608 *Ultimum Vale or The Third Book of Ayres* that the Commonwealth was "but a well tunde Song where all partes doe agree." Quoted in Marsh, *Music and Society*, 45.

48. Ortiz, *Broken Harmony*, 164.

this exposure is a "scathing critique."[49] *The Tempest* uses the tropes of magic, theater, and music to explore Prospero's authority, but in revealing his artful mechanisms, it does not simultaneously condemn them all. Prospero himself is famously eager to admit that his shows are but an "insubstantial pageant," but he does not deny that the "baseless fabric" of his vision had real power over Ferdinand and Miranda (4.1.155, 151). The theory of the music of the spheres, theatrical magic, and state-organized religion may all gain their power to enchant via lies and deception, but their effects need not only be negative. Formerly feuding brothers have reached a tenuous peace and father and son are reunited with renewed affection: musical chords and theatrical tableaux may be staged tricks, yet they contain their own truth. If the "truest poetry is the most faining," as Touchstone asserts in *As You Like It*, it is also the case that the lies behind theater and music and religion can create human magic (3.3.16). When Prospero acknowledges how insubstantial his shows are and drowns his book, he forswears his role as creator of illusion (magician, playwright, musician, priest) to join the merely human ranks where other kinds of miracles happen: those brought on by the hard work of communication and collaboration between people.

The play's final moments gesture to the way in which artists themselves need liberation, as Prospero's music-maker asks for his freedom one more time. "Where The Bee Sucks," Ariel's only song in *The Tempest* that manifests his own volition (rather than the service of Prospero), is full of pastoral conventions that would be familiar to early modern playgoers: bees and blossoms and summertime. Sung in Robert Johnson's original musical setting, the air is, as Lindley points out, a high art version of Caliban's mockery of a freedom song.[50] The song expresses Ariel's desire to rest, and to turn into a form that can lie "in a Cowslips bell." The audience is thus reminded that the actor's body has little connection to Ariel's future liberated form, a form that will allow him to sleep within a flower. At the same time, the song's lyrics use fairy clichés, and Johnson's musical setting is melodically and tonally typical of seventeenth century art songs: images and sounds are drawn from the *human* world, from secular poetic and musical conventions, making them easily comprehensible to Prospero and the audience.[51]

---

49. McAdam also argues that "while apparently eschewing a concept of magic as proto-science, he [Shakespeare in the late plays] treats it seriously as a form of psychological and ideological control." "Magic and Gender in Late Shakespeare," 243.

50. Lindley, *Shakespeare and Music*, 231. Robert Johnson's setting can be found in Duffin, *Shakespeare's Songbook*, 454–56.

51. Lindley points out that Johnson's setting responds to the metrical change to triple-time in the last two lines of the lyrics, "underlining the sense of release of which the lyric speaks." Lindley,

Prospero's response to Ariel's final song—which is also the last music of the play proper—indicates the tension between his attachment toward his (musically expressed) authority and his commitment to recognizing debts and to keeping his promise: "Why that's my dainty *Ariell*: I shall misse/Thee, but yet thou shalt have freedome" (5.1.95–96). Prospero's sadness at losing Ariel corresponds to his sadness at overthrowing his charms—but his willingness to both drown his book and liberate his captive spirit indicates that he has learned to listen to and empathize with Ariel and the humans for whom Ariel had advocated. As the play's final action, Prospero grants Ariel his freedom: "Then to the Elements/Be free, and fare thou well" (5.1.318–19). To yield authority and admit the power of lies is to liberate others while learning that the enslaver has debts to the enslaved.

After liberating Ariel, it remains for Prospero to acknowledge his debt to the audience members who have believed in his powers, to humble himself before them in a final act of self-effacement. This begins with him admitting that he has rid himself of the powers to manipulate others and joined the human ranks of his family and the audience themselves: "Now my Charmes are all ore-throwne,/And that strength I have's mine owne./Which is most faint" (Epilogue 1–3). In yielding his own authority, Prospero cedes the magical deceptions of theater, music, and religion, the very deceptions that have brought out the play's reconciliations: "now I want [lack]/ Spirits to enforce: Art to inchant" (Epilogue 13–14). Echoing Lancelot Andrewes and other church authorities who sought a compromise between church-controlled authority over music's powers and quiet, individual responsibility for salvation, the play ultimately demonstrates that even enforced enchantment may have social, if not spiritual, benefits.

Prospero has learned that his freedom is dependent on familial ties and the listening ears of a wider world. Whether or not we map the near-retired Shakespeare himself onto the character, one can see in Prospero's epilogue the notion of an artist—a playwright, a musician, an actor—acknowledging that his powers over an audience depend on their willingness to listen. At the story's end, a ship of people leave the isle of controlled, orchestrated sounds to forge a new harmony enabled by the hard, human work of listening and cooperation. It is a "brave new world" that allows myriad understandings of the power of music and religion to enchant, but in which the master director has exposed the deceptions inherent in such projects and stepped aside.

Shakespeare and Music, 230. For another musicological analysis of Johnson's setting, see Fox-Gold, "Other Voices," 265.

The Winter's Tale echoes *The Tempest* in its use of music as a means of exploring the power of man-made art. It also combines magical and religious discourse in its handling of musical issues, presenting another tyrant who needs to learn to listen to myriad sounds before he is able to participate in the tenuous harmonies of reunion.

Sicilia's Silences

When Archidamus notes the "great difference betwixt our *Bohemia*, and your *Sicilia*" at the start of *The Winter's Tale* (1.1.3–4), he may as well be marking the acoustic contrast between the countries.[52] Leontes's Sicilia, in the first three acts, prescribes no performed music. Leontes is more affected by what he sees than by what he hears; in addition to ignoring the truth of these voices, he cannot apprehend music's veracities.[53] In the first three acts, the tone-deaf and out-of-tune Leontes rejects the sounds of music both earthly and divine. When he suspects that Hermione is sleeping with his friend Polixenes, he imagines an unchaste version of his wife's study of practical music. In ignoring the oracle, he rejects the ideas of speculative music. In *The Winter's Tale*, musics practical and speculative (even if those speculations are man-made myths) possess both the power to deceive and the power to heal. In the final scene, those powers conjoin. While *The Winter's Tale* shares *The Tempest*'s ambivalence about the powers of art, its final message affirms that, flawed though they may be, artistic collaborations are perhaps society's most useful projects.

In the beginning, Leontes's inability to listen to others—and his related rejections of music and ideas about music—amplifies his jealous tyranny. His first pangs of irrational jealousy are felt as rhythmic, discordant frenzy: "my heart daunces,/But not for joy; not joy" (1.2.109–10). A few lines later, he perverts the image of his wife playing the virginals—a harpsichord-like instrument frequently played by upper-class women in early modern England—to frantically interrupt his own thoughts about his son's paternity. Leontes

---

52. I quote from "The Winter's Tale," *The Norton Facsimile of the First Folio of Shakespeare*, ed. Charlton Hinman (New York: W. W. Norton & Company, 1996), and cite line numbers from Stephen Orgel's edition, *The Winter's Tale: Oxford World Classics* (Oxford: Oxford University Press, 1996).

53. Gina Bloom points out that Leontes is deaf to others, "too distracted by his own internal monologue of suspicion to listen to the many voices that insist on Hermione's innocence." *Voice in Motion: Staging Gender, Shaping Sound in Early Modern England* (Philadelphia: University of Pennsylvania Press, 2007), 123.

imagines his wife's hands intimately playing on those of Polixenes: "still Virginalling/Upon his Palme?" (1.2.124–25).[54] Virginals were almost always associated with upper-class women, even though men sometimes played them as well; songs for the virginals were associated with the domesticity and refinement of the chaste gentlewoman who studied the instrument and gave it its name.[55] As such, the turning of Polixenes's hand into the instrument itself suggests a subversion of sexual norms.[56] A seventeenth-century satire called "A Musicke Lecture at the Schools" suggests that women's study of music would tune and refine their souls, manners, and looks: "Thus Ladyes as your Looking-glasses corrects an extravagant hair, and instructs you by the benefit of scarlett to make an harmony of Red and white in your cheekes; so musicke puts your soules into tune, meaning your crooked manners and making that which was before a stone, a Jewell in your casketts."[57] In Leontes's projection, however, the dignity and very soul of his upper-class, musically-trained wife has been degraded. He imagines a perverted music that is not there, stoking his jealousy with the phantom sounds of ill-mannered, adulterous discord.

Leontes's musical metaphors continue as he tells Mamillius to "Goe play (Boy) play: thy mother playes, and I/Play too; but so disgrac'd a part, whose issue/Will hisse me to my Grave" (1.2.184–87). Encompassing a range of significations, Leontes's "play" thus puns on child's recreation, on the actor's craft, and on the playing of musical parts. The sound of a bastard child hissing Leontes to his grave is immediately followed by the explicitly musical "Contempt and Clamor/Will be my Knell" (ll. 187–88). In his delusion, Leontes progresses from frenzied dance music to perverted virginal playing to the judgmental cacophony of hisses and church bells that accompany his

---

54. A similarly sexually explicit use of the word occurs in Lewis Wager's *Life and Repentance of Mary Magdalene*, when Infidelity asks Mary "can you play not on the virginals," to which the fallen woman responds that "there is no instrument but that handle I can." "The Life and Repentaunce of Mary Magdalene," in *Reformation Biblical Drama in England*, ed. Paul Whitfield White (New York: Garland Publishing, 1992), ll. 839, 884.

55. See Marsh, *Music and Society*, 18 on the gendering of virginals and other early modern instruments. The title of a contemporary Byrd composition is revealing: *Parthenia, or the Maydenhead of the first musicke that ever was printed for the virginals* (Loathberry, UK: G. Lowe, 1613?). For more on the associations of upper-class women and virginals, see Linda Austern, "Women's Musical Voices in Sixteenth-Century England," *Early Modern Women: An Interdisciplinary Journal* 3 (2008): 127–52.

56. For Thomas Nash, lascivious lower-class London women were characterized by the fact that they were not taught "what belongs to a Needle, Violl, Virginall, or Lute." *Quaternio, or a Fourefold Way to a Happie Life* (London, 1633), 155.

57. "A Musicke Lecture at the schools" (1642) in *Mischellaneous official papers and letters*, Add MS 37999, British Library, 67r.

burial. His mind, his family, and his country have seemingly fallen out of tune, the metaphorical dissonance of Sicilia resembling the popular early modern sense of discord as social and political unrest.[58]

While Leontes corrupts popular musical pastimes to express his paranoia in the first act, the play's third act features his rejection of speculative music. Leontes is unwilling to accept the authority of the ceremonial, "unearthly" sounds in the highly classicized scene in which he hears the oracle's pronouncements. The reports on the oracle in act 3, scene 1 suggest that music had been heard at Delphos.[59] Dion reminisces, "O, the Sacrifice,/ How ceremonious, solemne, and un-earthly/It was i'th'Offring" (3.1.6–8). "Solemn" is often used in Shakespeare's late plays to cue offstage music of mysterious origins: for example, the invisible music in *The Tempest* is thrice called "solemn," while "solemn music" similarly appears in both *Cymbeline* and *Henry VIII*.[60] That the oracle is also "ceremonious" suggests that it staged a sort of classical musical rite powered by mathematical proportions of sounds in affinity with the universe's spheres.

Cleomenes describes the oracle's truthful pronouncement itself as acoustically overwhelming:

> But of all, the burst
> And the eare-deaff'ning Voyce o'th'Oracle,
> Kin to Joves Thunder, so surpriz'd my Sence,
> That I was nothing. (3.1.8–11)

The play's pre-classical setting evokes Pythagorean and Platonic theories of the music of the spheres, still popular poetically in 1611, even as Bacon and others began to question them as myth. John Taverner's 1611 lecture speaks of the way ancient music was able to "surpize" sense and body in a way that's been lost in contemporary practice: ". . . Antiquity was want to couch excellent inventions under the harmoney of their notes, by the means as it were

---

58. The word "discord" is popular in plays about political unrest, and occurs five times in *1 Henry VI*. In *Troilus and Cressida*, Ulysses says "Take but degree away, untune that string/and hark what discord follows" (1.3.109–10). For a history of this metaphor, see Hollander, *The Untuning of the Sky*, 245–66.

59. J. H. P. Pafford suggests that music is "sensed as having been in the background at the pronouncement of the Oracle," and certainly Dion and Cleomenes's dialogue supports this notion. "Music and Songs in *The Winter's Tale*," *Shakespeare Quarterly* 10.2 (Spring 1959): 161.

60. Alan Dessen and Leslie Thomson find thirty-five uses of "solemn music" in early modern drama. *A Dictionary of Stage Directions in English Drama 1580–1642* (Cambridge: Cambridge University Press, 1999), 206.

by a double force captivating the sense & affections. Wee have noe such thing in our musicke."[61] The reported oracle thus calls on the notion, expressed also in Faustus's memories of Homer's song, that there was a potency to music of the classical past that has been lost.

Leontes's initial rejection of this powerful oracle indicates an unwillingness to acknowledge any voice but his own. That by 1611 ancient oracles were known fictions highlights the notion—shot throughout the play—that even superstitious lies may contain the truth; it's a notion Macbeth evokes before his doom when he says that the Weird Sisters' prophecy about Birnan Wood coming to Dunsinane offered "lies like truth" (5.5.43). More precisely, belief in the oracle would have required Leontes to humble himself, to see beyond his own needs: belief in its authority would have prevented tragedy. If one were to map contemporary religious implications onto this idea, it becomes apparent that the powers of art and religion to deceive can, at times, encourage humility, empathy, and cooperation.

Many critics, most recently Phebe Jensen, have argued that Leontes rages against images in the first three acts of the play.[62] But Leontes proves equally unreceptive to sounds. While Leontes is iconoclastic, anti-theatrical, and anti-festive, as Jensen claims, he is also tone deaf. In Sicilia, dance music has lost its joy, domestic entertainments have been perverted, and not even the solemn sounds and "ear-deaff'ning Voyce o' th'Oracle" affect the king's dangerous convictions. Leontes rejects the making of art—music is perverted, stories and myths are rejected. Yet, while magic—musical, theatrical, and spiritual—gets spurned as an illusion, it is artful illusion itself that restores the king to his wife at the play's end, when he is "mocked with art." But before the play introduces the penitent Leontes of act 5, it boldly exposes artfulness as a tool of trickery and treacherous deceit.

Bohemian Rhapsodies

Exemplifying puritanical critiques of music, Autolycus and his sheep-shearing fans reveal popular music to be an aid to lechery, idolatry, and thievery. At the same time, music promotes love and the re-formation of community.

61. John Taverner, "Praelections musical in aedibus Greshamensibus" (1610–11) MS 2329, Sloane Collection, British Library, London, 51B.

62. Jensen writes, "in the play's first three acts, Leontes' diseased iconoclasm exaggerates the extreme Reformation position against both images and festive sport." *Religion and Revelry in Shakespeare's Festive World* (Cambridge: Cambridge University Press, 2008), 197.

Bohemia in the spring looks and sounds like the English countryside, both the real, Jacobean countryside and that pastoral fantasy of the past popular in early modern poetry, romance, and drama.[63] If, as was likely the case, pre-show and inter-act music was played by the King's Men's consort, the contrast between the music-less world of Sicilia and the musical world of the contemporary London theater would have been marked.[64] When music is at last played *within* the Bohemian scenes of act 4, the noisy acoustic world of England's rural and local present is brought into the play. Suddenly, the offstage musicians are playing bagpipes, pipes, and tabors, actors are singing, and some of them are likely playing instruments onstage, too.[65]

Autolycus, the leader of Bohemia's musical revelry, is a thieving, peddling ballad seller. He is also essential to the play's redemptive final acts, swapping clothes with Florizel so the boy can travel safely with him and Perdita to Sicilia. Indeed, it is Autolycus's theatrical and musical skills—his stories, his feigning, his singing—that move the play toward its conclusion. Where Ortiz argues that Autolycus's musical performances "contaminate Paulina's musical spell in the finale," I suggest that Autolycus actually prefigures the notion, so crucial to that finale, that the lies of art can do good.[66] Act 4 is filled with music that dramatizes several puritanical objections to musical arts, even as it presents what tends to be the play's most memorable scene.[67] The music includes several kinds of popular song—narrative ballads, three-men songs, peddlers' cries, and country dances. As several cultural historians and musicologists have recently asserted, ballad melody creates extra-textual meaning.

---

63. The Old Shepherd's remembrance of his dead wife's singing, dancing, and hospitality on this annual celebration also mark the scene as a traditional springtime festivity: "upon this day, she was both Pantler, Butler, Cooke/Both Dame and Servant: Welcom'd all: serv'd all,/Would sing her song, and dance her turne" (4.4.53–69); there is also Perdita's reference to "Whitsun-Pastorals" (4.4.134).

64. German patron Frederic Gershow, who visited Blackfriars in 1602, wrote: "For a whole hour preceeding the play one listens to a delightful musical entertainment on organs, lutes, pandoras, mandores, viols, and flutes." The translation by Dr. C. W. Wallace is printed in Morrison Boyd, *Elizabethan Music and Musical Criticism* (Westport, CT: Greenwood Press, 1962), 201. William Prynne protested this new practice, seeing that the London theaters were too associated with "amorous, obscene lascivious lust-provoking songs . . . melodiously chanted out upon the Stage between each severall Action." *Histrio-mastix*, 261.

65. The clown's servant mentions all three instruments, which were likely used in the scene, 4.4.183–85. For more on actors' musical training, see Lindley, *Shakespeare and Music*, 100–102.

66. Ortiz, *Broken Harmony*, 183.

67. Simon Forman's account of the play ends with a paragraph on Autolycus; rather than commenting on act 5, his lasting impression of the play is "beware of trustinge feined beggars or fawning fellows." *Booke of Plaies and Notes thereof per formans for Common Pollicie*, MS Ashmole 208, Bodleian Library. Four hundred years of performance history attest to the impact of act 4, and when I directed the play in central California in 2015, it was indeed the fourth act that garnered the most excitement.

Paying attention to the known and probable melodies of Autolycus's songs reveals that the sonic hermeneutics of the scene are complex and self-aware, providing a conscious assertion of the artfulness of this popular entertainment.[68]

The role of Autolycus was likely first played by the clown actor Robert Armin, a known singer who originated other musical roles like Feste in *Twelfth Night*. Tiffany Stern's work has shown that Armin (if it was he) would have learned his part in isolation, revealing his voiced and bodied performances of the solo songs in limited group rehearsals and the actual performance.[69] The actor playing Autolycus is thus particularly visible in this role: character and actor share an ability to entertain, to improvise.[70] Autolycus simultaneously reminds the audience of the power of charismatic actors, of the power of the ballads sung and sold outside the theater, and also of other profane musics enjoyed in streets and taverns.

With his ballad selling and singing, Autolycus represents one of early modern England's most popular art forms. By 1600 there were between six hundred thousand and three million ballads in circulation, by one scholar's estimate.[71] As Bruce Smith points out, these ballads were bought, sold, and sung a mere fifteen feet from the Globe stage, but their form was an old one even then.[72] Ballads served and continued to perform a number of social functions, both affecting and reflecting their society. They told tall tales, as in Autolycus's ballad about the singing fish, and were politically and religiously charged, praising the Reformation's progress or lamenting the decline of traditional religion; they were a source of sensationalist news and a useful tool of propaganda.[73] Mopsa's gullibility regarding their inherent truth attests

---

68. See, for example, Bruce Smith, "Shakespeare's Residuals: The Circulation of Ballads in Cultural Memory," in *Shakespeare and Elizabethan Popular Culture*, eds. Stuart Gillespie and Neil Rhodes (London: Arden, 2006), 193–217; Ross Duffin, "Ballads in Shakespeare's World," in *"Noyses, sounds, and sweet aires": Music in Early Modern England*, ed. Jessie Ann Owens (Washington, DC: The Folger Shakespeare Library, 2006), 32–47; and Marsh, *Music and Society*, 288–327.

69. Tiffany Stern, *Rehearsal from Shakespeare to Sheridan* (Oxford: Clarendon Press, 2000), 10 and passim.

70. See also Harry Berger Jr.'s chapter, "Imaginary Audition and Metatheater," in *Imaginary Audition: Shakespeare on Stage and Page* (Berkeley: University of California Press, 1989), 74–103.

71. Tessa Watt, *Cheap Print and Popular Piety, 1550–1640* (Cambridge: Cambridge University Press, 1991), 11, 42. See also Natascha Wurzbach, *Rise of the English Street Ballad* (Cambridge: Cambridge University Press, 1990), and Patricia Fumerton and Anita Guerrini, eds., *Ballads and Broadsides in Britain, 1500–1800* (Aldershot, UK: Ashgate, 2010).

72. Smith, *Acoustic World*, 169. Andrew Taylor's book *The Songs and Travels of a Tudor Minstrel: Richard Sheale of Tamworth* explains how minstrelsy evolved into balladry, so that the old tradition did not die out but rather was adapted. (York, UK: York Medieval Press, 2012).

73. Autolycus brags: "Here's another ballad of a Fish, that appeared upon the coast, on wensday the fourescore of April, fortie thousand fadom above water, & sung this ballad against the hard

to their communicative power: "Pray now buy some: I love a ballet in print, a life, for then we are sure they are true," she implores the Shepherd's Son (4.4.258–59). Autolycus's ballads thus call to mind the credulity of consumers of art and the benign lies created by artistic fictions, raising a specter of themes important to the play's improbable conclusion.

The acoustic properties of the songs Autolycus sings are as varied as their subject matter. Early modern ballad tunes are generally written in either Dorian (minor) or Ionian (major) modes. Early seventeenth-century music theorist Charles Butler suggests that tunes in the Dorian mode incite the listener to "sobrieti, prudence, modesti, and godliness," while Ionian songs stimulate "honest mirth and delight."[74] Autolycus's many tunes employ both modes—demonstrating the character and actor's versatility as well as the effectiveness of music itself in inciting multiple passions and emotions.

The melody of Autolycus's first song, "When Daffodils Begin to Peere," is now unknown, but its lyrics and placement at the very start of the play's lengthy musical sequencing means that it was probably upbeat and in a major/Ionian key, as in Ross Duffin's suggested setting taken from the contemporaneous Fitzwilliam virginal book.[75] After finishing his lusty musical soliloquy, Autolycus returns to a new song a moment later:

> *But shall I go mourne for that (my deare)*
> *the pale Moone shines by the night,*
> *And when I wander here, and there*
> *I then do most go right.* (4.3.15–18)

While the melody for this song does not survive either, the switch from the sunny scene of "Daffodils" to the moonlit night—when vagabonds, like Autolycus himself, were safe to wander—suggests that perhaps a more mysterious minor/Dorian key would be appropriate. The standardized meter of these songs means that Armin or any actor could change the melodies whenever he wanted, substituting the newest fashionable tune for an old one, and perhaps playing with audience expectation for the tune by using different words. Autolycus's first scene ends with "Jog On," a contemporaneously popular song, the merry and major tune of which, usually called *Hanskin*, is

---

hearts of maids: it was thought she was a Woman, and was turn'd into a cold fish, for she wold not exchange flesh with one that lov'd her: The Ballad is very pittifull, and as true" (4.4.274).

74. Charles Butler, *The Principles of Music, in Singing and Setting* (London, 1636), 1–2.

75. Duffin, *Shakespeare's Songbook*, 440.

known.[76] The melody's leaps, including repeated perfect fourths and synco-
pated rhythms, suit lyrics that celebrate free ranging along the "footpath
way" and Autolycus's successful pickpocketing of the Shepherd's Son. He
uses music to aid in, lament, and celebrate his vagabond life.

In his musical introduction to the audience, Autolycus recalls the many
musical vices we have seen from earlier plays. Singing of "doxies" (available
women), "pugging" (thieving), and "tumbling in the hay" in his first song
and vagabondage in his second, and then stealing another man's purse by
feigning injury and celebrating his theft with song, his musical actions continue that dramatic tradition. They also bring to life the ballad monger and
minstrel figures that were the source of much anti-theatrical and anti-music
wrath. George Puttenham's complaint is typical in conflating itinerant singers of stage and street: "the small & popular Musicks sung by these *Canta-
banqui* [itinerant singers] . . . they be used in Carols and rounds and such light
or lascivious Poems, which are commonly more commodiously uttered by
these buffoons or vices in playes then by any other person."[77] Autolycus's
similarities to morality vice figures stem from his fondness for women, and
his thieving, feigning, peddling, and singing.

Shakespeare's thieving peddler is perhaps most reminiscent of Bale's Infidelity, whose entrance is framed by a ditty about broom selling. Like many
Protestant reformers, Bale railed against Catholic practices of selling
things—relics, indulgences, chantries—to souls who had been terrified into
buying them in order to reduce time in Purgatory for themselves or their
loved ones. Autolycus, too, sells items and songs; his wares as well as his techniques for hawking them are described in detail. Right before Autolycus
enters in act 4, scene 4, the servant reports: "Why, he sings 'em [ribbons,
lawns, and other merchandise] over as they were Gods, or Goddesses: you
would thinke a Smocke were a shee-Angell, he so chauntes to the sleeve-hand
[cuff] and the worke about the square [cloth covering] on't" (4.4.209–12);
the servant's description indicates that Autolycus embodies reformist critiques of the way popery profits off the selling of "enchanted" objects. For
his second entrance, he arrives "wearing a false beard" and singing "Lawne
as white as driven Snow," a peddler's song advertising "*gloves as sweete as Dam-
aske Roses/Maskes for faces, and for noses,*" as well as bracelets, necklaces, per-
fumes, and stomachers: "*Come buy of me, come: come buy, come buy,/Buy, Lads, or
else your Lasses cry: Come buy,*" the song ends (4.4.219, 221–22, 229–30).

---

76. Printed ibid., 230.
77. George Puttenham, *The arte of English poesie* (London, 1589).

Songs assist Autolycus's selling, a practice echoing Bale's Infidelity and other vices selling the idolatrous objects and experiences of Catholicism in reformist plays and polemics. And Autolycus does not just demonstrate the ability of peddlers and priests (or pardoners) to rip people off, he also shows how music enables him to stupefy listeners so he can pickpocket them. As he relates in his confessional soliloquy at the end of act 4, the Shepherd's Son practiced a ballad "till he had both Tune and Words, which so drew the rest of the Heard to me, that all their other Sences stucke in Eares: you might have pinch'd a Placket, it was sencelesse" (4.4.603–6). Autolycus demonstrates longstanding reformist fears about music's ability to mesmerize people into getting ripped off by the tricksters of the street and traditional religion, but the tricks of act 4's ballad-filled Bohemia are benign compared to the treachery of the silent Sicilia of the previous acts.[78]

Autolycus's ballads also bring people together: they demonstrate that the immense popularity of balladry allowed it to function as an equalizer of sorts. Melody moved more freely across social strata and the religious spectrum than lyrics, and the melodies that Autolycus sings before religiously diverse audiences echo musics both traditional (and Catholic) and contemporary (and Protestant). Autolycus's diverse melodies and rhymes appeal to listeners across religious and economic boundaries.

The sheepshearing scene's most musically complex vocal song, "Get You Hence," was likely an original melody by Robert Johnson, a composer associated with the Lord Chamberlain's household and then with the King's Men; Johnson wrote songs for The Tempest and likely collaborated with Shakespeare on The Winter's Tale. The Dorian melody survives and it is (to most critics' ears) surprisingly mournful.[79] The representation of complex three-part singing performed by a ballad monger and two shepherdesses challenges the notion of the rustic simplicity of country art. The song slows down the frantic scene, exposing the considerable emotional power of contemporary music. The lyrics are dark: a deep man's voice orders both of the competing women to "get you hence" and refuses their treble questioning, "wh[i]ther?, o wh[i]ther?, wh[i]ther?" (4.4.295, 297). As the clown's amazed servant reports, Autolycus "hath songs for man, or woman, of all sizes" (4.4.193). His

---

78. Autolycus's constant sartorial changes also recall vices that don disguises in plays like King Johan or Respublica. As one who wears disguises, Autolycus demonstrates not only the dangers of disguise, as Protestant moralities do, but also that such deceit has its advantages. After all, Florizel and Perdita would not have made it back to Sicilia without the help of Autolycus.

79. Printed in Duffin, Shakespeare's Songbook, 165–66. Lindley argues that Johnson's melody might not have been the one used in original performance, Shakespeare and Music, 167–68, and Ortiz responds to the complexities of the melody question, Broken Harmony, 210.

contrasting melodies, the songs' stories of springtime sex, of trickery, of lost love, and his sung promises of fine clothing, decoration, and related success in love, all suggest popular music's capacity to narrate, mock, sell, inform, deceive, and mourn. Both the tunes and the clothes Autolycus sells offer possibility to their buyers: textiles and ballad texts alike can deceive and also charm, as the play demonstrates.

Feeling the Music

As we have seen, profane music's abilities to charm and deceive were precisely what bothered both the outright anti-musical and those who worked to supplant profane music with sacred song. Popular ballads are "wanton," the "snares of unclennesse," Miles Coverdale alleges in his preface to the *Goostly Psalmes and Spirituall Songes*.[80] To "H.S.," balladry "poisons the world" because it can "tickle up the ears of people."[81] Those who wrote, sold, bought, and performed ballads were condemned as lower class, and further associated with crime, alehouses, and ribald sexuality.[82] However, there are surviving collections of low-class ballads and catches that were printed for eager gentry and nobility.[83] Even the most highbrow gentlefolk appear to have enjoyed this derided lowbrow entertainment, and melody moved freely across confessional divides. All members of an audience, regardless of social standing, were likely to tap their toes and enjoy the familiar melodies. Playing this music on the stage, Autolycus calls attention to the community-forming function of popular music both on stage and off.

The fact that Autolycus's music also may have inspired kinesthetic experiences furthers its community-forming function, and links it to the scene's dances. Two participants in those dances are Perdita and Florizel, who with their youthful lust embody the ability of music to transcend (apparent) class boundaries and to promote lechery. In the story of *The Winter's Tale*, though, any role dance might play in bringing the offspring of Leontes and Polixenes together is surely redeemed. Bruce Smith's recent suggestion that ballads

---

80. Miles Coverdale, *Goostly psalmes and spirituall songes* (London, 1535), preface.

81. H.S. *To the Musicioners, the Harpers, the Minstrels, the Singers, the Dancers, the Persecutors* (London, 1658), 8.

82. For example, the playwright Henry Chettle, who may have been in the business of printing ballads, nonetheless stigmatizes ballad-sellers who travelled "in every corner of Cities and market Townes of the Realme singing and selling of ballads . . . and with-drawing people from christian exercises, especially at faires markets and such publike meetings." *King-harts Dreame* (London: 1593), C1r.

83. For descriptions of these collections, see Marsh, *Music and Society*, 194–95.

were often danced—the word "ballad," like "ballet," comes from the French "ballere" meaning "to dance"—indicates that the fourth act's musical sequencing might feature smaller dances during these ballads in addition to the shepherd and shepherdess dance and the anti-masque. Using his own work on mirror neurons in *Phenomenal Shakespeare*, Smith suggests that watching the dancers perform dances and dance tunes on stage would produce kinetic subjectivity in audience members, who would feel and recall their own experiences dancing.[84]

The dances of the massive sheepshearing scene are reminiscent of Rogationtide (like Whitsun, a post-Easter holiday), when country parishes blessed newly planted crops by ringing bells, processing, and feasting.[85] Rogationtide had been suppressed under Edward VI, but after Mary had encouraged it, the tradition persisted through the reigns of Elizabeth, James, and Charles I. If the types of dancing at these springtime festivities were not standardized, they were always interactive, involving large groups of people moving together with simple movements. It would have been easy for London actors to replicate the sort of circle and square dancing choreography of country dances, which were becoming increasingly popular in urban settings. This type of dancing, like all dancing, was much derided by reforming polemicists: regarding country dancing in particular, Phillip Stubbes asks, "what clipping, what culling, what kissing and bussing, what smooching and slavering one of another, what filthie groping and uncleane handling is not practised in those dancings?"[86] The shepherd and shepherdess dance would have been noisy, filling the space with the full sound of the King's Men's consort, augmented perhaps by onstage actors playing tabors and recorders, the sounds of the actors' feet thumping the wooden stage, and likely the audience's whooping and clapping, too.

Yet, while the scene represents lowbrow country dancing, it also mimics royal entertainments. Before the satyrs' dance, the Old Shepherd's servant introduces the twelve locals who have "made themselves all men of hair" in order to present a dance, proclaiming that "[o]ne three of them, by their owne report (Sir,) hath danc'd before the King" (4.4.320–21, 332–33). The reference is likely an in-joke, recalling the recent (1 January 1611) perfor-

---

84. Bruce Smith, "Putting the 'Ball' Back in Ballads" (paper given at "Living English Broadside Ballads, 1550–1750: Song, Art, Dance, Culture," Huntington Library, San Marino, CA., April 5, 2014); and *Phenomenal Shakespeare* (London: Wiley-Blackwell, 2010), 151–52.

85. Smith calls Rogationtide a way that communities "formally marked their aural boundaries." *Acoustic World,* 32.

86. Phillip Stubbes, *Anatomie of Abuses* (London, 1585), 22.

mances of Ben Jonson and Indigo Jones's masque *Oberon* before the Jacobean court.[87] The King's Men likely took roles in the masque so, plausibly, the joke is made funny by its truth. The dance would have been accompanied by the consort, providing the audience with an opportunity to hear a fine ensemble playing courtly instrumental music, a type of music newly popular with the rise of the printing press and increased attention from composers to non-vocal musical art forms.[88] *The Winter's Tale*'s representation of the sort of country dancing popularly performed in the court thus blurs distinctions between royal and peasant, town and country, and the aristocracy's continued enjoyment of the lowbrow entertainments they pretended to despise.[89] Depending on the performance venue, rural celebrations of community identity are either reproduced before the court, or the King's private entertainments are brought to the economically diverse patrons of the Globe and Blackfriars. In theatrical performances, this mixture of secular and sacred, upper- and lower-class music can be juxtaposed, performed by and for heterogeneous audiences who are briefly synchronized by their shared aural, visual, and psycho-kinetic experience. This scene's dances reveal that there are only superficial differences between the entertainments of court and of country parish, between the new and the traditional, the royal and the lower class.

While courtly dancing was defended and even praised by the upper class, country dancing was continuously derided by reformers like Stubbes, Northbrooke, and Prynne. Phebe Jensen suggests that the rural traditions represented in act 4, scene 4—the country dancing, the singing, Perdita's reference to Whitsun—assert the vitality and validity of traditions long called papist and backwards by reformers.[90] Jensen argues that by representing traditions

---

87. John Long has further pointed out that the entire sequence of songs, dances, monologues, and dialogue in act 4, scenes 3 and 4 structurally resembles *Oberon. Shakespeare's Use of Music: The Final Comedies* (New York: Da Capo Press, 1977), 69–70.

88. See Suzanne Lord, *Music from the Age of Shakespeare: A Cultural History* (Westport, CT: Greenwood Press, 2003), 129. This early Jacobean royal indulgence in country dances had both precedent and antecedent. Elizabeth I enjoyed "a pleasant daunce with Taber and Pipe" on her visit to Sussex in 1591, and later, Charles II held a ball at which were performed "country dances, the King leading the first . . . which was, says he, 'cuckolds all a-row,' the Old dance of England." Elizabeth's experience is quoted in Francis Rust, *Dance in Society: An Analysis of the Relationship between the Social Dance and Society in England from the Middle Ages to the Present Day* (London: Routledge, 1969), 47. Samuel Pepys describes Charles II's entertainments: Pepys, *Diary of Samuel Pepys*, vol. 3, eds. R.C. Latham and W. Mathews (London: HarperCollins, 1995), 300–301.

89. In Marsh's words, "In all periods, members of the self-styled social elite will tend to disparage the culture of their supposed inferiors while simultaneously espousing it with some degree of disquiet," *Music and Society*, 21.

90. Jensen, *Religion and Revelry*, 194–233. Jensen cites numerous Protestant tracts that associate the practice and history of festive traditions like Whitsun with popish idolatry.

of festivity, Shakespeare aesthetically, if not theologically, aligns himself with old religion.[91] But the scene also suggests an aesthetics that is, like the play, generically inclusive, catholic in the other sense of the word.

Percy Scholes and others have shown that there was a disjunction between idealized proposals and actual practice when it came to Puritanical attitudes toward music.[92] Shakespeare puts a contemporary Puritan in this scene, one that represents the sort who compromised (hypocritically, perhaps) on music. The clown explains that the shearers are "most of them means [tenors] and basses—but one Puritan amongst them, and he sings Psalmes to horne-pipes" (4.3.42–44). The practice of singing psalms to profane tunes (and instruments) was common in early modern England, yet a contentious issue. The less-than-inspiring psalm tunes from the mid-sixteenth century caused some Reformers to set psalms to popular ballads, in hopes that they would catch on in a more popular form. Most psalms sung in church since around 1559 had been set to ballad meter and could easily fit Autolycus's tunes. Many reforming polemicists were concerned about this conciliatory practice, deriding any mix of scurrility with divinity, be it profaned psalms or the secular entertainments of traditional feast days.[93]

The fourth act of *The Winter's Tale* explores the complications that arise from religiously diverse communities creating sacred and profane art together, foregrounding the productive overlap of divine and bawdy that creates and maintains a community of kings and ballad mongers, sinners and moralists. As discussed in chapter 2, since the early years of the English Reformations, reformers indulged in and could not entirely divorce themselves from musical experience. The joke about Puritans playing psalms to hornpipes points to the affective—one might say irresistible—power of music as much as to the hypocrisy of religious fanaticism. *The Winter's Tale* asserts such kinship with England's acoustic past, while also acknowledging the myriad other sounds, Protestant too, that make a community.

Perdita demonstrates throughout the sheepshearing scene that she has inherited her father's anti-festive streak, opposing transformation, costuming, artistic expression, and hybridity. In rejecting such things, she is unknowingly

---

91. Ibid., 5.

92. See Percy Scholes, *The Puritans and Music: In England and New England* (Oxford: Clarendon Press, 1934; 1969).

93. Beth Quitslund argues that the joke is that it is anti-social and wrong for a Puritan to sing psalms outside of church, quoting a 1619 tract called *Preparation to the Psalter* that calls singing metrical psalms to secular tunes blasphemy. Again, I surmise that frequent protests of the practice likely mean that it was being done. *The Reformation in Rhyme: Sternhold, Hopkins and the English Metrical Psalter, 1547–1603* (Aldershot, UK: Ashgate, 2008), 232.

denouncing that which will bring her back to her parents. Her resistance to musical festivity is also important to mark. Perdita was a baby without a real lullaby; perhaps that is why she is skeptical of music, and hesitates to "sing her song, and dance to her turne" as the Old Shepherd's deceased wife once had on such days (4.4.58).[94] When Perdita enters into a debate about nature and art with the disguised Polixenes, she echoes Michel de Montaigne by stating that she is against the cultivated hybridization of flowers, or any effort on human's part to improve nature: carnations and such flowers are "Natures bastards . . . and I care not to get slips of them" (4.4.83, 84–85).[95] Perdita is herself, in some ways, a hybrid: a genetic mixture of Leontes and Hermione, birthed in nobility and raised in country poverty. When she at last succumbs to the music, she dances "featly," like a country girl, but with a remove, like she is "too Noble for this place" (4.4.178, 159). Ignorant of her origins, of her own pied-ness, Perdita is resistant to interference with nature, but *human* artfulness ultimately brings her to her true identity, and her father and mother.

Against calls for natural purity, for unadorned churches and unaccompanied psalms, *The Winter's Tale* iterates a trope of polyphony, of hybridized art forms, of messy disguises and morally ambiguous tricks.[96] Shakespeare's play, taken as a whole, argues against Perdita's view that human art is corrupting, and sides with Polixenes, who asserts that human art is natural, it can be that "which do's mend Nature: change it rather, but/The Art it selfe, is Nature" (4.4.96–97).[97] The ballads, songs, and dances of the Bohemian scene interrupt the stoic aurality of the play's previous acts. Dancing reclaims its joy, and the fact that instrumental pastimes may be lusty is celebrated rather than scorned. Music's ability to bring people together, even to enchant them into believing lies, leads the play to its final musical performance. The characters return to Sicilia in distress, but the sonic and interpersonal disorder created by the musical theatrics of act 4 are all necessary to bring about the literal and figurative harmonies of the final act.

---

94. Before abandoning the baby Perdita, Antigonus laments "thou'rt like to have/A lullabie too rough" (3.3.53).

95. Orgel points out that Montaigne's essay "Of the Cannibals" argues that wild fruits have the most natural properties and we have "bastardized" them. "Introduction," 172.

96. Gary Schmidt explores the notion of a hybrid aesthetics—from creatures like centaurs to tragicomedies—pervading the literature and culture of early modern England in *Renaissance Hybrids: Culture and Genre in Early Modern England* (Farnham, UK: Ashgate, 2013).

97. That is, humans are natural, and human art aids nature to become even more beautiful. Orgel quotes Puttenham's similar argument from *The Art of English Poesy* that art is an "aide and coadjutor to nature." Orgel, "Introduction," 172.

Music Awakes Her

The reanimation of Hermione, her statue's transformation into the living wife thought dead, is activated by music. The innocent, upper-class, musically-trained Hermione resembles another of Shakespeare's falsely accused, Desdemona. Othello recalls that his wife, "an admirable Musitian . . . will sing the Savagenesse out of a Beare," but all the audience hears her sing is a plangent lament before her murder (4.1.89). In *The Winter's Tale*, the wrongly accused wife reappears to the sound of music, and the melodies prove redeeming rather than foreboding. The savageness of the bear remains, but the final acoustic mode of *The Winter's Tale* is one of fragile concord, a concord that sounds of the early modern notion that discord makes harmony more beautiful. The music of the final scene exceeds contemporary religious debates, combining a vaguely pagan setting and pre-Christian ideas with a Catholic aesthetic and a reformed idea of grace.[98]

That Leontes should be ready to receive the graces of the play's finale has much to do with his sixteen years of contrition, a repentance that is based on the false premise of his wife's death. Leontes shares with Alonso a transformation for the better that is inspired by a lie. That Paulina's final act is so explicitly artful—and musical—embodies the sense to which the reconciliations music facilitates are of a piece with its power to enchant and deceive. If, for reformist polemicists and Marlowe, music's deceptive qualities make it condemnable, for Shakespeare, it is the very deceptiveness of art that leads people to the imaginative realm wherein they might create a better world.

Paulina commands, "Musick; awake her: Strike," and Hermione is stone no more (5.3.98). Paulina's line cues the play's instrumentalists; the line sounds like the Clown's call before the Shepherd's dance, "Not a word, a word, we stand upon our manners, Come, strike up" (4.4.166–67). The Clown cues onstage actors, instrumentalists who play the parts of musical shepherds; offstage musicians would likely augment their playing. In the world of the play, then, the music is diegetic and logical—it comes from the Shepherds. But when Paulina cues music in act 5, scene 3, she only cues the offstage musicians, for no actor in this scene would be holding or playing an instrument.

---

98. Many other scholars have argued for Shakespeare's hybridized, inclusive version of Christianity and its social exigencies, often especially citing the late plays. Kastan describes Shakespeare's plays as having "an inclusive and theologically minimalist Christianity that resisted religious rigor and valued social accord," and cites the fact that scholars are starting to focus more on what joined Christians in early modern England rather than on what divided them. *Will to Believe*, 37, 75. See also Thomas Betteridge, "Writing Faithfully in a Post-Confessional World," in *Late Shakespeare 1608–1613*, eds. Andrew J. Power and Rory Loughnane (Cambridge: Cambridge University Press, 2013), 225–42.

Andrew Gurr's research suggests that in public performance this music would have come from the music room above the stage of Blackfriars, or from the Globe's retrofitted curtained music room in the balcony above the stage.[99] So, in any public performance, the sounds cued by Paulina came from above the players' and audience members' heads while the musicians were hidden from view: a staged acoustic miracle.[100]

"Strike" (as opposed to the Clown's "strike up") is often a cue for stringed instrumentalists, who strike their strings with bows.[101] It is possible that a consort of viols sounded at this moment, evoking the relatively recent English taste for wordless, stringed music that had been inherited from the Italian repertoire.[102] Even if viols were not played here, the context all but requires a mixture of other *bas* (soft, for a chamber) instruments such as lute, harp, and flute as opposed to the *haut* (loud, for the outdoors) instruments such as tabor, pipe, and shawm/hautboy probably used in act 4. After the louder and more varied sounds of act 4, the audience hears a simpler harmony, likely in the Ionian mode.

Paulina's music, defying the intellect to perform a seemingly celestial transformation of stone into corruptible flesh, calls on the long tradition that considers music to be the most efficient means for allowing humans to contact the divine or to revive the dead. This idea of a mutuality between humans and the heavens conveyed through musical harmony persisted popularly despite scientific challenges to the idea.[103] Throughout Shakespeare's plays, music is referred to in or accompanies several moments involving miracle and death, for example, the "Musicke of the Spheres . . . most heavenly Musicke" that Pericles hears when he is reunited with *his* lost daughter (5.1.229, 232), or the music Queen Katherine cues in *Henry VIII* when she imagines her death, "on that Coelestiall Harmony I go too" (4.2.80).

Shakespeare calls on these traditions when choosing to accompany the miraculous magic of the "dead" statue's transformation into the living Hermione with music. This moment possesses emotional power not just because of its climactic status in the narrative; the music resonates with intellectual and popular traditions of music's divine mysteries. A few years before *The Winter's Tale* was written, Thomas Wright wrote a treatise explaining four reasons for music's affective power. He calls on classical, pre-Christian, and new scientific

---

99. Gurr, *The Shakespearean Stage*, 97, and Gurr, *The Shakespearian Playing Companies*, 367–68.

100. A similar effect could have perhaps been staged at court, where no expense was spared.

101. This cue is explained in more detail in Long, *Shakespeare's Use of Music*, 91.

102. On the evolution of viols and their music, see Peter Holman, *Four and Twenty Fiddlers: The Violin at the English Court 1540–1690* (Oxford: Clarendon Press, 1993), 12.

103. For a discussion of this theory with regards to this scene, see Ortiz, *Broken Harmony*, 188–90.

ideas in order to refute attacks on music by nonconforming reformers. For Wright, music is powerful because: it is in sympathy with the soul's heaven-like proportions (a classical idea used in natural magic); God, in His prov-idence, gave sound a spiritual quality (a Christian idea); soundwaves physically affect the body, passing through the ears to the heart where they "beateth and tickleth it in such a sort, as it is moved with semblable pas-sions" (a contemporary scientific idea); and finally, because it affects men differently, provoking bad men to lust but lifting a good man to heaven (a notion from early modern social theories found in many defenses of music).[104] *The Winter's Tale* dramatizes Wright's arguments, combining an-cient settings with contemporary musical arts and sciences. While the re-vival of Hermione suggests music's heaven-like proportions and spiritual quality, the representation of so many musical forms throughout the play has demonstrated music's somatic power, its ability to "tickle the heart" in a va-riety of ways.

Music is a crucial part of the magic (as Leontes will call it) of Hermione's sudden animation, a magic that many have suggested is coded Catholic.[105] Much has been written about the way this magic disenchants or affirms Cath-olic sacramentality and aesthetics (and indeed, whether or not the scene is magic at all). While many have also debated whether or not the resurrection and its music are "real," I think that this question is beside the point in the-

---

104. Thomas Wright, *The Passions of the Minde in Generall (1604)*, ed. Thomas O. Sloan (Ur-bana: University of Illinois Press, 1971), 163–71.

105. Julia Lupton argues that any Catholicism suggested in the scene is cancelled because the statue trick is a hoax; Huston Diehl similarly suggests that the forbidden rituals of Catholicism are demystified and contained in this scene. Lupton, *Afterlives of the Saints: Hagiography, Typology, and Re-naissance Literature* (Palo Alto, CA: Stanford University Press, 1996), 217; Diehl, *Staging Reform, Re-forming the Stage: Protestantism and Popular Theater in Early Modern England* (Ithaca, NY: Cornell University Press, 1997), 232. Karen Sawyer Marsalek and Alice Dailey both read the scene in the context of medieval cycle drama in Marsalek, "English Resurrection Drama and *The Winter's Tale*," in "*'Bring furth the pagants': Essays in Early English Drama Presented to Alexandra F. Johnston*, eds. Marsalek and David Klausner (Toronto: University of Toronto Press, 2007), 271–91; and Dailey, "Easter Scenes from an Unholy Tomb: Christian Parody in *The Widow's Tears*," in *Marian Moments in Early Modern British Drama*, eds. Regina Buccola and Lisa Hopkins (Aldershot, UK: Ashgate, 2007), 127–39. For Jennifer Waldron, the scene reflects the important role of the believer's body in the Protestant faith, and Charles Moseley points out that any audience member would associate Sicily, in 1611 under Spain's jurisdiction, with Catholicism and Bohemia with Protestants. Waldron, *Reforma-tions of the Body: Idolatry, Sacrifice, and Early Modern Theater* (New York: Palgrave Macmillan, 2013), 55; and Moseley, "The literary and dramatic contexts of the last plays," in *The Cambridge Companion to Shakespeare's Last Plays*, ed. Catherine M. S. Alexander (Cambridge: Cambridge University Press, 2009), 57. I agree with Alison Shell, who suggests that in combining Christian and pagan elements with its requirement of repentance and faith in miracles but not faith in Christ, the scene is doc-trinally open. Shell, *Shakespeare and Religion*, 211.

atrical experience. The audience *knows* that Hermione is an actor, and they know that the invisible music comes from human musicians—the curtain was likely drawn for the pre-show and inter-act musical interludes. The tricks have been revealed, but as with a Penn and Teller show, they are no less amazing for that. Human art—practical music as opposed to celestial music, theatrical spectacle as opposed to miracle—does not exclude or deny magic (or divinity). It rather assigns human agency in creating affective experience in collaboration with nature (and perhaps God's heavens). Whether the sounds of the voice and viol resonate with God's music or not is left to an audience member to feel and consider, as are the nature of the truths behind Hermione's resurrection. Art may be a benign deceit, celestial harmony may be a fiction, but to be "mocked with art" is to be open to transformation.

Leontes's response to the statue's transformation into his wife—"if this be Magick, let it be an Art/Lawfull as Eating" (5.3.110–11)—may thus be heard as something like a plea for artistic and religious freedom: let the statues and songs and plays created in churches, homes, and playhouses be lawful; let us marvel in our capacity to create things that affect others; let aesthetic experience be open to interpretation.[106] While Ortiz argues that Autolycus's "bawdy, morally barren" music—which makes him "an ideal lightning rod for Puritan critiques of art"—thus "contaminate[s] Paulina's musical spell," I argue that Autolycus and his music are central to the comic spring that melts the tragic winter, so that Autolycus's art is rather redeemed in the end.[107] Describing Autolycus's relationship with his songs, the shepherds' servant had said that he "utters them as he had eaten ballads" (4.4.186–87). Autolycus's art seems so natural as to be a part of his very passion: let *that* scorned music, Leontes's plea says, be lawful, too. All arts—music, theater, dance, sculpture—are as vital to ancient Sicilia and Jacobean England as food, and no more in need of justification than the humans who create and consume them.

---

106. Focusing on visual and verbal aspects of the play, several other scholars have also argued that the play's final scene argues for the power of visual art—see Piero Boitani, *The Gospel According to Shakespeare*, trans. Vittorio Montemaggi and Rachel Jacoff (Notre Dame, IN: University of Notre Dame Press, 2013), 88; and Hester Lees-Jeffries, *Shakespeare and Memory* (Oxford: Oxford University Press, 2013), 194—and on the power of fiction and words—see Eric S. Mallin, *Godless Shakespeare* (London: Continuum, 2007), 67; Susannah Brietz Monta, " 'It is requir'd you do awake your faith': Belief in Shakespeare's Theater," in *Religion and Drama in Early Modern England: The Performance of Religion on the Renaissance Stage*, eds. Jane Hwang Degenhardt and Elizabeth Williamson (Farnham, UK: Ashgate, 2011), 133; and Gillian Woods, *Shakespeare's Unreformed Fictions* (Oxford: Oxford University Press, 2013), 208.

107. Ortiz, *Broken Harmony*, 183.

Leontes *needs* music in his kingdom—Hermione's playing, Perdita's dancing, his singing subjects. As John Taylor sums up: "'Tis Concord keeps a Realme in Stable stay/But Discord brings all Kingdomes to decay."[108] While the play presents plenty of discord, the music accompanying Hermione's reanimation suggests a new concord, a new music, for Sicilia. The harmonies created by various voices recall the anonymous "Treatise on Church Music's" argument that people's naturally diverse vocal ranges imply that there should be harmonies in church music: "Nature having disposed all voices both of men and children into fyve kindes. . . . These fyve kindes being the naturall voyces of all, both men, women, and children, I say, I demaund whether is it not more for edification . . . by causinge every one to singe his part allotted to him by nature, rather then to have voyces violated, and drawne out of their naturall compasse."[109] In other words, the fact of human vocal diversity—implying functional differentiation among singers—suggests that harmony may be woven into the fabric of the natural order itself.

Harmony created from diversity is not unlike the precarious unity binding Jacobean England together, with its recent history of civil and religious strife. Forgiveness and compromise, so crucial to the play's plot, were also central to the creation of the fragile peace of 1611. *The Winter's Tale*'s representations of human musical creation assert a social, community-defining function for song, dance, and musical-magical sciences that soften (but by no means preclude) the smaller squabbles about how the psalms should be sung or whether or not ballad mongers are criminals. The play was also first performed around the time Prince Henry was invested as Prince of Wales and his marriage negotiations opened; Charles Moseley suggests that the play's "resolution of the sins of the fathers by the hopes vested in their children" supports "the idea of a union of the conflicting confessions."[110] The early modern theater resembled the church not because, as reforming polemicists claimed, it shared in Catholic ritual's ability to deceive, but rather because its practitioners—through words, sounds, and sights—could produce the affective power of religious experience. Later in 1611, *The Winter's Tale* was performed at court on the anniversary of the Gunpowder Plot, and it was performed again soon after the sudden death that befell Prince Henry, James's son and heir. The idea that art has the power to reconcile fractured com-

---

108. Taylor, *All the Workes*, vol. 2, 19–20. In *An Answer of the Most Reverend Father in God*, Cranmer describes Catholicism as discord, sung out of tune with a "shamefull jarre."

109. "Treatise on Church Music," 8v–9r.

110. Moseley, "The literary and dramatic contexts," 57.

munities and assuage grief is thus not only internal to the play itself but also a part of its performance history.

That human-made art has redemptive power is half the point. Forgiveness is also a human act: the grace of Hermione is a human creation, Leontes's contrition an act of will. Sarah Beckwith has argued that the final scene restages mystery plays that present Christ's resurrection, and that *The Winter's Tale* replaced a Catholic model of forgiveness—priestly absolution through Christ's Eucharistic body—with a forgiveness that takes the form of a reconciled community.[111] For Beckwith, the resurrections of *The Winter's Tale* and other late plays involve complex encounters with the characters' pasts: the subject thought dead (Hermione) is the vehicle of redemption for the one (Leontes) whose actions had appeared to lead to irredeemable harm.[112] The play rejects Jean Calvin's exclusion of the human in his reformed version of grace, and shows that human forgiveness is, in Beckwith's words, "rather the *medium* of grace."[113] Hermione, as has often been noted, is associated with grace throughout the play. Her first declaration of (human) love for Leontes, in her own words, was "grace indeed" (1.2.104). When she first speaks after animating, Hermione asks the gods to give her daughter their grace: "You Gods looke downe,/And from your sacred Viols poure your graces/Upon my daughters head" (5.3.121–23).[114] Hermione's initial acts of love, Paulina's miracle or benevolent deceit, the bringing of Perdita back to Sicilia: all required human agency. People, not gods (or God) have orchestrated the final reconciliation, as intentionally constructed as a statue, as artful as a song.

The ambiguity of Hermione's reappearance and the irrevocability of the deaths of young Mamillius and Paulina's beloved Antigonus complicate the scene's final reconciliation, yet the music of the scene establishes a tonality of harmony created out of discord. As Alison Shell, looking at Paulina's final speech that still mourns for Antigonus, argues, the play asks us to "rejoice at exceptional grace, but in passing—and perhaps with dangerous compassion—it also deplores the fact that grace is exceptional."[115] Early modern

---

111. Sarah Beckwith, *Shakespeare and the Grammar of Forgiveness* (Ithaca, NY: Cornell University Press, 2011), 128–46.

112. Ibid., 131–35.

113. Ibid., 144. Shell also notes that critiques and departures from high Calvinism gained ground in the early seventeenth century and are mirrored in *The Winter's Tale* as well as *Two Noble Kinsmen*. *Shakespeare and Religion*, 197.

114. It is interesting to note the orthography of our modern word "vials" in the Folio, for it implies a pun on musical viols and the instruments of heaven.

115. Shell, *Shakespeare and Religion*, 215.

theories of harmony often required discordant sounds as well as sweet ones. For Charles Butler, "a Discord . . . in Musick" can "mak[e] the Concord following the sweeter."[116] Like the play's mix of popular balladry, courtly entertainments, and celestial music, harmony itself was defined for the early moderns as that which "joyneth and accordeth diverse thinges that seeme contrary."[117] The play's final, fragile resolution—binding its religiously and socially diverse audience in a shared musical temporality—suggests that divisiveness and diversity do not exclude the possibilities of forgiveness. These reconciliations can also be understood as the complex hybridization of distinct forms. When Perdita calls humanly cultivated flowers "nature's bastards" (4.4.83), her protest against botanical hybridity echoes the Calvinist resistance to human artistic interference with God's nature, to mixtures of profane and sacred, to the pied-ness of most popular piety. The play as a whole promotes the opposite view, one that sees human artistic collaboration with each other and with nature as munificent—perhaps even a form of grace. The early seventeenth century's tenuous compromises between myriad religious perspectives, the coexistence of psalms and profane ballads and dances, the combination of traditional festivities, moral dramas, and masques that create Jacobean theater: all are acts of collaborative creation.

Throughout the chapters of this book, we have seen how music can inspire rebellion or reconcile diverse souls, how it can incite lusty dancing or evoke a transcendent sense of the sacred. Its multifarious effects are what make it such a powerful—if also controversial—resource of the theater, and of the marketplace, tavern, and church. Why music should be such a contested, complicated, and powerful theatrical and religious tool is perhaps best summed up by theologian Don Saliers: "music is first and foremost a human practice."[118] Asserting that music and theology are practices enacted in the diverse minds and hearts of people, Saliers asks, "might this require attention to the dissonant, the tension-filled, and the difficult truths as well as the harmonious, the beautiful, and the praiseworthy?"[119] Indeed, it is the *humanity* of the theater, with its bodies on stage performing words and music written by humans and for the benefit of human souls, that aligns theater with religious and musical practices. As we have seen, this essential truth was

116. Charles Butler, *The Principles of Music*, 51.
117. Stephen Batman, *Batman upon Bartholome, his Booke De Proprietatibus Rerum* (London, 1582), 424.
118. Don Saliers, *Music and Theology* (Nashville: Abingdon Press, 2007), xi.
119. Ibid., xii.

appreciated, exploited, and often feared by the playwrights, composers, and theologians of the long sixteenth century. The theater's ability to stage harmonies reveals the horror, beauty, and poignancy of the fact that the power of religion and music—a power to move people to acts both terrible and generous—is rooted in the fact that those enterprises, too, are made and remade by humans, sounded and felt in their resonant bodies.

BIBLIOGRAPHY

Primary Sources

The Accession and Coronation and Marriage of Mary Tudor as Related in Four Manuscripts of the Escorial. Translated by C. V. Malfatti. Barcelona: C. V. Malfatti, 1956.

Ambrose. *Explanatio psalmorum.* Edited by M. Petschenig. *Corpus Scriptorum Ecclesiasticorum Latinorum* 61. 1919.

Ascham, Roger. *Toxophilus the schole of shootinge contayned in two books.* London, 1545.

Augustine. *Confessions.* Translated by R. S. Pine-Coffin. New York: Penguin Books, 1987.

Avison, Charles. *An Essay on Musical Expression.* London, 1752.

Bacon, Francis. *Bacon, Selected Philosophical Works.* Edited by Rose-Mary Sargent. Indianapolis: Hackett, 1999.

Bale, John. *The Actes of Englysh votaryes.* 1551.

———. *An answere to a papystycall exhortacyon.* Antwerp: S. Mierdman, 1548.

———. *A Christian Exhortation unto Customable Swears.* Antwerp: Widow of C. Ruremond, 1543.

———. *The Complete Plays of John Bale.* Edited by Peter Happé. 2 vols. Cambridge: D. S. Brewer, 1985–86.

———. *The Dramatic Writings of John Bale, Bishop of Ossory.* Edited by John S. Farmer. London: Early English Text Society, 1907.

———. *The Epistel exhortatorye of an Inglyshe Chrystian.* London, 1548.

———. *The Image of both Churches.* London: Thomas East, 1570.

———. *King Johan.* Edited by Barry B. Adams. San Marino, CA: Huntington Library, 1969.

———. *Kynge Johan* (manuscript facsimile). Materialen zue Kunde des älteren englischen Dramas 25. Vaduz: Kraus Reprint Ltd., 1963.

———. *The pageant of Popes, contayning the lyves of all the bishops of Rome.* London: T. Marshe, 1574.

———. *The vocacyon of Johan Bale to the bishoprick of Ossorie in Irelande.* Rome, 1553.

Barlow, William. *Rede me and be nott wrothe for I saye no thynge.* Strasbourg: Johann Schott, 1528.

Batman, Stephen. *Batman upon Bartholome, his Booke De Proprietatibus Rerum.* London, 1582.

Becon, Thomas. *The jewel of joye.* London, 1550.

The Bible and Holy Scriptures conteyned in the Olde and Newe Testament. Geneva, 1561.

Bodenham, John. *Bel-vedére, or, The Garden of the muses.* London, 1600.

Boethius. *Fundamentals of Music.* Translated by Calvin M. Bower and Claude V. Palisca. New Haven, CT: Yale University Press, 1989.

The booke of the common prayer and administracion of the sacramentes, and other rites and ceremonies of the Churche: after the use of the Churche of England. London, 1549.

The Book of Common Prayer: the Texts of 1549, 1559, and 1662. Edited by Brian Cummings. Oxford: Oxford World Classics, 2013.

Bownde, Nicholas. *The Doctrine of the Sabbath.* London, 1595.

Bray, Gerald, editor. *Documents of the English Reformation.* Minneapolis: First Fortress Press, 1994.

Breton, Nicholas. *The Soule's Harmony.* London, 1602.

Browne, Sir Thomas. "Religio Medici." In *The Major Works,* edited by C. A. Patrides, 57–161. New York: Penguin Books, 1977.

Butler, Charles. *The Principles of Music, in Singing and Setting.* London, 1636.

Calvin, John. *Ecclesiastical Advice.* Edited by Mary Beaty and Benjamin Farley. Louisville, KY: John Knox Press, 1991.

———. *Institute of Christian Religion.* London: Reinolde Wolfe & Richarde Harison, 1561.

Cantus Ayeres or Phantasticke Spirites for three voices. London: William Barley, 1608.

Castiglione, Baldassare. *The Book of the Courtier from the Italian of Count Baldassare Castiglione.* London, 1561.

The catechisme that is to say, ane co[m]mon and catholik instructioun of the christin people in materis of our catholik faith and religion. Saint Andrews, 1552.

Certayne questions demaunded and asked by the noble realme of Englande. London, 1555.

Chettle, Henry. *King-harts Dreame.* London, 1593.

Christopherson, John. *An exhortation to all menne to take hede and beware of rebellion wherein are set forth the causes.* London, 1554.

Chrysologus, Peter. *Sermones.* Edited by Alexander Olivar. 3 vols. *Corpus Christianorum, series latina* 24A. Turn-hout, Belgium: Brepols, 1975–82.

Church of England. *Injunctions geven by the Quenes Majestie.* 1559.

"A Comedy Called Misogonus." In *Six Anonymous Plays,* edited by John S. Farmer, 133–244. London: Early English Drama Society, 1906.

Cooper, Thomas. *An admonition to the people of England wherein are ansvvered, not onely the slaunderous untruethes, reprochfully uttered by Martin the libeller, but also many other crimes by some of his brood.* London, Christopher Barker, 1589.

Coverdale, Miles. *Goostly psalmes and spirituall songes drawen out of the holy Scripture, for the comforte and consolaycon of soch as love to rejoyce in God and his Worde.* London, 1535.

Coxe, Francis. *A short treatise declaring the destestable wickedness of magical sciences.* London, 1561.

Cranmer, Thomas. *An Answer of the Most Reverend Father in God Thomas Archebyshop of Canterburye . . . unto a craft and sophistical cavillation devised by Stephen Gardiner.* London: Reynolde Wolfe, 1551.

Cressy, David and L. A. Ferrell, editors. *Religion and Society in Early Modern England: A Sourcebook.* New York: Routledge, 1996.

Davies, John. *Orchestra or a Poeme of dauncing Judicially proving the true observation of time and measure.* London, 1596.

Dickinson, Emily. *The Poems of Emily Dickinson.* Edited by R. W. Franklin. Cambridge: Belknap Press, 1999.

"The Digby *Mary Magdalene.*" In *Early English Drama: An Anthology*, edited by John C. Coldewey, 186–252. New York: Garland Publishing, 1993.

The Digby Plays: Facsimiles of the Plays in Bodley MSS Digby 133 and e. Museo 130. Edited by Donald C. Baker and John L. Murphy. Medieval Drama Facsimiles 3. Leeds, UK: University of Leeds, 1976.

Dives and Pauper. Edited by Priscilla Heath Barnum. Oxford: Early English Text Society, 1976.

Donne, John. *Devotions.* London, 1624.

——. *Poems, by J. D. With elegies on the authors death.* London: 1633.

The English Broadside Ballad Archive (EBBA). www.ebba.english.ucsb.edu.

Elyot, Thomas. *The Boke named the Gouerner.* London, 1537.

——. *The dictionary of syr Thomas Eliot knight.* London, 1538.

Erasmus, Desiderius. *De ciuilitate morum puerilium (Manners for Children).* 1532.

——. *The Essential Erasmus.* Translated and introduced by John P. Dolan. London: Meridian Books, 1964.

Feuillerat, Albert, editor. *Documents Relating to the Revels at Court in the Time of King Edward VI and Queen Mary: The Loseley MSS.* Vaduz: Kraus Reprint, 1963.

Foxe, John. *Actes and monuments of matters most speciall and memorable.* London, 1563.

Fulwell, Ulpian. *The Dramatic and Miscellaneous Writings of Ulpian Fulwell.* Edited by John S. Farmer. London: Early English Drama Society, 1906.

——. *The first parte, of the eyghth liberall science: entituled, Ars adulandi, the arte of flatterie with the confutation therof. . . .* 1579.

——. "Like Will to Like Quoth the Devil." In *Two Moral Interludes*, edited by Peter Happé, 49–108. Oxford: Malone Society Reprints, 1991.

——. *A pleasant enterlude, intituled, Like will to like quoth the Deuill to the collier. . . .* 1587.

Gosson, Stephen. *Plays Confuted in Five Actions.* London, 1582.

——. *The School of Abuse* (1579). Edited by Arthur Freeman. New York: Garland, 1973.

——. *The School of Abuse* (1587). Edited by Edward Arber. London, 1869.

Greville, Fulke. *The Life of the Renowned Sir Philip Sidney.* London, 1651.

Hooker, Richard. *The works of Mr. Richard Hooker.* London, 1566.

Hooper, John. *Early Writings of John Hooper.* Edited by S. Carr. Cambridge: Cambridge University Press, 1843.

Hudson, Anne, editor. *Selections from English Wycliffite Writings.* Toronto: University of Toronto Press, 1997.

Jonson, Ben. "Every Man in His Humour." In *Ben Jonson: Five Plays*, edited by G. A. Wilkes, 1–97. Oxford: Oxford University Press, 1988.

"King Darius." In *Early English Dramatists: Anonymous Plays.* Early English Drama Society, 3rd series, edited by John. S. Farmer, 42–92. London: Early English Drama Society, 1904.

Lok, Henry. *Ecclesiastes, othervvise called The preacher Containing Salomons sermons or commentaries (as it may probably be collected) vpon the 49. Psalme of Dauid.* London, 1597.

Machyn, Henry. *The Diary of Henry Machyn, Citizen and Merchant-Taylor of London from AD 1550 to AD 1563.* Edited by J. G. Nichols. London: Camden Society, 1848.

The Macro Plays: The Castle of Perseverance, Wisdom, Mankind. Edited by Mark Eccles. Early English Text Society 262. Oxford: Oxford University Press, 1969.

Marlowe, Christopher. "Doctor Faustus." In *Christopher Marlowe: The Complete Plays*, edited by Frank Romany and Robert Lindsay, 341–96. London: Penguin Books, 2003.

——. *Doctor Faustus: A- and B-texts.* Edited by David Bevington and Eric Rasmussen. Manchester, UK: Manchester University Press, 1993.

——. *The Tragicall History of D. Faustus.* London, 1604. Reprinted in facsimile for Menston, UK: Scolar Press Limited, 1970.

——. *The Tragicall History of the Life and Death of Doctor Faustus.* London, 1616. Reprinted in facsimile for Menston, UK: Scolar Press Limited, 1970.

Meredith, Peter and John E. Tailby, editors. *The Staging of Religious Drama in Europe in the Later Middle Ages: Texts and Documents in English Translation.* Kalamazoo, MI: Medieval Institute Publications, 1983.

Misogonus. Edited by Lester E. Barber. New York: Garland Publishing, 1979.

More, Thomas. *Utopia.* London, 1684.

Morley, Thomas. *Plaine and Easie Introduction to Practicall Music.* New York: W. W. Norton & Company, 1973.

Mulcaster, Richard. *Positions wherein those primitive circumstances be examined, which are necessary for the training up of children.* London, 1581.

"A Musicke Lecture at the schools." (1642) MS 37999. Miscellaneous official papers and letters, British Library, London.

Nash, Thomas. *Quaternio, or a Fourefold Way to a Happie Life.* London, 1633.

A new and mery enterlude, called the triall of treasure. London, 1567.

Northbrooke, John. *Spiritus est vicarious Christi in Terra.* London, 1577 (?).

"De Papa." In *The English Works of Wyclif Hitherto Unprinted*, edited by F. D. Matthew, 458–82. Oxford: Early English Text Society, 1902.

Parker, Matthew. *The whole Psalter translated into English metre, which contayneth an hundreth and fifty Psalmes.* 1567.

Pepys, Samuel. *Diary of Samuel Pepys.* Edited by R. C. Latham and W. Mathews. 11 vols. London: HarperCollins, 1995.

Phillip, John. "The Comedy of Patient and Meek Grissill." In *A Gathering of Griseldas: Three Sixteenth Century Texts*, edited by Faith Gildenhuys, 75–152. Ottawa: Dovehouse Editions, 1996.

Philpot, John. *A trew report of the dysputacyon had & begonne in the convocacyon hows at london among the clargye there assembled.* London, 1554.

The Play of Wisdom: Its Texts and Contexts. Edited by Milla Cozart Riggio. New York: AMS Press, 1998.

Playford, John. *A breefe introduction to the skill of musick for song & viol.* London, 1654.

Ponet, John. *A shorte treatise of politike power*. London, 1556.

Praise of Musicke, wherein besides the antiquitie, dignitie, delectation, & vse thereof in ciuill matters, is also declared the sober and lawfull vse of the same in the congregation and church of God. Oxford, 1585.

"Of Prelates." In *The English Works of Wyclif Hitherto Unprinted*, edited by F. D. Matthew, 52–107. Oxford: Early English Text Society, 1902.

Preston, Thomas. *A Critical Edition of Thomas Preston's Cambises*. Edited by Robert Carl Johnson. *Elizabethan & Renaissance Studies* 23. Salzburg: Institut für Englische Sprache und Literatur, 1975.

Prynne, William. *Histrio-Mastix*. London, 1633.

Puttenham, George. *The arte of English poesie*. London, 1589.

Records of Early English Drama: Ecclesiastical London. Edited by Mary C. Erler. Toronto: University of Toronto Press, 2008.

Records of Plays and Players in Norfolk and Suffolk, 1330–1642. Edited by David Galloway and John Wasson. Malone Society Collections 11. Oxford: Oxford University Press, 1981.

Rhodes, John. *An Answere to a Romish Rime lately printed: Wherein are contayned Catholike question to the Protestant*. Simon Stafford: London, 1602.

Ridley, Nicholas. *Certen godly, learned, and comfortable conferences, betwene the two Reverende father and holy Martyrs of Christe*. London, 1556.

Rogers, Thomas. *A Golden Chaine*. London, 1587.

S., H. *To the Musicioners, the Harpers, the Minstrels, the Singers, the Dancers, the Persecutors*. London, 1658.

Sarum Mass Book: A New English Version with Gregorian Chant. Austin: Saint Hilarion Guild Press, 1990.

Scot, Reginald. *The discoverie of witchcraft*. London, 1584.

S[eager], F[rancys]. *Certayne Psalmes select out of the Psalter of David, and drawen into Englyshe Metre, with Notes to every Psalme in iiij parts to Syne, by F. S*. London, 1553.

The second tome of homilees of such matters as were promised, and intituled in the former part of homilees. Set out by the aucthoritie of the Queenes Maiestie: and to be read in every parishe church agreeably. London, 1571.

Shakespeare, William. "The Life of Henry the Fift." In *The First Folio of Shakespeare (1623): The Norton Facsimile*, 422–49. New York: W. W. Norton and Company, 1996.

——. "The Life of King Henry the Eighth." In *The First Folio of Shakespeare (1623): The Norton Facsimile*, 559–86. New York: W. W. Norton and Company, 1996.

——. "Measure for Measure." In *The First Folio of Shakespeare (1623): The Norton Facsimile*, 79–102. New York: W. W. Norton and Company, 1996.

——. "The Merchant of Venice." In *The First Folio of Shakespeare (1623): The Norton Facsimile*, 181–202. New York: W. W. Norton and Company, 1996.

——. "The Merry Wives of Windsor." In *The First Folio of Shakespeare (1623): The Norton Facsimile*, 57–78. New York: W. W. Norton and Company, 1996.

——. "A Midsummer Night's Dream." In *The First Folio of Shakespeare (1623): The Norton Facsimile*, 163–80. New York: W. W. Norton and Company, 1996.

——. "Othello, the Moor of Venice." In *The First Folio of Shakespeare (1623): The Norton Facsimile*, 818–47. New York: W. W. Norton and Company, 1996.

——. "Pericles, Prince of Tyre." London, 1609.

——. "The Second Part of Henry the Sixt." In *The First Folio of Shakespeare (1623): The Norton Facsimile*, 474–500. New York: W. W. Norton and Company, 1996.

——. "The Tempest." In *The First Folio of Shakespeare (1623): The Norton Facsimile*, 19–37. New York: W. W. Norton and Company, 1996.

——. *The Tempest: Arden Shakespeare*, 3rd edition. Edited by Virginia Mason Vaughan and Alden T. Vaughan. Bloomsbury, UK: Arden Shakespeare, 2011.

——. "The Tragedy of Hamlet." In *The First Folio of Shakespeare (1623): The Norton Facsimile*, 760–90. New York: W. W. Norton and Company, 1996.

——. "The Tragedy of Macbeth." In *The First Folio of Shakespeare (1623): The Norton Facsimile*, 739–59. New York: W. W. Norton and Company, 1996.

——. "Troilus and Cressida." In *The First Folio of Shakespeare (1623): The Norton Facsimile*, 587–600. New York: W. W. Norton and Company, 1996.

——. "The Winter's Tale." In *The First Folio of Shakespeare (1623): The Norton Facsimile*, 295–321. New York: W. W. Norton and Company, 1996.

——. *The Winter's Tale: Oxford World Classics*. Edited by Stephen Orgel. Oxford: Oxford University Press, 1996.

Sternhold, Thomas and John Hopkins. *The whole booke of Psalmes, collected into Englysh metre by T. Starnhold, I. Hopkin, & others . . . .* London, 1562.

Strype, John. *Annals of the Reformation and Establishment of Religion and Other Various Happy Occurrences in the Church of England.* London: Edward Symon, 1735.

Stubbes, Philip. *Anatomie of Abuses.* London, 1585.

——. *The theater of the Popes monarchie wherein is described as well the uncleane lives of that wicked generation. . . .* London: Thomas Dawson, 1585.

Taswell, William. *The propriety and usefulness of sacred musick: a sermon preach'd in the cathedral-church of Gloucester.* 1742.

Taverner, John. "Praelections musical in aedibus Greshamensibus." (1610–11) MS 2329, Sloane Collection. British Library, London.

Taverner, Richard. *An Oration gradulatory made upon the joyfull proclayming of the moste noble Princes Quene Mary Quene of Englande.* London, 1553.

"Three Middle English Sermons from the Worcester Chapter Manuscript F. 10." Edited by D. M. Grisdale. *Leeds School of English Language Texts and Monographs* 5. Leeds, UK: Titus Wilson, 1939.

A Treatise of Miraclis Pleyinge. Edited by Clifford Davidson. Kalamazoo, MI: Medieval Institute Publications, 1993.

"Treatise on Church Music." MS 18 B XIX. Royal Collection. British Library, London, 1610?

"Trial of Treasure." In *A Select Collection of Old English Plays*, edited by W. Carew Hazlitt. Volume 3, 257–301. London: Reeves and Turner, 1874.

The Trial of Treasure. Edited by Peter Happé. Scarborough, UK: Malone Society Reprints, 2010.

Tudor Royal Proclamations. Edited by Paul L. Hughes and James F. Larkin. Vol. 2. New Haven, CT: Yale University Press, 1969.

Udall, Nicholas. *The Dramatic Writings of Nicholas Udall.* Edited by John S. Farmer. London: Early English Drama Society, 1906.

———. "Ralph Roister Doister." Reprinted in *Materials for the Study of the Old English Drama* 16. Edited by G. Scheurwegh. Vaduz: Kraus Reprint Ltd., 1963.

———. *Respublica: An Interlude for Christmas 1553.* Edited by W. W. Greg. London: Early English Text Society, 1952.

———. "Royster Doyster." In *Tudor Plays: An Anthology of Early English Drama,* edited by Edmund Creeth, 215–314. New York: Anchor Books, 1966.

Vermigli, Pietro. *A treatise of the cohabitacyon of the faithfull with the unfaithful.* 1555.

Wager, Lewis. "The Life and Repentaunce of Mary Magdalene." In *Reformation Biblical Drama in England,* edited by Paul Whitfield White, 1–66. New York: Garland Publishing, 1992.

Wager, William. "The Longer Thou Livest." In *The Longer Thou Livest and Enough Is as Good as a Feast,* edited by R. Mark Benbow, 1–78. Lincoln: University of Nebraska Press, 1967.

———. *A very mery and pythie commedie, called the longer thou livest, the more foole thou art.* London, 1569.

The Wakefield Pageants in the Towneley Cycle. Edited by A. C. Cawley. Manchester, UK: Manchester University Press, 1958.

Winstanley, William. *The Lives of the most famous English poets.* London, 1687.

"Wisdom." In *Early English Drama: An Anthology,* edited by John C. Coldeway, 68–104. New York: Garland Publishing, Inc., 1993.

"Wisdom." In *Two Moral Interludes: The Pride of Life and Wisdom,* edited by David Klausner, 39–72. Kalamazoo, MI: Medieval Institute Publications, 2009.

Wright, Thomas. *The Passions of the Minde in Generall (1604).* Edited by Thomas O. Sloan. Urbana: University of Illinois Press, 1971.

Wriothesley, Charles. *A Chronicle of England During the Reigns of the Tudors.* Edited by William Douglas Hamilton. London: Camden Society, 1875.

Wyclif, John. *The English Works.* Edited by Frederic David Matthew, Early English Texts Society ser. 74. Reprinted Millwood, New York: Kraus, 1975.

———. "Of Feigned Contemplative Life." In *Fourteenth Century Verse and Prose,* edited by Kenneth Sisam, 119–28. Oxford: Clarendon Press, 1950.

The York Plays. Edited by Richard Beadle. London: Edward Arnold, 1982.

Secondary Sources

Adorno, Theodor. *Introduction to the Sociology of Music.* Translated by E. B. Ashton. New York: Seabury Press, 1976.

Aers, David. *Sanctifying Signs: Making Christian Tradition in Late Medieval England.* Notre Dame, IN: University of Notre Dame Press, 2004.

———and Sarah Beckwith. "The Eucharist." In *Cultural Reformations: Medieval and Renaissance Literary History,* edited by Brian Cummings and James Simpson, 153–65. Oxford: Oxford University Press, 2011.

Ahnert, Ruth. *The Rise of Prison Literature in the Sixteenth Century.* Cambridge: Cambridge University Press, 2013.

Albright, Daniel. *Music Speaks: On the Language of Opera, Dance, and Song.* Rochester, NY: University of Rochester Press, 2009.

Alter, Jean. *A Sociosemiotic Theory of Theatre.* Philadelphia: University of Pennsylvania Press, 1990.

Anglo, Sydney. "An Early Tudor Programme for Plays and Other Demonstrations against the Pope." *Journal of the Warburg and Courtauld Institutes* 20.1/2 (1957): 176–79.

Aston, Margaret. "Lollard Women Priests?" In *Lollards and Reformers: Images and Literacy in Late Medieval Religion*, edited by Margaret Aston, 49–70. London: Hambledon, 1984.

——and Colin Richmond. "Introduction." In *Lollardy and the Gentry in the Later Middle Ages*, edited by Margaret Aston and Colin Richmond, 1–27. New York: St. Martin's Press, 1997.

Atlas, Allan. *Renaissance Music: Music in Western Europe, 1400–1600.* New York: W. W. Norton, 1998.

Auden, W. H. "Music in Shakespeare." In *The Dyer's Hand and Other Essays.* New York: Random House, 1948; 1962.

Austern, Linda Phyllis. "'Art to Enchant': Musical Magic and its Practitioners in English Renaissance Drama." *Journal of the Royal Musical Association* 115, no. 2 (1990): 191–206.

——. "'For Musicke is the Handmaid of the Lord': Women, Psalms, and Domestic Music-Making in Early Modern England." In *Psalms in the Early Modern World*, edited by Linda Phyllis Austern, Kari Boyd McBride, and David L. Orvis, 77–114. Aldershot, UK: Ashgate, 2011.

——. *Music in English Children's Drama of the Later Renaissance.* Philadelphia: Gordon and Breach Science Publishers, 1992.

——. "Nature, Culture, Myth, and the Musician in Early Modern England." *Journal of the American Musicological Society* 51, no. 1 (1998): 1–47.

——. "'Tis Nature's Voice': Music, Natural Philosophy and the Hidden World in Seventeenth-Century England." In *Music Theory and Natural Order from the Renaissance to the Early Twentieth Century*, edited by Suzannah Clark and Alexander Rehding, 30–67. Cambridge: Cambridge University Press, 2001.

——. "Women's Musical Voices in Sixteenth-Century England." *Early Modern Women: An Interdisciplinary Journal* 3 (2008): 127–52.

——and Kari Boyd McBride and David L. Orvis. "Introduction." In *Psalms in the Early Modern World*, edited by Linda Phyllis Austern, Kari Boyd McBride, and David L. Orvis, 1–36. Aldershot, UK: Ashgate, 2011.

Austin, J. L. *How to do Things with Words.* Cambridge: Cambridge University Press, 1962; 1975.

Ayers, P. K. "The Protestant Morality Play and the Problems of Dramatic Structure." *Essays in Theatre* 2 (1984): 94–110.

Badir, Patricia. "Medieval Poetics and Protestant Magdalenes." In *Reading the Medieval in Early Modern England*, edited by Gordon McMullan and David Matthews, 205–19. Cambridge: Cambridge University Press, 2007.

Baker, Donald. "Is *Wisdom* a 'Professional' Play?" In *The* Wisdom *Symposium: Papers from the Trinity College Medieval Festival*, edited by Milla Cozart Riggio, 67–86. New York: AMS Press, 1986.

Bakhtin, Mikhail. *The Dialogic Imagination.* Translated by Caryl Emerson and Michael Holquist. Austin: University of Texas Press, 1981.

Barber, C. L. *Creating Elizabethan Tragedy: The Theater of Marlowe and Kyd.* Chicago: University of Chicago Press, 1988.

——. "The Form of Faustus' Fortunes Good or Bad." *The Tulane Drama Review* 8, no. 4 (1964): 92–119.

Barber, Lester. "Anthony Rudd and the Authorship of *Misogonus*." *English Language Notes* 12, no. 4 (1975): 255–60.

——. "Introduction." In *Misogonus*, edited by Lester E. Barber, 7–27. New York: Garland Publishing, 1979.

Barnum, Priscilla Heath. "Introduction." In *Dives and Pauper*, edited by Priscilla Heath Barnum, ix–xvii. Oxford: Early English Text Society, 1976.

Bartels, Emily. *Spectacles of Strangeness: Imperialism, Alienation, and Marlowe.* Philadelphia: University of Pennsylvania Press, 1993.

—— and Emma Smith. *Christopher Marlowe in Context.* Cambridge: Cambridge University Press, 2013.

Bauer, Walter. *Orthodoxy and Heresy in Earliest Christianity.* Translated by Georg Strecker, edited by Robert A. Kraft and Gerhard Krodel. Philadelphia: Fortress Press, 1971.

Beadle, Richard, editor. *The Cambridge Companion to Medieval English Theatre.* Cambridge: Cambridge University Press, 2007.

Beckwith, Sarah. *Shakespeare and the Grammar of Forgiveness.* Ithaca, NY: Cornell University Press, 2011.

——. *Signifying God: Social Relation and Symbolic Act in York Corpus Christi Plays.* Chicago: University of Chicago Press, 2001.

Bennett, Jacob. "The Meaning of the Digby Mary Magdalene." *Studies in Philology* 101, no 1. (2004): 38–47.

Bernard, G. W. *The Late Medieval English Church: Vitality and Vulnerability Before the Break With Rome.* New Haven, CT: Yale University Press, 2012.

Betteridge, Tom. *Literature and politics in the English Reformation.* Manchester, UK: Manchester University Press, 2004.

——. "Staging Reformation Authority: John Bale's *King Johan* and Nicholas Udall's *Respublica*." *Reformation and Renaissance Review* 3 (2000): 34–58.

——. "Writing Faithfully in a Post-Confessional World." In *Late Shakespeare 1608–1613*, edited by Andrew J. Power and Rory Loughnane, 225–42. Cambridge: Cambridge University Press, 2013.

Bevington, David. " 'Blake and wyght, fowl and fayer': Stage Picture in *Wisdom, Who is Christ.*" In *The* Wisdom *Symposium: Papers from the Trinity College Medieval Festival*, edited by Milla Cozart Riggio, 18–38. New York: AMS Press, 1986.

——. *From* Mankind *to Marlowe: Growth of Structure in the Popular Drama of Tudor England.* Cambridge, MA: Harvard University Press, 1962.

——. "*Misogonus* and Laurentius Bariona." *English Language Notes* 2 (1964): 9–10.

——. "The Performance History." In *Doctor Faustus: A Critical Guide*, edited by Sara Munson Deats, 41–71. London: Continuum, 2010.

——. "Political Satire in the Morality *Wisdom Who is Christ.*" *Renaissance Papers* (1964): 41–51.

——. "Staging the Reformation: Power and Theatricality in the Plays of William Wager." In *Interludes and Early Modern Society: Studies in Gender, Power, and Theatricality*, edited by Peter Happé and Wim Hüsken, 353–80. Amsterdam: Rodopi Press, 2007.

——. *Tudor Drama and Politics: A Critical Approach to Topical Meaning.* Cambridge, MA: Harvard University Press, 1968.

——and Eric Rasmussen. "Introduction." In *Doctor Faustus: A- and B-texts*, edited by David Bevington and Eric Rasmussen, 1–102. Manchester, UK: Manchester University Press, 1993.

Black, Jonathan. "The Divine Office and Private Devotion in the Latin West." In *The Liturgy of the Medieval Church*, edited by Thomas J. Heffernan and E. Ann Matter. 2nd ed., 41–64. Kalamazoo, MI: Medieval Institute Publications, 2005.

Blackburn, Ruth H. *Biblical Drama under the Tudors*. The Hague: Mouton, 1971.

Blank, Paula. *Broken English: Dialects and the Politics of Language in Renaissance Writings.* New York: Routledge, 1996.

Blatt, Thora. *The Plays of John Bale: A Study of Ideas, Techniques, and Style.* Copenhagen: C.E. Gas, 1968.

Bloom, Gina. *Voice in Motion: Staging Gender, Shaping Sound in Early Modern England.* Philadelphia: University of Pennsylvania Press, 2007.

Boitani, Piero. *The Gospel According to Shakespeare.* Translated by Vittorio Montemaggi and Rachel Jacoff. Notre Dame, IN: University of Notre Dame Press, 2013.

Bond, R. Warwick. *Early Plays from the Italian.* New York: Benjamin Bloom, 1911.

Bossuyt, Ignace. "The Art of Give and Take: Musical Relations between England and Flanders from the 15th to 17th Centuries." *The Low Countries: Arts and Society in Flanders and the Netherlands, a Yearbook* (1993–94): 39–50.

Boyd, Morrison. *Elizabethan Music and Musical Criticism.* Westport, CT: Greenwood Press, 1962.

Brandt, Bruce. "The Critical Backstory." In *Doctor Faustus: A Critical Guide*, edited by Sara Munson Deats, 17–40. London: Continuum, 2010.

Brantley, Ben. "Missionary Men with Confidence in Sunshine." *New York Times*, March 25, 2011, sec. C.

Bray, Roger. "England i, 1485–1600." In *European Music 1520–1640*, edited by James Haar, 487–508. Woodbridge, UK: Boydell & Brewer, 2006.

——. "Sacred Music to Latin Texts." In *Music in Britain: The Sixteenth Century*, edited by Roger Bray, 46–93. Oxford: Blackwell, 1995.

——. "William Byrd's English Psalms." In *Psalms in the Early Modern World*, edited by Linda Phyllis Austern, Kari Boyd McBride, and David L. Orvis, 61–76. Aldershot, UK: Ashgate, 2011.

Brokaw, Katherine Steele. "Ariel's Liberty." *Shakespeare Bulletin* 26, no. 1 (2008): 23–42.

Brown, Pamela A. and Peter Parolin, editors. *Women Players in England, 1500–1660: Beyond the All-Male Stage.* Aldershot, UK: Ashgate, 2008.

Bryant, J. C. *Tudor Drama and Religious Controversy.* Macon, GA: Mercer University Press, 1984.

Burton, Jonathan. *Traffic and Turning: Islam and English Drama, 1579–1624.* Newark: University of Delaware Press, 2005.

Butler, Judith. *The Psychic Life of Power.* Palo Alto, CA: Stanford University Press, 1997.

Butterworth, Philip. *Magic on the Early English Stage.* Cambridge: Cambridge University Press, 2005.

Byville, Eric. "How to Do Witchcraft with Speech Acts." *Comparative Drama* 45, no. 2 (2011): 1–33.

Carlson, Marvin. *The Haunted Stage: The Theatre as Memory Machine.* Ann Arbor: University of Michigan Press, 2001.

Carpenter, Nan Cooke. "Music in 'Doctor Faustus': Two Notes." *Notes and Queries* 195, no. 9 (1950): 180–81.

Carpenter, Sarah. "*Respublica.*" In *The Oxford Handbook of Tudor Drama*, edited by Thomas Betteridge and Greg Walker, 514–30. Oxford: Oxford University Press, 2012.

Carter, Susan. "The Digby Mary Magdalen: Constructing the Apostola Apostolorum." *Studies in Philology* 106, no. 4 (2009): 402–19.

Cartwright, Kent. "Humanist Reading and Interpretation in Early Elizabethan Morality Drama." *Allegorica* 28 (2012): 9–31.

———. *Theater and Humanism: English Drama in the Sixteenth Century.* Cambridge: Cambridge University Press, 1999.

Catto, Jeremy. "After Arundel: The Closing or the Opening of the English Mind?" In *After Arundel: Religious Writing in Fifteenth-Century England*, edited by Vincent Gillespie and Kantik Ghosh, 43–54. Turnhout, Belgium: Brepols Publishers, 2011.

Cavanagh, Dermot. "The Paradox of Sedition in John Bale's *King Johan.*" *English Literary Renaissance* 31, no. 2 (2001): 171–91.

———. "Political Tragedy in the 1560s: *Cambises* and *Gorboduc.*" In *The Oxford Handbook of Tudor Literature*, edited by Mike Pincombe and Cathy Shrank, 488–503. Oxford: Oxford University Press, 2009.

Cerny, Lothar. "Music and Magic: the Restoration of Hermione in Shakespeare's *The Winter's Tale.*" *Anglistentag Stuttgart Proceedings* (1992): 223–35.

Chambers, E. K. *The Mediaeval Stage.* Oxford: Oxford University Press, 1903.

Charlton, Kenneth. "'False Fonde Bookes, Ballades and Rimes': An Aspect of Informal Education in Early Modern England." *History of Education Quarterly* 27, no. 4 (1987): 449–71.

Charney, Maurice. "The Children's Plays in Performance." *Research Opportunities in Renaissance Drama* 18 (1975): 19–23.

Charry, Brinda. "Recent Perspectives on *The Tempest.*" In *The Tempest: A Critical Reader*, edited by Alden T. Vaughan and Virginia Mason Vaughan, 61–92. London: Bloomsbury Arden, 2014.

Cheney, Patrick. "Introduction: Marlowe in the twenty-first century." In *The Cambridge Companion to Christopher Marlowe*, edited by Patrick Cheney, 1–23. Cambridge: Cambridge University Press, 2004.

Clopper, Lawrence. *Drama, Play, and Game: English Festive Culture in the Medieval and Early Modern Period.* Chicago: University of Chicago Press, 2001.

——. "English Drama: From ungodly *ludi* to sacred play." In *The Cambridge History of Medieval English Literature*, edited by David Wallace, 739–66. Cambridge: Cambridge University Press, 1999.

Coldewey, John. "The Digby Plays and the Chelmsford Records." *Research Opportunities in Renaissance Drama* 18 (1975): 103–21.

——. Introduction to *Early English Drama: An Anthology*. Edited by John C. Coldeway. New York: Garland Publishing, Inc., 1993.

——. "The non-cycle plays and the East Anglian tradition." In *The Cambridge Companion to Medieval English Theatre*, edited by Richard Beadle and Alan Fletcher, 211–34. Cambridge: Cambridge University Press, 2008.

Cole, Andrew. *Literature and Heresy in the Age of Chaucer.* Cambridge: Cambridge University Press, 2008.

Coleman, David. *Drama and the Sacraments.* Basingstoke, UK: Palgrave Macmillan, 2007.

Coletti, Theresa. "'Curtesy Doth It Yow Lere': The Sociology of Transgression in the Digby *Mary Magdalene.*" *English Literary History* 71, no. 1 (2004): 1–28.

——. *Mary Magdalene and the Drama of Saints: Theatre, Gender, and Religion in Late Medieval England.* Philadelphia: University of Pennsylvania Press, 2004.

Corthell, Ronald and Frances Dolan, Christopher Highley, and Arthur Marotti, editors. *Catholic Culture in Early Modern England.* Notre Dame, IN: University of Notre Dame Press, 2007.

Cox, John D. *The Devil and the Sacred in English Drama, 1350–1642.* Cambridge: Cambridge University Press, 2000.

——. *Shakespeare and the Dramaturgy of Power.* Princeton, NJ: Princeton University Press, 1989.

Craig, John. "Psalms, groans, and dog whippers: the soundscape of worship in the English parish church, 1547–1642." In *Sacred Space in Early Modern Europe*, edited by Will Coster and Andrew Spicer, 104–23. Cambridge: Cambridge University Press, 2005.

Craik, T. W. *The Tudor Interlude: Stage, Costume, and Acting.* Leicester, UK: Leicester University Press, 1962.

Cressy, David. *Birth, Marriage, and Death: Ritual, Religion, and the Life-Cycle in Tudor and Stuart England.* Oxford: Oxford University Press, 1997.

Cummings, Brian. *The Literary Culture of the Reformation: Grammar and Grace.* Oxford: Oxford University Press, 2002.

——. *Mortal Thoughts: Religion, Secularity, and Identity in Shakespeare and Early Modern Culture.* Oxford: Oxford University Press, 2013.

——. "Protestant Allegory." In *The Cambridge Companion to Allegory*, edited by Rita Copeland and Peter T. Stuck, 177–90. Cambridge: Cambridge University Press, 2010.

——, editor. *The Book of Common Prayer: the Texts of 1549, 1559, and 1662.* Oxford: Oxford World Classics, 2013.

——and James Simpson, editors. *Cultural Reformations: Medieval and Renaissance Literary History.* Oxford: Oxford University Press, 2011.

Cunich, Peter. "The Dissolutions and their Aftermath." In *A Companion to Tudor Britain*, edited by Robert Tittler and Norman Jones, 221–37. Oxford: Wiley-Blackwell, 2009.

Cutts, John P. "Music and the Supernatural in 'The Tempest': A Study in Interpretation." *Music & Letters* 39, no. 4 (1958): 347–58.

Dailey, Alice. "Easter Scenes from an Unholy Tomb: Christian Parody in *The Widow's Tears*." In *Marian Moments in Early Modern British Drama*, edited by Regina Buccola and Lisa Hopkins, 127–39. Aldershot, UK: Ashgate, 2007.

d'Amico, Jack. *The Moor in English Renaissance Drama.* Tampa: University of South Florida Press, 1991.

Davenport, W. A. *Fifteenth-Century English Drama: The Early Moral Plays and their Literary Relations.* Cambridge: D. S. Brewer, 1982.

Davidson, Clifford. "*Doctor Faustus* at Rome." *Studies in English Literature, 1500–1900* 9, no. 2 (1969): 231–39.

——. "Improvisation in Medieval Drama." In *Improvisation in the Arts of the Middle Ages and Renaissance*, edited by Timothy McGee, 193–221. Kalamazoo, MI: Medieval Institute Publications, 2003.

——. "The Middle English Saint Play and its Iconography." In *The Saint Play in Medieval Europe*, edited by Clifford Davidson, 31–122. Kalamazoo, MI: Medieval Institute Publications, 1986.

Davis, Alex. "Shakespeare's Clowns." In *Shakespeare and Elizabethan Popular Culture*, edited by Stuart Gillespie and Neil Rhodes, 67–91. London: Arden, 2006.

Dean, David. "Elizabethan Government and Politics." In *A Companion to Tudor Britain*, edited by Robert Tittler and Norman Jones, 44–60. Oxford: Wiley-Blackwell, 2009.

Deats, Sara Munson, editor. *Doctor Faustus: A Critical Guide.* London: Continuum, 2010.

——. " 'Mark this show': Magic and Theater in Marlowe's *Doctor Faustus*." In *Placing the Plays of Christopher Marlowe: Fresh Cultural Contexts*, edited by Sara Munson Deats and Robert A. Logan, 13–24. Aldershot, UK: Ashgate, 2008.

——and Robert A. Logan, editors. *Placing the Plays of Christopher Marlowe: Fresh Cultural Contexts.* Aldershot, UK: Ashgate, 2008.

Debax, Jean-Paul. "*Respublica*: pièce catholique?" *Caliban* 24 (1987): 27–47.

Degenhardt, Jane Hwang. *Religion and Drama in Early Modern England: The Performance of Religion on the Renaissance Stage.* Farnham, UK: Ashgate, 2011.

Derrida, Jacques. *Of Grammatology.* Translated by Gayatri Chakravorty Spivak. Baltimore: Johns Hopkins University Press, 1997. First published 1974.

Dessen, Alan and Leslie Thomson. *A Dictionary of Stage Directions in English Drama 1580–1642.* Cambridge: Cambridge University Press, 1999.

Dewar-Watson, Sarah. "Marlowe's Dramatic Form." In *Christopher Marlowe in Context*, edited by Emily C. Bartels and Emma Smith, 49–56. Cambridge: Cambridge University Press, 2013.

Dickens, A.G. *Reformation Studies*. London: Hambledon Press, 1982.

Diehl, Huston. *Staging Reform, Reforming the Stage: Protestantism and Popular Theater in Early Modern England*. Ithaca, NY: Cornell University Press, 1997.

Dillon, Janette. *Language and Stage in Medieval and Renaissance Drama*. Cambridge: Cambridge University Press, 1998.

Dixon, Mimi Still. " 'Thys Body of Mary': 'Femynyte' and 'Inward Mythe' in the Digby *Mary Magdalene*." *Medieavalia* 18 (1995): 221–44.

Dollimore, Jonathan. *Radical Tragedy: Religion, Ideology, and Power in the Drama of Shakespeare and his Contemporaries*. Brighton, Sussex: Harvester Press, 1984.

Doring, Tobias. *Performances of Mourning in Shakespearean Theater and Early Modern Culture*. Basingstoke, UK: Palgrave Macmillan, 2006.

Dudley, Martin R. "Sacramental Liturgies in the Middle Ages." In *The Liturgy of the Medieval Church,* edited by Thomas J. Heffernan and E. Ann Matter. 2nd ed., 193–218. Kalamazoo, MI: Medieval Institute Publications, 2005.

Duffin, Ross W. "Ballads in Shakespeare's World." In *"Noyses, sounds, and sweet aires": Music in Early Modern England*, edited by Jessie Ann Owens, 32–47. Washington, DC: The Folger Shakespeare Library, 2006.

——. *Shakespeare's Songbook*. New York: W. W. Norton & Company, 2004.

Duffy, Eamon. "Bare ruined choirs: remembering Catholicism in Shakespeare's England." In *Theatre and Religion: Lancastrian Shakespeare*, edited by Richard Dutton, Alison Findlay, and Richard Wilson, 1–39. Manchester, UK: Manchester University Press, 2003.

——. "The Conservative Voices in the English Reformation." In *Christianity and Community in the West: Essays for John Bossy*, edited by Simon Ditchfield, 87–105. Burlington, VT: Ashgate, 2001.

——. *Fires of Faith: Catholic England under Mary Tudor*. New Haven, CT: Yale University Press, 2009.

——. *The Stripping of the Altars: Traditional Religion in England 1400–1580*. New Haven, CT: Yale University Press, 2005.

Dumitrescu, Theodor. *The Early Tudor Court and International Musical Relations*. Aldershot, UK: Ashgate, 2007.

Dunn, Catherine. "The Function of Music in Shakespeare's Romances." *Shakespeare Quarterly* 20, no. 4 (1969): 391–405.

Dutton, Richard and Alison Findlay and Richard Wilson, editors. *Theatre and Religion: Lancastrian Shakespeare*. Manchester, UK: Manchester University Press, 2003.

Duxfield, Andrew. "*Doctor Faustus* and Renaissance Hermeticism." In *Doctor Faustus: A Critical Guide,* edited by Sara Munson Deats, 96–110. London: Continuum, 2010.

Eccles, Mark. "Ulpian Fulwell." *Studies in Philology* 79, no. 4 (1982): 51–53.

——. "William Wager and his Plays." *English Language Notes* 18, no. 4 (1981): 258–62.

Edgerton, William L. "The Apostasy of Nicholas Udall." *Notes and Queries* 195 (1950): 223–26.

———. *Nicholas Udall*. New York: Twayne Publishers, 1965.

———. "Nicholas Udall in the Indexes of Prohibited Books." *The Journal of English and Germanic Philology* 55, no. 2 (1956): 247–52.

Edmundson, Todd. "Prospero's Exile and the Tempest of the English Reformation." *Religion and the Arts* 14 (2010): 252–66.

Emmerson, Richard K. "Dramatic History: On the Diachronic and Synchronic in the Study of Early English Drama." *Journal of Medieval and Early Modern Studies* 35, no. 1 (2005): 39–66.

Enders, Jody. *The Medieval Theater of Cruelty*. Ithaca, NY: Cornell University Press, 1999.

Fabel, Kirk M. "Questions of Numismatic and Linguistic Signification in the Reign of Mary Tudor." *Studies in English Literature, 1500–1900* 32, no. 2 (1997): 237–55.

Fairfield, Leslie. *John Bale: Mythmaker for the English Reformation*. West Lafayette, IN: Purdue University Press, 1976.

Falco, Raphael. "Medieval and Reformation Roots." In *A Companion to Renaissance Drama*, edited by Arthur F. Kinney, 239–56. Oxford: Blackwell Publishing, 2004.

Fincham, Kenneth and Nicholas Tyacke. *Altars Restored: The Changing Face of English Religious Worship, 1547–c. 1700*. Oxford: Oxford University Press, 2007.

Findon, Joanne. "Mary Magdalene as New Custance?" *English Studies in Canada* 32, no. 4 (2006): 25–50.

Finney, Gretchen Ludke. *Musical Backgrounds for English Literature: 1580–1650*. New Brunswick, NJ: Rutgers University Press, 1962.

Fischer-Lichte, Erika. *The Semiotics of Theater*. Bloomington: Indiana University Press, 1992.

Flanigan, C. Clifford, Kathleen Ashley, and Pamela Sheingorn. "Liturgy as Social Performance: Expanding the Definitions." In *The Liturgy of the Medieval Church*, edited by Thomas J. Heffernan and E. Ann Matter. 2nd ed., 635–52. Kalamazoo, MI: Medieval Institute Publications, 2005.

Fletcher, Alan J. *Drama, Performance, and Polity in Pre-Cromwellian Ireland*. Toronto: University of Toronto Press, 2000.

———. *Preaching and Politics in Late-Medieval England*. Dublin: Four Courts Press, 1998.

Folkerth, Wes. *The Sound of Shakespeare*. London: Routledge, 2002.

Forest-Hill, Lynn. "Maidens and Matrons: The Theatricality of Gender in the Tudor Interludes." In *Interludes and Early Modern Society: Studies in Gender, Power, and Theatricality*, edited by Peter Happé and Wim Hüsken, 43–71. Amsterdam: Rodopi, 2006.

Foster, Brett. "Hell is Discovered: The Roman Destination of Doctor Faustus." In *Christopher Marlowe the Craftsman: Lives, Stage, and Page*, edited by Sarah K. Scott and Michael Stapleton, 179–98. Surrey, UK: Ashgate, 2010.

Fox, Alistair. *Politics and Literature in the Reigns of Henry VII and Henry VIII.* Oxford: Blackwell, 1989.

Fox-Gold, Jacquelyn. "Other Voices: The Sweet, Dangerous Air(s) of *The Tempest*." *Shakespeare Studies* 24 (1996): 241–75.

Friesen, Ryan Curtis. *Supernatural Fiction in Early Modern Drama and Culture.* Brighton: Sussex Academic Press, 2010.

Fumerton, Patricia and Anita Guerrini, editors. *Ballads and Broadsides in Britain, 1500–1800.* Aldershot, UK: Ashgate, 2010.

Gair, Reavley. *The Children of Paul's: the Story of a Theatre Company, 1553–1608.* Cambridge: Cambridge University Press, 1982.

——. "The Conditions of Appointment for Masters of Choristers at Paul's (1553–1613)." *Notes and Queries* 27, no. 2 (1980): 116–24.

Gates, Daniel. "Unpardonable Sins: The Hazards of Performative Language in the Tragic Cases of Francesco Spiera and *Doctor Faustus*." *Comparative Drama* 38, no. 1 (2004): 59–81.

Gatti, Hilary. "Bruno and Marlowe: *Doctor Faustus*." In *Christopher Marlowe: Longman Critical Reader*, edited by Richard Wilson, 246–65. London: Longman, 1999.

Gerhardt, Ernst. "No Quycker Merchaudyce than Lybrary Bokes: John Bale's Commodification of Manuscript Culture." *Renaissance Quarterly* 60, no. 2 (2007): 408–33.

Gharavi, Lance, editor. *Religion, Theatre, and Performance.* New York: Routledge, 2012.

Gibson, Gail McMurray. "The Play of *Wisdom* and the Abbey of St. Edmunds." In *The* Wisdom *Symposium: Papers from the Trinity College Medieval Festival*, edited by Milla Cozart Riggio, 39–66. New York: AMS Press, 1986.

——. *The Theater of Devotion: East Anglian Drama and Society in the Late Middle Ages.* Chicago: University of Chicago Press, 1989.

Gildenhuys, Faith. "Introduction." In *A Gathering of Griseldas: Three Sixteenth Century Texts*, edited by Faith Gildenhuys, 11–74. Ottawa: Dovehouse Editions, 1996.

Giles-Watson, Maura. "The Singing 'Vice': Music and Mischief in Early English Drama." *Early Theater* 12, vol. 2 (2009): 57–90.

Gillespie, Stuart. "Shakespeare and Popular Song." In *Shakespeare and Elizabethan Popular Culture*, edited by Stuart Gillespie and Neil Rhodes, 174–92. London: Arden, 2006.

Gillespie, Vincent. "Venus in Sackcloth: *The Digby Mary Magdalene* and *Wisdom* Fragment." In *The Oxford Handbook of Tudor Drama*, edited by Thomas Betteridge and Greg Walker, 72–92. Oxford: Oxford University Press, 2012.

Gouk, Penelope. *Music, Science and Natural Magic in Seventeenth-Century England.* New Haven, CT: Yale University Press, 1999.

Gourley, Brian. "Carnivalising Apocalyptic History in John Bale's *King Johan* and *Three Laws*." In *Renaissance Medievalisms*, edited by Konrad Eisenbichler, 169–90. Toronto: Centre for Reformation and Renaissance Studies, 2009.

Granger, Penny. "Reading her Psalter: The Virgin Mary in the N-Town Play." In *Psalms in the Early Modern World*, edited by Linda Phyllis Austern,

Kari Boyd McBride, and David L. Orvis, 61–76. Aldershot, UK: Ashgate, 2011.

Grantley, Darryll. *English Dramatic Interludes 1300–1580: A Reference Guide.* Cambridge: Cambridge University Press, 2004.

——. "Saints and miracles." In *The Cambridge Companion to Medieval English Theatre*, edited by Richard Beadle and Alan Fletcher, 263–86. Cambridge: Cambridge University Press, 2008.

——. "*The Winter's Tale* and Early Religious Drama." *Comparative Drama* 20, no. 1 (1986): 17–37.

Green, Andrew. "Sound and Music in *The Tempest*." *English Review* 13 (2002): 2–5.

Green, Ian. "'All people that on earth do dwell, Sing to the Lord in cheerful voice': Protestantism and Music in Early Modern England." In *Christianity and Community in the West: Essays for John Bossy*, edited by Simon Ditchfield, 148–64. Burlington, VT: Ashgate, 2001.

Greenblatt, Stephen. *Hamlet in Purgatory.* Princeton, NJ: Princeton University Press, 2001.

Greg, W. W. "Introduction." In *Respublica: An Interlude for Christmas 1553*, edited by W. W. Greg, vii–xxi. London: Early English Text Society, 1952.

Griffiths, Jane. "Counterfet Countenance: (Mis)representation and the Challenge to Allegory in Sixteenth-Century Morality Plays." *Yearbook of English Studies* 38, no. 1/2 (2008): 17–33.

Griffiths, Trevor R. "'This Island's Mine': Caliban and Colonialism." In *Critical Essays on Shakespeare's* Tempest, edited by Alden T. Vaughan and Virginia Mason Vaughan, 130–51. London: Bloomsbury Arden, 2014.

Guinle, Francis. "'Where Angels fear to Tread': Allegory and Protestant Ideology in *The Longer Thou Livest, the More Fool Thou Art* (1559) and *Enough is as Good as the Feast* (1560)." In *Tudor Theatre: Allegory in the Theatre*, edited by Peter Happé, 145–58. Bern: Peter Lang, 2000.

Gurr, Andrew. *Playgoing in Shakespeare's London.* Cambridge: Cambridge University Press, 1987; 1996.

——. *The Shakespearean Stage 1574–1642.* Cambridge: Cambridge University Press, 1970.

Guynn, Noah. "The Wisdom of Farts: Ethics and Politics, Carnival and Festive Drama in Late Medieval and Early Modern France." Paper circulated for Merced Seminar in the Humanities, University of California-Merced, Merced, CA, December, 2013.

Gwynn, Dominic. "The Classical British Organ 1500–1660." *The Tracker* 52, no. 4 (2008): 18–23.

Hadfield, Andrew. *Literature, Politics, and National Identity: Reformation to Renaissance.* Cambridge: Cambridge University Press, 1994.

Haigh, Christopher. *English Reformations: Religion, Politics, and Society under the Tudors.* Oxford: Clarendon Press, 1993.

Haines, John. "Why Music and Magic in the Middle Ages?" *Magic, Ritual, and Witchcraft* 5, no. 2 (2010): 149–72.

Halpern, Richard. "Marlowe's Theater of the Night: Marlowe's Faustus and Capital." *English Literary History* 71, no. 2 (2004): 455–95.

Handelman, Don. *Models and Mirrors: Towards an Anthropology of Public Events*. New York: Berghahn Books, 1998.

Hanna, Judith Lynne. *The Performer-Audience Connection: Emotion to Metaphor in Dance and Society*. Austin: University of Texas Press, 1983.

Happé, Peter. *English Drama Before Shakespeare*. New York: Longman, 1999.

——. "Introduction." In *Tudor Interludes*, edited by Peter Happé, 7–34. New York: Penguin Books, 1972.

——. "Introduction." In *The Complete Plays of John Bale*, edited by Peter Happé, 1–28. Vol. 1. Cambridge: D. S. Brewer, 1985–86.

——. *John Bale*. Amherst: Twayne Publishers, 1996.

——. "John Bale and the Practice of Drama." *Reformation* 18, no. 1 (2013): 7–20.

——. "John Bale's Lost Mystery Cycle." *Cahiers Elizabethan* 60 (2001): 1–12.

——. "Laughter in the Court: Four Tudor Comedies (1518–1585), from Skelton to Lyly." *Tudor Theater* 6 (2002): 11–27.

——. "Rejecting and Preserving Bale's *John the Baptist*." Paper presented at the International Medieval Congress, Leeds, UK, July 3, 2013.

——. *Song in Morality Plays and Interludes*. Lancaster, UK: Medieval Theatre Monographs, 1991.

——. "Tragic Themes in Three Tudor Moralities." *Studies in English Literature* 5, no. 2 (1965): 207–27.

Harper-Bill, Christopher. *The Pre-Reformation Church in England 1400–1530*. Harlow, UK: Longman, 1989.

Harris, Jonathan Gill. *Untimely Matter in the Time of Shakespeare*. Philadelphia: University of Pennsylvania Press, 2009.

Harrison, Carol. *The Art of Listening in the Early Church*. Oxford: Oxford University Press, 2013.

Hassel, R. Chris, Jr. *Shakespeare's Religious Language: A Dictionary*. New York: Continuum, 2005.

Healy, Thomas. "*Doctor Faustus*." In *The Cambridge Companion to Christopher Marlowe*, edited by Patrick Cheney, 174–92. Cambridge: Cambridge University Press, 2004.

Heetderks, Angela. "Witty Fools and Foolish Wits: Performing Cognitive Disability in English Literature, c. 1380–c. 1602." PhD diss., University of Michigan, 2014.

Heffernan, Thomas J. "The Liturgy and the Literature of Saints' Lives." In *The Liturgy of the Medieval Church*. 2nd ed., edited by Thomas J. Heffernan and E. Ann Matter, 65–94. Kalamazoo, MI: Medieval Institute Publications, 2005.

Helms, Dietrich. "Henry VIII's Book: Teaching Music to Royal Children." *The Musical Quarterly* 92, no. 1/2 (2009): 118–35.

Higman, Francis. "Music." In *The Reformation World*, edited by Andrew Pettegree, 491–504. London: Routledge, 2000.

Hill, Eugene D. "The First Elizabethan Tragedy: A Contextual Reading of 'Cambises.'" *Studies in Philology* 89, no. 4 (1992): 404–33.

Hill-Vasquez, Heather. *Sacred Players: The Politics of Response in the Middle English Religious Drama*. Washington, DC: The Catholic University of America Press, 2007.

Hirschfeld, Heather. *The End of Satisfaction: Drama and Repentance in the Age of Shakespeare*. Ithaca, NY: Cornell University Press, 2014.

Hollander, John. *The Untuning of the Sky: Ideas of Music in English Poetry, 1500–1700*. Princeton, NJ: Princeton University Press, 1961.

Holmes, Peter. *Resistance and Compromise: The Political Thought of Elizabethan Catholics*. Cambridge: Cambridge University Press, 1982.

Holsinger, Bruce. "Liturgy." In *Oxford Twenty-First Century Approaches to Literature: Middle English*, edited by Paul Strohm, 295–314. Oxford: Oxford University Press, 2007.

——. "Lollard Ekphrasis: Situated Aesthetics and Literary History." *Journal of Medieval and Early Modern Studies* 35, no. 1 (2005): 67–89.

——. *Music, Body, and Desire in Medieval Culture: Hildegard of Bingen to Chaucer*. Palo Alto, CA: Stanford University Press, 2001.

Honigmann, Ernst. *Shakespeare: The Lost Years*. Manchester, UK: Manchester University Press, 1985.

Hornback, Robert. "A *Dirige* and Terence 'In the Briers': Mock-Ritual and Mock-Classicism as Iconoclastic Translation in Udall's *Ralph Roister Doister*." *Research Opportunities in Medieval and Renaissance Drama* 48 (2009): 22–47.

——. "Lost Conventions of Godly Comedy in Udall's Therites." *Studies in English Literature, 1500–1900* 47, no. 2 (2007): 281–303.

——. "Reformation Satire, Scatology, and Iconoclastic Aesthetics in *Gammer Gurton's Needle*." In *A Companion to Tudor Literature*, edited by Kent Cartwright, 309–23. Chichester, UK: Wiley-Blackwell, 2010.

Hornbeck, J. Patrick II. *What is a Lollard?: Dissent and Belief in Late Medieval England*. Oxford: Oxford University Press, 2010.

House, S.B. "Cromwell's Message to the Regulars: the Biblical Trilogy of John Bale, 1537." *Renaissance and Reformation* 26 (1991): 123–38.

Howard, Jean and Paul Strohm. "The Imaginary 'Commons.'" *Journal of Early Medieval and Early Modern Studies* 37, no. 3 (2007): 549–77.

Howe, Nicholas, editor. *Ceremonial Culture in Pre-Modern Europe*. Notre Dame, IN: University of Notre Dame Press, 2007.

Hoxby, Blaire. "Allegorical Drama." In *The Cambridge Companion to Allegory*, edited by Rita Copeland and Peter T. Stuck, 191–208. Cambridge: Cambridge University Press, 2010.

Hudson, Anne. *The Premature Reformation: Wycliffite Texts and Lollard History*. Oxford: Clarendon Press, 1988.

Hughes, Andrew. "Liturgical Drama: Falling between the Disciplines." In *The Theatre of Medieval Europe*, edited by Eckehard Simon, 42–62. Cambridge: Cambridge University Press, 1991.

Hunt, Alice. *The Drama of Coronation: Medieval Ceremony in Early Modern England*. Cambridge: Cambridge University Press, 2008.

Hunt, Maurice. *Shakespeare's Religious Allusiveness: Its Play and Tolerance*. Aldershot, UK: Ashgate, 2004.

Ilnitchi, Gabriela. "Music and the Liturgy." In *The Liturgy of the Medieval Church*, edited by Thomas J. Heffernan and E. Ann Matter. 2nd ed., 589–612. Kalamazoo, MI: Medieval Institute Publications, 2005.

Jackson, Ken and Arthur Marotti. "Introduction." *Shakespeare and Religion: Early Modern and Postmodern Perspectives*, edited by Ken Jackson and Arthur Marotti, 1–24. Notre Dame, IN: University of Notre Dame Press, 2011.

James, Jamie. *The Music of the Spheres: Music, Science, and the Natural Order of the Universe*. New York: Grove Press, 1993.

Jameson, Fredric. *The Political Unconscious: Narrative as a Socially Symbolic Act*. Ithaca, NY: Cornell University Press, 1981.

Jensen, Ejner. "The Boy Actors: Plays and Playing." *Research Opportunities in Renaissance Drama* 18 (1975): 5–11.

Jensen, Phebe. *Religion and Revelry in Shakespeare's Festive World*. Cambridge: Cambridge University Press, 2008.

Johnson, Robert Carl. "Introduction." In *A Critical Edition of Thomas Preston's Cambises*, edited by Robert Carl Johnson, 1–44. *Elizabethan & Renaissance Studies* 23. Salzburg: Institut für Englische Sprache und Literatur, 1975.

Johnston, Alexandra F. "Tudor Drama, Theatre and Society." In *A Companion to Tudor Britain*, edited by Robert Tittler and Norman Jones, 430–37. Oxford: Wiley-Blackwell, 2009.

——. "*Wisdom* and the Records: Is there a Moral?" In *The* Wisdom *Symposium: Papers from the Trinity College Medieval Festival*, edited by Milla Cozart Riggio, 87–102. New York: AMS Press, 1986.

Jones, Norman. "Religious Settlements." In *A Companion to Tudor Britain*, edited by Robert Tittler and Norman Jones, 238–53. Oxford: Wiley-Blackwell, 2009.

Jones, Robert C. "Dangerous Sport: the Audience's Engagement with Vice in the Moral Interludes." *Renaissance Drama* 6 (1973): 45–64.

——. "Jonson's *Staple of News* Gossips and Fulwell's *Like Will to Like*: 'The Old Way' in a 'New' Morality Play." *Yearbook of English Studies* 3 (1973): 74–77.

Jorgens, Elise Bickford. "The Singer's Voice in Elizabethan Drama." In *Renaissance Rereadings: Intertext and Context*, edited by Maryanne Cline Horowitz, Anne J. Cruz, and Wendy A. Furman, 33–50. Urbana: University of Illinois Press, 1988.

Juhász-Ormsby, Ágnes. "The Books of Nicholas Udall." *Notes and Queries* 56, no. 4 (2009): 507–12.

Jurkowski, Maureen. "Lollardy and Social Status in East Anglia." *Speculum* 82, no. 1 (2007): 120–52.

Justice, Steven. "Eucharistic Miracle and Eucharistic Doubt." *Journal of Medieval and Early Modern Studies*. 42, no. 2 (2012): 307–32.

——. "Lollardy." In *The Cambridge History of Medieval English Literature*, edited by David Wallace, 662–89. Cambridge: Cambridge University Press, 1999.

Kastan, David Scott. "'Holy Wurdes' and 'Slypper Wit': John Bale's *King Johan* and the Poetics of Propaganda." In *Rethinking the Henrican Era: Essays on Early Tudor Texts and Contexts*, edited by Peter Herman, 267–82. Urbana: University of Illinois Press, 1994.

——. *A Will to Believe: Shakespeare and Religion*. Oxford: Oxford University Press, 2014.

Kaufman, Peter Iver. "The Protestant Opposition to Elizabethan Religious Reform." In *A Companion to Tudor Britain*, edited by Robert Tittler and Norman Jones, 271–88. Oxford: Wiley-Blackwell, 2009.

Kelly, Stephen and Ryan Perry. "Devotional Cosmopolitanism in Fifteenth-Century England." In *After Arundel: Religious Writing in Fifteenth-Century England*, edited by Vincent Gillespie and Kantik Ghosh, 363–80. Turnhout, Belgium: Brepols Publishers, 2011.

Kendall, G. Yvonne. "Ornamentation and Improvisation in Sixteenth-Century Dance." In *Improvisation in the Arts of the Middle Ages and Renaissance*, edited by Timothy McGee, 170–91. Kalamazoo, MI: Medieval Institute Publications, 2003.

Kernan, Alvin. *The Playwright as Magician: Shakespeare's Image of the Poet in the English Public Theater.* New Haven, CT: Yale University Press, 1979.

Kertzer, David. *Ritual, Politics and Power.* New Haven, CT: Yale University Press, 1988.

Kewes, Paulina. "Marlowe, History, and Politics." In *Christopher Marlowe in Context*, edited by Emily C. Bartels and Emma Smith, 138–54. Cambridge: Cambridge University Press, 2013.

Kieckhefer, Richard. *Magic in the Middle Ages.* Cambridge: Cambridge University Press, 1989.

Kim, Hyun-Ah. *Humanism and the Reform of Sacred Music in Early Modern England.* Aldershot, UK: Ashgate, 2008.

King, Pamela. "Morality Plays." In *The Cambridge Companion to Medieval English Theatre*, edited by Richard Beadle and Alan Fletcher, 235–62. Cambridge: Cambridge University Press, 2008.

King'oo, Clare Costley. *Miserere Mei: The Penitential Psalms in Late Medieval and Early Modern England.* Notre Dame, IN: University of Notre Dame Press, 2012.

Kirkman, Andrew. *The Cultural Life of the Early Polyphonic Mass: Medieval Context to Modern Revival.* Cambridge: Cambridge University Press, 2010.

Kitsch, Aaron. "Bastards and Broadsides in *The Winter's Tale*." *Renaissance Drama* 30 (2001): 43–71.

Kittredge, G. L. "The 'Misogonus' and Laurence Johnson." *Journal of English and Germanic Philology* 3, no. 3 (1901): 335–41.

Klausner, David. Introduction to *Two Moral Interludes: The Pride of Life and Wisdom* (TEAMS Edition). Edited by David Klausner, 1–8. Kalamazoo, MI: Medieval Institute Publications, 2009.

Knapp, Jeffrey. "Preachers and Players in Shakespeare's England." *Representations* 44 (1993): 29–59.

——. *Shakespeare's Tribe: Church, Nation, and Theater in Renaissance England.* Chicago: University of Chicago Press, 2002.

Kümin, Beat. "Sacred Church and Worldly Tavern: Reassessing an Early Modern Divide." In *Sacred Space in Early Modern Europe*, edited by Will Coster and Andrew Spicer, 17–38. Cambridge: Cambridge University Press, 2005.

Kuriyama, Constance. *Christopher Marlowe: A Renaissance Life.* Ithaca, NY: Cornell University Press, 2002.

Lake, Peter with Michael Questier. *The Antichrist's Lewd Hat: Protestants, Papists, and Players in Post-Reformation England*. New Haven, CT: Yale University Press, 2002.

Lamb, Edel. *Performing Childhood in Early Modern Theater: The Children's Playing Companies, 1599–1613*. New York: Palgrave Macmillan, 2009.

Last, Suzan. "Marlowe's Literary Double Agency: *Doctor Faustus* as a Subversive Comedy of Error." *Renaissance and Reformation* 24 (2000): 23–44.

Lawton, David. "Christopher Marlowe, Doctor Faustus." In *The Oxford Handbook of Tudor Drama*, edited by Thomas Betteridge and Greg Walker, 161–74. Oxford: Oxford University Press, 2012.

——."Voice After Arundel." In *After Arundel: Religious Writing in Fifteenth-Century England*, edited by Vincent Gillespie and Kantik Ghosh, 133–51. Turnhout, Belgium: Brepols Publishers, 2011.

Leaver, Robin A. *Goostly Psalmes and Spirituall Songes: English and Dutch Metrical Psalms from Coverdale to Utenhove, 1535–1566*. Oxford: Oxford University Press, 1987.

——. "The Reformation and Music." In *European Music 1520–1640,* edited by James Haar, 317–400. Woodbridge, UK: Boydell & Brewer, 2006.

Lees-Jeffries, Hester. *Shakespeare and Memory*. Oxford: Oxford University Press, 2013.

Leher, Seth. " 'Representyd no in yower syght': The Culture of Spectatorship in Late Fifteenth Century England." In *Bodies and Disciplines: Intersections of Literature and History in Fifteenth-Century England*, edited by Barbara Hanawalt and David Wallace, 29–62. Minneapolis: University of Minnesota Press, 1996.

Le Huray, Peter. *Music and the Reformation in England 1549–1660*. Cambridge: Cambridge University Press, 1978.

Lennam, Trevor. "The Children of Paul's, 1551–1582." *Elizabethan Theatre* 2 (1970): 20–36.

Lin, Erika. *Shakespeare and the Materiality of Performance*. New York: Palgrave, 2012.

Lindley, David. "Music, Masque, and Meaning in *the Tempest*." In *The Court Masque*, edited by David Lindley, 47–59. Manchester, UK: Manchester University Press, 1984.

——. *Shakespeare and Music: Arden Critical Companions*. London: Arden, 2006.

Lipton, Emma. "Performing reform: Lay piety and the marriage of Mary and Joseph in the N-Town cycle." *Studies in the Age of Chaucer* 23 (2001): 407–35.

Loades, David. "The Personal Religion of Mary I." In *The Church of Mary Tudor*, edited by Eamon Duffy and David Loades, 1–32. Aldershot, UK: Ashgate, 2006.

Logan, Robert. "The State of the Art: Current Critical Research." In *Doctor Faustus: A Critical Guide*, edited by Sara Munson Deats, 72–95. London: Continuum, 2010.

Long, John H. *Shakespeare's Use of Music: The Final Comedies*. New York: Da Capo Press, 1977.

Loomba, Ania and Martin Orkin, editors. *Post-Colonial Shakespeares*. London: Routledge, 1998.

Lord, Suzanne. *Music from the Age of Shakespeare: A Cultural History*. Westport, CT: Greenwood Press, 2003.

Lupton, Julia. *Afterlives of the Saints: Hagiography, Typology, and Renaissance Literature*. Palo Alto, CA: Stanford University Press, 1996.

——. "Creature Caliban." *Shakespeare Quarterly* 51, no.1 (2000): 1–23.

MacCulloch, Diarmaid. *The Later Reformation in England 1547–1603*. Basingstoke, UK: Palgrave Macmillan, 2000.

——. *Tudor Church Militant: Edward VI and the Protestant Reformation*. London: Allen Lane, 1999.

MacLure, Millar. *Marlowe: The Critical Heritage*. London: Routledge, 1979.

Maguire, Laurie and Aleksandra Thostrup. "Marlowe and Character." In *Christopher Marlowe in Context*, edited by Emily C. Bartels and Emma Smith, 39–48. Cambridge: Cambridge University Press, 2013.

Maisano, Scott. "New Directions: Shakespeare's Revolution—*The Tempest* as Scientific Romance." In *The Tempest: A Critical Reader*, edited by Alden T. Vaughan and Virginia Mason Vaughan, 165–94. London: Bloomsbury Arden, 2014.

Mallin, Eric S. *Godless Shakespeare*. London: Continuum, 2007.

Margulis, Elizabeth Hellmuth. *On Repeat: How Music Plays the Mind*. Oxford: Oxford University Press, 2014.

Marotti, Arthur. *Religious Ideology and Cultural Fantasy: Catholic and Anti-Catholic Discourses in Early Modern England*. Notre Dame, IN: University of Notre Dame Press, 2005.

——. "Shakespeare and Catholicism." In *Theatre and Religion: Lancastrian Shakespeare*, edited by Richard Dutton, Alison Findlay, and Richard Wilson, 218–41. Manchester, UK: Manchester University Press, 2003.

Marsalek, Karen Sawyer. "English Resurrection Drama and *The Winter's Tale*." In *"Bring furth the pagants": Essays in Early English Drama Presented to Alexandra F. Johnston* edited by Karen Sawyer Marsalek and David Klausner, 271–91. Toronto: University of Toronto Press, 2007.

Marsh, Christopher. "'At it ding dong': Recreation and Religion in the English Belfry, 1580–1640." In *Worship and the Parish Church in Early Modern Britain*, edited by Natalie Mears and Alec Ryrie, 151–72. Surrey, UK: Ashgate, 2013.

——. *Music and Society in Early Modern England*. Cambridge: Cambridge University Press, 2011.

Marshall, John. "Her Virgynes, as many as man wylle": Dance and Provenance in Three Late Medieval Plays, *Wisdom / The Killing of the Children / The Conversion of St Paul*." *Leeds Studies in English* 25 (1994): 111–48.

Marshall, Peter. "Confessionalization, Confessionalism, and Confusion in the English Reformation." In *Reformating Reformation*, edited by Thomas F. Mayer, 43–64. Surrey, UK: Ashgate, 2012.

——. "The Reformation, Lollardy, and Catholicism." In *A Companion to Tudor Literature*, edited by Kent Cartwright, 15–30. Oxford: Wiley-Blackwell, 2010.

Massey, Dawn. "'Veritas filia Temporis': Apocalyptic Polemics in the Drama of the English Reformation." *Comparative Drama* 32, no. 1 (1998): 146–75.

Mazzio, Carla. *The Inarticulate Renaissance: Language Trouble in an Age of Eloquence.* Philadelphia: University of Pennsylvania Press, 2009.

McAdam, Ian. "Magic and Gender in Late Shakespeare." In *Late Shakespeare 1608–1613*, edited by Andrew J. Power and Rory Loughnane, 243–61. Cambridge: Cambridge University Press, 2013.

McCarthy, Jeanne. "Disciplining 'Unexpert People': Children's Dramatic Practices and Page/Stage Tensions in Early English Theatre." *The International Shakespeare Yearbook* 10 (2010): 143–64.

——. " 'The Sanctuary is Become a Plaiers stage': Chapel Stagings and Tudor Secular Drama." *Medieval and Renaissance Drama in England* 21 (2008): 56–86.

McCarthy, Kerry. *Byrd.* Oxford: Oxford University Press, 2013.

McCoy, Richard. *Faith in Shakespeare.* Oxford: Oxford University Press, 2013.

McCullough, Peter. "Music Reconciled to Preaching: A Jacobean Moment?" In *Worship and the Parish Church in Early Modern Britain*, edited by Natalie Mears and Alec Ryrie, 109–30. Surrey, UK: Ashgate, 2013.

McNeill, W. H. *Keeping Together in Time: Dance and Drill in Human History.* Cambridge, MA: Harvard University Press, 1995.

McSheffrey, Shannon. *Gender and Heresy: Women and Men in Lollard Communities, 1420–1530.* Philadelphia: University of Pennsylvania Press, 1995.

——. "Heresy, Orthodoxy, and English Vernacular Religion 1480–1525." *Past and Present* 186 (February 2005): 47–80.

Miller, Edwin Shephard. "The Antiphons in Bale's Cycle of Christ." *Studies in Philology* 48, no. 3 (1951): 629–38.

——. " 'Magnificat Nunc Dimittis' in *Misogonus*." *Modern Language Notes* 60, no. 1 (1945): 45–47.

——. "*Roister Doister*'s 'Funeralls.' " *Studies in Philology* 43, no. 1 (1946): 42–58.

——. "The Roman Rite in Bale's *King Johan*." *Publications of the Modern Language Association* 64 (1949): 802–33.

Mills, David. "Wit to Woo: The Wit Interludes." In *Interludes and Early Modern Society: Studies in Gender, Power, and Theatricality*, edited by Peter Happé and Wim Hüsken, 163–90. Amsterdam: Rodopi, 2006.

Milner, Matthew. *The Senses and the English Reformation.* Surrey, UK: Ashgate, 2011.

Milsom, John. "Music, Politics and Society." In *A Companion to Tudor Britain*, edited by Robert Tittler and Norman Jones, 492–508. Oxford: Wiley-Blackwell, 2009.

——. "William Mundy's 'Vox Patris Caelestis' and the Accession of Mary Tudor." *Music & Letters* 91, no. 1 (2010): 1–38.

Minear, Erin. *Reverberating Song in Shakespeare and Milton.* Aldershot, UK: Ashgate, 2011.

Minh-ha, Trinh T. *Women, Native, Other: Writing Postcoloniality and Feminism.* Bloomington: Indiana University Press, 1989.

Minnis, Alastair. " 'Respondet Waltherus Bryth . . .': Walter Brut in Debate on Women Priests." In *Text and Controversy from Wyclif to Bale: Essays in Honour of Anne Hudson*, edited by Helen Barr and Ann M. Hutchison, 229–50. Turnhout, Belgium: Brepols Publishers, 2005.

Mitchell-Buck, Heather S. "Tyrants, Tudors, and the Digby Mary Magdalen." *Comparative Drama* 48, no. 3 (2014): 241–59.

Monson, Craig. "Reading Between the Lines: Catholic and Protestant Polemic in Elizabethan and Jacobean Sacred Music." In *"Noyses, sounds, and sweet aires": Music in Early Modern England*, edited by Jessie Ann Owens, 78–89. Washington, DC: The Folger Shakespeare Library, 2006.

Monta, Susannah Brietz. "'It is requir'd you do awake your faith': Belief in Shakespeare's Theater." In *Religion and Drama in Early Modern England: The Performance of Religion on the Renaissance Stage*, edited by Jane Hwang Degenhardt and Elizabeth Williamson, 115–37. Farnham, UK: Ashgate, 2011.

Montrose, Louis. *The Purpose of Playing: Shakespeare and the Cultural Politics of the Elizabethan Theatre*. Chicago: University of Chicago Press, 1996.

Moran, Andrew. "Eating and Synaesthesia in The Winter's Tale." *Religion and the Arts* 9, no. 1/2 (2005): 38–61.

Morehen, John. "English Church Music." In *Music in Britain: The Sixteenth Century*, edited by Roger Bray, 94–146. Oxford: Blackwell, 1995.

Moseley, Charles. "The literary and dramatic contexts of the last plays." In *The Cambridge Companion to Shakespeare's Last Plays*, edited by Catherine M. S. Alexander, 47–70. Cambridge: Cambridge University Press, 2009.

Muir, Edward. *Ritual in Early Modern Europe*. Cambridge: Cambridge University Press, 2005.

Mullaney, Steven. *The Reformation of Emotions in the Age of Shakespeare*. Chicago: University of Chicago Press, 2015.

Munro, Ian. "Theater and the Scriptural Economy in *Doctor Faustus*." In *The Return of Theory in Early Modern English Studies: Tarrying with the Subjunctive*, edited by Paul Cefalu and Bryan Reynolds, 296–318. New York: Palgrave Macmillan, 2011.

Munro, Lucy. "Music and Sound." In *The Oxford Handbook of Early Modern Theater*, edited by Richard Dutton, 543–59. Oxford: Oxford University Press, 2009.

Murakami, Ineke. *Moral Play and Counterpublic: Transformations in Moral Drama, 1465–1599*. New York: Routledge, 2010.

Narey, Wayne. "Metatheatricality on the Medieval Stage." *Medieavalia* 18 (1995): 387–406.

Neill, Michael. "'Noises, Sounds, and sweet airs': The Burden of Shakespeare's Tempest." *Shakespeare Quarterly* 59, no. 1 (2008): 36–59.

——. "*The Tempest*: 'Hush, and be mute': Silences in *The Tempest*." In *Late Shakespeare 1608–1613*, edited by Andrew J. Power and Rory Loughnane, 88–107. Cambridge: Cambridge University Press, 2013.

Neuss, P. V. "The Sixteenth-Century English 'Proverb Play.'" *Comparative Drama* 18, no. 1 (1984): 1–18.

Nichols, Ann Eljenholm. *Seeable Signs: The Iconography of the Seven Sacraments 1350–1544*. Woodbridge, UK: Boydell Press, 1994.

Nisse, Ruth. *Defining Acts: Drama and the Politics of Interpretation in Late Medieval England*. Notre Dame, IN: University of Notre Dame Press, 2005.

Norland, Howard B. *Drama in Early Tudor Britain 1485–1558*. Lincoln: University of Nebraska Press, 1995.

——. "'Lamentable tragedy mixed ful of pleasant mirth': The Enigma of 'Cambises.'" *Comparative Drama* 26, no. 4 (1992–93): 330–43.

Oettinger, Rebecca Wagner. *Music as Propaganda in the German Reformation*. Aldershot, UK: Ashgate, 2001.

Oliver, Leslie Mahin. "William Wager and *The Trial of Treasure*." *Huntington Library Quarterly* 9, no. 4 (August 1946): 419–29.

Orgel, Stephen. "Introduction." In *The Winter's Tale: Oxford World Classics*, edited by Stephen Orgel, 1–88. Oxford: Oxford University Press, 1996.

Ortiz, Joseph. *Broken Harmony: Shakespeare and the Politics of Music*. Ithaca, NY: Cornell University Press, 2011.

Owens, Jessie Ann. "Introduction: Soundscapes of Early Modern England." In *"Noyses, sounds, and sweet aires": Music in Early Modern England*, edited by Jessie Ann Owens, 8–19. Washington, DC: The Folger Shakespeare Library, 2006.

Oxford English Dictionary (OED). www.oed.com.

Pafford, J. H. P. "Music and Songs in *The Winter's Tale*." *Shakespeare Quarterly* 10, no. 2 (1959): 161–75.

Page, Daniel Bennett. "Uniform and Catholic: Church Music in the Reign of Mary Tudor (1553–58)." PhD diss., Brandeis University, 1996.

Palmer, D. J. "Magic and Poetry in *Doctor Faustus*." *Critical Quarterly* 6 (1964): 56–67.

Parker, John. *The Aesthetics of Antichrist: From Christian Drama to Christopher Marlowe*. Ithaca, NY: Cornell University Press, 2007.

——. "Faustus, Confession, and the Sins of Omission." *English Literary History* 80, no. 1 (2013): 29–59.

——. "Persona." In *Cultural Reformations: Medieval and Renaissance Literary History*, edited by Brian Cummings and James Simpson, 592–608. Oxford: Oxford University Press, 2011.

Paulson, Julie. "A Theater of the Soul's Interior: Contemplative Literature and Penitential Education in the Morality Play *Wisdom*." *Journal of Medieval and Early Modern Studies* 38, no. 2 (2008): 253–83.

Peery, William. "A Prayer for the Queen in *Roister Doister*." *University of Texas Studies in English* 17 (1948): 222–23.

——. "Udall as Timeserver I." *Notes and Queries* 194, no. 6 (1949): 119–21.

——. "Udall as Timeserver II." *Notes and Queries* 194, no. 7 (1949): 138–41.

Pettegree, Andrew. *Reformation and the Culture of Persuasion*. Cambridge: Cambridge University Press, 2005.

Pineas, Rainer. "John Bale's Nondramatic Works of Religious Controversy." *Studies in the Renaissance* 9 (1962): 218–33.

——. "The Polemical Drama of John Bale." In *Shakespeare and the Dramatic Tradition: Essays in Honor of S.F. Johnson*, edited by W. R. Elton and William B. Long, 194–210. Newark: University of Delaware Press, 1989.

Pittenger, Elizabeth. " 'To Serve the Queere': Nicholas Udall, Master of Revels." In *Queering the Renaissance*, edited by Jonathan Goldberg, 162–89. Durham, NC: Duke University Press, 1994.

Poole, Kristen. "*Dr. Faustus* and Reformation Theology." In *Early Modern English Drama: A Critical Companion*, edited by Garrett Sullivan Jr., Patrick Cheney, and Andrew Hadfield, 96–107. Oxford: Oxford University Press, 2006.

——. "Garbled Martyrdom in Christopher Marlowe's 'The Massacre at Paris.' " *Comparative Drama* 32, no. 1 (1998): 1–25.

Potter, Lois. *The Revels History of Drama in English 1500–1576*. London: Methuen, 1980.

Potter, Robert. *The English Morality Play: Origins, History and Influence of a Dramatic Tradition*. London: Routledge & Kegan Paul, 1975.

Potter, Ursula. "Tales of Patient Griselda and Henry VIII." *Early Theatre* 5, no. 2 (2002): 11–28.

Power, Andrew J. and Rory Loughnane, editors. *Late Shakespeare 1608–1613*. Cambridge: Cambridge University Press, 2013.

Preedy, Chloe Kathleen. *Marlowe's Literary Scepticism: Politic Religion and Post-Reformation Polemic*. London: Arden Shakespeare, 2012.

Questier, Michael C. *Conversion, Politics and Religion in England, 1580–1625*. Cambridge: Cambridge University Press, 1996.

Quitslund, Beth. *The Reformation in Rhyme: Sternhold, Hopkins and the English Metrical Psalter, 1547–1603*. Aldershot, UK: Ashgate, 2008.

Rankin, Mark. "Introduction: The Presence of John Bale in Tudor Historical and Literary Scholarship." *Reformation* 18, no. 1 (2013): 21–35.

——. "Narrative and the Nature of Reading in John Bale's Response to a Sixteenth-Century Reader of *The Vocacyon of Johan Bale* (1553)." *Reformation* 18, no. 1 (2013): 21–35.

Rankin, Susan. "Naturalis concordia vocum cum planetis: Conceptualizing the Harmony of the Spheres in the Early Middle Ages." In *Citation and Authority in Medieval and Renaissance Musical Culture: Learning from the Learned*, edited by Suzannah Clark and Elizabeth Eva Leach, 3–22. Woodbridge, UK: Boydell, 2005.

Rastall, Richard. *The Heaven Singing*. Vol. 1 of *Music in Early English Religious Drama*. Cambridge: D. S. Brewer, 1996.

——. *Minstrels Playing* Vol. 2 of *Music in Early English Religious Drama*. Cambridge: D. S. Brewer, 2001.

Remnant, Mary. "Musical Instruments in Early English Drama." In *Material Culture and Medieval Drama*, edited by Clifford Davidson, 141–94. Kalamazoo, MI: Medieval Institute Publications, 1999.

Rex, Richard. *The Lollards*. Basingstoke, UK: Palgrave Macmillan, 2002.

Richards, Judith M. *Mary Tudor*. London: Routledge, 2008.

Richmond, Colin. "East Anglian Politics and Society in the Fifteenth Century: Reflections, 1956–2003." In *Medieval East Anglia*, edited by Christopher Harper-Bill, 183–208. Woodbridge, UK: The Boydell Press, 2005.

Richmond, Velma Bourgeois. *Shakespeare, Catholicism, and Romance*. New York: Continuum, 2000.

Riggio, Milla Cozart. "The Staging of *Wisdom*." In *The* Wisdom *Symposium: Papers from the Trinity College Medieval Festival*, edited by Milla Cozart Riggio, 1–17. New York: AMS Press, 1986.

Riggs, David. "Marlowe's Life." In *The Cambridge Companion to Christopher Marlowe*, edited by Patrick Cheney, 24–40. Cambridge: Cambridge University Press, 2004.

Roberts, Gareth. "'An Art Lawful as Eating'?: Magic in *The Tempest* and *The Winter's Tale*." In *Shakespeare's Late Plays: New Readings*, edited by Jennifer Richard and James Knowles, 124–44. Edinburgh: Edinburgh University Press, 1999.

Robinson, J. W. *Studies in Fifteenth-Century Stagecraft*. Kalamazoo, MI: Medieval Institute Publications, 1991.

Rollins, Hyder Edward. "The Date, Author, and Contents of a Handfull of Pleasant Delights." *Journal of English and Germanic Philology* 18, vol. 1 (1919): 43–59.

Romany, Frank and Robert Lindsay. "Introduction." In *Christopher Marlowe: The Complete Plays*, edited by Frank Romany and Robert Lindsay, 341–96. London: Penguin Books, 2003.

Rossano, Matt. "The Esssential Role of Ritual in the Transmission and Reinforcement of Social Norms." *Psychological Bulletin* 138 (2012): 529–49.

Rutledge, Douglas F. "*Respublica*: Rituals of Status Elevation and the Political Mythology of Mary Tudor." *Medieval and Renaissance Drama in England* 5 (1991): 55–68.

Rutter, Tom. *The Cambridge Introduction to Christopher Marlowe*. Cambridge: Cambridge University Press, 2012.

Sabol, Andrew J. "A Three-Man Song in Fulwell's *Like Will to Like* at the Folger." *Renaissance News* 10 (1957): 139–42.

Saliers, Don. *Music and Theology*. Nashville: Abingdon Press, 2007.

Saliers, Don and Emily Saliers. *A Song to Sing, A Life to Live: Reflections on Music as Spiritual Practice*. San Francisco: Jossey-Boss, 2005.

Sanders, Norman, Richard Southern, T. W. Craik, and Lois Potter. *The Revels History of Drama in English 1500–1576*. London: Methuen, 1980.

Savage, Kay. "Stage Directions: Valuable clues in the exploration of Elizabethan performance practice." *Studies in Theater and Performance* 28, no. 2 (2008): 161–82.

Scarisbrick, J. J. *The Reformation and the English People*. Oxford: Basil Blackwell, 1984.

Scherb, Victor. *Staging Faith: East Anglian Drama in the Later Middle Ages*. Madison, NJ: Fairleigh Dickinson University Press, 2001.

Schmidt, Gary. *Renaissance Hybrids: Culture and Genre in Early Modern England*. Farnham, UK: Ashgate, 2013.

Scholes, Percy. *The Puritans and Music: In England and New England*. Oxford: Clarendon Press, 1934. Reprinted 1969.

Schreyer, Kurt. *Shakespeare's Medieval Craft: Remnants of the Mysteries on the London Stage*. Ithaca, NY: Cornell University Press, 2014.

Schwartz, Regina. *Sacramental Poetics at the Dawn of Secularism: When God Left the World*. Palo Alto, CA: Stanford University Press, 2008.

Schwyzer, Philip. "Paranoid History: John Bale's *King Johan*." In *The Oxford Handbook of Tudor Drama*, edited by Thomas Betteridge and Greg Walker, 499–513. Oxford: Oxford University Press, 2012.

Seng, Peter. *The Vocal Songs in the Plays of Shakespeare: A Critical History*. Cambridge, MA: Harvard University Press, 1967.

Shapiro, Michael. "Early Boy Companies and Their Acting Venues." In *The Oxford Handbook of Early Modern Theater*, edited by Richard Dutton, 121–35. Oxford: Oxford University Press, 2011.

Shell, Alison. *Oral Culture and Catholicism in Early Modern England*. Cambridge: Cambridge University Press, 2007.

——. *Shakespeare and Religion*. London: Arden, 2010.

Shepherd, Simon. *Marlowe and the Politics of Elizabethan Theater*. Brighton: The Harvester Press, 1986.

Shrank, Cathy. "John Bale and reconfiguring the 'medieval' in Reformation England." In *Reading the Medieval in Early Modern England*, edited by Gordon McMullan and David Matthews, 179–92. Cambridge: Cambridge University Press, 2007.

Simpson, James. "John Bale, *Three Laws*." In *The Oxford Handbook of Tudor Drama*, edited by Thomas Betteridge and Greg Walker, 109–22. Oxford: Oxford University Press, 2012.

——. *Reform and Cultural Revolution: Oxford English Literary History*. Oxford: Oxford University Press, 2002.

Sinfield, Alan. *Faultlines: Cultural Materialism and the Politics of Dissident Reading*. Oxford: Clarendon Press, 1992.

——. *Literature in Protestant England, 1560–1660*. London: Croom Helm, 1983.

Smeeton, Donald Dean. *Lollard Themes in the Reformation Theology of William Tyndale*. Kirksville, MO: Sixteenth Century Essays & Studies, 1986.

Smith, Bruce. *The Acoustic World of Early Modern England: Attending to the O-Factor*. Chicago: University of Chicago Press, 1999.

——. *Phenomenal Shakespeare*. London: Wiley-Blackwell, 2010.

——. "Putting the 'Ball' Back in Ballads." Paper given at "Living English Broadside Ballads, 1550–1750: Song, Art, Dance, Culture," Huntington Library, San Marino, CA, April 5, 2014.

——. "Shakespeare's Residuals: The Circulation of Ballads in Cultural Memory." In *Shakespeare and Elizabethan Popular Culture*, edited by Stuart Gillespie and Neil Rhodes, 193–217. London: Arden, 2006.

——. "What means this noise?" In *"Noyses, sounds, and sweet aires": Music in Early Modern England*, edited by Jessie Ann Owens, 20–31. Washington, DC: The Folger Shakespeare Library, 2006.

Smith, Melissa. "Personifications of Plague in Three Tudor Interludes: *Triall of Treasure, The Longer Thou Liuest, the More Foole Thou Art*, and *Inough Is as Good as a Feast*." *Literature and Medicine* 26, no. 2 (2007): 364–85.

Sofer, Andrew. *Dark Matter: Invisibility in Drama, Theater, and Performance*. Ann Arbor: University of Michigan Press, 2013.

Solberg, Emma Maggie. "Madonna, Whore: Mary's Sexuality in the N-Town Plays." *Comparative Drama* 38, no. 3 (2014): 191–219.

Somerset, Fiona. "Wycliffite Spirituality." In *Text and Controversy from Wyclif to Bale: Essays in Honor of Anne Hudson*, edited by Helen Barr and Ann M. Hutchison, 375–86. Turnhout, Belgium: Brepols Publishers, 2005.

Soule, Lesley Wade. *Actor as Anti-Character: Dionysius, the Devil, and the Boy Rosalind*. Westport, CT: Greenwood Press, 2000.

Southern, Richard. *The Staging of Plays Before Shakespeare*. New York: Theatre Arts Books, 1973.

Spinrad, Phoebe. *The Summons of Death on the Medieval and Renaissance English Stage*. Columbus: Ohio State University Press, 1987.

Sponsler, Claire. "The Culture of the Spectator: Conformity and Resistance to Medieval Performances." *Theatre Journal* 44, no. 1 (1992): 15–29.

Starr, G. A. "Notes on 'Respublica.'" *Notes and Queries* 8 (1961): 290–92.

Stern, Tiffany. *Rehearsal from Shakespeare to Sheridan*. Oxford: Clarendon Press, 2000.

Stevens, John. *Music & Poetry in the Early Tudor Court*. London: Methuen and Co Ltd, 1961.

Stewart, Alan. *Close Readers: Humanism and Sodomy in Early Modern England*. Princeton, NJ: Princeton University Press, 1997.

Streete, Adrian. *Protestantism and Drama in Early Modern England*. Cambridge: Cambridge University Press, 2009.

Streitberger, W. R. *Court Revels, 1485–1559*. Toronto: University of Toronto Press, 1994.

Stroup, Thomas. "Ritual in Marlowe's Plays." *Comparative Drama* 7, No. 3 (1973): 198–221.

Summit, Jennifer and David Wallace. "Rethinking Periodization." *Journal of Medieval and Early Modern Studies* 37, no. 3 (2007): 447–51.

Sutherland, N. M. "The Marian Exiles and the Establishment of the Elizabethan Regime." *Archive for Reformation History* 78 (1987): 253–85.

Swift, Daniel. *Shakespeare's Common Prayers: The Book of Common Prayer and the Elizabethan Age*. Oxford: Oxford University Press, 2013.

Tannenbaum, Samuel. "A Note on *Misogonus*." *Modern Language Notes* 45, no. 5 (1930): 308–10.

———. *Shakespearian Scraps and Other Elizabethan Fragments*. New York: Columbia University Press, 1933.

Tarantino, Elisabetta. " 'Between Peterborough and Pentecost': Nonsense and Sin in William Wager's Morality Plays." In *Nonsense and Other Senses: Regulated Absurdity in Literature*, edited by Elisabetta Tarantino, 55–85. Newcastle upon Tyne, UK: Cambridge Scholars, 2009.

Taylor, Andrew. "The Reformation of History in John Bale's Biblical Dreams." In *English Historical Drama, 1500–1660: Forms Outside the Canon*, edited by Teresa Grant and Barbara Ravelhofer, 58–97. Basingstoke, UK: Palgrave Macmillan, 2007.

———. *The Songs and Travels of a Tudor Minstrel: Richard Sheale of Tamworth*. York, UK: York Medieval Press, 2012.

Temperley, Nicholas. " 'If any of you be mery let hym synge psalmes': the Culture of Psalms in Church and Home." In "*Noyses, sounds, and sweet aires*": *Music in*

Early Modern England, edited by Jessie Ann Owens, 90–100. Washington, DC: The Folger Shakespeare Library, 2006.

———. *The Music of the English Parish Church*. Cambridge: Cambridge University Press, 1979.

Thiemann, Ronald F. "Sacramental Realism: Relocating the Sacred." In *Reforming Reformation*, edited by Thomas F. Mayer, 65–80. Farnham, UK: Ashgate, 2012.

Thomson, John A. F. "Knightly Piety and the Margins of Lollardy." In *Lollardy and the Gentry in the Later Middle Ages*, edited by Margaret Aston and Colin Richmond, 95–111. New York: St. Martin's Press, 1997.

———. *The Later Lollards, 1414–1520*. Oxford: Oxford University Press, 1965.

Tomlinson, Gary. *Music in Renaissance Magic: Toward a Historiography of Others*. Chicago: University of Chicago Press, 1993.

Vanhoutte, Jacqueline. *Strange Communion: Motherland and Masculinity in Tudor Plays, Pamphlets, and Politics*. Newark: University of Delaware Press, 2003.

Vaughan, Alden T. and Virginia Mason Vaughan. *The Tempest: A Critical Reader*. London: Bloomsbury Arden, 2014.

———. Introduction to *The Tempest: Arden Shakespeare*, edited by Virginia Mason Vaughan and Alden T. Vaughan. 3rd ed., 1–160. Bloomsbury, UK: Arden Shakespeare, 2011.

Vaughan, Virginia Mason. "The Critical Backstory: What's Past is Prologue." In *The Tempest: A Critical Reader*, edited by Alden T. Vaughan and Virginia Mason Vaughan, 13–48. London: Bloomsbury Arden, 2014.

Vitkus, Daniel. *Turning Turk: English Theater and the Multicultural Mediterranean 1570–1630*. New York: Palgrave Macmillan, 2003.

Vitz, Evelyn Birge. "The Liturgy and Vernacular Literature." In *The Liturgy of the Medieval Church*, edited by Thomas J. Heffernan and E. Ann Matter. 2nd ed., 503–63. Kalamazoo, MI: Medieval Institute Publications, 2005.

Von Rosador, Kurt. "The Sacralizing Sign: Religion and Magic in Bale, Greene, and the Early Shakespeare." *The Yearbook of English Studies* 23 (1993): 30–45.

Waldron, Jennifer. *Reformations of the Body: Idolatry, Sacrifice, and Early Modern Theater*. New York: Palgrave Macmillan, 2013.

Walker, Greg. *Plays of Persuasion: Drama and Politics at the Court of Henry VIII*. Cambridge: Cambridge University Press, 1991.

———. *The Politics of Performance in Early Renaissance Drama*. Cambridge: Cambridge University Press, 1998.

Wallace, David, editor. *Cambridge History of Medieval Literature*. Cambridge: Cambridge University Press, 1999.

Walsh, Brian. "Marlowe and the Elizabethan Theatre Audience." In *Christopher Marlowe in Context*, edited by Emily C. Bartels and Emma Smith, 68–79. Cambridge: Cambridge University Press, 2013.

Warley, Christopher. "Reforming the Reformers: Robert Crowley and Nicholas Udall." In *The Oxford Handbook of Tudor Literature*, edited by Mike Pincombe and Cathy Shrank, 273–90. Oxford: Oxford University Press, 2009.

Warner, Christopher J. "John Bale: Bibliographer between Trithemius and the Four Horsemen of the Apocalpse." *Reformation* 18, vol. 1 (2013): 36–47.

Warren, Roger. "Rough Magic and Heavenly Music: the Tempest." In *Critical Essays on Shakespeare's* The Tempest, edited by Virginia Mason Vaughn and Alden Vaughn, 152–89. New York: G.K. Hall, 1998.

Watkins, John. "The Allegorical Theatre: Moralities, Interludes and Protestant Drama." In *The Cambridge History of Medieval English Literature*, edited by David Wallace, 767–92. Cambridge: Cambridge University Press, 1999.

Watt, Tessa. *Cheap Print and Popular Piety, 1550–1640*. Cambridge: Cambridge University Press, 1991.

Wegman, Robert. *The Crisis of Music in Early Modern Europe, 1470–1530*. New York: Routledge, 2008.

Weimann, Robert. "'Moralize Two Meanings' in One Play: Divided Authority on the Morality Stage." *Medievalia* 18 (1995): 427–50.

——. *Shakespeare and the Popular Tradition in the Theater: Studies in the Social Dimension of Dramatic Form and Function*. Baltimore: The Johns Hopkins University Press, 1978.

Wells, Robin Headlam. *Elizabethan Mythologies: Studies in poetry, drama, and music*. Cambridge: Cambridge University Press, 1994.

Wentersdorf, Karl P. "The Allegorical Role of the Vice in Preston's 'Cambises.'" *Modern Language Studies* 11, no. 2 (1981): 54–69.

West, William. "Intertheatricality." In *Early Modern Theatricality*, edited by Henry Turner, 151–72. Oxford: Oxford University Press, 2013.

Westfall, Susanne. *Patrons and Performance: Early Tudor Household Revels*. Oxford: Clarendon Press, 1990.

Wheat, Cathleen H. "A Poore Help, Ralph Roister Doister, and Three Laws." *Philological Quarterly* 28 (1949): 312–19.

White, Paul Whitfield. *Drama and Religion in English Provincial Society, 1485–1660*. Cambridge: Cambridge University Press, 2008.

——. "Marlowe and the Politics of Religion." In *The Cambridge Companion to Christopher Marlowe*, edited by Patrick Cheney, 70–89. Cambridge: Cambridge University Press, 2004.

——. "Reforming Mysteries' End: A New Look at Protestant Intervention in English Provincial Drama." *Journal of Medieval and Early Modern Studies* 29, no. 1 (1999): 121–87.

——. *Theater and Reformation: Protestantism, Patronage, and Playing in Tudor England*. Cambridge: Cambridge University Press, 1993.

——. "Theater and Religious Culture." In *The New History of Early English Drama*, edited by John D. Cox and David Scott Kastan, 133–51. New York: Columbia University Press, 1997.

Whitelock, Anna. *Mary Tudor: Princess, Bastard, Queen*. New York: Random House, 2009.

Wiggins, Martin. *British Drama 1533–1642: A Catalogue*. 3 vols. Oxford: Oxford University Press, 2012.

Williamson, Beth. "Sensory Experience in Medieval Devotion: Sound and Vision, Invisibility and Silence." *Speculum* 88, no. 1 (2013): 1–43.

Willis, Jonathan. "'By These Means the Sacred Discourses Sink More Deeply into the Minds of Men': Music and Education in Elizabethan England." *History* 94, no. 3 (2009): 294–309.

———. *Church Music and Protestantism in Post-Reformation England: Discourses, Sites and Identities.* Aldershot, UK: Ashgate, 2010.

———. "Protestant Worship and the Discourse of Music in Reformation England." In *Worship and the Parish Church in Early Modern Britain,* edited by Natalie Mears and Alec Ryrie, 131–50. Surrey, UK: Ashgate, 2013.

Wilson, Christopher R. and Michela Calore. *Music in Shakespeare: A Dictionary.* London: Continuum, 2007.

Wilson, Richard, editor. *Christopher Marlowe: Longman Critical Reader.* London: Longman, 1999.

———. *Secret Shakespeare: Studies in theater, religion, and resistance.* Manchester, UK: Manchester University Press, 2004.

Wiltermuth, S. S. and Chip Heath. "Synchrony and Cooperation." *Psychological Science* 20 (2009): 1–5.

Winkelman, Michael. "*Respublica*: England's Trouble about Mary." *Comitatus: A Journal of Medieval and Renaissance Studies* 22 (2002): 77–98.

Winkler, Amanda. *O Let us Howle Some Heavy Note: Music for Witches, the Melancholic, and the Mad on the Seventeenth-Century English Stage.* Bloomington: Indiana University Press, 2006.

Winn, James A. *Unsuspected Eloquence: A History of the Relations Between Poetry and Music.* New Haven, CT: Yale University Press, 1981.

Wong, Katrine K. *Music and Gender in English Renaissance Drama.* New York: Routledge, 2013.

Wood, Andy. *The Memory of the People: Custom and Popular Sense of the Past in Early Modern England.* Cambridge: Cambridge University Press, 2013.

Wooding, Lucy. "The Marian Restoration and the Mass." In *The Church of Mary Tudor,* edited by Eamon Duffy and David Loads, 227–57. Aldershot, UK: Ashgate, 2006.

———. *Rethinking Catholicism in Reformation England.* Oxford: Clarendon, 2000.

Woods, Gillian. "Marlowe and Religion." In *Christopher Marlowe in Context,* edited by Emily C. Bartels and Emma Smith, 222–31. Cambridge: Cambridge University Press, 2013.

———. *Shakespeare's Unreformed Fictions.* Oxford: Oxford University Press, 2013.

Woolf, Rosemary. *The English Mystery Plays.* London: Routledge and Kegan Paul, 1972.

Wootton, David. "Introduction." In *Christopher Marlowe: Doctor Faustus with the English Faust Book,* edited by David Wootton, vi–xxiii. Indianapolis: Hackett Publishing, Inc., 2005.

Wort, Oliver. *John Bale and Religious Conversion in Reformation England.* London: Pickering and Chatto, 2013.

Worthen, W. B. "Disciplines of the Text/Sites of Performance." *The Drama Review: The Journal of Performance Studies* 39, no. 1 (1995): 13–28.

Wright, Louis B. "A Political Reflection in Phillip's *Patient Grissell.*" *Review of English Studies* 4, no. 16 (1928): 424–28.

Wulstan, David. *Tudor Music*. London: J. M. Dent and Sons, 1985.

Wurzbach, Natascha. *The Rise of the English Street Ballad, 1550–1650*. Cambridge: Cambridge University Press, 1990.

Wylde, Jacqueline. "Singing a New Song in *The Shoemaker's Holiday*." In *Religion and Drama in Early Modern England: The Performance of Religion on the Renaissance Stage*, edited by Jane Hwang Degenhardt and Elizabeth Williamson, 39–54. Farnham, UK: Ashgate, 2011.

Young, Alan R. *The English Prodigal Son Plays: A theatrical fashion of the sixteenth and seventeenth centuries*. Salzburg: Institut für Anglistik ind Amerikanistk Universität, 1979.

Zagorin, Perez. *Ways of Lying: Dissimulation, Persecution, and Conformity in Early Modern Europe*. Cambridge, MA: Harvard University Press, 1990.

Zieman, Katherine. *Singing the New Song: Literacy and Liturgy in Late Medieval England*. Philadelphia: University of Pennsylvania Press, 2008.

Zim, Rivkah. *English Metrical Psalms: Poetry as Praise and Prayer 1535–1601*. Cambridge: Cambridge University Press, 1987.

Zlatar, Antoininia Bevan. *Reformation Fictions: Polemical Protestant Dialogues in Elizabethan England*. Oxford: Oxford University Press, 2011.

Zysk, Jay. "The Last Temptation of Faustus: Contested Rites and Eucharistic Representation in *Doctor Faustus*." *Journal of Medieval and Early Modern Studies* 43, no. 2 (2013): 335–67.

Sound and Video Recordings

Barton, John, director. "King Johan." *The First Stage*, Box N. Dover Publications 99717-0, vinyl LP set. Released in 1970.

——. "Mary Magdalene." *The First Stage*, Box M. Dover Publications 99711-1, vinyl LP set. Released in 1970.

——. "Mind, Will, and Understanding." *The First Stage*, Box M. Dover Publications 99711-1, vinyl LP set. Released in 1970.

——. "Ralph Roister Doister." *The First Stage*, Box N. Dover Publications 99719-7, vinyl LP set. Released in 1970.

Benedictine Monks of Santo Domingo de Silos. *Gregorian Chant: The Definitive Collection*. Milan Records, compact disc, compiled 2008.

Dufay Collective. *A L'Estampida*. Avie Records, compact disc. Released in 2004.

——. Compact disc accompanying Christopher Marsh, *Music and Society in Early Modern England*. Cambridge University Press, 2010.

Ensemble Plus Ultra. *William Byrd: Gradualia (1607)*. Musica Omnia, compact disc. Released in 2008.

The Hilliard Ensemble. *Music for Tudor Kings: Henry VII and Henry VIII*. Musical Concepts, compact disc. Released in 2008.

Marlowe, Christopher. *Doctor Faustus*. Globe Theatre on Screen, directed by Jules Maxwell. Kultur Video, 2013. DVD.

Oberlin, Russell, et al., *Music of the Middle Ages, vol. 6: English Polyphony of the Fourteenth and Fifteenth Centuries*. Lyrichord Discs Inc. Recorded 1991, released on compact disc in 1994.

Salm, vol. 1: Gaelic Psalms from the Hebrides of Scotland. Celtic America LLC, compact disc. Released in 2005.

Compact disc accompanying Ross Duffin, *Shakespeare's Songbook.* New York: W. W. Norton & Company, 2004. Various artists.

Swailes, Alex and Keith Swailes. *Northumberland Alone.* Ally Lee, compact disc. Released in 1999.

Tallis Scholars. *Christmas With the Tallis Scholars.* Gimell, 2 compact discs. Released in 2003.

——. *John Browne: Music from the Eton Choirbook.* Gimell, compact disc. Released in 2005.

——. *The Tallis Scholars Sing William Byrd.* Gimell, 2 compact discs. Released in 2007.

Tudor Age Music. Various artists. Griffin, compact disc. Released in 2010.

Index

CPSIA information can be obtained at www.ICGtesting.com
Printed in the USA
BVOW08*0722290616

453353BV00006B/3/P